The United Nations
(A Study of International Organisation)

by

Prem Arora

Sixth Thoroughly Rivised Editiion

HEED PUBLICATIONS
Your partner in success

Printed in India

Corporate Office:
V-27/17 (Basement),
DLF City Phase-III,
Gurgaon, Haryana-122002
e-mail: cosmosbookhive@gmail.com

MRP: ₹350/ -

Bulk Sales

Cosmos Bookhive offers e xcellent d iscounts o n t his b ook w hen o rdered i n q uantity f or bulk purchases or special sales. Cosmos Bookhive books may be purchased for educational, business, or sales promotional use. For general information on our other products and services or to obtain technical support, please contact: 124-4371455, +91-9811282855 or cosmosbookhive@gmail.com and you can also buy books from online bookstore at www.CosmosBookhive.com.

PREFACE TO SIXTH EDITION

The warm reception accorded to the first edition of this book has encouraged me to thorough by revise the book. Certain dimensions which had escaped my notice in the first edition of the book have been added in the presence edition. Effort has been made to incorporate latest facts and developments to make the book update and more useful for the students and teachers of United Nations. My task of revisions of the book was rendered easy on account of numerous suggestions sent by esteemed readers. I convey my gratitude to these readers and hope that in future also they will continue to send their valued suggestions.

The establishment of the United Nations in 1945 was a turning point in the history of international system. It reflected the determination of the member states to eradicate the scourge of war and conduct their relations on a different footing. But since its establishment conflicting opinions have been expressed about the role of the United Nations. Its critics say that the United Nations has failed to achieve its main objective of maintaining world peace and proved quite ineffective on account of great power diplomacy, regional groupings and military pacts. On the other hand, its admirers claim that the United Nations has solid accomplishments to its credit. Its peace-keeping forces have contained hostilities; it helped the colonial people to attain independence and full sovereignty; provided shelter and relief to the refugees; promoted respect for human rights by adopting large number of instruments; expanded and codified international law; eradicated several diseases, etc. An effort has been made in this work to encompass the shortcomings and achievements of the United Nations and to provide a fair assessment of its working.

The book has been designed as a textbook for students of graduate and post-graduate classes offering UNITED NATIONS/INTERNATIONAL ORGANISATION as a subject. In the preparation of this book the author has drawn from various standard works, journals and periodicals and tried to present the matter in systematic and lucid form. For the benefit of students and teachers who are interested in making detailed study. of various aspects a list of further readings has been provided at the end of each chapter. The book shall also be useful for the candidates taking up various competitive examinations as well as general readers interested in acquiring an insight into the working of the United Nations.

In the end I must thank my publishers **COSMOS BOOKHIVE (P) LTD** for bringing out this edition with rapid speed.

(PREM ARORA)

Contents

Chapter 1

DEVELOPMENT OF INTERNATIONAL ORGANISATION

The urge for peace and self-preservation has inspired man to devise institutions for greater international cooperation and avoidance of confrontation. Though this process of evolving international organisations has existed for long it received a special impetus as a result of the scientific and technological developments during the past few centuries. However, in the present century this international cooperation assumed new dimensions with the emergence of the League of the Nations and the United Nations. It would not be wrong to say that the League represented the culmination of the long process of the evolution of international organisation. However, it also radically differed from the institutions created during the past few centuries.

Meaning of International Organisation.

According to Potter the term international organisation refers to "the aggregate of procedures and organs for expressing the unification of nations." He draws a distinction between apparent and international organisations and says that any degree of international unity or community which w6uld supersede national interest, policy and action would satisfy this concept as, for example a mere International custom or an international agreement. He asserts that it is not essential that any strictly international organ should be involved in this process. On the other hand the term is often used to refer to the agencies and procedures deliberately set up as the expression of fundamental international organisation. Jacob and Atterton hold that international organisations are in reality "associations of sovereign states. They have governmental functions to perform, but they do not have the powers normally assumed by the governments."

Characteristics of International Organisation

Thought the international organisations may differ in their structure and functions they possess certain common characteristics. The main characteristics of international organisations are follows:

First, membership of international organisations is generally open only to sovereign states. The delegates who participate in the deliberations of these international organisations are nominated by the government and act according to their directions. Thus they represent the views of the various governments in the deliberations of the organisation. However sometimes certain technical experts are also appointed as delegates to the international organisation and they express views in their individual capacity. Similarly sometimes non-sovereign states are also admitted as members of international organisation. For example Byelorussia and Ukraine, two Republics of the Soviet Union were admitted as members of the United Nations, even though they lacked sovereign character. Another notable point is that in case of countries which have two governments, *de facto* and *de jure,* the government which enjoys effective control over the state's territory is usually provided representation in the international organisation. But often this rule is violated due to political considerations. For example National Government continued to represent China in the United Nations even though it had lost control over the mainland of China, because of the political manoeuvring of the United States and her allies. It was only in the 1970's that People's Republic of China could get representation in the United Nations after improvement of its relations with the United States. Thus we can say that usually the membership of international organisation is available only to sovereign states, but certain exceptions can always be possible.

Secondly, all the member states are treated as equal members irrespective of their size, population, wealth or power. The members are entitled to the same rights and privileges. Thus all the members of the United Nations have been granted equal status under the U.N. Charter. However, this principle of equality has been violated in the composition of the Security Council where five major powers - the USA, the USSR, the UK, France and the People's Republic of China, have been accorded special status and granted power of veto on matters of importance to be decided by the Security Council. Similarly, all the members of the United Nations do not make equal financial contribution towards the expenses of the United Nations. The various members are expected to make contribution. in accordance with their capacity. Likewise in the International Monetary Fund and the International Bank for Reconstruction and Development the members have been given votes in proportion to their shares. This obviously implies that rich and powerful countries are able to exert greater influence in the United Nations. But it is also true that in most of the other international agencies the states are Treated as equal irrespective of their size, population or power.

Thirdly, the international organisations lack binding force. This implies that the international organisations cannot compel the member states to abide by their decisions. They can merely make recommendations to the member states, which may or may not be followed. The states follow these recommendations if it suits them. Further, the international agencies cannot interfere in the domestic jurisdiction of the member states. Thus we can say that the international organisations rack authority to compel the member states to abide by their decisions. However, this should not be construed to mean that the international agencies cannot take any measures to enforce their decisions. For example the Universal Postal Union can compel its members to abide by its decision by prescribing exclusion from the union as a penalty for failure to comply with the prescribed regulations. Similarly the International Bank and the International Monetary Fund can impose sanctions against the members who fail to carry out their decisions. Likewise even the Security Council has been vested with the power to make binding decisions with regard to maintenance of peace and security.

Finally, an international organisation primarily seeks to promote intergovernmental collaboration. As 'sovereignty' is still a dominant feature of the modern-state system, the international organisations try to secure voluntary cooperation of the member states with a view to reconciling the viewpoints of various states and bring about necessary agreement among them. The U. N. Charter specifically lays down that 'the United Nations shall be the centre for harmonising the actions of the nations in the attainment of common ends'. It even stipulates these ends which include the maintenance of international peace and security, development of friendly relations among nations on the basis of equal rights and self determination of the people, and international cooperation for solving international problems of economic, social, cultural or humanitarian character.

DEVELOPMENT OF INTERNATIONAL ORGANISATION

The origin of international organisation can be traced back to the earliest periods of recorded history. We get sufficient evidence in the histories of India, China, Mesopotamia and Egypt regarding the existence of diplomatic practices, commercial relations, treaties of alliances etc. These treaties of the past, according to Mangone, are the first steps towards the formation of international organisation.

Greek Period

The Greeks formed the first formal organisation known as Amphietyonic Lea e in the early sixth century B. C. for the regulation of inter-state relations, avoiding war and for promoting international unity. In 477 the maritime states of Asia Minor Aegean Island, the Cycles, Euboea and other city states on the shores of Thrace and Propontes formed a confederation known as Delos. The members of this confederation contributed ships and men for the maintenance of a common navy. A little later the Greeks formed the Achaean League of the Hellenese which had 70 states, enjoying full autonomy as its members. It may be noted that these organisations of the Greeks were confined only to the Greek states and outside states were excluded.

The Roman Period

The Romans contributed to the growth of international organisation in an indirect manner. They evolved certain military, administrative and legal techniques which provided the basis for the growth of international organisation insofar as they included members of other race and nationalities also.

Alliance of Christian Powers

The lawlessness which was created after the decline of Roman Empire encouraged fresh efforts for the creating of new organisations for preservation of order. In 1305 Pierre Dubories, a French lawyer, proposed an alliance of the Christian powers. He also suggested the establishment of a Permanent Court of Arbitration for the settlement of differences among the members. Thereafter a number of alliances and associations were formed but generally they lacked adequate machinery for inter-state cooperation. Some of the important associations formed during the medieval period were Hanseatic League, and Uncleus (a League formed by the Swiss cantons of Uri, Schwyz and Ulterwaiden).

The Grand Design

The most ambitious project which constituted a milestone on the road to development of international organization was the Grand Design, an organisation of fifteen Christian Republics which was formed at the instance of Henry IV in 1603 to eliminate war and settle disputes peacefully. This scheme, however, failed as it was too radical and narrow. It was essentially a European Organisation because its members were European states and was by no means a universal organisation.

Treaty of Westphalia and Internationational Organisation

The Treaty of Westphalia (1648) was the next important milestone in the development of international organisation. Though this treaty did not formally create any international organisation and made no bid to resolve the social and economic problems of the states which arose as a result of the havoc of warfare, yet it opened a new era in international relations by uniting the various European states in diplomatic conference. As Mangone has observed "The Congress of Westphalia had little resemblance to the intricate Organisation of the twentieth century peace conference. No officer presided, no committees were formed, no votes were taken. But the cities of negotiation including the route between Muster and Osnabruck, were neutralized from the war while both papal Nuncial Chigi and Ambassador Contarine of Venice acted as mediators for plenipotentiaries in Muster. Of the greatest importance to international organisation, however, were the gathering of hundreds of envoys in the diplomatic conference which represented practically every political interest in Europe and the achievement by negotiation rather than by the dictation of two great and multilateral treaties which legalized the new order of European international relations."

Peace Of Utrecht

The next important step in the direction of establishing international organisation was taken by the Peace of Utrecht in 1713 which accorded international sanction to new dynasties and gave a serious setback to imperial aspirations. Thus the Protestant succession to British throne was accepted by France, the Elector of Brandenburg took the title of Prussia and Victor Amadeus got Nice and was also proclaimed the king of Sicily.

Apart from these measures certain scholars and philosophers also presented their plans for the creation of international Organisation during the seventeenth and eighteenth centuries. Some of the important plans presented included *Essay Towards the Present and Future Peace of Europe* by William Penn in 1693; *Project to Bring Perpetual Peace in Europe* by Saint Pierre in 1712; *Pleafor an Universal and Perpetual Peace* by Bentham in 1793; and *Perpetual Peace* by Kant in 1795.

DEVELOPMENT OF INTERNATIONAL ORGANISATION IN NINETEENTH CENTURY

Congress of Vienna (1815)

The development of international or ganisations received a special impetus in the nineteenth century due to profound changes in political, economic and social conditions. In the wake of the industrial revolution there was a tremendous increase in production which in turn resulted in heavy growth in trade and penetration of European powers in different parts of the world. This resulted in the creation of a complex worldwide economic network, which influenced the growth of international institutions in four ways. First, the increase in international transactions enhanced the risk of conflicts and wars among the states. To avoid these wars the states evolved instruments of international arbitration. Secondly, they felt the need for certain common rules and regulations for the purposes of patenting inventions, classifying goods for customs duties and deciding exchange rates between currencies. To deal with these aspects a number of public international unions were created in the nineteenth century. Thirdly, realising that the sovereign rights of the states posed a serious obstruction in the way of efficient conduct of international business it was decided to set up General Postal Union in 1875 (which was succeeded by Universal Postal Union in 1878) for smooth transmission of postal items across frontiers. Fourthly, the interdependent nature of the economies of various countries to settle their rivalries in their mutual interest. This led to the establishment of international commissions to regulate the trade of specific commodities like sugar. In the social sphere this feeling of inter-dependence encouraged the states to cooperate with each other in control of diseases. These efforts culminated in the establishment of International Office of Public Hygiene in 1907.

The nineteenth century witnessed more concrete steps in the direction of creation of international organisation. The first important step in this direction was the Congress of Vienna (1815). This Congress not only made a political settlement but also tackled a variety of social and economic problems. Above all it evolved a procedure for its working. The Congress also provided a threefold classification of diplomatic envoys and made the European states admit the principle of basic equality of all states. The Congress also for the first time evolved the procedure of having a Presiding Officer and Committees for the conduct of its business. Proper invitations for participation in Congress of Vienna "unwittingly.... lay the foundations of a political and international system which for a century shaped the course of European and to some extent of world affairs."

Above all this the Congress also evolved a mechanism for the enforcement of the terms of settlement arrived at Vienna. It created a *Quadruple Alliance* consisting of Austria, Great Britain, Prussia and Russia which was subsequently converted into *quintuple Alliance* with in inclusion of France. The Congress of Vienna contributed to the evolution of international organisation in three ways. First, it forced an alliance to enforce peace after the war. Secondly, it started the practice of holding conferences of great powers at fixed intervals to preserve peace. Thirdly, it emphasised the principle that the maintenance, of peace depended on collaboration of big powers.

The Concert of Europe

As noted above the Congress of Vienna marked the beginning of an age of consultations in international sphere. In 1815, Tsar Alexander concluded a Holly Alliance with Prussia and Austria with a view to conducting the domestic as well as international relations in accordance with principles of Christian morality. In 1818 the Czar put forward the ideal of League of Nations at the Aix-la-Chappelle Congress. This League was expected to put down with firmness all threats to the domestic revolutions. The Aix-la-Chappelle Congress also considered numerous other questions relating to international slave trade, the depredations of the Barbary pirates, emancipation of jews, quarrels between Spain and Portugal, revolt of the Spanish American colonies etc. Thus it demonstrated the utility of resolving the differences and problems through international consultations. After Aix-la-Chappelle the powers of Europe held conference at Troppau in 1820, Laibach in 1821 and Verona in 1822. Though these conferences did not prove as successful as the Congress of Aix-la-Chappelle, yet the practice of holding international conferences by the states of Europe in times of peace to regulate their political views and interests was firmly established. The Concert played a significant role in resolving various issues such as independence of Belgium (1830); independence of Greece (1837); maintenance of status of Egypt as part of Turkish Empire (1841); recognition of territorial integrity of Ottoman Empire (1853); regulation of navigation of Danube etc. The concert of Europe continued to hold meetings at regular interval still 1914 and greatly contributed to the preservation of peace by preventing the outbreak of wars. By that time "the practice of International Conferences in times of peace among the states of Europe, to regulate their political views and interests, had been firmly established." Commenting on the importance of the Concert of Europe Prof. Mangone observed "though the conferences had neither the power nor the inclination to decide and settle all the questions, but the net achievement of clarifying the issues and adjusting a number of them by friendly discussion among the assembled Great Powers indicated the utility of international consultations."

Cheever describes the formation of the Concert of Europe as a landmark in the history of international Organisation on three counts. First, though

G. J. Mangone, A *Short History of International Organisation,* p. 42

the Concert was formed during the war, it continued, even after hostilities had ceased, to enforce peace. Secondly, periodic conferences were instituted when the great powers agreed to renew their meetings at fixed intervals. Thirdly, despite the suspicion of the smaller powers it was generally agreed that the maintenance of peace depended on this sort of big power collaboration. These notions were carried over into both the League and the U. N. But probably, the most important contribution of the Concert of Europe was that it produced the prototype of a major organ of modem international organisation.

The Hague Conferences

The Hague Conferences of 1899 and 1907 also played a major role in the creation of the present International organization. The Hague Conferences of 1899 attended by 26 states worked out a Convention for the Pacific Settlement of International Disputes. It provided for establishment of an ad hoc International Commission of Inquiry to which the parties could refer their disputes. It also made provision of Permanent Court of Arbitration. The Hague Conference of 1907 attended by 44 states took still more significant steps in the direction of creation of international organisation. It for the first time convened a meeting of the representatives of all the constituted states to discuss problems of common interest for the good of entire mankind. This Conference can be considered as the First General Assembly of the States.

The Hague Conferences of 1899 and 1907 had three fold significance. In the first place, these conferences treated the small states as independent and equal partners for the first time. Secondly, these conferences emphasised the need of avoiding war and mitigating the evils and barbarities of war. For this purpose the two conferences tried to clarify and codify the rules for the conduct of war, and thus placed international law on a new footing. Thirdly, these conferences provided permanent agencies and devices for settlement of disputes among the states.

According to Palmer and Perkins, the importance of the Hague Conferences of 1890 and 1907 lay in the fact that they "represented a transitional step from *ad hoc* conferences and specialized international organizations towards the League of Nations, the first great experiment of an organization open to all states and without a special purpose and character."

Public International Unions

The creation of a number of international administrative agencies and public international unions in the later half of the nineteenth century and early twentieth century was another significant step in the direction of development of international organisations. These agencies and unions were primarily created to meet the growing need of co-operation in economic and social spheres. Over 30 international unions were established between 1865 and 1914. some of the notable agencies and organisations created for this purpose include the European Commission for Danube (1856); The International

D. S. Cheever and H. F. Havilland, *Organising for Peace* p. 35
Palmer and Perkins, *International Relations,* p.320

Bureau of Telegraphic Administration (1868); the Universal Postal Union (1875); the International Copyright Union (1886); the International Office of Health (1903); International Institute of Agriculture (1905) etc. Some of these international bodies and agencies are still working, while the functions of others have been taken over by different agencies of the United Nations.

The international public or administrative unions were engaged in variety of activities. They served as clearing houses of information, centres for discussion on common problems and tried to bring about co-ordination among the policies of various states by laying down certain minimum standards. These unions possessed some common features which are given below.

1. These international unions were created through multilateral treaties and clearly defined the rights and duties of the members. They also provided an institutional framework for the attainment of stated objectives
2. These unions were voluntary in character and held faith in the principle of equality of member states.
3. Most of these unions possessed three organs viz.(i) a conference comprising of all the members. The Conference meet at regualr intervals and laid down the basic policy (ii) a Council which was the main executive organ; and (iii) and a secretariat (comprising of international civil servants) which looked after the routine functions of the union.
4. All the decisions were taken by majority vote, with each member enjoying equal voting rights.
5. Some of the organisations enjoyed a distinct legal status. They could own property, and enjoyed the right to sue and be sued. These organisations also enjoyed some diplomatic immunities.
6. The finances of these organisations were provided by the member states either on the basis of their ability to pay or on the basis of equality or a combination of the above two formulas.
7. The decisions of the Unions were taken either in the form of resolutions which were transmitted to the members for compliance; or draft-international treaties, which came into force after ratification by the member states.

The Public International Unions supplemented the administrative work of the national governments and tried to provide certain services to the governments. No doubt they lacked the authority to frame laws and impose taxes, yet they greatly stimulated experimental development of functional innovations of international relations. They introduced several organisational concepts which left a deep impact on future international organisations. For example the Bureau of the International Telegraph Union established in 1868 served as a model for secretariat of several international organisations in subsequent years. According to Inis L Claude Jr, this development of permanent staff to give continuity to the organisation, to carry out functions of research, correspondence and publication, and to prepare the business and make arrangement for future conferences, was the crucial step in the transformation of international organisations from sequences of disconnected conferences into genuine institutions. Above all the Public International Unions promoted a feeling of cooperation among the sovereign states.

The League of Nations

The League of Nations, which was created after the first World War, was one of the most comprehensive institution of international organisation. It combined in itself the different organisations. The League of Nations also differed from the previous institutions insofar as the latter were merely agencies of consultations, whereas the League marked the beginning of collaboration. According to Mangone the main difference between international organisation before and after the League of Nations lies in the achievement of a permanent agency through which states could collaborate continuously on the grave problems which affected the peace of the world. However, certain scholars do not see the League of Nations in any way different from the previous international organisations. For example Vandenbosch and Hogan have observed "....the League of Nations was not a new and marvellous invention so far as its structure and methods were concerned, since ample precedents for these may be found in preceding international institutions." Similarly other scholars have also noted several similarities between the institutions of the League of Nations and earlier institutions.

For example to them the Council of the League was a replica of the Concert of Europe and the General Assembly was merely a realisation of the plans of the Hague Statesmen to create a General Conference of Nations. Similarly the secretariat was merely an extension of the idea of the International Bureau which formed part of the earlier unions. Again the Permanent Court of International Justice envisaged in the covenant of the League was largely based on the ideas expressed at the Hague Conferences about the International Judicial Organ. However, it cannot be denied that 'the League did provide for the first time a comprehensive system, with the union in one institution of a number of separate elements which had previously existed in a piecemeal fashion. "Further more, it made a radical departure from the earlier institutions insofar as it laid "emphasis on the principle of collective security, in contrast to the traditional nineteenth century principle of neutrality of third states towards belligerents engaged in an international conflict."

An impartial observer will admit that it is wrong to undermine the importance of the League of Nations by asserting that it was merely a continuation of the earlier institutions. Actually it deserves credit for having created bodies like General Assembly and Permanent Court of International Justice, which had so far existed in thought only. It also goes to the credit of the League of nations that it pulled together separate lines of development into a coherent system. Above all, the significance of the League lies in the fact that it made a bid to improve the procedures and assist the operation ofthe world political system. It also introduced radical changes in the multi-state system. The Mandate System introduced by the League of Nations helped the backward communities to escape annexation by big powers. Henceforth the big powers were to treat these territories as the sacred trust of civilisation and could not annex them without the consent of the League of Nations. For about two decades the League worked as an effective institution and could boast of a number of achievements in the political, economic and social fields. No doubt, ultimately the League failed and its structure showed many weaknesses, but this does not undermine its contribution to the growth of international organisation. The mere fact that the United Nations created after the second World War was largely based on the League of Nations bears a testimony to the importance of the League as a body of international standing.

The development of international organisation culminated in the formation of the United Nations Organization in 1945 with a view to promoting international co-operation and establishing international peace and security. Though the United Nations largely borrowed from the League, in matters of Organisation and functions it certainly marked an improvement over the League of Nations. It is clear from the preceding account that international organisations like the League of Nations and the United Nations which emerged in the present century were largely based on the principles evolved during the nineteenth century namely, general system of international organisation, combination of great power council, universal conferences, specialised functional units and permanent staff. According to Mangone without the experience of the nineteenth century, without the practices and procedures of international consultation for one hundred years, without the example of the international agencies created in two or three generations, the world would never have built such a rare device as the League of Nations and the United Nations.

CLASSIFICATION OF INTERNATIONAL ORGANISATIONS

In view of the presence of a large variety of international organisations in the present day world, their classification poses a serious problem. Different scholars have tried to classify these international agencies and institutions on the basis of different principles.

1. **On *the basis of Functions.*** On the basis of functions of international organisations, scholars have classified them as political, administrative and judicial. The political organisations are primarily concerned with the preservation of international peace and security. The United Nations is one such Organisation. The administrative organisations on the other hand have very limited aims and objectives and work merely as administrative agencies. The Trusteeship Council is an example of Administrative International Organisation. The judicial institutions perform certain judicial functions and try to resolve the differences among members. The Permanent Court of international Justice and the International Court of Justice are instances of this type of international organisation. Critics regard the classification on the basis of functions as unscientific because it is indeed difficult to draw a line of distinction

See Gerard J. Mangone, *A Short History of International Organisation,* pp. 1-20 between the various types of functions performed by an international organisation.

2. ***On the basis of Field of Operation.*** Some scholars have classified international organisations on the basis of their field of operation as global and regional. A global Organisation is a much broader Organisation which has usually a universal membership and extensive jurisdiction. Such a global organisation can have within its jurisdiction several regional organizations. The United Nations is the best example of global organisation. It has within it several regional bodies like the Regional Commissions of the Economic and Social Council, the Economic Commission for Asia, the Far East, Europe, Latin America, Africa etc. The regional organisations on the other hand cover a much narrower area. They are usually confined to some particular region and under take very limited functions. These organisations are usually formed by states with similar objectives. The NATO, the Warsaw Treaty Organisation, the ASEAN, and the SAARC are outstanding examples of regional organisations.

3. ***On the basis of Government or State Treaties.*** The third basis for the classification of international organisations is whether the treaty which created them has been concluded by the states or the governments. If the organisation is created on the basis of a treaty concluded between the states it involves all the organs of the government viz., the legislature, the executive (administration) as well as the government. The prominent examples of international organisations created through inter-state treaties are the Food and Agricultural Organisation, the World Health Organisation, etc. On the other hand if the organisation is created through a treaty concluded by the governments, only the administrative wing of the government is involved. The International Monetary Fund is the best example of international organisation created through inter government treaty. It may be noted that usually only international organisations of nonpermanent nature are created through intergovernmental treaties viz. the United National Rehabilitation Administration. Sometimes the governments enter into treaties to create international organisations to overcome the constitutional hurdles.

4. ***On the basis of Membership and Activity.*** Certain scholars like Norman Hill have also classified international organisations on the basis of their membership and activity. On the basis of membership Hill classifies the international organisations as bilateral, regional or universal. The bilateral organisations are usually created by two states through agreement. The best examples of this type of organisation are the Joint Commission for U.S. and Canada, the Anglo-Egyptian Condominium for Sudan etc. The regional organisations are created by the member states of a particular region. The best examples of regional organisations are the O. A. S., ASEAN, SAARC, etc. The universal organisations have universal membership. The League of Nations and the United Nations are the best examples of universal international organisations.

On the basis of activities of organisations they are broadly classified as general and functional. The general organisations pursue much broader objectives as compared to the functional organisations. The United Nations, O. A. S., ASEAN, SAARC etc. are examples of general organisations. On the other hand the International Telegraph Union, General Postal Union, ILO, FAO, UNESCO, WHO etc. are examples of the functional organisations.

It is clear from the above discussion that no single principle can be followed for the classification of international organisations. No wonder scholars have tried to base the classification of international organisations on different principles viz. on the basis of their area of operation, the manner of their creation, and the nature of the functions performed by them.

FURTHER READINGS

Inis L. Claude — *Swords into Ploughshares*

Gerald J. Mangone — *A Shot History of International Organisation*

H. Nicholas — *The United Nation as a Political Institution*

Robert E. Biggs and Jack C. Plano — *The United Nations : International Organization and World Politics*

U. N. publication — *Everyone's United Nations*

D. S. Cheever and H.F. Havilland — *Organising for Peace*

Chapter 2

THE LEAGUE OF NATIONS

Alarmed by horrors of the first world war leading statesmen of the world decided to evolve some sort of an organisation to save humanity from the horrors and destruction of yet another war in future. However, the genesis of the League can be traced in the various peace movements in the nineteenth century viz. the Congress of Vienna (1814-15), The Holy Alliance (1815), the concert of Europe (1815-22), the European Commission (1856), the International Telegraphic Union (1856), the Universal Postal Union (1874), the American Union (1890), and the permanent Court of Arbitration at the Hague (1899), and others. However, the League of Nations differed from these earlier organisations in as far as it combined in one institution a number of separate elements which had previously existed in a piecemeal fashion. It also differed from these organisations because it laid emphasis on principle of collective security rather than neutrality which was a basic feature of organisations of nineteenth century. Further, it provided regular occasions for the representatives of member states to meet and discuss their common problems as well as the matters which were likely to endanger world peace.

President Wilson of the US was a strong proponent of the League of Nations. In one of his Fourteen Points he insisted "a general association of nations must be formed under specific covenants for the purpose of providing mutual guarantees of political independence and territorial integrity to great and small states alike." It was at President Wilson's insistence that the covenant of the League was made part of the peace. treaties concluded at the end of the first world war.

Aims and Objects

The aims and objects of the League of nations were outlined in the Preamble to the Covenant and included the following (i) achievement of international peace and security; (ii) prevention of recurrence of war in future by establishing relations between different nations on the principles of equality, justice and honor; (iii) promotion of international co-operation in the social, intellectual and material field to make human life better and noble; and (iv) promotion of respect for international law in the conduct of relations among states.

Membership

The League had two types of members – original and non-original. The states and dominions who were either signatories to the various peace treaties or actually acceded to the Covenant before 20 March 1920 were regarded as original members. In all there were 43 original members' of the League. The non-original members included the states who were neither original members not joined the League before 20 March 1920. In all 17 states were admitted as members in this category. It is noteworthy that a number of states were also denied membership in this category on various grounds. The Covenant also contained provisions regarding withdrawal and expulsion of states from the League. In all 16 states withdrew from the League during its existence of 19 years. On the other hand the USSR was expelled from the League following her aggression against Finland in 1939.

Organs of the league

The League consisted of three main organs–the Assembly, the Council and the Secretariat. In addition it had two autonomous organs (Permanent Court of International Justice and ILO), and a number of subsidiary and auxiliary organs viz. Mandates Commission, International Tariff Commission, International Economic and Fiscal Commission etc.

The General Assembly was the deliberative wing of the League. Each member state sent three representatives to the Assembly even though it enjoyed only one vote. Generally the Assembly met annually but special sessions of the Assembly could be convened as and when required. The main functions assigned to the Assembly included the following (i) Deliberation on all matters falling within the sphere of the League including discussion on various political, economic and technical questions which had a bearing on international interests and international peace; (ii) Formulation of annual budget and apportionment of expenses among various member states; (iii) Admission of new members of League of Nations by two-thirds majority; (iv) Election of temporary members of Council every year; (v) Election of 15 Judges of International Court for nine years; (vi) Ratification of appointment of Secretary General appointed by the Council; (vii) Changes in the rules and regulations of the League through amendment of the Covenant; (viii) Advise the members to reconsider treaties which had become inapplicable; and (ix) Exercise of necessary supervision over the working of the Council. Thus the functions assigned to the Assembly were purely of an advisory nature.

The Council was the executive organ of the League, even though it also performed certain quasi-judicial functions. The Council consisted of five permanent and four non-permanent members. But as the US did not join the League the strength of permanent members was reduced to four. The four permanent members of he League were Great Britain, France, Italy and Japan. The strength of the permanent as well as non-permanent members could be increased by the Assembly. Actually Germany and the USSR were made permanent members and the strength of non-permanent members was raised to eleven.

The Council met thrice a year in the months of January, May and September. The meetings of the Council were presided over by the President elected by the Council from its members in alphabetical order. The Council could also hold emergency meetings to deal with situations which posed a threat to world peace. Though the meetings of the Council were held in public, it could also hold its meetings in camera. All procedural matters were decided by the Council by majority vote while all important decisions required unanimity.

The main functions assigned to the Council included (i) Preventive action to check situations which posed threat to world peace; (ii) Suggestion of measures to be taken by the members of the League for the preservation of territorial integrity of the member states; (iii) Mobilisation of sanctions against Covenant breaking states; (iv) Formulation of plans for the reduction of parmanents kepping in view the geographical situation and circumstances of each state; (v) Advise how the evil effect of manufacture of munitions and implements of war by private enterprises could be prevented; (vi) Suggest military sanctions against states guilty of violating the provisions of the Covenant, including their expulsions; (vii) Inquire into disputes brought before the Council or to refer the same to the Assembly; (viii) Nomination of additional permanent members of the Council; (ix) Nomination of the Secretary General subject to the approval of his appointment by the Assembly; (x) Execution of arbitral awards; (xi) Defining of scope of authority or control to be exercised by the Mandatory Powers under the mandate system; (xii) Direction of the work of the Secretariat and receipt of reports from subsidiary organs of the League.

The Secretariat looked after the routine day-to-day administrative work of the League. It worked under the overall control of the Secretary General.

The Secretary General was assisted by Deputy Secretary General, three Under Secretaries and other staff drawn from various states and recruited by the Secretary General. The employees of the Secretariat were entitled to all diplomatic privileges and immunities available to diplomatic envoys of various countries. The main functions of the Secretariat included (i) registration and publication of treaties concluded by members and non-members; (ii) provision of necessary information and data to various organs and delegates of the League; (iii) preparation of agenda for meetings of various bodies and making arrangements for these meetings; (iv) to encourage members to settle disputes through negotiations; (v) to communicate the decisions and agreements concluded by the League to the member States for their ratification; (vi) to coordinate activities of various organs of the League; and (vii) publication of minutes of the Assembly and Council proceedings in the Journal of the League. In addition to the above three organs the League of Nations Machinery comprised two other major agencies viz. the Permanent Court of International Justice and the ILO. The Permanent Court of International Justice consisted of a benches of 15 judges, who were appointed by the Council and Assembly of the League jointly. The Court considered several cases which were referred to it by the government and also made significant advisory pronouncements. ILO, tried to lay down the minimum international standards for working and living conditions. It also examined the reports form member states regarding implementation of conventions adopted by it. This organisation became the first specialised agency of the United Nationals in 1946.

Functioning of the League of Nations

As the League was formed primarily to preserve international peace and promote co-operation among the member states, it tried to develop open, just and honourable relations among the members and encouraged them to act in accordance with international law. For the attainment of its objectives the League of Nations (i) Formulated plans for the reduction of national armaments; (ii) Encouraged members to respect territorial integrity and political independence of all members; (iii) Encouraged settlement of intentional disputes through peaceful means. If a member state resorted to war in violation of the provisions of the Covenant, its action was to be taken as a war against all members of the League, and action could be taken against the erring state in the form of severance of trade and financial relations as well as armed action. In extreme cases the League could also expel the state from membership of the League as Russia was expelled in 1940 following invasion on Finland. (iv) It was to work for bringing about peaceful changes by impressing on member states to reconsider their existing treaties in the context of the changed international conditions; (v) League ensured well being of the people of Mandate Territories by insisting in annual reports from Mandatory Power and making suitable suggestions for the improvement of conditions of people in these territories; (vi) It took necessary measures for the promotion of human welfare by taking measures for the protection of public health; encouraging research in medicine and various kinds of diseases; assisting various countries in dealing with serious diseases like typhus, cholera small pox etc; All this suggests that the League was to impress on the member states that they must co-operate with each other for the solution of common problems.

The League during its short life of 19 years made considerable achievements in the political, social, humanitarian and economic spheres. In the political sphere it successfully resolved a number of disputes among the member states. It also promoted collective security and tried to tackle problem of disarmament. The League during its existence handled over 40 disputes between different states. Though the League did not meet with uniform success in all these cases, it certainly succeeded, in resolving disputes involving small states. Some ofthe important disputes handled by the League included Osland Island dispute between Sweden and Finland; dispute over Eupen and Malmedy between Germany and Belgium; Mosul Boundary dispute between Turkey and Iraq; Corfu Island dispute between Italy and Greek; dispute due to Greek invasion of Belgium; dispute over Gran Chaco between Bolivia and Paraguarsy; conflict over nationality law of England and France between Great Britian and France; Manchurian crisis which assumed serious dimensions due to occupation of Manchuria by Japan; crisis which arose due to Italy's attack on Ethiopia; dispute over Vilna city between Poland and Lithuania; dispute over upper Silesia; case of Hungarian optants between Hungary and Rumania; dispute between Albania and Yugoslavia ; dispute over Faworzias district between Poland and Czechoslovakia; Austro-German Customs Union between Great Britain, France and Austria; etc. It is noteworthy that the League was comparatively more successful during the period 1924-30 when the major powers extended full support to its action. However, thereafter the major powers tried to promote their own interests, which naturally rendered the League less effective.

The other political achievements of the League included ensuring of proper administration of Mandate Territories and protection of interests of the people of mandatory territories. The League also tried to promote collective security by encouraging Treaty of Mutual Assistance (1923), the Geneva Protocol (1924), Locarno Treaties (1925), Kellogg-Briand Pact (1928) and General Act (1928). Though these steps did not meet with uniform success, they certainly contributed to the power and prestige of the League. The League sought to tackle the problem of disarmament by setting up a permanent Advisory Committee to formulate a programme of disarmament, but could not achieve much success. The League also sought to protect the minorities in different countries and appointed a three member committee to look into the complaints of the minorities. The complaints received by the Committee were taken up with the concerned government and an effort was made to resolve the issue amicably.

But probably the most notable achievement of the League in the political field was successful administration of the Saar Valley through a Governing Commission. Ultimately in 1935 the Commission held a plebiscite in the Saar valley and the people decided by over 90 per cent votes in favour of union with Germany. In case of the free city of Danzig however the League could not prove effective because frequent conflicts took place between Germany and Poland over this territory.

In the social and economic fields also the League did meritorious work. It set up a Permanent Health Organisation in 1923 to protect public health through international co-operation. The Organisation encouraged research in medicine and various kinds of diseases and made significant contributions to the eradication of malaria, smallpox, leprosy, rabies, cancer, tuberculosis, syphilis, heart diseases etc. It sought to regulate the trade in narcotic drugs and restricted trade in opium. The League not only took important steps in the direction of abolition of slavery but also paid considerable attention to the improvement of the condition of workers. It also sought to protect the interests of women and children. For this purpose it adopted a number of conventions. It even paid attention to the problem of resettlement and rehabilitation of refugees. With the help of philanthropist organisations like Red Cross, Children Fund etc. it secured settlement of large number of refugees in Armenia, Austria, Greece, Hungary, Turkey etc. The League was responsible for the repatriation of about 500,000 prisoners of war to their homelands. The League also encouraged co-operation amongst the scientists, artists, teachers, writers etc. of various countries with a view to promoting progress of general civilisation and human knowledge. For this purpose it organised periodical conferences, lectures and published relevant material.

In the economic sphere the League made a serious bid to rehabilitate the world economy which was badly shaken during the first world war. It appointed a number of committees and commissions to delve deep into the matter. It even organised a Conference at Brussels where numerous steps were suggested to control inflation, eliminate wasteful expenditure, balancing the budget and return to gold standards. In 1927 it held the Second World Economic Conference which made useful suggestions for free flow of labour, capital and goods in all countries. In 1933 the League organised a Monetary and Economic Conference in London to take stock of economic problems confronting different countries. Some of the other economic problems where the League did commendable job related to handling of problem of counterfeiting, falsification in gold prices etc. The League even held some of the countries to rehabilitate their economies by rendering them necessary assistance. Some of the countries which were provided assistance included Austria, Hungary, Greece, Bulgaria etc. The League even tried to encourage international travel and laid down rules and regulations for smooth travel amongst different countries. The League also tried to simplify the frontier formalities for passengers and goods traffic to facilitate international traffic.

It is evident from the preceeding account that the League of Nations did commendable job in the political, social, economic and cultural spheres. It is true that in the political sphere the League failed to keep the big powers like Japan, Italy, Germany and Russia under check, but its achievements in the social, economic and cultural spheres were indeed commendable. According to Cordell Hull 'The League of Nations has been responsible for more humanitarian and scientific endeavour than any other organisation in history.

Failure of the League

Despite its numerous achievements in the social, economic and cultural spheres, the League failed to achieve its main objective viz. 'save the succeeding generations from the scourge of war', because within two decades of its establishment the world was confronted with the second world war and the League could not do anything. The main causes which contributed to the failure of the League were as follows:

1. In the first place, as the League of Nations was made a part of the peace treaties concluded at the end of first world war, this gave rise to several suspicions in the minds of the vanquished powers, who looked upon the League as an instrument for the maintenance of status quo. Even the neutral states who never aligned themselves with the war aims of the Allies looked upon the League with suspicion.
2. Secondly, the failure of the U.S. to join the League of Nations (because the American Senate refused to ratify the Treaty of Versailles) also rendered the League ineffective because members like England became quite lukewarm in their support to the League.
3. Thirdly, the lack of universal character also rendered the League ineffective. At no time all the big powers were members of the League. At

the time of its establishment Germany, Russia, Austria and Turkey were kept out of the League which naturally gave them the impression that it was an organ for the preservation of fruits of victory and maintaining status quo. No doubt subsequently these powers were admitted as members of the League, but at no time all the major powers were members of the League. This naturally rendered the League of Nations less effective.

4. Fourthly, the various member states looked upon the League of Nations as a convenient tool for the promotion of their interests rather than a forum for international co-operation. Thus France wanted to use the League to keep Germany weak and supported Italy's action in Abyssinia to gain a potentiality against Germany. Britain wanted to use the League for preservation of balance of power. Germany joined the League to get the humiliating terms of the Treaty of Versailles expunged. Potter has observed 'It was not the League of the Nations, but the nations of the League which failed'.

5. Fifthly, the Organisational defects of the League of Nations also contributed to the failure of the League. The Covenant accepted war as a normal method for settlement of international disputes by permitting to resort to defensive war. Further, under the Covenant a country could be held guilty of resorting to war only through a unanimous resolution of the Council, which was not possible in view of persistent political rivalry among the various member states. The lack of an international force which could help the League to enforce its decisions also rendered it ineffective. Further, under the Covenant the League could not take immediate action. It had to wait for some time before it could initiate action, which often resulted in various powers adopting rigid stand on the issue which was not easy to change subsequently. Above all the Covenant accorded equal status to all the member states irrespective of their size and resources, which was naturally resented by the big powers. Naturally they were not willing to assume major responsibility for the resolution of the conflict.

6. Narrow nationalistic interests encouraged the people of different countries to support even undesirable activities of their national governments. Thus the people of Japan, Italy, Germany and Russia supported their governments in their aggression, without realising that it posed a serious threat to world peace. Likewise the people of England, France and the United States did not favour the involvement of their governments in the conflicts with the Axis powers because of purely selfish considerations. This naturally rendered the League of Nations less effective.

7. The economic depression of the 1930's also contributed to failure of the League. It not only caused serious financial difficulties for the League but also encouraged the states like Japan and Germany to resort to programme of militarism on the plea of providing employment to their people. The League could hardly do anything to check all this. This resulted in piling of armaments which ultimately jeopardized world peace

and contributed to the collapse of the League of Nations.

8. Deliberate flouting of the Covenant of the League by the big powers and the failure of the League to keep powers like Japan, Italy and Germany under check greatly undermined the faith of the smaller states in the League. They were convinced that the League could not protect them against the big powers and they must find other methods to protect themselves.
9. The shabby treatment meted out to powers like Italy and Turkey at the peace settlement of 1919-20 made them suspicious about the intentions of the League. As these powers were not happy with the peace settlement they were determined to flout the authority of the League at the first available opportunity.
10. Above all, it has been argued that the League failed because it was ahead of time. The states were not willing to compromise with their sovereignty and still considered that national interests were paramount. They agreed to accept the Covenant of the League because they did not want to displease the American President (Wilson) who had rendered great service to the Allies during the first world war and was largely responsible for their victory over the Axis powers.

Though the League of nations became a casualty of the second world war, but the ideals which it sought to promote, the hope to which it gave rise, the method it devised, the agencies created, have become an essential part of the political thinking of the civilized world and their influence will survive until mankind enjoys a unity transcending the division of states and nations."

FURTHER READINGS

E. H. Carr — *International Relations between the two World Wars*

J. I. Knudson — *A History of the League of Nations*

F. Pollock — *The League of Nations*

George Scott — *The Rise and Fall of the League of Nations*

C. K. Webster and S. Herbert — *The League of Nations in Theory and Practice*

Chapter 3

ORIGIN OF THE UNITED NATIONS AND ITS PURPOSE

Establishment of U. N.

The foundations of the United Nations were laid on the ashes of the League of Nations. The League's failure to avert war and promote the cause of peace encouraged the statesmen of the world to reiterate the conviction of the people all over the world to work out for enduring peace. The task was rendered easy because by this time even the United States of America was willing to enter a system of collective security. Though the statesmen could have thought of reviving or improving the League of Nations, they decided to start afresh due to several reasons. First, they thought that psychologically it would be better to establish a new Organisation than revive an Organisation to which the stigma of failure was attached. Secondly, it would have been absolutely necessary to revive the covenant in the changed conditions. It was felt that it would be easier to draft a new document than to modify the old one. Thirdly, U.S. President Roosevelt felt that the American people would be willing to join a new world Organisation rather than join the League which had evoked bitter political controversy in the U.S.A. Fourthly, it was realised that no security organisation could be effective unless all the Great Powers were members of the Organisation. As Russia had been expelled from the League of Nations in 1939, she would have been reluctant to join the League of Nations. Hence it was felt desirable to have a new international organisation in the form of United Nations.

Inter – Allied Declaration

The first step in the direction of establishment of United Nations was taken in June 1941 when the representatives of Australia, Canada, New Zealand, South Africa and the United Kingdom and the exiled governments of Belgium, Czechoslovakia, Greece, Luxembourg, Netherlands, Norway, Poland, Yugoslavia and France joined the Inter-Allied Declaration in London. They asserted that "the only true basis of enduring peace is the willing co-operation of free peoples in a world in which, relieved of the menace of aggression, ail may enjoy economic and social security". These representatives asserted their intention "to work together and with other free people, both in war and peace, to this end."

The Atlantic Charter

The next important step in the direction of the United Nations was take in August 1941 when President Roosevelt of the USA Prime Minister Winston Churchill, of Great Britain, signed the Atlantic Charter on a battleship in the North Atlantic. The Charter outlined eight general principles on the basis of which the future world order was to be raised.

(1) The two leaders stated "after the final destruction of the Nazi tyranny they hoped for a peace that would enable all nations to dwell in safety within their own boundaries and would ensure that all people in all lands could live out their lives in freedom from fear and want.'

(2) They asserted that their countries do not seek any aggrandisement– territorial or other.

(3) All the nations must abandon the use of force because peace could not be maintained if nations continue to use arms to threaten aggression outside their frontiers.

(4) Disarmament was essential 'pending the establishment of a wider and permanent system of general security'. The two governments promised to aid and encourage all other practicable measures which will lighten for peace-loving people the crushing burden of armaments.

(5) The two governments asserted that they respect the right of all people to choose the form of government under which they will live, and they wish to see sovereign rights and self-government restored to those who have been forcibly deprived of them.

(6) Peace should enable all men to transverse the high seas and oceans without hindrance.

(7) They will endeavour to further the enjoyment by all states of access on equal terms to the trade and raw materials of the world which are needed for their economic prosperity.

(8) They expressed desire to bring about the fullest collaboration between all nations in the economic field with the object of security for all, improved labour standards, economic advancement and social security.

Declaration by the United Nations

The signing of the Declaration of United Nations on 1 January 1942 by representatives of 26 nations involved in fighting against the Axis powers was the next important step in the direction of formation of United Nations. In this Declaration the signatory governments proclaimed their support for the purpose and principles of the Atlantic Charter and their conviction that complete victory over their enemies was essential for the defence of life, liberty, independence, religious freedom, human rights and justice and that they were engaged in a 'common struggle against the savage and brutal forces seeking to subjugate the world'. The representatives of these 26 nations pledged to employ all military and economic resources against those members of the Tripartite Pact and its adherents, with which their government was at war; to cooperate with the other signatories; and not to make a separate armistice or peace with the enemies.

The Declaration was left open for signature by other nations which were or may render material assistance and contributions in the struggle for victory over Hitlerism.

Moscow Declaration

On 30 October 1943 the Foreign Ministers of Soviet Union (Molotov), the United Kingdom (Anthony Eden), and United States (Cordell Hull), and China's Ambassador to Soviet Union (Too Ping Sheung) signed the Moscow Declaration. The four governments proclaimed that they "recognize the necessity of establishing at the earliest practicable date a general international organisation, based on the principle of the sovereign equality of all peace-loving States, and open to membership by all such States, large and small, for the maintenance of international peace and security." According to Vendenbosch and Hogan "from the point of view offering a new international Organisation this document was very important, since its statements on this subject were more specific than those of the Atlantic Charter, and it also definitely committed the Soviet Union to active cooperation in establishing a security organisation."

Teheran Conference

In November 1943 President Roosevelt, Prime Minister Churchill, and Premier Stalin met at Teheran and issued a joint statement on 1 December 1943 by which they accepted the supreme responsibility to make a peace which will command the goodwill of the overwhelming mass of the people of the world and banish the scourge and terror of war for many generations. They further sought the co-operation and active participation of all nations, large and small, whose peoples in heart and mind were dedicated to the elimination of tyranny and slavery, oppression and intolerance.

Dumbarton Oaks Conference

Concrete plans for the creation of the United Nations were drawn up at the Dumbarton Oaks Conference held at Washington from 21 August 1944 to 7 October 1944. The proceedings of the Conference can be broadly divided into two phases. During the first phase the representatives of the United States, the United Kingdom and the Soviet Union conferred for six weeks on the main outlines of the proposed international organisation. In the second phase the representatives of the Soviet Union were dropped and replaced by those of China. The proposals for the establishment of a General International Organisation were published on 9 October 1944 and were sent to all other governments for review. These proposals can very well be considered the first draft of the United Nations Charter. However, these proposals were briefer than the final Charter, particularly in respect to economic and functional aspects.

At this Conference the four powers agreed on proposals for the aims, structure and functioning of the world organisation. It was agreed that China, France, the Soviet Union and the United Kingdom would be permanently represented on the Council. However, these powers could not reach any agreement on the voting procedure to be followed in the Council.

The Yalta Conference

In February 1945 President Roosevelt, Prime Minister Churchil and Marshal Stalin met at Yalta and took up the question of voting procedure in the Security Council, which had remained unsolved at Dumbarton Oak. They also drafted a plan for the occupation and control of defeated Germany and for keeping order in liberated Europe. The 'veto' formula, later embodied in the UN Charter was also finalised at the Yalta Conference. At Yalta a system of trusteeship limited to the following three categories was agreed upon (i) Former mandates of the League of Nations (these were former colonies of Germany and Turkey which had been put under the supervision of the League), some of which had not yet gained independence. (2) Territories to be taken from Germany and Japan after world war II (3) Territories which the present colonial powers would voluntarily put under the supervision of the projected United Nations trusteeship system. The Conference, however, reassured the British that no part of their empire would be put under the control of the United Nations without their consent.

The Yalta Conference also deliberated on voting and decision-making procedures and decided that the permanent members of the Security Council should be given the right of veto, except on procedural matters. The procedural matters should be decided by majority of 7 of the 11 members. At the Conference, the Soviet Union agreed that parties to a conflict should not have veto in the Security Council when the issue was a matter of peaceful settlement of a dispute. But when the Security Council considered any enforcement action, the parties to the conflict would also have right to vote.

It was announced at the Yalta Conference that a conference of United Nations would be called to meet at San Francisco in the United States on 25 April 1945 to prepare the charter of such an Organisation, along the lines proposed in the informal conversations held at Dumbarton Oaks.

San Francisco Conference

The Dumbarton Oaks proposals were studied by the nations of the world, both individually and collectively. The representatives of 20 Latin American countries met at Mexico City between 21 February and 8 March 1945 and adopted a set of points to be taken into consideration in the drawing up of the charter of the proposed Organisation. Similar talks were held in London among the representatives of the British Commonwealth from 4 to 13 April 1945 where the participants concluded that Dumbarton Oaks proposals provide the basis for a charter, and also asserted that improvement and expansion were called for in certain respects.

The San Francisco Conference, which marks the culmination point in the emergence of the United Nations, started on 25 April. This conference officially known as United Nations Conference on International Organisation was held under the chairmanship of Edward Stesttinius, the U.S. Secretary of State. The Conference was attended by 260 representatives from 50 states. The Conference met for two months in full session and in small committees. It considered the Dumbarton Oaks proposals, the Yalta Agreement and amendments proposed by various governments. Out of these deliberations emerged the 111 article Charter. At the plenary session the delegates unanimously adopted the Charter of the United Nations on 25 June. The signing ceremony took place the next day at the auditorium of the Veterans' Memorial Hall. The Charter actually came into force four months later on 24 October 1945 when the permanent members of the Security Council and majority of the other signatories had filed their instruments of ratification.

THE PURPOSES AND PRINCIPLES OF THE UNITED NATIONS

The purposes of the United Nations are set forth in Article 1 of the Charter. These include the following:

1. Maintenance of international peace and security.
2. Development of friendly relations among nations.
3. International co-operation in solving problems of economic, social, cultural and humanitarian nature; promotion and encouragement of respect for human rights and fundamental freedom.
4. To act as a centre for harmonising the actions of nations to achieve the above ends.

It will be observed from the above list of purposes of the United Nations, that maintenance of international peace and security has been given first place, because in its absence the other purposes of the United Nations cannot be realised. For the purpose of maintenance of international peace and security, the UN can take effective collective measures for the prevention and removal of threats to peace, and for the suppression of acts of aggression or other breaches of peace, and to bring about any peaceful means, and in conformity with the principles of justice and international law, adjustments or settlement of international disputes of situations which might lead to a breach of peace.

In the second place UN seeks to develop friendly relations among nations based on respect for the principle of equal rights and self-determination of the people and can take other appropriate measures to strengthen universal peace. Both the above purposes of the United Nations are essentially political in character because they have a direct bearing on the struggle for power among the nations.

The third purpose of the United Nations is to ensure international cooperation for solving international problems of economic, social, cultural or humanitarian nature. It promotes and encourages respect for human rights and assures fundamental freedom to all without distinction of race, sex, language or religion.

Finally, the United Nations is expected to act as centre for the coordination of various international economic, social, cultural activities. It is noteworthy that the United Nations alone does not coordinate all these activities. A number of other organisations also play a vital role in this regard. However, the charter expects the UN to be the centre of all these activities.

For the attainment of the above purposes the UN acts in accordance with certain principles which have been outlined in Article 2 of the UN Charter. These principles include the following:

1. The Organisation is based on the principle of the sovereign equality of all its members.

2. The members shall fulfil in good faith the obligations assumed by them in accordance with the present Charter.

3. All members shall settle their international disputes by peaceful means in such a manner that international peace and security, and justice are not endangered.

4. All members shall refrain in their international relations from the threat or use of force against the territorial integrity or political independence of any state, or in any other manner inconsistent with the purposes of the United Nations.

5. All members shall give the United Nations every assistance in any action it takes in accordance with the present Charter, and shall refrain from giving assistance to any state against which the United Nations is taking preventive or enforcement action.

6. The Organisation shall ensure that states which are not members of the United Nations act in accordance with these.

7. The Organisation shall not intervene in matters essentially within the domestic jurisdiction of any state. This provision shall not, however, prejudice the application of enforcement action with respect to threats to peace, breaches of peace and acts of aggression.

It shall be desirable to know how far the above principles have actually been adhered to. As regards the principle of sovereign equality of states, though the UN Charter has accorded equal representation to the States in the General Assembly and they enjoy equal votes, but this principle has been compromised by according 'veto' power to the big five members of the Security Council. With regard to the second principle also the members of the UN have not fully lived up to their obligations set forth in the Charter and their commitment has merely proved to be a pious wish. With regard to the third principle though the members have made use of instruments like negotiation, enquiry, mediations, conciliation, arbitration and judicial settlement for the settlement of their disputes, they have also made use of regional agencies or arrangements for the protection of their interests. The members have also followed the fourth principle of refraining from the use of force against territorial integrity or political independence of other states. Members have also generally shown readiness to assist the United Nations in any action it proposed to take in accordance with the Charter. The UN has also tried to ensure that the non-members act in accordance with the principles of the UN Charter and thus impart universal character to the Organisation. Finally, the principle that the UN shall not intervene in matters which fall within the domestic jurisdiction of a state, has seriously restricted the authority of the Organisation. It is indeed difficult to determine when a particular issue falling within the jurisdiction of the state may cease to be a matter of national concern alone and assume international dimensions.

HOW FAR UNITED NATIONS IS AN IMPROVEMENT OVER LEAGUE OF NATIONS

Though both the League of Nations and the United Nations aimed at promotion of international co-operation and establishment of international peace and security, yet they differed from each other in many ways.

1. First, the UN Charter in comparison to the Covenant of the League is a much longer document. As against 26 articles of the Covenant, the UN Charter has 111 articles. This is due to the fact that the UN Charter has discussed the matters in greater detail. The UN Charter sometimes even resorts to repetitions for emphasis.
2. Secondly, the League at no stage had all great powers as its members. Only two of the five powers at a time became members of the League. On the other hand the UN included all the super powers of the post world war II period as members.
3. Thirdly, with regard to the structure also the two differ. Whereas the League had three principal organs viz. the Assembly, the Council and the Secretariat, the UN has six principal organs viz. the General Assembly, the Security Council, the Economic and Social Council, the Trusteeship Council, the International Court of Justice and the Secretariat. No doubt, the League also provided for a permanent Court of International Justice, but it did not form integral part of the League. Even the Mandates Commission under the League was quite different from the Trusteeship Council provided under the UN Charter.
4. Whereas the Covenant of the League did not draw any distinction between the powers of the Council and the Assembly, the UN Charter has clearly divided the powers of the General Assembly and the Security Council. The General Assembly is mainly responsible for making recommendations for international peace and security, election of non-permanent members of the Security Council, admission of new members, election of the members of various agencies of the United Nations, budgetary matters etc. On the other hand the Security Council is mainly responsible for the maintenance of international peace and security.
5. The voting procedure under the League and the UN also fundamentally

differs. Under the Covenant decisions were taken by the Assembly as well as the Council by unanimity of the members present and voting. On the other hand under the UN Charter the General Assembly decides ordinary matters by simple majority and decides all important matters by two-thirds majority. The decisions of the Security Council on all procedure matters are taken by affirmative votes of nine members, while all other matters are decided by affirmative vote of nine members, which includes the concurring votes of the permanent members.

6. The procedure for amendment of Covenant and UN Charter also fundamentally differed. Amendments in the Covenants could take place only after they were ratified by the members of the League whose representatives composed the Council and by the members of the League whose representatives composed the Assembly. These amendments were not binding on the parties which recorded dissent. However, such states ceased to be the members of the League. On the other hand the UN Charter can be amended by two-thirds majority of the members of Assembly, and has to be ratified by two-thirds members of the United Nations, including all the permanent members of the Security Council, in accordance with their respective constitutions.

7. The Covenant contained a provision for withdrawal of membership. A member state could withdraw from the membership of the League after giving a notice of two years of its intention to do so. Further, a state ceased to be a member of the League if it voted against and refused to ratify an amendment. On the other hand the UN Charter does not contain any specific provision for withdrawal. Further, a member of the UN does not cease to be its member if it refuses to ratify an amendment to the Charter. On the other hand an amendment, adopted by the General Assembly is binding on all the members.

8. The Covenant of the League did not concede right of individual or collective self-defense to the members. The UN Charter on the other hand specifically recognises the right of individual or collective self-defence in the event of armed attack against a member of the UN until the Security Council takes measures necessary for the maintenance of international peace and security. However, the measures taken by the members in the exercise of right of self-defence have to be immediately reported to the Security Council and do not in any way affect the authority and responsibility of the Security Council.

9. Under the Covenant the members could decide whether another member had violated its obligations and whether enforcement measures, not involving the use of armed forces, should be adopted or not. But under the UN Charter this task has been assigned to the Security Council which has to decide whether there exists a threat to the peace or not. Once the Security Council takes a decision in this regard the members of the UN are duty bound to support the enforcement action of the Security Council.

10. The League Council did not enjoy any power to take action in the event

of armed aggression under the Covenant. But under the UN Charter the Security Council can take immediate action.

11. The activities of the League were mainly confined to the political sphere, even though it also undertook some minor social, economic and cultural functions. On the other hand the UN lays great emphasis on the economic, social, cultural and humanitarian activities. For this purpose special body has been provided in the form of Economic and Social Council. No such organ existed under the Covenant.

12. The Covenant did not contain any provisions with regard to human rights and fundamental freedoms. On the other hand the UN Charter attaches great importance to human rights and fundamental freedoms. In fact the General Assembly of the UN proceeded to adopt a 'Declaration of Human Rights' which stipulates the various rights and freedoms which the members are expected to make available to their citizens.

13. The League paid very little attention to the interests of the dependent people. It adopted a mandate system with a view to protecting and prom6ting the interests of dependent people, but it played only limited role. The UN Charter on the other hand contains very elaborate provisions with regard to dependent people. The Charter contains Declaration regarding Non-Self-governing Territories which is binding on all the members of the UN which administer such territories. These members are obliged to promote the social, economic and cultural welfare of the inhabitants and to prepare them for self-government as rapidly as possible. Even the Trusteeship System under the UN is an improvement over the Mandate System provided under the League, and the Trusteeship Council enjoys more extensive powers than those enjoyed by the Mandates Commission under the League.

14. The Covenant did permit regional arrangements for securing the maintenance of peace, but the provisions under the Covenant were quite passive and ambiguous. On the other hand, the UN Charter accords greater recognition to the regional arrangements for the maintenance of peace and security. It specially enjoins on the members entering regional arrangements to achieve pacific settlement of local disputes through regional arrangements or by such regional agencies before referring them to the Security Council. On the other hand, the Security Council is also expected to 'encourage the development of pacific settlement of local disputes through such regional arrangements or by such regional agencies either on the initiative of the states concerned or by reference from the Security Council.'

It is clear from the preceding discussion that the UN Charter constitutes a definite improvement over the Covenant of the League. As Hartmann has observed 'the United Nations is, so far as its vital functions are concerned, an improved version of League.'

FURTHER READINGS

H. Nicholas	*The United Nations as a Political Institution*
Inis L. Claude	*Swords into Ploughshares*
A. Vendenbosch and W.N. Hogan	*The United Nations*
Gerard J. Mangone	*A Short History of International Organisation*
Asha Hans	*The United Nations*
U. N. Publication	*Everyone's United Nations*
Evan Luard	*A History of the United Nations*
Ruth B. Russel	*A History of the United Nations Charter*

Chapter 4

GENERAL ASSEMBLY

Composition

The General Assembly is the apex body of the United Nations. It has been described as 'the town meeting of the world' because all the members of the United Nations are *ipso facto* members of the General Assembly. Each member has a single vote even though each state can send five representatives to the Assembly. These representatives are the nominees of their respective governments. The Charter does not impose any restriction on the member states with regard to the appointment of the delegates to the General Assembly except that article 8 enjoins upon the states not to make any discrimination on the basis of sex. These representatives have to act in accordance with the instructions, of their respective governments and are responsible to them. Thus the General Assembly is more of a diplomatic conference than a legislative body.

President

The General Assembly at its first session elects a President for a term of twelve months. As a matter of convention, the President is taken from a minor country. It may be noted that though the President is elected by the General Assembly, in reality the choice of the candidate for the post of President is made through private consultations before the session of the Assembly and a candidate who is acceptable to the majority of the members is elected as President. It is noteworthy that during the initial years close contests took place for the office of Presidentship. But now the Presidentship of the Assembly is rotated among five group of sates viz African Asian ; Eastern; European; Lotin American ; Western European ; and of others.

Vice-Presidnents and Charimen of Standing Committees

In addition to the President, the General Assembly at its first session also elects 21 Vice-Presidents and seven Chairmen for the seven Standing Committees. All these officials, along with the President constitute the General Committee, which acts as the steering committee for each session. This committee acts as advisory body to the President. However, its recommendations are not binding on the President. It mainly advises the President with regard to agenda and priorities of debates, allocation of items to the seven committees, coordination of work of the standing committees, fixing date for adjournment of Assembly and assistance to the President in the discharge of his responsibilities.

While nominating the seventeen Vice-Presidents of General Assembly effort is made to provide representation to all the areas. Usually seven members are taken from Asian and African states; one from Eastern European states; three from Latin American states; two from Western European and other states; and five seats are given to five permanent members of the Security Council. Likewise, the Chairmanship of the Seven Committees is also allocated on the basis of these areas

Sessions of Assembly

The regular session of the General Assembly is held once is held once a year. The session commences on the third Tuesday in September and continues until mid-December. In addition special sessions of the Assembly can be called at the request of the Security Council, a majority of member states or one member state with the concurrence of the majority. Emergency special session of the Assembly can be called within 24 hours of a request by the Security Council on vote of any nine of its members, or by a majority of the member states.

Voting

Decisions on all important questions are taken by two-third majority of the members present and voting. Some of the important matters which fall in this category include recommendations on peace and security; election of members of the Security Council, the Economic and Social Council and the Trusteeship Council ; admission, suspension and expulsion of member states; trusteeship questions and budgetary matters. The other matters can be decided by simple majority.

Agenda

The General Assembly conducts its business on the basis of the agenda which is prepared by the Secretary General in the month of July. The Secretary General has not much discretion with regard to the determination of the agenda because there are certain items which must find their place on the agenda. Thus the agenda of the Assembly invariably includes Annual Report of the Secretary General, reports of other organs of the United Nations, items proposed by members of the United Nations. Further, this agenda is reviewed by the General Committee of the Assembly to avoid overlapping and repetition.

Committees of Assembly

As the General Assembly is quite a large body where effective deliberations are not possible, it works through Committees. The matters are allocated to the various committees on the advice of the General Committee. The main Committees of the General Assembly, in addition to the General Committee are:

First Committee (Disarmament and related International Security matters)

Special Political Committee

Second Committee (Economic and Financial matters)

Third Committee (Social, Humanitarian and Cultural matters)

Fourth Committee (Decolonisation matters)

Fifth Committee (Administrative and Budgetary matters)

Sixth Committee(Legal matters)

It may be noted that certain questions are considered in the plenary meetings of the Assembly itself rather than being referred to the Committees of the Assembly. Even the matters which are considered by the Committees and submitted to the Assembly are voted on in the plenary meetings. Usually resolutions are adopted in the plenary meetings by acclamation or without vote; but votes can also be taken by roll call.

General Debate

The Annual Session of the General Assembly starts with a general debate. This general debate, according to Nicholas is rare moment for seizing the spotlight and putting a point of view that might otherwise be ignored. If one of the advantages of the U. N. is that the world comes flooding in there, making of Turle Bay a kind of synthesis of the seven seas, the General Debate is, if not an indispensable, at least an established and convenient channel for this. Of course member states present themselves exclusively in the guise in which they wish to be known, but this too is an aspect of reality – one often neglected in ambassadorial dispatches and intelligence reports.

It may be noted that the General Assembly does not have any effective rules for the conduct of the general debate. The Chairman of the Assembly exercises discretion in this context.

He has to call upon the speakers in the order in which they signify their desire to speak. Although the President can call upon a delegate to be relevant, but generally he refrains from making use of this power due to fear of provoking resentment of the members. Instead the President has preferred the gentler method of urging, requesting and appealing to the delegates to secure their compliance. Again, the President cannot impose any time-restriction on a speaker. This can be determined by the Assembly by majority vote. Similarly it is the Assembly which determines how many times a member can speak. Though the proceedings of the Assembly may give the impression that it works like a legislature, but actually it lacks most of the legislative ingredients like parties, whips, government and opposition, front-benchers and back-benchers etc. Further the principle of responsibility, is also conspicuously absent in its operation.

Functions and Powers

The General Assembly performs varied and extensive functions which can be conveniently studied under the following heads.

Deliberative Functions

The General Assembly can discuss any question or matter within the scope of the UN Charter and relating to any organ of the United Nations. It can also invite the attention of the Security Council to the situations which are likely to endanger international peace and security and recommend measures for the peaceful adjustment of situation which is likely to disturb the friendly relations between nations.

The General Assembly can also initiate studies and make recommendations for (a) promoting international co-operation in political arena and encourage progress of international law and its codification; (b) promoting international co-operation in the economic, social, cultural, educational and health fields and assisting in realisation of human rights and fundamental freedom for all without discrimination of race, sex, language or religion. The deliberative functions of the Assembly according to Vandenbosch and Hogan, implies two things. First, it entails the power to ascertain the facts and information necessary for the discussion. Secondly, its deliberations may go beyond mere discussion and may result in certain recommendations. In other words the General Assembly can make recommendations and also conduct investigations for promoting international co-operation.

The recommendations of the General Assembly do not possess any legal sanction and are merely an expression of opinion or advice of the Assembly, which is not binding on the member states. Further, though the General Assembly enjoys extensive powers with regard to discussion on world problems, it cannot intervene in matters falling within the domestic jurisdiction of the states. But in view of the growing inter-dependence of internal and foreign affairs, it is not always easy to say what really falls under the 'domestic jurisdiction'. For example, in 1948 India lodged a complaint with General Assembly regarding maltreatment of Indian minority in South Africa, but the South African Government challenged the right of the Assembly to consider the issue on the plea that the matter essentially relates to 'domestic jurisdiction'. Despite this the General Assembly proceeded to adopt a resolution in December 1946 and insisted that the treatment of the Indian minority should be in accordance with international obligations, including the provisions of the Charter. It is a different matter that the South African Government refused to implement the resolution on the ground that the matter did not fall within the competence of the General Assembly.

Competence of the General Assembly.

The General Assembly has also performed certain legislative functions, even though the UN Charter did not assign any legislative functions to the Assembly. In fact, sometimes the member states agree in advance to accept the recommendations of the Assembly. This actually happened in the case of the Italian colonies when an agreement could not be reached by the United States, Great Britain, France and the Soviet Union regarding their disposal, and they referred the issue to the General Assembly with an understanding that the recommendations of the Assembly would be binding on the parties.

Supervisory Functions

The supervisory functions of the General Assembly include the power to exert control and regulate the working of other organs and agencies of the United Nations. It receives and considers annual and special reports from other organs of the United Nations. Thus the Security Council reports to the General Assembly the measures decided upon or taken for the maintenance of international peace and security. Likewise the Economic and Social Council has to obtain the approval of the General Assembly before convening International Conferences, while concluding agreements with Specialized Agencies or while seeking advisory opinion of the International Court of Justice. Even the Trusteeship Council operates under the supervision of the General Assembly. The General Assembly also enjoys the power to lay down regulations for the appointment of the staff of the Secretariat. In short, it can be said the General Assembly exercises overall control or supervision over the principal organs of the United Nations and its specialised agencies.

Financial Functions

The General Assembly enjoys important financial powers. It apportions expenses among the member states and approves the budget of the United Nations. Thus with its power of financial control, it is able to review the working of other organs of the United Nations. The responsibility for the financial and budgetary arrangements of the specialised agencies of the Organisation also rests with the General Assembly. Control over finances gives the General Assembly the power to supervise and control the activities of other organs and agencies of the organisation.

Electoral Functons

The electoral functions of the General Assembly include the admission of new members and selection of members of other organs. It admits new members to the UN on the recommendations of the Security Council. It may be noted that no new member can be admitted without an affirmative vote of the General Assembly. The – General Assembly can also suspend a member on the basis of recommendations of the Security Council on the ground of violating the principles of the UN charter continuously. The General Assembly also elects members of several other organs. Thus it elects ten nonpermanent members of the Security Council; the judges of the International Court of Justice for a period of nine years in concurrence with the Security Council. It also appoints the Secretary General on the recommendations of the Security Council.

The Constituent Functions

The General Assembly enjoys significant power with regard to amendment of the Charter. Amendments to the UN Charter can be carried out by the General Assembly by two-third majority of its members. However, these amendments have to be ratified by two-thirds of the members of the United Nations, including all permanent members of the Security Council, in accordance with their constitutional process. The General Assembly can convene a general conference, in concurrence with the Security Council, to review the original Charter. For the discharge of these duties the General Assembly can establish various committees and subsidiary organs. Some of the committees which have been setup by the General Assembly in this regard include the Political and Security Committee, Economic and Financial Committee, Social Humanitarian and Cultural Committee, Trusteeship Committee, Administrative and Budgetary Committee, Legal Committee, the General Committee and the Credentials Committee. For tackling specific problems the General Assembly can also establish ad hoc committees.

UNITING FOR PEACE RESOLUTION OF 1950 AND CHANGED ROLE OF THE ASSEMBLY

A remarkable change took place in the powers and role of the General Assembly following adoption of 'Uniting for Peace Resolution' on 3 November 1953. This resolution was introduced by the United States apprehending that the Soviet Union's use of veto in the Security Council would certainly block any action similar to the one taken in Korea. The resolution laid down that if the Security Council, because of lack of unanimity of the permanent members, fails to perform the primary responsibility for maintenance of peace and security, in any case when there appears to be threat to peace, breach of peace or act of aggression, the General Assembly shall consider the matter immediately with a view to making appropriate recommendations to the members for 'collective measures', including, in the case of breach of peace or act of aggression, the use of armed forces when necessary to maintain or restore international peace and security.

The resolution provided that if the General Assembly is not in session at the time, it may meet in emergency special sessions within twenty-four hours of the request thereof. Such emergency special sessions shall be convened if requested by the Security Council on the vote of any seven members, or by a majority of the members of the United Nations. The resolution provided for the establishment of a fourteen-nation Peace Observation Commission to observe and report on dangerous situations in any part of the world. It urged the member-states to maintain in their armed forces special elements which could be made available for the United Nations service on call of the Security Council or the General Assembly. The resolution urged the members to renew their fidelity to the world organisation, honour its decisions and promote respect for human rights.

It may be noted that the Uniting for Peace Resolution could be adopted only because the Soviet delegation had absented from the Security Council, as a protest against its refusal to grant seat to Communist China. However, subsequently even Soviet Union confirmed this practice during the Suez Crisis of 1956 when she supported the Assembly's action against the votes of Britain and France. Thus the Uniting for Peace Resolution greatly strengthened the position of the General Assembly vis-a-vis the Security Council. By virtue of this resolution the General Assembly became the ultimate custodian of collective security measures. Henceforth the General Assembly could determine by two-thirds majority when and where a threat to world peace exists and what joint measures should be taken to counter the threat. Thus the United Nations "reverted to the precedent of the League, where responsibility rested on both a smaller representative organ and the entire body of the states in the organization, whichever was able to function more effectively." (Jacob and Atherton)

The Uniting for Peace Resolution procedure was again used in 1958 during the Jordan and Lebanon crisis and a UN Observation Group was sent to defuse the crisis and deter foreign infiltration.

The position of the General Assembly suffered a setback in the wake of Congo crisis in the early 1960's when the Uniting for Peace Resolution could not be effectively applied due to financial veto and deadlock in the Assembly. As a result, once again the smaller powers started looking towards Security Council for an effective role. The enormous expansion of membership of the Assembly also rendered it ineffective on account of its unwieldy size.

Further, henceforth Soviet Union started making less frequent use of veto in the Council which reduced the need for an alternative agency. Above all, the Security Council members were keen to retain their special influence in the Security Council and naturally encouraged the restoration of the Council's supremacy on questions of security. Despite this there were occasional Special Assemblies on the questions of Rhodesia (1965), South-West Africa (1967) and North South issues (1974-75).

The change in the composition of membership of the United Nations had its impact on the working of the General Assembly and it started devoting greater attention to the discussion of problems concerning development. The other important problems which attracted the attention of the General Assembly include political rights, racial discrimination, human rights etc. In recent years the General Assembly has also taken up for discussion several new subjects which were never discussed by the Assembly in earlier years. This include issues like outer space, the environment, satellite broadcasts, natural resource surveys, population control, application of science to development, sovereignty over natural resources etc.

Evaluation

The General Assembly occupies a predominant position among the organs of the United Nations. It not only exercises supervision over the organs like the Secretariat, the Trusteeship Council and the Economic and Social Council, but also provides direct guidance. It is true that the Assembly does not exercise any direct control over the Security Council and the International Court of Justice, but these organisations have been assigned only specific powers. On the other hand the General Assembly has the right to discuss and take decision on any matter mentioned in the UN Charter.

The predominance of the General Assembly is further evident from the fact that most of the subsidiary bodies of the United Nations as well as its normal; organs have to submit reports to the General Assembly.

In the political sphere the predominance of the General Assembly is assured by its large membership and representation of various member states on terms of equality. This has made the weak states pin their hopes on this body because they can influence its decisions on account of their number. Taking advantage of their majority in the UN, the developing countries have tried to use it to further their own interests and sought transfer of resources from the developed to the developing world. Above all, the General Assembly has greatly influenced the process of world politics by providing the norms within which the states operate for the attainment of their goals.

FURTHER READINGS

H.G. Nicholas	*The United Nations as a Political Institution*
A.Vandenbosch and W. N. Hogan	*The United Nations*
Sydney D. Bailey	*The General Assembly of the United Nations*
M. J. Peterson	*The General Assembly in World Politics*
Ruth B. Russel	*The General Assembly, Patterns, Problems and Prospects*

Chapter 5
THE SECURITY COUNCIL

The Security Council is often described as the enforcement wing of the United Nations. It is primarily responsible for the maintenance of international peace and security. For this purpose, its services can be requisitioned any time. This naturally implies that the Security Council has to work continuously so that it can take quick action in the event of threat to international peace or security.

Composition

The Security Council is a much smaller body than the General Assembly. Initially it consisted of eleven members - five permanent members (United States, United Kingdom, U. S. S. R., France and Nationalist China) and six non-permanent members elected by the General Assembly for a term of two years. The strength of the non-permanent members was raised to ten in 1965. Thus at present the Security Council comprises 15 members - five permanent and ten non-permanent. The five permanent members are China, France, Russia, USA and United Kingdom. The non-permanent members of Security Council are not eligible for immediate re-election. While electing the nonpermanent members of the Security Council, the General Assembly takes into account the contributions of the members towards the maintenance of international peace and security. It also ensures that different geographical regions get equitable representation in the Security Council.

Each member of the Security Council has one vote. Decisions on procedural matters are taken by affirmative vote of at least nine members, while decisions on substantive matters are taken by the votes of nine members, which must also contain the concurring votes of all the permanent members. The Presidency of the Security Council is held by each member of the Security Council in alphabetical order for a period of one month.

FUNCTIONS AND POWERS

The UN Charter has entrusted the responsibility of maintenance of international peace and security to the Security Council. For this purpose all the members of the United Nations are committed to carry out the decisions of the Security Council. It is noteworthy that while all other organs of the United Nations can merely make recommendations to the governments of the member states, the Security Council alone has been vested with the power to take decisions which the member states are obliged to carry out. The main functions of the Security Council can be conveniently studied under the following heads.

Deliberative Functions

In the first instance the Security Council has the power to discuss and investigate any dispute or situation and make recommendation to the member states to settle their disputes by peaceful means. Disputes or situations likely to endanger international peace and security may be brought to the attention of the Security Council by any member of UN, by the General Assembly, or by the Secretary General. Even non-member states can bring the dispute before the Council, provided they accept in advance the obligations of peaceful settlement contained in the UN Charter. It may be noted that a state which is a member of the United Nations, but not of the Security Council, can also take part in the proceedings of the Security Council when it is considering a matter which affects the interest of that country. Even a state which is not a member of the UN can be invited to take part in the discussions of the Council if it is a party to the dispute being considered by the Security Council. However, such states cannot take part in voting.

The Security Council can also take up general questions regarding maintenance of international peace and security. It is responsible for framing plans for the establishment of a system for the control of armaments. The United Nations Atomic Energy Commission was set up by virtue of a resolution of the General Assembly, but it is responsible to and operates under the supervision of the Security Council.

Enforcement Functions

The Security Council has been vested with important enforcement powers. When the Security Council finds that a peaceful settlement among the disputant countries is not possible, it can decide upon measure which it considers necessary for the maintenance of order and restoration of international peace and security. On account of this power, the Security Council is often described as the, 'enforcement arm' of the United Nations. While taking up adequate measures, Security Council first tries to resolve the dispute without involving the use of armed forces. For this purpose it can adopt measures like complete or partial interruption of economic relations, severing of rail, sea, air, postal, radio and other communication links; and snapping of diplomatic relations. When these measures fail to produce the desired effect, the Security Council can take such action by air, sea or land forces, as may be necessary for the maintenance or restoration of international peace and security. Such action may include blockade, demonstrations and other operations by air, sea or land forces of members of the United Nations.

It may be noted that though the Security Council can urge the member nations to apply sanctions against an aggressor, there is no guarantee that the states will answer the call. In this regard Article 43 of the UN Charter enjoins upon all members of the United Nations to make available to the Security Council, on its call and in accordance with the special agreement or agreements, armed forces, assistance and facilities, including rights of passage necessary for the purpose of maintaining peace and security. However, such agreement could not be concluded due to differences among the super powers, and thus these provisions have remained inoperative.

To assist the Security Council on all questions relating to its military requirements for the maintenance of international peace and security, a Military Staff Committee has been established. This Committee also assists the Security with regard to employment and command of forces at its disposal, the regulation of armaments and possible disarmament. This Committee comprises the Chief of Staff of the permanent members of Security Council or their representatives.

It may be observed that though the Charter grants the states the right to have recourse to individual or collective self-defence in the event of an armed attack against them, they are not expected to exercise this right until the Security Council has taken measures necessary to maintain international peace and security. Thus the main thrust of the enforcement duties of the Council is not to envisage specific terms of settlement of individual disputes, but maintenance of international peace and security.

Electoral Functions

The Security Council enjoys extensive electoral powers which pertain to admission of new members and the constitution of other organs of the United Nations. The new members to the world body can be admitted by the General Assembly only on the recommendation of the Security Council. By virtue of this power the Security Council refused to recommend admission of Albania, Bulgaria, Hungary, Rumania etc. as members of the United Nations. The Security Council also takes part in the election of judges of the International Court of Justice. It also makes recommendations regarding the appointment of the Secretary General. Again the recommendation of the Security Council is essential for the suspension of a member of the United Nations by the General Assembly.

Role of the Security Council

Though the UN Charter made the Security Council the most important organ of the United Nations, it has not been able to play the role which was envisaged for it. Since its inception, the Security Council has not only held fewer sessions but the scope of the political issues considered by it has considerably narrowed down. Palmer and Perkins have rightly observed "Although the Security Council was envisaged central agency of the United Nations, it has not been able to play its expected role. The reason is clear, instead of great power unanimity on which the United Nations was predicted, the postwar years have brought major rights and disagreement among the most powerful States of the world. Under these circumstances, the Security Council, in which five permanent members possess an individual veto, has been unable to function effectively. Since the Korean war and the return of the Russian representative to the Security Council on August 1, 1950, the Council has faded into background and its place has been taken in considerable measure by the unwieldy General Assembly, which was not designed to play a major role in the Security field."

Two factors contributed to the reduction of the importance of Security Council in the 1950's. First, adoption of uniting for Peace Resolution by the General Assembly in 1950 which provided that if the Security Council fails to exercise its primary responsibility for the maintenance of international peace and security, due to lack of unanimity of the permanent members, the matter shall be immediately considered by the General Assembly with a view to making appropriate recommendations to the members for collective measures. This resolution made the General Assembly the ultimate custodian of collective security and rendered the Security Council less effective. Secondly, the development of powerful regional security alliances outside the United Nations like NATO, SEATO, Warsaw Treaty, etc. also greatly contributed to the reduction of importance of the Security Council. The growth of these alliances was not only indicative of lack of unity among permanent members of the Security Council but also lack of confidence of the members in the efficacy of the Security Council as an instrument of collective security.

Thirdly, the admission of a large number of independent Afro-Asian countries as members of the United Nations has tilted the balance in favour of the General Assembly. The newly emerged Afro-Asian countries have used the General Assembly to end colonialism, promote human rights and disarmament. In view of their large strength even the major powers have attached great importance to their views and made a bid to win their support.

In the 1960's once again the Security Council started playing more effective role towards the maintenance of peace and security. During the Congo crisis of 1960 most of the important decisions such as dispatch of forces to assist the Congolese government etc. were taken by the Council. Again in October 1962 during the Cuban crisis the Security Council played a leading role. In 1964 on the issue of Cyprus also the Security Council took the decision to send peace-keeping force to take over the responsibility from the British forces. In the subsequent years also the Security Council continued to play effective role in the resolution or handling of various disputes such as question of South Africa and Rhodesia, war in Vietnam in January 1966, the Arab-Israel War of 1967, the India-Pakistan war of 1971 and conflict in Middle East in 1973. The growing importance of the Security Council in the 1960's is further evident from the fact that the number of non-permanent members was raised from 6 to 10 to provide greater representation to the newly independent countries of Asia and Africa.

In recent years there has been a growing feeling among members that the Security Council must be made an effective body as was originally envisaged by the U.N. Charter. For this purpose, it is proposed its powers should be revised, the composition of the Security Council should be changed, the system of 'veto' should be replaced by equal voting rights for all the members of the Security Council. It is also suggested that the Security Council can be made more effective by making greater use of informal techniques like

N.D. Palmer and H. C. Perkins, *International Relations,* p.358

private meetings of the Council, the appointment of conciliators, and by making a bid to reconcile the conflicting interests of the parties before the issue actually comes up for consideration before the Security Council.

RELATIONS BETWEEN GENERAL ASSEMBLY AND SECURITY COUNCIL

The UN Charter has entrusted the responsibility for the maintenance of international peace and security to the Security Council, even though it is required to submit annual reports to the General Assembly with regard to the measures taken by it for the purpose. However, the General Assembly cannot pass any judgement on the action taken by the Security Council. Hence in no way the Security Council is subject to overriding authority of the General Assembly.

The relationship between the Security Council and the General Assembly as envisaged under the U.N. Charter, underwent a change following passage of the Uniting for Peace Resolution in 1950. After the passage of this resolution the General Assembly came to wield very extensive powers in the event of Security Council failing to exercise its primary responsibility of maintenance of international peace and security due to lack of unanimity of permanent members in any case where there appeared to be a threat to peace, breach of peace or act of aggression. This decline in the powers of the Security Council was halted in the sixties and it once against started playing important role in the settlement of international disputes. Thus it played an important role in the handling of crisis in Cuba, Congo, Cyprus, Santo Domingo and India-Pakistan. Security Council also played a prominent role during the Middle East crisis.

The size of the Security Council also gives it an advantage over the General Assembly which is an unwieldy body and meets only for three or four months. onwards the close of the year, while the Security Council is well organised and functions continuously. Therefore, as Prof. Nicholas has observed "In a world where undeclared and lightning war appears henceforth to be the rule rather than the exception, an agency which can respond at once, however, inadequate, is always likely to remain at least a forum of first resort, and on issues on which the Super Powers have the last say, often of last resort too.' (H.G. Nicholas. *The United Nations as a Political Institution,* p. 97)

THE PROBLEM OF VETO

One provision of the UN Charter which has evoked maximum controversy pertains to veto in the Security Council. This controversy has existed from the very inception of the United Nations and has still remained unresolved. For a proper understanding of this problem it shall be desirable to have an idea about the provisions of the UN Charter in this regard.

Article 27 of the UN Charter which deals with the voting procedure provides (i) that each member of the Security Council shall have one vote; (ii) that the decision of the Security Council on procedural matters shall be made by an affirmative vote of seven members; (iii) that decisions of the Security Council on all other matters shall be made by an affirmative vote of seven members, including the concurring votes of the permanent members, provided that in decision under Charter VI and under paragraph 3 of Article 52, a party to a dispute shall abstain from voting. There was hardly any difference of opinion among the members at Dumbarton Oaks with regard to (i) and (ii). There was also agreement on the general principle contained in the third point, except with regard to exceptions enumerated under this point. While the United States took the position that in voting on a substantive question involving pacific settlement a party to a dispute should not be allowed to vote, the Russians took the stand that the principle of big-power unanimity should apply to all substantive matters. However, the differences between the two powers were reconciled in the form of Yalta Formula. Under this formula the parties to a dispute were excluded from voting on a matter of pacific settlement, but not when the enforcement measures were involved. No enforcement action could be taken without the concurrence of the five permanent members.

Some scholars have justified the principle of unanimity among the permanent members on practical grounds. It has been argued that "the leading industrial nations have almost a monopoly of the means of waging a modem global war. If a reasonable degree of co-operation exists among them, it is difficult to see how a large scale war could occur. If, however, they disagree to the point of fighting each other, the obvious result would be a Third World War". It was further argued that "co-operation among the permanent members is essential if the Security Council is to perform its functions. Since its decisions are to be taken by a procedure of voting, the outcome of the voting on a resolution indicates whether or not the necessary agreement exists. If all the members vote the same way, this shows that they agree on the measures to be taken. If some vote for and some against a proposal this shows that they disagree and therefore are not prepared to co-operate in the suggested course of action."

At the San Francisco Conference also there were differences between the small and the big powers with regard to the voting procedure. Some of the smaller countries objected to the voting procedure on the ground it violated the principle of 'sovereign equality' of all the members. They expressed the fear that this would weaken the Security Council by creating the likelihood that the Security Council may not be able to discharge its duties due to a deadlock over the veto. They argued that since no coercion or even legal or binding decisions could be made in this realm, the unanimity of the permanent members was necessary. On the other hand the Great Powers opposed the enforcement action against themselves. They, argued that if such an action became necessary, it would mean a general war and the United Nations would be destroyed. They contended that no enforcement action should be taken against other states without big power unanimity.

Thus the 'veto' provision evoked strong controversy between the Great Powers and the small states. But, as Vandenbosch and Hogan have observed "all the advantages were on the side of the former (Great Powers), for the reason that a United Nations Organisation could function effectively only with all the Great Powers as members; with one or two of the Great Powers absent it would have little, if any, value. Before this inexorable fact the small states had to bow. They were able to effect many changes, most of them improvements, in the Dumbarton Oaks Proposals, but they were unable to dislodge the Great Powers from the predominant position the latter had created for themselves in that document.'

The General Assembly was not happy with the 'veto provisions' and adopted a resolution in April 1949 recommending that the Security Council should consider a number of questions as procedural and the members should consult each other to avoid the veto, which should be exercised only in matters of vital importance. The only impact of this resolution was that the members agreed to consult each other in advance. It also led to an important change in the original plan whereby abstention was not to be regarded as veto, despite a clear reference of concurring votes of the permanent members in the UN Charter.

Effects Of Veto

Almost all the major powers have made use of the 'veto' with the USSR topping the list. Most of the vetoes were applied on the question of membership of the United Nations. Sometimes vetoes were also applied to the same question in successive years. The frequent exercise of' veto' indicated that there were sharp differences between the USA and the USSR, which naturally undermined the effectiveness of the Security Council. On account of East-West differences the Security Council could not make effective use of its powers in disputes like Congo, Berlin, Palestine, Indo-China, Hungary, Suez etc. It also prevented harmonious relations among the permanent members of the Security Council, which was a basic prerequisite for peace, and gave rise to cold war. As a result the states were reluctant to refer their disputes to the Security Council. It has been argued that had there been no 'veto' probably the pacific settlement of disputes would have been encouraged. However, it is erroneous to argue that if there had been no veto, the Security Council would have worked more effectively. It is a matter of common knowledge that even the General Assembly, where the big Five have no 'veto' power, has also not succeeded in obtaining compliance of all its recommendations.

Demand For Abolition Of Veto

In view of the various complications of the provisions concerning 'veto' by the Five Big Powers, a demand has been made for its abolition. It has been argued that the 'veto' provisions have stood in the way of successful working of the United Nations. This is, however, not correct. The success of the United Nations depends on its ability to influence the actions of the member states. If the states are not willing to accept its recommendations, the changing of voting procedure would not do any good. The veto is a symptom of the disagreement rather than its cause and its abolition would not do much good. However, certain modifications may be effected in the application of the veto. Thus veto should be abolished with regard to membership and pacific settlement of disputes. Similarly, it would be desirable to allow the Council to determine the existence of threat to or a breach of peace or an act of aggression through procedural vote, but it would certainly not be desirable to permit the Security Council to decide upon sanctions without the concurrence of the permanent members. The real solution of the problem does not lie in the abolition of the veto but in promoting sufficient co-operation among the members, specially the Great Powers. It is indeed difficult to imagine that the Big Powers would agree to the abolition of the 'veto'.

ASSESSMENT OF SECURITY COUNCIL

At the time of the inauguration of the UN Charter high hopes were expressed about the capacity of the Security Council to maintain international peace and security. But in actual practice its performance, particularly during the last 30 years, has been far less impressive. No doubt the UN Charter had called upon all members of the UN to make available to the Security Council, armed forces assistance and facilities, but this arrangement has proved quite unworkable and the members could not reach any agreement on the composition of a U.N. force. Even if such a force had been created, it would not have been possible to make effective use of such force due to differences among permanent members.

It is true that the Security Council has not been able to play an effective enforcement role, however its central position in the international arena cannot be denied. Whenever there is any conflict the member states turn to the Security Council. Even if the Security Council is not able to immediately halt the fighting or resolve the dispute, it certainly brings to bear the weight of outside opinion and prevents further aggravation of the situation. It helps in tiding over the crisis situations by encouraging the individual powers and groups of nations to find **a** negotiated settlement. Quite often the Security Council succeeded in achieving consensus on issues like Cyprus, Congo and the Middle East where the interests of the Powers were not too divergent. It is true that on other issues where the interests of the Big Powers were difficult to reconcile, it could not achieve much success viz. on the issues of Hungary and Vietnam.

The Security Council, whose position had been some what undermined following adoption of Uniting for Peace Resolution in 1950, has started reasserting itself in recent years. Its role on the question of Rhodesia and Iraqi annexation of Kuwait as well as the Middle East has been quite effective. It also played an important role in bringing an end to the policy of apartheid in South Africa. The Security Council can play an even more effective role in future if the strength of the permanent members is increased and seats are provided to countries like Japan, Germany, Brazil and India.

FURTHER RADINGS

A. Vandenbosch and W. N. Hogan	*The United Nations*
H. G. Nicholas	*The United Nations as a Political Institution*
Sydney D. Bailey	*The Procedure of the UN Security Council*
Nicol Davidson	*UN Security Council : Towards Greater Effectiveness*

Chapter 6

THE ECONOMIC AND SOCIAL COUNCIL

The framers of the UN Charter were fully conscious of the importance of social and economic conditions for the preservation of world peace. Therefore they provided for the establishment of the Economic and Social Council to coordinate the economic and social work of the United Nations and its specialised agencies and institutions. The Economic and Social Council is one of the six principal organs of the United Nations and operates under the authority of the General Assembly. Article 55 of the UN Charter enjoins on the United Nations to create conditions of stability and well-being, which are necessary for peaceful and friendly relations among nations based on respect for the principle of equal rights and self determination of the people by promoting (a) higher standards of living, full employment and conditions of economic and social progress and development; (b) solutions of intertional economic, social, health and related problems and in international cultural and educational cooperation; and (c) universal respect for and observance of human rights and fundamental freedoms for all without distinction of race, sex, language or religion.

Composition

The Economic and Social Council at present consists of 54 members. Each year the General Assembly elects 18 members for a period of three years but the retiring members are eligible for immediate re-election. Originally the Council comprised 27 members. Its strength was raised to 27 in 1965 and 54 in 1973. No criteria have been laid down for the election of members by the General Assembly. However, the General Assembly tries to give representation to variety of social, economic, cultural and geographical interests. In addition, the Council can invite any member of the UN to take part in its deliberations, on any matter of particular concern to that member, without right to vote.

The Council elects a President for one year from among its members. Usually the President is taken from a country which is not a great power.

All the decisions of the Council are taken by simple majority with each member enjoying one vote.

The Council generally holds two month-long sessions every year. One session is held in New York and the other is held in Geneva. During the remaining part of the year the Council carries on its work through its subsidiary bodies – commissions and committees, which meet at regular intervals and report back to the Council.

Functions of the Economic and Social Council

The Council performs variety of functions through studies and reports, discussions and recommendations and coordination.

1. It can make or initiate studies and reports with respect to international economic, social, cultural, educational, health and related matters. Thus the Council has made studies regarding the problems of refugees, the world shortage of housing, the reconstruction of devastated areas and the economic status of women. These studies and reports are very helpful in handling the problems.
2. Secondly, the Economic and Social Council makes recommendations to the General Assembly, the members of the United Nations and specialised agencies with regard to international economic, social, cultural, educational, health and related matters. It can also make recommendations for the purpose of promoting respect for and observance of human rights and fundamental freedom for all. It may be noted that the recommendations of the Council are not binding on the members.
3. Thirdly, the Economic and Social Council can prepare draft conventions for submission to the General Assembly with respect to matters falling within its competence. Such draft conventions have proved quite useful in concluding international agreements. Some of the important conventions drafted by the Economic and Social Council relate to Prevention and Punishment of Crime of Genocide and Protocol relating to the Status of Stateless Persons.
4. Fourthly, the Economic and Social Council convenes international conferences both on its own initiative as well as on instructions from the General Assembly. These conferences can be both intergovernmental and non governmental and usually pertain to matters not falling within the domestics jurisdiction of the members. Some of the important conferences convened by the Economic and Social Council include the World Population Conference (1954), the U. N. Scientific Conference on Conservation and Utilisation of Resources etc. The Council can also call conferences of regional character on subjects like health, trade. transport, employment, refugees, stateless persons etc.
5. Fifthly, the Council coordinates the work of the specialised agencies of the United Nations. These specialised agencies are created through inter-governmental agreements and have wide international responsibilities. Some of the specialised agencies, whose work is supervised by the Economic and Social Council include the International Labour Organisation (ILO), Food and Agricultural Organisation (FAO), International Civil Aviation Organisation (I.C.A.O.), United Nations Educational,

Scientific and Cultural Organisation (UNESCO), International Bank for Reconstruction and Development (IBRD), International Monetary Fund (IMF), World Health Organisation (WHO), Universal Postal Union (U.P.U.), Intentional Telecommunication Union (ITU), World Meteorological Organisation(WMO), International Finance Corporation(I.F.C.), Inter Government Martime Consultative Organisation (IMCO), International Refugee Organisation(I.R.O.) etc. It may be noted that all these specialised agencies of the United Nations have their own constitutions, spheres of action, budget and staff. They have distinct identities and are completely autonomous. However, they have been brought into relationship with the UN through agreement negotiated by the Economic and Social Council and approved by the General Assembly. This enables the Council to coordinate the work of various agencies. This coordination is essential because the activities of these agencies are not mutually exclusive and involve a considerable degree of overlapping and concern different phases of the same problem. Thus the Economic and Social Council plays a key role in developing the prerequisites of stable world order.

Subsidiary Bodies of the Council

The subsidiary bodies of the Economic and Social Council include five regional commissions, six functional commissions, six standing committees, and other standing expert bodies.

Regional Commissions

The Council has five Regional Commissions. These are Economic Commission for Africa with headquarters at Addis Ababa (Ethiopia), Economic and Social Commission for Asia an Pacific (with headquarters at Bangkok, Thailand), Economic Commission for Europe (Geneva, Switzerland), Economic Commission for Latin America and the Caribbeans (Santiago, Chile), and the Economic and Social Commission for Western Asia (Baghdad, Iraq). These Commissions have similar functions with regard to their respective areas. The main objective of these Commissions is to initiate and participate in measures for facilitating concerted action for economic and social development in order to raise the level of economic activity and advance the levels of living and to maintain and strengthen economic relations among their members and other countries. The Commissions can establish with the approval of the Council such agencies as they may deem appropriate, for the discharge of their responsibilities.

Functional Commissions.

The Council has six Functional Commissions viz. Statistic Commission; the Population Commission; the Commission for Social Development; the Commission on Human Rights; the Commission on the Status of Women; and the Commission on Narcotic Drugs. The Commission on Human Rights has a Sub-Commission on Prevention of Discrimination and Protection of Minorities.The Commission on Narcotic Drugs has a Sub-Commission on Illicit Drug Traffic and Related Matters in the Near and Middle East. The Statistical Commission promotes the development of national statistics, the coordination of statistical work, and the development of central statistical services; and advises the organs of the UN on general questions of statistical information. The Population Commission studies and advises on the size and structure of populations, the interplay of demographic factors and policies, designed to influence the size and structure of population and changes therein. The Commission for Social Development advises on social policies of a general character on vital social problems and on related required measures. The Commission on Human Rights and its Sub-Commission on Prevention of Discrimination and Protection of Minorities, submits proposals, recommendations and reports regarding international Bill of Rights, the protection of Minorities and prevention of discrimination. The Commission on the Status of Women prepares recommendations and reports on promotion of women's rights in political, economic, civil, social and educational fields. The Commission on Narcotic Drugs assists in exercising powers of supervision over the application of international conventions and agreements dealing with narcotic drugs. It advises the Council on all matters pertaining to the control of narcotic drugs and prepares such draft on international conventions as may be necessary from time to time.

Standing Committees.

The Economic and Social Council has six Standing Committees. These include (i) The Committee for Programmer and Coordination which advises and assists the Council in the discharge of its coordination function and keeps under review the activities of the United Nations and its related agencies and programmers. It reviews programmes and procedures in particular sector on a system-wise basis as well as the interaction of different sectors in order to ensure that programmes in a particular sector respond to the objectives set forth in the General Assembly resolution. It particularly reviews the programme planning, implementation of programmes, their evaluation and effectiveness of the coordination machinery. The Committee is expected to continuously review further steps required to implement within the United Nations the recommendations of the Ad hoc Committee of Experts to examine the finances of the United Nations and the Specialized Agencies concerning the development of an integrated system of long-term planning, programming and budgeting.

(ii) The Committee on Non-governmental Organisations and on negotiations with inter-governmental agencies, recommends the status of individual Non-governmental Organisations and is called whenever it is necessary to negotiate an agreement with a newly created agency.

(iii) The Committee on Housing, Building and Planning examines reports and makes recommendations to the Governments and United Nations bodies. It promotes research in the field of housing related community facilities and physical planning.

(iv) The Committee on Natural Resources lays down guidelines, examines reports, analyses existing resolutions and makes recommendations in areas related to the natural resources.

(v) The Committee on Science and Technology for Development promotes international cooperation. It encourages formulation of overall policy and evaluates and reviews policies and new developments in the field of science and technology.

(vi) The Committee on Review and Appraisal, assists the Council and the General Assembly in the overall review and appraisal of the UN Development Decades. The Committee also examines the obstacles and reasons for shortfalls identified in the various sectoral and regional reviews; and recommends on the basis of such reviews and its own conclusions, measures to overcome the obstacle and shortfalls, including new or revised goals and policy measures required

Expert Bodies

Finally Economic and Social Council has a number of standing expert bodies on sujects like crime prevention and control; development planning, international cooperation in tax matters and transport of dangerous goods. The Committee on Crime Prevention and Control advises policies and international action in the area of crime prevention. The Committee for Development Planning evaluates programmes in their progress, analyses major trends and studies individual questions in the area of economic planning, programmes and projections. The Advisory Committee on the Application of Science and Technology to Development reviews programmes and suggests practical measures for such application. It also advises on desired changes in the area of science and technology. The Ad Hoc Group of Experts on Tax Treaties explores ways and means for facilitating the conclusion of tax treaties between the developed and developing countries. The Meeting of Experts on the United Nations Programme in Public Administration works in close collaboration with specialised agencies and non-governmental organisations and formulates programmes in the field of public administration. It also examines the Secretary General's proposals in public administration for the Development Decades. The Committee on Experts on the Transport of Dangerous Goods not only revises and updates the list of dangerous goods but also considers the Pxisting transportation practices and studies problems relating to packing and other related matters.

Relations with Non-governmental Organisations

The UN Charter authorises the Economic and Social Council to hold consultations with non-governmental organisations concerned with matters falling within its competence. The Council feels that these organisations with their special experience and technical knowledge can render valuable service to the Council in its work. Over 600 non-governmental organisations have been accorded consultative status by the Council. These non-governmental organisations broadly fall into three categories. First, there are organisations which are concerned with most of the Council's activities and are closely linked with the economic and social activities of the area which they represent. They can submit items for inclusion in the provisional agenda of the Council and can also send observers to all the public meetings of the Council.

Secondly, there are organisations which have special competence in specific fields of activity of the Council. They cannot submit items for the provisional agenda of the Council, even though they can participate as observers in the public meetings. Thirdly, there are organisations which can make occasional contribution to the Council, its subsidiary organs or other UN bodies.

Co-ordinations of UN System

The Economic and Social Council plays a central promotional and coordinating role with regard to the UN system, viz. United Nations, UNCTAD, UNIDO, UNDP, UNEP, UNICEF and other UN organs. It also plays an important role in developing the political will and taking the political decisions necessary to launch and maintain broad international actions in which the co-operation of various parts of the system is required. The coordinating function of the Economic and Social Council also implies that it can obtain reports from the specialised agencies and arrange for the representatives of the specialised agencies to participate in its deliberations to vote.

It may be noted that co-ordination of the working of various agencies of the UN has been the main preoccupation of the Council, For this purpose in 1946 the Council set up an inter-agency coordinating committee under Secretary General. Subsequently this committee was renamed as Administrative Committee on Coordination. In addition a Programme Coordination Committee, has been set up. The main task of this committee is to consider the annual reports of agencies as well as the Administrative Committee on Coordination.

Evaluation of its Working

Though the UN Charter has accorded the Economic and Social Council the status of principal organ of the United Nations, it functions under the authority of the General Assembly. In fact its activities resemble the activities of the committees of the Assembly so much that often a charge of duplication of duties is levelled against it. In recent years the Economic and Social Council has tended to assume more extensive role and held discussions on issues like housing, human rights, narcotic drug control, water resources, desertification, population problems, trade, industrial development, literacy, refugees, science and technology etc. The Council has also produced studies which have helped to overcome the dearth of statistical and other kinds of information on economic and social conditions in the world. On the basis of its deliberations and studies, it has formulated recommendations which have formed the basis of various resolutions or declarations adopted by the General Assembly. Thus the Council plays a quasi-legislative role. It is true it cannot make law, but it has played an important role in helping the members of the United Nations develop laws.

The two subjects which have attracted regular attention of the Economic Council and have been frequently debated by it, relate to economic development and human rights. The Council has impressed on the developed countries the need to provide necessary assistance to the developing countries for their development. It has also impressed on the various governments the need to provide more rights to its citizens. But probably the most important contribution of the Economic and Social Council has been that it has provided useful statistical and other data on economic and social conditions. On the basis of this data it has also adopted certain resolutions and declarations, which once endorsed by the General Assembly are submitted to the member-states for ratification. Viewed in this context the ECOSOC has played an important role in the development of international law. Despite this it cannot be denied that the Council enjoyed very limited powers only. It can only study, discuss and recommend but not enforce its decisions, for which it is completely dependent on the General Assembly.

Giving an assessment of the Economic and Social Council, Arther Lewis has observed "Since there is absence of any power to legislate on economic and social matters, the Economic and Social Council is bound to be a forum of discussion from which recommendations ensure. Although the Economic and Social Council attempted too much and has diversified its activities greatly, yet it has substantial achievements to its credit e.g., the UNICEF, the UN Refugee Fund, the Technical Assistance Board, the U.N. Relief and Works Agency and the Special Fund for Economic Development all have performed singularly useful task. it may well be that whatever the major political issues can be resolved and the Security Council and the General Assembly assume a formal role, ECOSOC will come to the fore as the most active and useful organ of the U.N."

FURTHER READINGS

Geirard J. Mangone (ed) — *UN Administration for Economic and Social Programmes*

Martin Hill — *The United Nations System Coordinating its Economic and Social Work*

Palmer and Perkins — *International Relations*

Walter R. Sharp — *The United Nations Economic and Social Council*

Chapter 7

TRUSTEESHIP COUNCIL AND TRUSTEESHIP SYSTEM

The Trusteeship Council has been indicated as one of the principal organs of the United Nations in the UN Charter. But actually it works as an auxiliary organ of the General Assembly insofar as it supervises the administration of the non-strategic trust territories, and as an auxiliary organ of the Security Council with regard to strategic areas.

Composition

The Charter did not prescribe the size of the Council and merely provided that the Trusteeship Council must reflect a balance between members that administer Trust Territories and members that do not. To ensure this balance it was provided that the General Assembly may elect for three years as many members as may be necessary to ensure that the total membership of the Trusteeship Council is equally divided between those members of the United Nations which administer trust territories and those which do not. As the number of Trust Territories and of administering countries has decreased, the Council become smaller. The Council elects a president from amongst the representatives of the members of the Council. In addition it also elects a Vice-President from amongst the representatives of members of the Council. Each member of the Council has only one vote. It is noteworthy that even though the permanent membrs of the Security Council are also the permanent members of the Trusteeship Council, they do not enjoy any 'veto' power. All the decisions of the Trusteeship Council are taken by majority vote of the members actually present. and voting. Generally the Trusteeship Council meets once a year but special sessions can be convened at any time on the request of the majority of the members. The proceedings of the Council are conducted in accordance with the rules and procedure determined by the Council itself. With the completion of the process of decolonisation the strength of the Trusteeship Council is now confined to only five permanent members of the Security Council. It is expected that within few years the Trusteeship Council shall be wound up.

Functions And Powers

The functions and powers of the Trusteeship Council have been outlined in Article 87 of the Charter. Its functions include (i) consideration of reports submitted by the administering authority; (ii) acceptance of petitions and their examination in consultation with the administering authority; (iii) to arrange periodic visits to the respective trust territories at times agreed upon with the administering authority; and (iv) to take other action in conformity with the terms of the trusteeship agreements. It shall be desirable to study these functions of the Trusteeship Council in details.

Consideration of Reports from Administering authority

Under the UN Charter each administering authority is expected to submit an annual report for the territories under its control. In this report it provides information regarding political, economic, social and educational advancement of the inhabitants of the territory under its control. The Council studies these reports with the help of specialised agencies and makes necessary suggestions. On the basis of these reports, the Council drafts a report of its own which is incorporated in its annual report to the General Assembly in the case of non-strategic territories and areas; and to the Security Council in respect of strategic areas, This report generally contains the recommendations of the Council as well as the individual views of members.

Receipt and Examination of Petitions

The Trusteeship Council receives and examines petitions from individuals as well as organisations in the trust territories. On receipt of petitions, the same are sent to the administering authority for comments before these are examined by the Council. These petitions can cover a wide range of subjects such as property claims and titles, denial of civil and human rights, racial discrimination, poor educational services and appeals for greater participation in local administration.

Visits to Trust Territories

The Trusteeship Council can also arrange periodic visits to the trust territories, at times agreed upon with the Administering Authority, to acquire firsthand in formation about the conditions and problems of the trust territories. Usually such missions are sent to each trust territory every two years. Commenting on the importance of such missions Profs. Palmer and Perkins say "Flying the UN flag, members of the Commission meet openly with spokesmen of the native people as well as with local officials, visit different sections of a territory and bring home to the people the fact that the UN is concerned with their welfare and is working for their eventual freedom. The missions also give representatives of the Trusteeship Council and the Secretariat an opportunity to make firsthand investigations of the areas for which they are responsible."

In addition to the above functions the Trusteeship Council can take any other action in conformity with the terms of the Trusteeship Agreements.

TRUSTEESHIP SYSTEM

After examining the organisation and functions of the Trusteeship Council, it shall be desirable to know about the Trusteeship System envisaged under the U. N. Charter. At the outset it may be pointed out that the Trusteeship System under the UN was a successor to the Mandate System provided under the League of Nations. However, it is wider in scope than the Mandate System provided under the League of Nations. Under the Trusteeship System the United Nations assumed broad responsibilities for the welfare of non-self-governing territories. Article 75 of the UN Charter provided "The United Nations shall establish under its authority an international trusteeship system for the administration and supervision of such territories as may be placed thereunder by subsequent individual agreement." The Charter stipulated that the following territories shall be placed under the trusteeship system:

(i) territories now held under mandate; (ii) territories which may be detached from enemy States as a result of Second World War; and (iii) territories voluntarily placed under the system by the States responsible for their administration. It was specified that the trusteeship system cannot apply to territories which have become members of the United Nations and whose relations are to be based on the principle of sovereign equality.

Objectives of Trusteeship System

According to the Charter the following are objectives of the trusteeship system.

1. To further international peace and security.
2. To promote the political, economic, social and educational advancement of the inhabitants of the trust territories and their progressive development towards self-government of independence as may be appropriate to the particular circumstances of each territory and its people and the freely expressed wishes of the people concerned, and as may be approved by the terms of each trusteeship agreement.
3. To encourage respect for all without distinction of race, sex, language or religion and to encourage recognition of the interdependence of the peoples of the world.
4. To ensure equal treatment in social, economic and commercial matters for all members of the United Nations and also equal treatment of the latter in the administration of justice without prejudice to the attainment of the foregoing objectives

Duties of Administering States

The duties of the States administering the trust territories were outlined in Article 73 of the UN Charter. It was emphasised that the interests of the inhabitants of the trust territories are paramount and the administering State must promote the well-being of the inhabitants of these territories. For this purpose they were expected (a) to ensure, with due respect for the culture of the people concerned, their political, economic, social and educational advancement, their just treatment and their protection against abuses; (b) to develop self-government, to take due account of the political aspirations of the people, and to assist them in the progressive development of their free political institutions according to the particular circumstances of each territory and its people and varying stages of advancement; (c) to further international peace and security; (d) to promote constructive measures of development, to encourage research and to co-operate with one another and, when and where appropriate, with specialised international bodies with a view to achieving the social, economic and scientific purposes set forth in this article; and (e) to transmit regularly to the Secretary General for information purposes, subject to such limitation as security and constitutional considerations may require, statistical and other information of a technical nature relating to economic, social and educational conditions in the territories for which they are respectively responsible. The information transmitted by the administering States is analysed by the UN Secretary General and is later on considered by the General Assembly. It may be noted that with the exception of certain strategic areas, which are the direct concern of the Security Council, the functions of the United Nations with regard to trust territories are performed by the General Assembly and more immediately by the Trusteeship Council. The manner in which the Trusteeship Council exercises supervision over the trust territories has already been dealt with above.

Operation of the Trusteeship System

Under the trusteeship System by the end of 1950, 10 Trusteeship Agreements had been approved by the General Assembly and one by the Security Council. As a result of these agreements approximately 20 million people living in these territories came under the purview of trusteeship. However, two of the former mandated territories of the days of League of Nations could not become part of the Trusteeship system. Palestine was excluded on account of dispute between the Jewish and Arab population, which led to the establishment of State of Israel in 1948. Similarly, Northwest Africa could not become a trust territory because no agreement could be reached regarding its incorporation.

It shall be desirable to know about the various trust territories and how they attained independence.

1. A part of Togoland was placed under-British administration. The Trusteeship Agreement for this territory was approved by the General Assembly in December 1946. A plebiscite was held there on 9 May 1955 in which the majority of people voted for union with neighbouring Gold Coast. After approval by the Assembly the territory was united with Gold Coast to form the new independent State of Ghana in March 1957.
2. Another part of Togoland was placed under French administration. The General Assembly approved the Trusteeship Agreement in December 1946. The government, which came to power following general elec-

tions, in April 1958 favoured independence. Following agreement between France and Togoland regarding independence, the Assembly resolved that the Trusteeship Agreement be terminated with effect from 27 April 1960. Togo became member of UN in September 1960.

3. A part of Cameroon was placed under French Administration. The Trusteeship Agreement was approved by the General Assembly in December 1946. In March 1959 the General Assembly voted to end the Trusteeship Agreement and on 1 January 1960 the territory became Republic of Cameroon. In September 1960 it was admitted to UN membership.

4. A part of Cameroon was placed under British administration. The Trusteeship Agreement was approved by the General Assembly on 13 December 1946. In the plebiscites held in Northern Cameroons and Southern Cameroons in February 1961 the Northern Cameroons by majority vote decided to join Nigeria while the majority in the Southern Cameroons decided to join the Republic of Cameroon. Accordingly in April 1961 the General Assembly decided to terminate the Trusteeship Agreement concerning the Cameroons under British administration with respect to Northern Cameroons as well as Southern Cameroons.

5. Somaliland was placed under Italian administration. The Trusteeship Agreement was approved by the General Assembly in December 1950. An elected Legislative Assembly drew up a Constitution for an independent Somalia which was approved in May 1960. In July 1960 it became independent.

6. Tanganyika was placed under British administration. Trusteeship agreement was approved by the General Assembly in December 1946. In May 1960 Tanganiyka attained internal self-government. In 1961 the Trusteeship Agreement was terminated and Tanganyika became an independent State and was admitted as member of United Nations. Subsequently in April 1964 Tanganyika, along with Zanzibar, formed the United Republic of Tanzania.

7. Western Samo was placed under administration of New Zealand. The Trusteeship Agreement for Western Samo was approved by the General Assembly in December 1946. In May 1961 in a UN supervised plebiscite the territory decided to become independent. The trusteeship agreement ceased to be in force on 1 January and Western Samo became an independent State. It was admitted as member of United Nations in December 1976.

8. Nauru was placed under the joint administration of Australia, New Zealand and United Kingdom. The Trusteeship Agreement was approved by the General Assembly in November 1947. A Legislative Council was created in January 1965 and a Legislative Assembly was elected in January 1968. Nauru became an independent State in January 1968 when the Trusteeship Agreement was terminated.

9. Ruanda-Urundi was placed under administration of Belgium. The General Assembly approved the Trusteeship Agreement for this territory in December 1946. The elections were held in Urundi in September 1961 and a government formed. In July 1962 the Assembly terminated the Trusteeship Agreement and Randa and Burundi emerged as two independent and sovereign States. In September 1962 the two were admitted as members of the United Nations.

10. New Guinea was placed under Australian administration. The General Assembly approved the Trusteeship Agreement in December 1946. In 1971 the Assembly of Papua and Trust territory of New Guinea decided to form Union of two territories to be named Papua New Guinea. In May 1973 an agreement was reached with Australia that self-government be granted in two stages. In December 1973 the Government of Australia transferred all internal powers to the territory, although it continued to have ultimate responsibility for the foreign affairs and defence of the territory. In September 1975 Papua New Guinea became an independent sovereign State and the Trusteeship Agreement was terminated with effect from that date. It was admitted as member of the UN in October 1975.

11. Trust territory of Pacific Islands was placed under the administration of United States. The Trusteeship Agreement for this territory was approved by the Security Council in April 1947. This territory known as Micronesia, comprised more than 2100 islands and a toll from three major archipelagoes: Marianas, the Carolines and the Marshalls. In December 1990 the Security Council decided to dissolve the trusteeship over the strategic Northern Marianas, Marshall Islands and Micronesia. However, the federated States of Micronesia and the Marshall Islands pressed for termination of agreement so that their governments could become more independent and gain worldwide diplomatic recognition. It may be noted that the two semi-independent nations have established diplomatic ties with several South Pacific countries and China. In 1994, Palau the last territory under the Trusteeship system also attained independence.

FURTHER READINGS

James N. Murray Jr	*The United Nations Trusteeship System*
George Thullen	*Problems of the Trusteeship System : A Study of Political Behaviour in the United Nations*
Inis L. Claude Jr	*Swords into Ploughshares*
United Nations publication	*Everyone's United Nations – A Handbook on the Work of the United Nations*

Chapter 8
INTERNATIONAL COURT OF JUSTICE

Composition

The International Court of justice is the principal judicial organ of the United Nations. It works according to a Statute which forms an integral part of the UN Charter. The Statute of the International Court of Justice is based on the statute of the Permanent Court of International Justice which was prepared by the League Council and unanimously approved by the League Council in 1920. It is noteworthy that after the Second World War several members pleaded for the continuance of the Permanent Court of International Justice on account of good work done by this body. However majority of the members were of the view that it would be better to start with a clean state. Therefore they decided to create a new Organisation. According to Eagleton the variations made in the Statute of the earlier Permanent Court of International Justice were "comparatively trivial and mostly for adaptation to the United Nations system.'

Membership

All the members of the United Nations are *ipso facto* members of the International Court of Justice. A State which is not a member of the United Nations can also become a party to the statute of the International Court of Justice upon the recommendations of the Security Council. The conditions for membership in each case are determined by the General Assembly. The conditions which have been laid down by the General Assembly for membership of the Council include (i) acceptance of the Statute and other obligations with respect to the Court which other members of the U.N. have accepted; and (ii) undertaking to contribute to the expenses an amount assessed by the General Assembly after consultation with the government concerned.

The Court consists of 15 judges elected by the General Assembly and the Security Council, voting independently. These judges are elected not on the basis of nationality, but on the basis of their qualifications and high moral character. Care is also taken to ensure that all the principal legal systems of the world get represented in the world court. Further, it has been provided that no two judges can be nationals of the same State. All this has been designed to ensure that no one country or group dominates the court.

Election

As regards the method of election, the initiative is taken by the Secretary General of the United Nations, who addresses a written request to the States which are parties to the present statute and to the members of the national groups asking them to nominate persons in a position to accept the duties of a member of the Court. These groups can nominate not more than four persons (not more than two from own nationality), in consultation with highest court of justice, its legal faculties and schools of law etc. On the basis of the names thus submitted the Secretary General of the United Nationals prepares a list of the persons in alphabetical order. Thereafter the General Secretary and the Security Council proceed independent of each other, to elect fifteen of these candidates. The candidates receiving absolute majority of vote in both the General Assembly and the Security Council are considered elected as judges.

Tenure

The Judges of the International Court of Justice are elected for a term of nine years. However, they are eligible for re-election. The term of the judges is so staggered that the tenure of only five judges expires after every three years. The vacancies thus falling vacant are also filled through regular elections. A judge elected to replace another member holds office for the remainder of his predecessor's term. It is noteworthy that though the judges of the International Court of Justice are taken from various States and the governments of these States take part in the nomination and election of these judges, but after their election the judges do not act as representatives of their respective countries nor do they act upon the instructions of their governments. They are treated as officials of the international judiciary and act accordingly. In fact each member of the Court, before entering upon his office, has to take a solemn declaration in the open court that he would exercise his powers impartially and conscientiously. The judges cannot take up any other occupation during their tenure of office.

Seat of Court

The International Court of Justice has its permanent seat at Hague. However, it can meet elsewhere also. The Court is permanently in session, except during the period of vacations. Generally the cases are heard by the full court, but it can also form chambers composed of three or four judges, to deal with specific categories of cases viz. labour cases and cases relating to transit and communications etc. The quorum of the court is nine. This implies that at least nine members must be present to hold the meeting of the Court.

Officals of Court and Procedure

The Court elects its own President and Vice-President for a term of three years. Both these officials a eligible for re-election. In addition to this the Court appoints are Registrar and such other officers as may deem necessary. The salary, allowances, etc. of these officials are determined by the

General Assembly and cannot be changed to their disadvantage during their term of office. The members are not permitted to engage in any other occupation during their term. On retirement the members are entitled to a pension. However, the statute is absolutely silent about the retirement age of the judges of International Court of Justice.

The Court takes all decisions by majority vote of the judges present and voting. The President of the Court does not exercise his vote, except in case of a tie. It may be noted that no party enjoys veto 'with regard to the decisions of the court. The statute also contains provision regarding the removal of judges. A judge can be removed from his office only by the unanimous vote of the other members of the court.

Functions and Powers

The International Court of Justice enjoys two types of powers viz. settlement of disputes and rendering of advisory opinion.

Settlement of Disputes

The Court hears all cases involving sovereign States which have accepted the Statute of the Court. The other states can also take their disputes to the Court on fulfillment of conditions laid down by the Security Council. It may be noted that there is no provision for automatic reference of the dispute to the court. The UN Charter merely imposes an obligation on the members to seek pacific settlement of international disputes which implies that the parties can make use of other judicial procedures also for the settlement of their disputes. However, the Charter enjoins on the members that they should as a matter of general rule refer legal disputes to the International Court of Justice (Art. 36).

Though the Court does not enjoy any compulsory jurisdiction, "the States, parties to the present statute, may at any time declare that they recognise it compulsory as and without special agreement, in relation to any other State accepting the same obligation, the jurisdiction of the Court in all legal disputes concerning (a) the interpretation of a treaty; (b) any question of international law; (c) the existence of any fact which, if established, would constitute a breach of an international obligation; (d) the nature of extent or the reparation to be made for the breach of an international obligation. In simple words the Statute permits the States to concede compulsory jurisdiction to the court either conditionally or unconditionally. Such an authority may be conceded for any length of period. It may be noted that usually the States conceding compulsory jurisdiction to the Court impose the conditions of reciprocity, which means that they accept the compulsory jurisdiction of the Court in a particular case on the condition that the other party to the dispute would also accept it.

Law Applied

The Court decides the cases referred to it in accordance with international law, international conventions, and the general principles of law recognised by civilised nations. In addition to this the Court also makes use of judicial decisions and teachings of highly qualified publicists of various countries to determine the rules of law. The Court is not bound by its earlier decisions and can take fresh look at the new cases.

The Court does not enjoy any enforcement power. It has to mainly rely on two factors for enforcement of its decisions First each member of the United Nations has an obligation to comply with the decision of the Court in any case to which it is a party. This implies that once a State has agreed to submit the case to the Court, it would accept the decision of the Court. Secondly the Security Council can undertake enforcement action to give effect to the judgements of the Courts. The UN Charter clearly stipulates that if any party to a case fails to perform the obligations incumbent upon it under a judgement rendered by the Court, the other party may have recourse to the Security Council, which may, if it deems necessary, make recommendations or decide upon measures to be taken to give effect to the judgement."

Advisory Opinion

The International Court of Justice also enjoys power to give advisory opinion to the General Assembly, the Security Council and other specialised agencies of the United Nations, on legal questions. While seeking such an opinion, the agency has to submit in writing the request containing an exact statement of the question upon which an opinion is required as well as all the documents likely to throw light upon the question. This means that the Court does not render advisory opinion on its own. Further, the advice ofthe Court is not binding on the organ seeking it. In fact the opinion given by the Court is more like an advice rather than a decision.

Assessment of the working of Court

Since the inauguration of the Court in 1946, over cases or disputes were referred to International Court of Justice. Out of these fifteen cases were the other then cases the Court found that the list for various reasons; while in the other ten cases the Court found that it did not enjoy jurisdiction over them. The remaining cases which were handled by the Court covered a wide range of topics and the Court after due deliberations gave its judgement in all, but four. Some of the important cases decided by the Court are given below.

The first case was brought before Court in 1948 on the recommendation of the Security Council and related to dispute over the mining of Corfu Channel between Albania and Great Britain. In this case two British destroyers while passing through the Corfu Channel struck mines in Albanian waters which resulted in serious damage to property and loss of 44 lives. The British Government demanded compensation from the Albanian government, while the Alabanian government charged the British of violating Albanian sovereignty by proceeding through the channel in spite of objections. Though initially Albania refused to submit the case to the Court, but subsequently accepted the jurisdiction of the Court. Thereupon the Court heard the arguments and examined witnesses and experts. Ultimately on 9 Aplil 1949, Court pronounced that Albania was responsible under international law for the damage and loss of human life, and asked Albania to pay necessary compensation.

Another important case which was brought before the Court during the initial years pertaining to dispute between Britain and Norway over fishing in certain areas of Norwegian coast. The Court held that the method employed by Norway in delimiting its territorial waters was not contrary to international law. In 1969, the Court at the request of Denmark, Netherlands and Federal Republic of Germany determined the principles and rules of international law applicable to the delimitation of the areas of the North Sea continental shelf pertaining to each of them. Likewise in 1974 the court held that Iceland was not entitled unilaterally to exclude the fishing vessels of the United Kingdom and the Federal Republic of Germany from areas between fishery limits agreed upon in 1961 and 60-mile limit proclaimed by Iceland in 1972. In 1985 in a case referred to it by Libyan Arab Jamahiriya and Malta, the Court decided upon the principles and rules of international law applicable to the delimitation of areas of the Mediterranean continental shelf pertaining to them.

In 1993 the Court determined the course of the maritime boundary in the area between Greenland the and Island of Jan Mayen dividing the continental shelf and fisheries zones of Denmark and Norway. Earlier in 1992 a Chamber of the Court gave a decision in dispute between El Salvador and Honduras on the questions of both land and maritime frontier delimitation.

The Court also gave several judgements on the question of diplomatic protection and rights of asylum. Some of the cases decided by the Court in this regard include case between Colombia and Peru in 1950; the dispute between France and United States regarding rights of US nationals in Morocco; the dispute regarding nationals between Liechtenstein and Guatemala in 1955; case regarding compensation put up by United States against Italy in 1989 regarding requisition of a company in Sicily, owned by the United States Corporations.

In 1973 Australia and New Zealand each brought a case against France concerning deposit of radioactive fallout from nuclear tests conducted by France in the atmosphere. The Court directed France to avoid such tests and later delivered judgement that France had undertaken to refrain from atmospheric nuclear testing after 1974.

In the case concerning seizure of US Embassy in Tehran and detention of diplomatic and consular staff, the Court provisionally decided in December 1979 that the embassy should be immediately given back and the detained staff released. Later in May 1980 it held that Iran had violated its obligation to the United States and must release the hostages, hand back the embassy and make reparations. But before the Court could fix the amount of reparation, the two States reached an agreement and withdrew the case.

In April 1984 Nicaragua instituted proceedings against United States in the Court and accused her of using military forces against Nicaragua and intervening in her internal affairs. Though US denied the jurisdiction of the Court, the Court called on US to refrain from action against Nicaraguan ports. In June 1986 the Court ruled that the US actions against Nicaragua were in breach of its obligations under international law and it was under an obligation to desist from those actions and to make reparations to Nicaragua. However, in 1991 Nicaragua withdrew its request that the Court should determine the form and amount of reparation.

In 1986 Nicaragua brought proceedings against Costa Rica and Honduras, alleging their responsibility in connection with armed activities in border areas. But these cases were also withdrawn following an agreement between the parties.

In 1992, Libya brought a case against the United Kingdom and the United States concerning the internatation or application of the 1971 Montreal Convention for the Suppression of Unlawful Acts against the Safety for Civil Aviation, Lockerbie, Scotland on 21 December 1988.

In 1993, Bosnia and Herzegovina brought a case against Yugoslavia (Serbia and Montenegro) concerning the application of the Convention on the Prevention and Punishment of Court called upon the parties to prevent further commission of the crime of genocide and further aggravation or extension of the dispute.

The International Court of Justice has also played a vital role in settlement of disputes through its advisory opinions. Thus on the issue of costs of peace-keeping forces, the Court advised that peace-keeping costs could be reckoned as normal expenses of the Organisation. With regard to disputes concerning admissions into the UN the Court confirmed that no admission could be made without the Security Council recommendation. On the question of South-West Africa, the Court advised that the Mandate awarded by the League to South Africa over South-West Aftica still existed and she must submit to the supervision of the mandate by the UN as successor to the League. It is a different matter that the South African Government did not submit to it. In 1970 the Security Council sought advisory, opinion on the issue of legal consequences of the presence of South Africa in Namibia in defiance of the Security Council decision. The Court gave the opinion that South Africa's presence in the territory was illegal and that other States were under an obligation to take no action which recognised South Africa's legal authority there. In 1988 the Court expressed the opinion that by virtue of the United Nations Headquarters Agreement, the United States was under obligation to submit to arbitration a dispute with was under obligation to submit to arbitration a dispute with the United Nations concerning an order to close the office of the Palestine Liberation Organisation observer mission in New York. In 1989 the Court rendered advisory opinion on the request of the Economic and Social Council on the applicability to a former rapporteur of a sub-commission of certain provisions of the Convention on the Privileges and Immunities of the United Nations. At present two requests for advisory opinion are pending with the Court with regard to matters referred to it by the World Health Organization concerning legality of the use by a state of nuclear weapons in armed conflict; and the one referred by the General Assembly concerning the legality of the threat or use of nuclear weapons

A perusal of some of the cases referred to above shows that the record of the International Court of Justice has not been quite impressive. Only a limited category of cases are brought before the Court. Even the number of cases which are being brought before the Court has considerably declined. Further, the lack of enforcement power has also rendered the working of the court less effective. It is true that under article 94 of the UN Charter, the Security Council can decide upon measures to be taken to give effect to the judgements of the Court, but it has never done so. This has naturally given rise to doubts about the desirability of taking the disputes to the Court. Instead States have preferred to take recourse to political settlement of disputes. This, however, does not take away the importance of the Court. It cannot be denied that the Court through its judgements has contributed to the growth of international law and contributed to the establishment of a more lawful world community in which mutual obligations are recognised. It is a different matter that to the majority of the people of the third world it appears that the Court is applying the code of the first world in the international arena. Their confidence in the judgements of the Court would increase only if it gives due regard to the laws and conventions of the third world countries and also convinces those from the developing countries that the law applied provides for change as well as stability and reflects a sense of justice. It must attach greater importance to the principle of equity in its judgements.

In conclusion, it can be said with Prof. Nicholas 'Despite the Court's acknowledged merits it has been far from fulfilling the high hopes entertained of it in some quarters at San Francisco and afterwards that its record to date is actually less impressive than that of its predecessor. The volume of business has been smaller and the cases that have been brought seem on the whole to have been less important than those brought before the permanent Court." (H.G. Nicholas, *The United Nations as a Political Institution)*

In spite of these limitations, it cannot be denied that the Court has 'contributed its mite to the golden collection of intentional organizations seeking peace and justice'.

FURTHER READINGS

H.G. Nicholas — *The United Nations as a Political Institution*

Goodrich and Simons — *The United Nations and the Maintenance of International Peace and Security*

Vandenbosch and Hogan — *The United Nations*

S. Rosenne — *The World Court : What it is and how it works*

D.W. Bowett — *The Law of International Institutions*

Chapter 9
THE SECRETARIAT

Composition

The Secretariat is one of the six principal organs of the United Nations. It comprises the Secretary General and such other staff as the Organisation may require. It provides services to the other organs of the United Nations namely the General Assembly, the Security Council, the Economic and Social Council and the Trusteeship Council as well as their subsidiary bodies. The Secretary General is appointed by the General Assembly on the recommendations of the Security Council. The other staff of the Secretariat is appointed by the Secretary General as per regulations laid down by the General Assembly. Generally while recruiting staff of the Secretariat great weightage is given to competence and integrity. However, due consideration is also given to wide geographical basis of recruitment. It may be noted that the staff permanently assigned to the Economic and Social Council, the Trusteeship Council and other organs of the United Nations also forms a part of the UN Secretariat.

The Secretariat is located at the headquarters of the United Nations in New York. It also has branch offices in Geneva, Vienna and Nairobi. The Secretariat also includes the regional commission's secretariats at Addis Ababa, Baghdad, Bangkok, Geneva and Santiago.

Functions of Secretariat

The main functions of the Secretariat include:

1. Production of reports and other documents containing information, analysis, historical background, research findings, policy suggestions etc. to facilitate deliberations and decision-making by other organs and their subsidiary bodies.
2. Provision of secretarial services to legislative organs and their subsidiary bodies.
3. Provision of meeting services to the legislative organs in accordance with the policies adopted by the General Assembly.
4. Provision of editorial, translation and document reproduction services for the issuance of UN documents in different languages.
5. Conduct of studies and provision of information that answers to the priority needs of the governments of member countries in meeting challenges in various fields.

6. Production of statistical publications, information bulletins and analytical work which the General Assembly has decided.

7. Organisation of conferences, expert group meetings and seminars on topics of concern to the international community.

8. Provision of technical assistance to developing countries.

9. Undertaking service missions to countries, areas or locations as authorised by the General Assembly or the Security Council.

10. To arrange for dissemination of information on United Nations activities and decisions among the public.

11. Provision of programme planning, financial, personnel, legal, management and general services which are essential for rational selection of work items and allocation of resources among them for effective, economic and efficient performance of the services and functions of the Secretariat.

While discharging the above functions the Secretariat gets involved in the policy formulation. The studies and reports prepared by the Secretariat serve as a useful input for the government policy. The UN officials engaged in international agencies greatly influence the decision making process through direct participation. In this regard probably the greatest influence is exercised by the staff of the World Bank, who not only frame the programme for discussion by the Executive Directors and Governing Board, but also secure approval for what the Bank President and his staff recommend. The agenda for the programme of UNESCO is likewise formulated by the Secretariat.

The U. N. officials also greatly influence the Organisation policy and world politics through quite diplomacy. These officials play a vital role in promoting agreement among States through quite discussions and reconciling their differences. They help in the formulation and adoption of resolutions by the U. N. Even after these resolutions are adopted the international officials try to seek compliance of these resolutions, by the member States. These officials also act as mediators, conciliators and conscious-builders and try to resolve the controversies between States. It is well known that in recent years the General Assembly and the Security Council have heavily banked on the Secretary General and his staff for resolving some of the outstanding disputes. The notable problems where their assistance was sought include Iran-Iraq War, Afghanistan, Kampuchea, Namibia, the Falkland Islands, Lebanon, the Middle East, Grenada, etc.

Professors Jacob and Atherton have highlighted the role of the international civil services thus "with its growing experience in the techniques of international administration, its relative permanence and continuity and its sense of direct responsibility for the various agencies operation, knits the organisations together and furnishes constant impetus to accomplishments for their objectives."

The Secretary General

As noted earlier, the Secretary General is the chief administrative officer of the Secretariat. He is appointed by the General Assembly on the recommendations of the Security Council. Usually before recommending the name of a candidate for the office of the Secretary General, the Security Council holds private discussions to find out a candidate acceptable to all the permanent members. However, the name recommended by the Security Council for the office of the Secretary General can be rejected by. the General Assembly.

Term

The UN Charter is silent about the term of office of the Secretary General. In the San Francisco Conference it was suggested that he should be appointed for a term of three years. However, this term was considered too short. It was argued that frequent re-elections would effect the independence of the Secretary General and force him to lay down office as soon as he gained experience. Therefore in January 1946 the General Assembly decided that the term of the Secretary General should be such that men of eminence and high attainment could take up this position. It was decided to appoint the first Secretary General for a term of five years with eligibility for reappointment. The General Assembly further expressed the view that it would be desirable that no member should offer a retiring Secretary General any governmental position in which the confidential information he has obtained might become a source of embarrassment to other members. Thus the Secretary General was given a term of five years which could be renewed or extended.

Trygve Lie, the first Secretary General was initially given appointment for five years but subsequently his term was extended by three years much against the wishes of USSR. After his death Dag Hammarskjold of Sweden became the Secretary General in 1953 and served till his death in a plane crash in 1961. U. Thant succeeded Hammarskjold, and remained in office till Jan. 1972 when he was replaced by Kurt Waldheim of Austria. Kurt Waldheim remained in office till 31 December 1981 and was succeeded by Javier Perez de Cuellar of Peru. In 1992 Boutros Ghali of Egypt became the sixth Secretary General. He served for only one term and was refilled by Kofi Anna of Ghana as the seventh Secretary General on 1 January 1997.

Powers and Functions

The U. N. Secretary General has been given more powers than enjoyed by his counterpart under the League of Nations. Furthermore, unlike Sir Eric Drummond, who did not assume responsibilities of direction and leadership during his term of over thirteen years, the first Secretary General of the United Nations (Trygve Lie), made full use of the powers vested in him by the UN Charter and provided a forceful leadership to the Organisation. The functions and powers of the Secretary General can be conveniently studied under the following heads.

1. **Administrative and Service Functions.** The Secretary General is responsible for the Organisation and direction of the activities of the Organisation. The staff of all the U. N. organs, excluding the International Court of Justice, falls under his purview. As such it is his responsibility to ensure that the various organs of the United Nations and their committees and conference work properly. For this purpose he draws provisional agenda, notifies about the meetings to various members, provides staff and facilities for the holding of meetings, examines the credentials of representatives and submits reports to the concerned organ. He also assists in the drafting of documents, resolutions and reports and provides legal and technical advice. He also takes necessary action on the resolutions passed by the General Assembly viz. communicates these resolutions to the member governments and ascertains the steps taken to implement these resolutions or recommendations.

   The responsibility for the registration of treaties and agreement entered into by the members of the United Nations also rests with the Secretary General. Article 102 of the UN Charter provides that "every treaty and every international agreement entered into by any member of the United Nations shall, as soon as possible, be registered with the Secretariat and published by it." Further, all multilateral treaties are also to be deposited with the Secretary General. It is the responsibility of the Secretary General to publish and notify all these treaties to the members of the United Nations.

   The Secretary General tries to maintain necessary liaison with the specialised agencies of the United Nations. For this purpose he holds meetings with the directors of these organizations and provides personnel for liaison purposes. He is responsible for exchange of documents and information as well as other functions.

2. **Financial Functions.** The Secretary General has been entrusted with important financial responsibilities. Subject to the authority of the General Assembly he prepares the budget of the United Nations. He allocates funds, controls expenditure, collects the contributions from members and acts as custodian of all the funds. He tries to develop common fiscal controls and financial practices in consultation with specialised agencies and undertakings.

3. **Representational Functions.** As the chief representative of the United Nations, the Secretary General, represents the UN in negotiations with other agencies and government. He also occupies a central position in the working of the various organs of the United Nations because the staff of these organisations and agencies is not only recruited but also controlled by the Secretary General. He also represents the U. N. before the International Court of Justice.

4. **Political Functions.** The Secretary General has also been assigned important political functions. Through these political functions he exercises profound influence on the formulation of the policy. It may be observed that this power of the Secretary General emanates from

Article 99 of the UN Charter which stipulates that "the Secretary General may bring to the attention of the Security Council any matter which in his opinion may threaten the maintenance of international peace and security." This article permits the Secretary General to submit for the consideration of the Security Council any dispute, situation or other matter which is not raised by a member of the Council. This enables the Secretary General to convene a meeting of the Security Council even when no other member of the Council demands such a meeting.

The Secretary General can also present information or state opinions on matters already under the consideration of the Security Council. It is well known that the Secretary General submitted a memorandum on the issue of Iran, when the question was already under consideration of the Security Council. Likewise in 1950 the Secretary General submitted proposals for the consideration of the Great Powers concerning representation of Red China in the United Nations.

Through his annual reports on the work of the Organisation also the Secretary General is able to exercise considerable amount of political influence. These reports are an important source of information on the accomplishments and problems of the United Nations, and usually form the basis for the opening debates of the General Assembly. In addition the Secretary General can also propose items for agenda of the General Assembly, the Security Council and the Trusteeship Council. All this enables him to exercise "initiative and influence by making proposals, effecting the establishment of priorities and advocating the viewpoints which he considers appropriate."

Changing Role

The office of the Secretary General has constantly grown since the establishment of the United Nations. Trygve Lie the first Secretary General played key role in the promotion of peace and took several initiatives to establish peace and security. In 1950 he drew the attention of the nations to the breach of peace at the 38th Parallel in Korea and convened meeting of the Security Council. He also formulated a ten point plan for accomplishment of peace in twenty years. However his efforts did not yield the desired results because he became unpopular with the Soviet Union and was ultimately forced to tender resignation in 1952.

Dag Hammarskjold, the second Secretary General preferred to play a more cautious role and tried to act strictly according to the principle of UN. Under the directions of the General Assembly he was called upon to secure implementation of cease-fire and withdrawal of British, French and Israeli forces from the Suez in 1956 to ensure peace. Thereafter he started playing more active role in the maintenance of peace. In 1958 he strengthened the UN Observer Group in Lebanon and transferred the dispute to the General Assembly because the Security Council was deadlocked. The General Assembly in its turn requested the Secretary General to make such practical arrangements which could help in upholding the purposes and principles of

Charter and thereby facilitate early withdrawal of foreign troops. In September 1959 once again it was Secretary General who drew the attention of the Security Council to the problem of Laos where foreign troops had infringed the borders. He ensured UN presence in Laos despite Soviet veto.

The position of the Secretary General which was some what undermined following adoption of Uniting for Peace Resolution, once again improved in the sixties. During the Congo crisis of July 1960 Secretary General Hanmmarskjold invoked the powers of the Secretary General under Article 99 of the Charter and requested a meeting of the Security Council. He recommended 'creation of ONUC, mainly composed of troops from African States. He also recommended withdrawal of Belgian troops from Congo because they were a source of tension. The Security Council not only accepted the above recommendations of the Secretary General but also authorised him to provide such military assistance as he may deem necessary.

The growing role of the Secretary General was criticised by Soviet Union and Khrushchev proposed TRIOKA in 1960 under which instead of one Secretary General, there were to be three Secretary Generals representing East, West plan and non-aligned blocs. However, this was rejected by Hammarskjold on the plea that it would substitute for an independent international Secretary General a triumvirate, each of whom would owe loyalty to the bloc that elects him and would rob the UN of its most distinctive dynamic and creative organ, and reduce the Secretariat to the level of a service agency for a Conference Organisation. In 1961, after Lumumba demanded continuance of Congo operation, Soviet Union again demanded continuance of Congo operation and dismissal of Hammarskjold. Despite this the Secretary General was given authority to reorganise the Congo national army and take all appropriate measures to prevent occurrence of civil war in Congo, including the use of force in the last report. Thus the Secretary General was given power even to intervene in the internal affairs. Due to efforts of the Secretary General the position in Congo considerably improved and an all-Congo government was installed under Adoula. But peace could not be established in Congo and soon Katanga announced withdrawal which led to fresh trouble. Secretary General Hammarskjold made personal bid to resolve the issue and undertook a personal visit to Tshombe (President of Katanga) to find a solution. However, he was killed in a plane crash which gave rise to doubts about the role of Secretary General in future.

The Secretary General U. Thant had to face serious problem in Congo due to outbreak of violence. Thereupon the Security Council authorised the Secretary General in November 1960 to remove the mercenaries through use of force. He not only established peace through use of UN forces but also proposed a plan of national reconstruction. Thereafter though O.N.U.C. continued in Congo for some time but ultimately these had to be withdrawn due to financial crisis. Under U. Thant the office of the Secretary General gained in prestige because he tried to keep good relations with both the great powers. Despite this he was criticised for his decision to remove UN peace-keeping forces from Sinai on the demand of President Nasser of Egypt in 1967.

Kurt Waldheim the fourth Secretary General played an important role as mediator. He organised and presided over talks beween the Turks and Greek communities in Cyprus and toured Middle East extensively to bring about settlement. During his tenure a number of constructive activities were also undertaken by the United Nations. These included provision of disaster relief, protection of international environment, administration of deep sea bed and running of a world university.

The fifth Secretary General Javier Perez de Cuellar was praised as well as criticised for his role. He played an important role in the withdrawal of Soviet troops from Afghanistan, conduct of free elections in Namibia, conduct of elections in Nicaragua. During his tenure five new peacekeeping operations were organised, which included two in the Middle East viz. the military observer team in Iran-Iraq border and the United Nations Iraq-Kuwait Observation Mission after the UN operation for liberation of Kuwait in 1991. It maybe noted that the Secretary General was able to play such an effective role chiefly due to changed international climate in which both United States and Soviet Union were willing to cooperate for the resolution of the long-standing disputes. However the position of the Secretary General was somewhat undermined during the Gulf crisis of 1990-91, when after repeated failure of Iraq to comply with the UN resolutions and withdraw troops from Kuwait, the UN passed a resolution calling on its members to use all possible means to liberate Kuwait if Iraq did not withdraw. As Iraq failed to heed this call, a UN multinational force went into action for the liberation of Kuwait, and achieved the desired success. However, during these operations the Secretary General found himself in embarrassing position because US did not keep him fully informed about the course of war. He even failed to stop the operations when the US led forces clearly overstepped their mandate.

The sixth Secretary General Dr Boutros Ghali of Egypt also played an active role in resolving the disputes and promoting greater co-operation among the member States. The present Secretary General Kofi Anna is also continuing the tradition of earlier Secretary Generals.

It is evident from the preceding account that the role of the Secretary General has undergone great transformation since the establishment of the United Nations. This transformation was made possible by a number of factors.

1. In the first place the UN Charter has given much latitude to the Secretary General by authorising him to bring any matter to the attention of the Security Council, which in his opinion poses a threat to world peace and security. This has enabled the Secretary General to play more important political role than his counterpart under the covenant of the League.
2. Secondly, the Secretary Generals have tended to assume more power through liberal interpretation of the powers assigned to them under the UN Charter. Thus Hammarskjold undertook a trip to Laos in 1959 in exercise of his powers vested in his office under Article 99 of the Charter. He asserted his right to carry out appropriate investigations regard-

ing developments in critical areas. Most of the developing countries have also supported the contention that the Secretary General should be permitted to forestall conflicts through use of his executive actions. This has naturally resulted in the expansion of his powers.

3. Thirdly, the failure of the Security Council, which was originally vested by the UN Charter with final authority to maintain international peace and security, due to cold war between two major powers, led to adoption of Uniting for Peace Resolution in 1950. It led to transfer of these powers to the General Assembly. But the General Assembly due to its large size and lack of effective powers, preferred to request the Secretary General to undertake these functions on its behalf. This naturally enhanced the powers and prestige of the Secretary General. Further, the various challenges posed to the UN have also enabled the Secretary General to assume more administrative responsibilities. It has also been able to play more effective role in mediation and considerable enhancement in the powers and prestige of the Secretary General.
4. Fourthly, the emergence of large number of independent States in Asia and Africa and their admission to the United Nations, has also contributed to the importance of the Secretary General because most of these States prefer the development and utilisation of the executive capacity of the Organisation. This has enabled the Secretary General to play the role of champion of the small States.
5. Fifthly, the personalities of various occupants of the office of Secretary General, have also exercised profound influence on the new role of the Secretary General. The first Secretary General (Trygve Lie) played a very positive role and did not hesitate to express his views openly even on controversial issues. This at times made him unpopular with Soviet Union. The second Secretary General (Dag Hammarskjold) acted with great diplomacy and fully exploited the powers vested in him. This won him the trust of both the powers and he was often entrusted with important diplomatic and executive duties. The third and the fourth Secretary Generals also by and large succeeded in keeping clear of Big Power politics and succeeded in winning great respect.
6. Finally, the actual course of world events, which often resulted in deadlocks between the General Assembly or the Security Council, also contributed to the importance of the Secretary General. In view of these deadlocks he was able to take greater initiatives with regard to peace-keeping and organisation of multinational cooperation. In the present context when the international crisis demands immediate action against threat of nuclear warfare, the Secretary General as an individual can take quick action. He can make use of Art. 99 of the Charter which permits him to take initiative for settlement of dispute without waiting for the General Assembly or the Security Council. It is true that the Secretary General does not enjoy any power to raise the finances and forces for promotion of peace, but he can certainly play an effective role in bringing the disputing parties to the negotiating table and identify appropriate areas of action by the United Nations.

It may be noted that the role which the Secretary General can play at any given time and in a particular situation depends on his personality as well as the political support which he is able to muster from various groups in the United Nations.

In conclusion we can say with Goodrich "there are definite advantages in having the Secretary General perform major political functions in the peace and security field. He is an official continuously on the job, presumably possessing qualifications of a political and personal nature which equip him for difficult diplomatic and administrative tasks. He has in the Charter a legal basis for taking initiative and assuming responsibilities. He has at his disposal a large and well qualified staff, representing a variety of experience and. national points of view. He is, therefore, in a position, acting directly or through chosen representatives, to mobilize a variety of, skills and experience, and with the traditions of an impartial and highly qualified international service to support him, to command the confidence and trust of governments."

FURTHER READINGS

Leon Gordenker	*The UN Secretary General and the Maintenance of Peace*
Arthur W. Roime	*The Secretary General in World Politics: The First Fifty Years*
Vandenbosch and Hogan	*The United Nations*
David A. Kay (ed)	*The United Nations Political System*
Inis L. Claude Jr	*Swords into Ploughshares*

(Leland M. Goodrich, 'The Political Role of the Secretary General' in David A. Kay *(ed), The United Nations Political System,* p. 138)

Chapter 10
UNITED NATIONS AND PROBLEM OF MEMBERSHIP

The provisions of the UN Charter pertaining to membership of UN have evoked great controversy. In fact even when the Charter was being finalised at the San Francisco Conference the representatives expressed opposite views on this issue. One group of representatives pleaded for universal membership of the United Nations and insisted that all the qualified states and dominions should be automatically admitted as members of the United Nations. The qualifications for membership, if any, should be determined by the Council. The Council should, however, insist only on technical qualifications and should not insist on any moral qualifications. The other group, however, held that the United Nations should admit only those states as members who had demonstrated certain moral standards before admission. They insisted that the States wishing to seek membership should file an application for admission, which could be accepted or rejected. In view of these conflicting views the UN Charter incorporated certain provisions regarding membership which sought to reconcile the above two views.

Provisions in UN Charter regarding Membership

Articles 3 to 6 of Charter deal with the membership. The Charter makes mention of two types of members–the original members and other members. The original members of the United Nations were the states which participated in the United Nations Conference on International Organisation at San Francisco, or had previously signed the Declaration by the United Nations of 1 January 1942, signed the present Charter and ratified the same. There was controversy regarding the inclusion of Soviet Republics, India and Philippines as original members of United Nations. However, ultimately, India and Philippines were admitted as original members of the United Nations even though they did not meet the traditional criteria of statehood. They were admitted in accordance with the suggestion that all self-governing states and dominions, accepting the obligations of membership, could become members of UN. Soviet Union insisted on the inclusion of all the 16 autonomous Soviet Republics as original members of UN, but US vehemently opposed it. Ultimately only two Republics of Soviet Union viz. Bylorussia and Ukraine were admitted as independent members of the United Nations.

The other members of the United Nations included the peace-loving states which accepted the obligations contained in the UN Charter and were in the judgement of the Organisation able and willing to carry out these obligations. The admission of such states to membership of the United Nations was effected through a decision of the General Assembly upon the recommendation of the Security Council. The Security Council makes such recommendation by a majority of seven members, including the concurring votes of the permanent members. A state admitted as member of the UN automatically acquires membership of the General Assembly, secures periodic representation in other organs and automatically becomes a party to the Statute of the International Court of Justice. It may be noted that a state applying for membership of the United Nations is not automatically granted the membership. The members of the General Assembly and Security Council take the decision not strictly in accordance with conditions enumerated in Article 4 of the Charter, but also take into account such political considerations as they consider relevant. In the early years of the United Nations a large number of states were ,'admitted as members of the UN without much difficulty. However, after the cold war between USA and USSR set in, both the states adopted an attitude of opposing membership of countries sponsored or supported by the opponent. The requests of Mongolian People's Republic, and Albania for membership of the UN were turned down in early fifties on the ground that the information regarding these states was not sufficient to show whether they were capable of discharging their obligations under the Charter. However subsequently both Albania and Mongolia were admitted as members in 1955 and 1963 respectively.

The General Assembly sought to resolve this deadlock over admission of new members and set up committees to examine the question of admission of members and use their good offices. However, the General Assembly failed to achieve much. Ultimately, it sought advice from the International Court of Justice on the question whether a new member can be admitted when the Security Council does not recommend the admission of a state due to failure of state to obtain the requisite majority or use of a negative vote by a permanent member of the Security Council. The International Court of Justice gave its opinion by 12 to 2 that membership of a state "cannot be effected by a decision of the General Assembly when the Security Council has made no recommendation for admission, by reason of the candidate failing to obtain the requisite majority or of the negative vote of permanent member upon a recommendation so to recommend."

Suspension of Members

Article 5 of the Charter stipulates that a member of the United Nations against which preventive or enforcement action has been taken by the Security Council may be suspended from the exercise of the rights and privileges of membership by the General Assembly upon the recommendation of the Security Council. However, the exercise of these rights and privileges can be restored by the Security Council.

Expulsion Of Members

Article 6 of the Charter deals with the expulsion of members. It stipulates that a member of the United Nations, which has persistently violated the principles contained in the present Charter may be expelled from the Organisation by the General Assembly upon the recommendation of the Security Council. It may be observed that so far none of the members has been suspended or dismissed.

Withdrawal Of Membership

The Charter is absolutely silent about withdrawal of membership. This has been interpreted to imply that the members are not entitled to withdraw from the membership of the United Nations once they join it. In January 1965, Indonesia withdrew from the United Nations and became the first state to do so. But subsequently Indonesia rejoined the United Nations.

Issue of Chinese Representation in UN

China was admitted as an original member of the United Nations in 1945. After the revolution of 1949 in China the Communists acquired control over the government of China at Peking, while the Nationalist government headed by Chiang-Kai-Shek fled to Formosa. A question naturally arose as to which of the two governments was entitled to represent China in the United Nations. This problem continued to plague the UN till 1971 and there was a persistent demand that the representatives of the Chinese Peoples Republic be seated as the representatives of the State of China in place of the Nationalist government which was in control of the island of Formosa only. It is noteworthy that strictly speaking the question of China was one of representation and not membership.

The western countries led by USA and Great Britain opposed the representation of the Chinese Peoples Republic in the United Nations on the basis of Article 4 of the Charter which lays down that a country to be eligible for membership of UN must be 'peace-loving' and 'able and willing' to carry out international obligations. These countries contended that the behaviour of red China since its birth had indicated that it was not a peace-loving country. It not only took aggressive military action against Korea, Taiwan, Tibet and states of South and South East Asia. Further, it pursued an aggressive and expansionist policy which was certainly against the purpose and principles of the UN Charter. The western countries asserted that the rightful claimant for seat in the UN was the law-abiding government of Republic of China, whose representative had been sitting in the United Nations since 1945 as a permanent member. They highlighted the war-like intentions of the government of Peking by pointing out that China had been training young men from Asia, Africa and Latin America in the art of 'guerrilla warfare', to be used against their own countries. They even used the views of Mao Tse Tung to confirm their contention that China was not a peace loving country. Mao Tse Tung had expressed his views about the world problems and asserted that "everything can be made to grow out of the barrel of a gun. The central duty and the highest form of revolution is armed seizure of political power and the settling of problems by means of war. This Marxist Leninist principle is universally correct, whether in China or foreign countries; it is always true."

On the other hand, those who supported representation of red China in the United Nations argued that under Article 4 of the UN Charter "an applicant for membership must be able and willing to carry out the obligation of membership." They contended that the Red China Government alone was capable of employing the resources and directing the people to fulfil the obligations of membership. They feared that if red China was kept out of the United Nations, a major conflict may ensue. In support of this view they argued that there was a common feeling that if USA had been member of the League of Nations, probably the second world war could have been avoided. Going by the same logic they argued that if Red China was not represented in the United Nations, it might contribute towards the Third World War. It was further argued that if China was admitted to UN, it would be easy to effect a change in her outlook and she can be persuaded to abandon war-like methods and follow rule of law. The representation of red China was also justified on practical grounds. As China was engaged in nuclear research, it was felt that her admission would bring her activities under international control. In case she was kept out of United Nations she might be forced to build a mighty fortress against its enemies which would certainly pose a serious threat to the peace and security of the world. In short they argued that whatever may be the legal justification for the exclusion of red China from the United Nations, it was not desirable to deny her representation in the world Organisation permanently.

This controversy regarding representation of red China in the United Nations persisted from 1950-1971 to seat Red China in the United Nations, but these attempts were foiled by United States which opposed the unseating of Chiang Kai Shek. The issue raised a critical stage in 1970 when the General Assembly voted by 51 to 49 votes for seating the people's Republic of China in the United Nations. However, United States took the stand that the admission of Red China was an important question and should be decided by a two-thirds majority. In 1971 United States effected a change in its China policy and proposed a Two Chinese Plan. According to this plan the permanent seat in the Security Council should be occupied by Red China while Republican China should be made an ordinary member of the United Nations. However, this plan of United States was rejected by both Mao Tse Tung and Chiang Kai Shek.

It was only after improvement of relations between China and USA and relaxation of trade and travel restriction between the two countries that Red China was given representation in United Nations in October 1971. The General Assembly by an overwhelming majority (76 to 35) decided to give seat in the Security Council as well as the General Assembly to the People's Republic of China, and evicted Taiwan. This marked an end of a prolonged struggle for getting a rightful place to the People's Republic of China.

Other Controversies Regarding Membership

In several other cases also there were controversies regarding the admission of new members either because doubts were expressed about their rightful status as states or their ability to provide a stable and effective government. For example the Arabstates objected to the admission of Israel as member on the ground that it lacked statehood because its borders were internally disputed. But as Israel's claim to statehood was accepted by all the members of the Security Council and more than two-thirds of the members of the General Assembly, Israel was given membership of United Nations. Likewise, Russia objected to the admission of Japan as member of UN on the plea that Japan was not a sovereign and independent state, as it was still under the control of the occupation forces. Soviet Union insisted that consideration of Japan's application for membership should be postponed until Japan concluded normal peace treaties with the USSR and the People's Republic of China. This objection of Soviet Union delayed admission of Japan as member of United Nation still 1956.

The applications of both Mongolian People's Republic and Albania were turned down by the UN in the early fifties on the grounds that the information regarding these states was not sufficient to show whether they were capable of fulfilling the obligations of the Charter. But ultimately Albania was admitted as member in 1955, while Mongolia gained membership in 1961.

The admission of Republic of Congo also evoked some controversy. The Security Council recommended that the Republic of Congo be admitted. This recommendation was made at a time when there did not exist any doubt about the existence of a legal and effective government in Congo. But when the matter came for discussion before the General Assembly in September 1960 and it voted to admit Congo to United Nations, serious doubts began to be expressed about the effectiveness of government in Congo due to existence of warring Congolese factions in the ongoing civil war in the state.

It is noteworthy that during the first ten years of existence the United Nations granted admission to only nine new members. This was largely due to emerging cold war when both the western and eastern blocs made use of their 'vetoes' to prevent the admission of members thought to be belonging to the other bloc. It was only after mid 1950's that the western coalition somewhat loosened and divisions appeared in the Soviet bloc, that the question of membership was viewed in a fresh perspective. By this time the Asian and African countries also started asserting themselves. In the context of the changed conditions a package deal was made and United States assented to the admission of 16 new members including several communist states. In the 1960's with. the relaxation of cold war, the membership of UN did not evoke much controversy and membership became more accessible.

Problem of Membership of Divided States

The divided states like Korea, Vietnam and Germany, also posed a problem of membership representation. In all these cases USA and Soviet Union took opposite stands. For example in the case of Korea, US maintained that the Government of South Korea was the only lawful government because it had been elected by the people and exercised effective control over that part of Korea. On the other hand Soviet Union argued that the South Korean government could not be granted membership of united Nations because it was a puppet government created through an illegal action of the United Nations. On account of this control North and South Korea could not be admitted as members of United Nations till 1991.

The Republics of North and South Vietnam were also denied admission as members of United Nations on the plea that they did not represent the states but were merely political factions. It was only after the East-West relations showed an improvement that the two parts of Vietnam were united and the unified Vietnam was admitted as member of UN in 1977. The question of admission of two Germanys as members of UN also posed problem for quite sometime. It was only after relations between two Germanys started improving in the 1960's that the two German states were admitted as members of UN by the General Assembly in September 1973.

Influx Of New States

During the period 1991-93 more than 25 new states were admitted as members of the United Nations. This because possible due to end of cold war as well as disintegration of Soviet Union and Yugoslavia. Most of these members are former Republics of Soviet Union-viz. independent Baltic Nations of Estonia, Latvia and Lithuania; and members of newly formed Commonwealth of independent States Moldovia, Kazakhstan, Myrgyzstan, Azerbaijan, Uzbekistan, Tajikistan, Turkmenistan, Armenia and Georgia.

The growth of membership of United Nations since l945 is given in the following table:

Years	Number of Members
1945	51
1946	55
1947	57
1948	58
1949	59
1950	60
1955	76
1956	80
1957	82
1958	83
1960	100
1961	104
1962	110
1963	112

1964	115
1965	118
1966	122
1967	123
1968	126
1970	127
1971	132
1973	132
1974	138
1975	144
1976	147
1977	149
1978	151
1979	152
1980	154
1981	157
1983	158
1984	159
1985	159
1986	159
1987	159
1988	159
1989	159
1991	166
1992	175
1993	183
1994	185

FURTHER READINGS

Inis Claude — *Swords into Ploughshares*

Peter R. Bachr and Leon Gordenker — *The United Nations*

Chapter 11

UNITED NATIONS AND INTERNATIONAL LAW

The present age is an age of internationalism in which the different states regularly come into contact with each other. To regulate the relations of states, both during times of peace as well as war, certain rules and regulations have been evolved over the past few centuries which are generally termed as international law. These rules regulate the mutual relations of the states according to certain accepted norms and prevent use of unnecessary force for the settlement of disputes. Most of the states observe these rules in their national interest. The United Nations which was created after the Second World War also aims at avoiding war and promoting co-operational relations among the member states. In fact the United Nations has played an important role in the development of international law in several ways. In the first instance the UN Charter has greatly contributed to the development of international law by setting forth several new principles of international law. Secondly, the various organs of the United Nations, have contributed to the growth of Intentional Law in several ways. Thus the UN Assembly has contributed to the growth of Intentional Law by adopting innovative resolutions; the International Law Commission has contributed towards the growth of international law through codification of existing rules of intentional law; the International Court of Justice has contributed to the growth of international law by enunciating new principles while adjudicating in different cases. Thirdly, the various specialised agencies of United Nations like the International Labour Organisation (ILO), International Telecommunication Union (ITU), the International Civil Aviation Organisation (ICAO), and International Maritime Organisation (IMO), etc. have greatly contributed to the development of international law by adopting rules of conduct in their respective fields. It shall be desirable to make a detailed study of the contribution of United Nations in the development of international law in all these spheres.

UN Charter and International Law

The UN Charter contributed to the strengthening and development of international law by reaffirming faith in the well-established rules of inter-state conduct, and enunciating certain principles of international conduct which the members of the international community were expected to observe. Some of the important principles of international law emphasised by the UN Charter include: (a) renunciation of the use of force by the member states to settle their disputes; (b) non-interference in the domestic or internal affairs of other states; (c) principle of sovereign equality of states and right of self determination of people; (d) principle of non-discrimination through emphasis on promotion e.g. of human rights and fundamental freedoms without discrimination as to race, sex, language or religion everywhere in the world; (e) promotion of international co-operation by encouraging progressive development of international law; (f) promotion of international co-operation in the economic, social, cultural, educational and health fields, etc. It is true that all these principles enunciated by the UN Charter were not entirely new and were already in vogue in some form or other, but their enunciation in a multilateral treaty of the statute provided them a legal status and international recognition which was indeed a significant development in the direction of development of international law.

Role of Various Organs of United Nations

The various organs and agencies of the United Nations have also greatly contributed to the development of international law in several ways. For example, the General Assembly of the United Nations has contributed to the development of international laws by adopting general legal conventions. For this purpose the UN Charter clearly entrusts the responsibility for initiating studies and making recommendations for the purpose of encouraging the progressive development of international law and its codification to the General Assembly. In pursuance of this responsibility the General Assembly set up an International Commission in November 1947. The Commission at that time comprised 15 members, now 34 mainly consisting of experts of law, who were elected by the General Assembly. The Commission was entrusted with two-fold functions viz. codification of the existing laws and progressive development of law.

As regards codification, the Commission was entrusted with the responsibility of codification of law of treaties, including their interpretation and binding force; arbitration procedure; the rights of the states on high seas and the question of territorial waters. Subsequently the Commission was also entrusted with the responsibility of examining issues pertaining to genocide, human rights, status of women and reparation for injuries suffered by the UN officials. It may be noted that on all these subjects a large body of precedents existed and the International Law Commission was merely expected to define the laws on these issues in more precise terms.

Though the International Commission set up for the purpose of codification of international law did not favour codification of all the existing laws and it decided to confine its activities only with regard to recognition of state, state succession, jurisdiction, immunities of states and their property, crimes committed abroad, high seas, territorial water, nationality, treatment of aliens, asylum law of treaties, arbitration procedure, state-responsibility, diplomatic immunities, consular immunities, etc. its efforts helped to clarify several obscure points of law.

The International Law Commission also helped in the development of new international law. It enunciated the principles applied in the Nuremberg trials. It outlined three categories of intentional crimes: (i) crimes against peace; (ii) crimes against humanity; and (iii) war crimes. It also insisted on the principle of individual accountability for these international crimes. The other notable contributions of the Commission included Draft Declaration on the Rights and Duties of the States, which outlined the basic rights of the states like independence, equality, jurisdiction over state territory, collective and individual self-defence against armed attack, etc.

Conventions Adopted by Assembly

Some of the important conventions adopted by General Assembly include the following.

1. *Genocide Convention:* In 1948 the General Assembly adopted Genocide Convention and declared genocide as a crime under international law. The convention included in genocide all killing, deliberate starvation, sterilisation and forcible decimation of human groups of people belonging to a particular culture. The convention was significant insofar as it brought even the internal actions of the states against their own citizens under the purview of international law.
2. *Human Rights Conventions.* The General Assembly also adopted a number of human rights conventions. The most prominent among these were the International Convention on the Elimination of all Forms of racial Discriminations 1966; the International Convention on the Suppression and Punishment of crime of apartheid in 1973; the Convention on Elimination of All Forms of Discrimination against Women in 1979; and the Convention on the Rights of the Child in 1991.
3. *General Assembly Resolutions.* In addition to the above Conventions, the General Assembly has been passing a wide range of resolutions every year, some of which insist on the application of the existing international law, while the others make laws. Some of the resolutions adopted by the General Assembly which can be included in the category of law-making resolutions include the General Assembly Resolution on the Declaration on the Granting of Independence to Colonial Countries and Peoples; the Declaration on the inadmissibility of Intervention in the Domestic Affairs of the State and the Protection of their Independence and Sovereignty; the Declaration of Principal of International Law concerning Friendly Relations and Cooperation among states in accordance with the Charter of UN and the General Assembly Resolution on Definition of Aggression.

Above all the General Assembly has contributed to the development of international law by setting up committees to examine specific legal matters. The Committees of the Assembly also examines the reports of the International Law Commission and makes specific suggestions on these recommendations.

UN Conferences and International Law

The Conferences convened by the United Nations have also contributed to the development of international law by adopting various conventions. Some of the conventions thus adopted include the following: (i)Vienna Convention on Diplomatic Relations and Treaties. Such conventions were adopted in 1961,1963 and 1969. All these conferences were provided draft texts by the International Law Commission at the instance of the UN General Assembly. (ii) UN Conferences also adopted three Laws of Sea Conventions in 1958, 1960 and 1982. These Conventions dealt with problems like ocean space and its uses, navigation and overflights, resource exploration and exploitation, conservation and pollution, fishing and shipping. The other issues dealt with by these conventions include defining of maritime zones, laying down rules for drawing sea boundaries, assigning legal rights, duties and responsibilities to state and providing machinery for settlement of disputes.

Another significant step in the direction of development of law of Sea was taken in 1982 when the United Nations Convention on the Law of the sea was signed by 117 states. More states signed this convention subsequently and by December 1984, 159 states and some other entities had signed it. The Convention came into force in November 1994 after it was ratified by the sixtieth state. The Convention was quite comprehensive in so far as it covered all ocean space and its uses viz. navigation and over flight, resource exploration and exploitation conservation and pollution, fishing and shipping. It also defined maritime zones, laid down rules for drawing sea boundaries, assigned legal rights, duties and responsibilities to the states and provided machinery for settlement of disputes.

The Convention on the Law of the Sea adopted in 1982 could not assume universal character because the industrialized countries continued to oppose the provisions relating to deep seabed continued to oppose the provisions relating to deep seabed mining. In fact the Convention of 1982 had placed all exploring and exploiting activities in the international sea bed Area under the control of the International Sea Bed Authority, which was authorized to conduct its own mining operations through its operating arm, the Enterprise or contract with private and state ventures to give them mining rights in the Area.

Several important conventions were also adopted by the United Nations in the field of Diplomatic Relations and Law of Treaties. Some of the important conventions adopted in this respect include the convention on Diplomatic relations adopted at Vienna in 1961; Convention on Consular Relations in 1963; Convention on Law of Treaties in 1968 and 1969; Convention on Prevention and Punishment of Crimes against Internationally Protected Persons, including Diplomatic Agents, adopted by General Assembly in 1969 and 1973. This was followed by Vienna Convention on Succession of States in Respect of Treaties adopted by General Assembly in 1977 and 1978. In 1983 Convention on Succession of States in respect of Stare Property, Archives and Debts was adopted at Vienna. In 1986 Vienna Convention on the Law of Treaties between States and International Organisations or between International Organisations was adopted.

International Trade Law

United Nations also took several steps to ensure smooth flow of international trade. In 1966 it established the United Nations Commission on International Trade Law (UNCITRAL) to promote the progressive harmonization and unification of the law of international trade. The main functions of this Commission include coordination of the work of international organizations active in the field of international trade law, promotion of wider participation in international conventions, and the preparation of new conventions and other instruments relating to international trade law. The Commission also offers training and assistance in international trade law by way of national or regional seminars, symposia or briefing missions. The Commission has paid special attention to the study and preparation of uniform rules in international commercial arbitration, international legislation on shipping, counter trade and procurement.

In 1974 the General Assembly adopted the Convention on the Limitation Period in the International Sale of Goods. The same was amended in 1980. In the meanwhile in 1978 United Nations Convention of Carriage of Goods by Sea, popularly known as Hamburg Rules, was adopted. In 1980 United Nations Conventions on Contracts for the International Sale of Goods was adopted. This was followed by United Nations Convention on the Liability of Operators of Transport Terminals in International Trade adopted at Vienna in 1991. In 1988 the General Assembly adopted the United Nations Convention on International Bill of Exchange of International Promissory Notes. The Commission adopted Model Law on International Commercial Arbitration in 1985, Model Law on International Credit Transfers in 1992; and Model Law on Procurement of Goods, Construction and Services in 1994; In 1992 the Commission prepared Legal Guide on International Counter Trade Transactions

Role of Specialized Agencies of UN

The specialised agencies of the UN have also played a prominent role in the development of international law. Some of these agencies have not only revolutionised international law in their fields but also established full legal machinery to enforce obedience to the laws generated in that field. Some of the specialised agencies of the UN which deserve special mention in this regard include International Maritime Organisation (IMO), the International Telecommunication Union (ITU), the International Labour Organisation (ILO), the International Civil Aviation Organisation (ICAO), etc.

It is evident from the preceding account that the UN has played an important role in the development and promotion of several legal innovations in the field of international law. On account of its international character the UN has promoted principles like universalism, human rights, common heritage of mankind, equality in international economic relations, etc.

Despite tremendous progress made by international law, it still suffers from several shortcomings and ambiguities. In the first place though the various states have tended to agree on general principles, on account of their divergent interests economic, military or social, they have often tended to come in conflict. Thus on the one hand the states have expressed faith in principle of human rights and on the other hand opposed intervention' in the domestic jurisdiction. Similarly the principles of self-determination by the people and assertion of faith in principle of territorial integrity of states are clearly opposed to each other.

Secondly, several areas of national conduct are not covered by international law which leaves sufficient scope for conflict between the states. Thus there is no agreement among states regarding the criteria for the recognition of new governments, the degree and type of intervention permissible in civil wars, rights over territorial waters, etc.

Thirdly there is great difference between theory and practice of international law. Often the treaties concluded by the states contain principles which are not easy to realise or practice. As a result often the treaties are either violated or flouted. There are no effective sanctions available with the international body to punish the states which flout the principles of international law. It is true that several devices have been evolved for the enforcement of international law since 1945, but they are far from effective. There is urgent need to build up a law abiding international community. In this regard apart from the United Nations, the various states, news-media, non-governmental agencies, individuals as well as the public opinion can play a vital role. However, it cannot be denied that the International Organisation in general and the UN in particular has played an important role towards the promotion of international law. As Prof. Louis Kenk in has observed "It has contributed to the ends which law pursues and to the law itself; it has helped to create an atmosphere of law fullness, to make law, promote its observance, deter violation. It has, I believe, helped maintain the basic requirements of the legal orders the prohibition of force between Nations." He further asserts that in future also 'the international Organisation will promote basic order and respect for law because they are in the common interest."

FURTHER READINGS

D.W. Bowett	*The Law of International Institutions*
Jacob Robinson	*'International Law and Organisation' in General Sources of Information*
J.G.Starke	*Introduction to International Law*
UN Publication	*Everyone's United Nations*
Daniel S. Cheever and H. Field Haviland Jr	*Organizing for Peace*

Chapter 12
BUDGET AND FINANCING OF UNITED NATIONS SYSTEM

Money is the lifeblood of any organization, be it national or international. In case of the United Nations it has posed a serious problem since its inception because 'the members are unwilling to give the Organisation the financial support for it to attain the strength it needs to preserve peace and advance the international good society." According to H. G. Nocholas "The United Nations finds itself short of money only because rich and powerful states have decided that it is in their interest to reduce it to such pecuniary embarrassment. And the reasons for their decision have very little to do with pressures from national treasuries; they reflect in all cases reasons of state electorate in foreign ministries." Before looking into the problem of UN finances, it shall be 'desirable to know about the provisions contained in the UN Charter with regard to finances of the United Nations.

Budgetary Provisions

Articles 17-19 of the UN Charter deal with the provisions regarding finances of the United Nations. Article 17 provides that the budget of the Organisation shall be considered and approved by the General Assembly. The expenses of the Organisation shall be borne by the members as apportioned by the General Assembly. The General Assembly shall consider and approve financial and budgetary arrangements with specialised agencies referred to in Article 57 and shall examine the administrative budgets of such specialized agencies with a view to making recommendation to the agencies concerned. Article 18 interalia provides that the budgetary questions shall be decided by the General Assembly by two-thirds majority. Article 19 stipulates that a member of the United Nations which is in arrears in the payment of the financial contributions to the Organisation shall have no vote in the General Assembly if the amount of its arrears equals or exceeds the amount of the contributions due from it for the preceding two full years. However, the General Assembly can permit such a member to vote, if it is satisfied that failure to pay is due to conditions beyond the control of the member.

An analysis of the above provisions of the Charter with regard to budget and finances highlights the following features: (i) The power to regulate the finances of the United Nations squarely rests with the General Assembly; (ii) all the members of the United Nations have a say in the allocation and expenditure of funds; (iii) no specific principles for apportionment of the expenses have been laid down and the same is determined by the General Assembly; (iv) the budget has to be approved by the General Assembly by two-thirds majority; (v) there is no single budget for the United Nations and the autonomous agencies prepare independent budgets; (vi) the members of the organisation which fail to pay their contribution for two years are debarred from voting in the Assembly. However, the Assembly can waive this disqualification if it is satisfied that the member has not made the payment due to conditions beyond its control.

Types of Expenditure

The expenditure incurred by the United Nations broadly falls into four categories.

1. *Regular Budget.* This refers to the budget pertaining to the United Nations Organisation and includes expenses on maintenance of headquarters, field missions, salaries, travel and transportation, equipment and supplies, printing and other expenses.
2. *Budget of Specialised Agencies.* Each of the Specialized Agency of the UN formulates its own budget. No doubt, the General Assembly is authorised to examine the budgets of these agencies and it can also make necessary recommendations to them in this regard, but generally the General Assembly has not much say in this regard.
3. *Voluntary Programmes.* Huge sums are spent on programmes of voluntary nature. These funds are usually collected through voluntary contribution from governments, organisations and even individuals. Such expenditure is not included in the regular budget. Some of the important programmes of this type include UN Expanded Programme for Technical Assistance, UNDP, UNICEF, etc.
4. *Enforcement Functions.* In addition to the above, the United Nations also spends huge amounts of money in carrying out the enforcement action. For this purpose the member states not only contribute money but also provide manpower, equipment, clothing, food, troops, etc.

Basis of Apportionment

The UN Charter has not specified the basis for apportionment of expenses. Therefore, in 1946 when the UN started its work, the need to find an equitable and satisfactory formula for appropriating of expenses was felt. Therefore, the General Assembly appointed a committee in 1946 to determine the contributions. For this purpose it laid down certain criteria viz. ability to pay as reflected by each state's total national income, per capita income, economic dislocation caused by the war after 1945 and foreign exchange earnings. All these criteria, except dislocation caused by war, still form the basis for determining assessments even now. However, in addition to this criteria, 'floor' and 'ceiling' limitations have also been added. The largest contributions to the UN budget is made by United States which contributes almost 25 percent of the regular budget. On the other hand a large number of underdeveloped countries contribute only 0.01 percent of the budget each. The poor countries have generally insisted that the contributions of the states should be determined strictly on the basis of a country's national income and ability to pay.

This arrangement of contribution to budget has been severely criticised by some of the major contributors to the budget. They have argued that the countries of the third world, which contribute the minimal are able to have larger say and decide as to how much should be spent and for what purpose. The seven richest countries which contribute almost 70 percent of the total budget can be easily outvoted by the developing countries which contribute only 30 per cent of the budget.

The imbalance in contribution has persisted since the inception of the United Nations. This imbalance further increased when the UN undertook peace keeping operations in the Middle East in 1956 and in Congo in 1960. The cost of these peace-keeping operations was much greater than even the regular budget and the major burden fell on the United States. Most of the States refused to make contribution on different pleas. For example the Soviet bloc countries as well as the Arab states insisted that the payment should be made only by the aggressors. The Latin American countries took the plea that the assessments were merely recommendations of the General Assembly and they were not legally obliged to comply with the same. France and Soviet Union took the stand that they would not pay their contributions because the decision regarding peace-keeping operation had not been taken by the Security Council. In view of these divergent stands of the members states on the question of contributions, in 1962 the General Assembly sought opinion of the International Court of Justice on the binding nature of the emergency assessments for the cost of peace keeping operations in the Middle East and Congo. The Court opined that these costs were 'expenses of the organisation' within the meaning of the Charter and the assessments were binding on the members.

On the basis of the opinion of the International Court of Justice, the General Assembly passed a resolution by an overwhelming majority. However, France refused to comply with the resolution and contended that if the Assembly were able to impose financial obligation on all members by two-thirds majority, it would take on the attributes of a super-state. In view of these developments United States announced its decision to oppose the right of delinquent states to vote at the nineteenth General Assembly in terms of article 19 of the Charter. In view of this threat the nineteenth session of General Assembly was postponed. In December 1964 when the assembly actually met, United States insisted that Soviet Union should not be permitted to exercise right of vote. A sort of stalemate was created. This stalemate ended when the Assembly unanimously authorised a budget at 1964 levels and urged the members to make voluntary contributions to meet the deficit. A committee of 33 members on peacekeeping was set up to find a way out of this constitutional and financial impasse. However, this committee also failed to find a financial solution and recommended that organisation's deficit should be made up by voluntary contributions. At the twentieth General Assembly,

United States acquiesced in the Soviet refusal. With the emergence of a strong group of third world countries, the General Assembly passed certain resolutions of doubtful legal or financial excessiveness. This convinced the United States that the viewpoint of Russia was not wrong. America realised the enforcement of articles 17 and 19 of the Charter would give the General assembly unlimited taxing powers and the maximum burden fell on the richest states.

As neither USA nor USSR carried out their pledges of voluntary contributions, this resulted in unpaid debts for peace-keeping touching the $50 million mark. A bid was made in 1965 to overcome the financial problems of the United Nations when at the initiative of the French Delegation an ad hoc committee consisting of 14 members was set up to examine the finances of the United Nations and the Specialised Agencies. The Committee was also asked to examine the administrative and budgetary procedures, the means of comparing and, if possible, standardizing their budgets and the financial aspects of their expansion with a view to avoiding needless expenditure. The Committee of Fourteen submitted two reports, one dealing with the financial situation of the United Nations Organisation and the second with the problem of coordination. These reports covered a vast array of problems including budget preparation, presentation and performance budget cycles, standardization of nomenclature, audit and inspection; programme planning and evaluation; co-ordination machinery, conferences, meetings and document action; and personnel. These recommendations led to the improvement in the administrative and budgetary practices of the United Nations system.

Despite this the financial position of the United Nations continued to deteriorate in the subsequent years. In his report to the General Assembly, the Secretary General observed "The organisation's financial situation is worse than ever before and steadily deteriorating. A main cause of the worsening situation is certain Governments continue to withhold contributions apportioned under the regular budget for the cost of servicing United Nations bonds and certain other activities which they consider to be improperly included in the regular budget."

In the mid 1980's the financial crisis of United Nations reached major proportions and its solvency was threatened because United States decided to withhold substantial arrears due to fund cuts mandated by the US Congress. United States insisted that it would persist with the cut until the UN adopted a system of weighted voting on budgetary matters. The things got further aggravated because several other countries fell in line with USA. Despite this the UN continued to work because several states like China, Soviet Union and other third world countries like India, decided to pay the long overdue debts to the United Nations. In 1986 the General Assembly, on the basis of report of Group of 18, carried out reforms in budgetary procedures and United States again started paying its **dues.**

However, thereafter again the financial position of the United Nations became quite precarious because of the continuing failure of many member states to pay, in full and on time, their assessed contributions to the regular budget or to peace-keeping operations. Despite this United Nations has been able to manage its operations mainly due to voluntary contributions from some of the countries and its Working Capital Fund (to which members states advance sums in proportion to their assessed contributions). Quite a large number of member states are still not contributing their share on regular basis. For example at the end of December 1994 only 75 states had paid their assessments for the regular budget in full, while 109 member states failed to discharge their statutory financial obligations to the United Nations. With regard to contribution to peace-keeping operations also members owed $ 1.3 billion at the end of 1994. The UN tided over the situation by delaying reimbursements to the states which had contributed troops for these peace keeping operations.

Preparation of Budget

The total amount of the budget and the factors determining the actual sum each state has to contribute, is decided by the General Assembly after considering a two-year budget proposal by the Secretary General together with the recommendations of a budgetary advisory committee and a programme and coordination committee. The proposals regarding regular budget are submitted by the individual departments to the Budget Division and the Office for Programme Planning and Coordination of the Secretariat. These offices pass on their recommendations to the Programme Planning and Budgeting Board chaired by the Secretary General. The recommendations of the board form the basis of the final budget recommended by the Secretary General.

Next the Budget is vigorously scrutinised by two subsidiary bodies of the General Assembly viz., the Advisory Committee on Administrative and Budgetary Questions (ACABQ) and Committee for Programme and Coordination (CPC). The Advisory Committee on Administrative and Budgetary Questions comprises 16 members who are experts in finance management and economics. These members are nominated by the respective governments to serve in their personal capacity. The Committee for Programme and Coordination comprises of 34 members. These expert members represent the views of their governments. These two committees analyse the budget from the point of view of its conformity with inter-governmental legislative mandates.

The Budget proposed by the Secretary General as well as the recommendations of the above two committees (ACABQ and CPC) to the Fifth Administrative and Budgetary Committee of the General Assembly, on which all the members of the United Nations are represented. The Fifth Administrative and Budgetary Committee scrutinises the budget proposals as well as recommendations of the committees and forwards its recommendations on budget to the General Assembly for final review and approval.

CONTROL OF EXPENDITURE

After the funds have been appropriated effort is made to ensure that the money is spent for the approved purpose and due economy observed. This is done by the secretariat which appoints financial officers who authorise expenditure and maintain proper records. In addition the Assembly has created a Joint Inspecting Unit, which looks into matters relating to efficiency of services and proper use of funds. This Unit comprises inspectors from 11 nations. The recommendations of the Joint Inspection Unit are discussed by the Fifth Committee or any other intergovernmental body directly concerned. All the expenditure of the United Nations is subject to double audit. First, the Secretariat conducts audit through its internal auditors. Secondly, there is a Board of External Auditors The findings of the Auditors and their recommendations are published and placed before the Assembly for its approval.

Independent Sources of Income

It has been observed in the preceding pages that the United Nations has been confronted with serious problem of funds due to large number of member-states withholding their contributions or refusing to make contributions for certain voluntary programmes. Therefore, certain scholars have pleaded that the UN must find some independent sources of income. Some of the important sources of revenue suggested by these scholars include: (i) Levying of charges for certain services rendered by the UN agencies. Thus the World Meteorological Organisation could charge fees for providing weather data. Likewise the International Telecommunication Union could charge some fee for issue of international radio licenses.

(ii) It could raise profits by exploiting the mineral and other forms of wealth in international water and sea beds by setting up UN International Investment Corporation in terms of Law of the Sea Treaty 1982.

(iii) Income from sale of rights to private companies or governments to exploit the resources of sea beds, or granting fishing, whaling and sealing rights in intentional waters.

(iv) It could charge tolls for various transportation and communication facilities provided to the members.

(v) Levy charges for use of outer space such as communicating satellites, meteorological system, etc.

However, the above proposals are not likely to find favour with all the members, and differences are bound to crop up among the members on account of their opposing interests. But one thing can be said with certainty that if the United Nations is to be saved there is need to improve its financial position and it must have certain independent sources of income. Prof. Eichlberger has rightly observed "The lessons of history dictate that the United Nations can only have the necessary sovereign independence and strength by having an independent source of income, in addition to the contributions made by the member states." (Clark M.'Eichlberger, U. N.: *The First Twenty Years, p. 139)*

FURTHER READINGS

David Singer	*Financing International Organisation: The United Nations Budget Process*
Johan G. Stoessinger	*Financing the United Nations System*
U.N. Publication	*Everyone's United Nations*
U.N. Publication	*United Nations, Image and Reality: Questions and Answers about Management, Finance and People*
Clark M. Eichlberger	*U.N.: The First Twenty Years*

Chapter 13
UNITED NATIONS AND HUMAN RIGHTS

For a long time guarantee and protection of human rights was the exclusive concern of the states. No doubt certain steps were taken at the international level between 16th and 20th century to protect the rights of nationals of states and to grant freedom of worship to religious minorities or even end the slave trade, but the real beginning in the direction of protection of human rights started only in the present century. The Covenant of the League made the "well-being and development" of subject peoples in mandated territories a matter of international concern and insisted on the mandate powers to 'secure just treatment of the native inhabitants of all their dependent territories'.

U. N. Charter and Human Rights.

The atrocities committed by the Nazis during the Second World War evoked greater interest in human rights and the UN Charter pledge to promote universal respect for the observance of human rights. The Preamble of the UN Charter reaffirms faith in the fundamental human rights, in the dignity and worth of human person, in the equal rights of men and women and of nations large and small. In addition to this the UN Charter contains references to the promotion of universal respect for human rights in several other articles. Article 13 enjoins on the General Assembly to assist in the realisation of human rights and fundamental freedom for all without distinction as to race, sex, language or religion. Article 55 dealing with International Economic and Social Cooperation also insists on universal respect for, and observance of, human rights and fundamental freedoms for all without distinction as to race, sex, language or religion. Article 68 enjoins upon the Economic and Social Council to set up commission for the promotion of human rights. Similarly Article 76 dealing with Trusteeship System insists on encouragement of respect for human rights and for fundamental freedoms for all without distinction as to race, sex, language or religion. All these provisions clearly shows the international body in the promotion of human rights.

It is noteworthy that the UN Charter does not contain any bill of rights. The list of rights was drawn by a Commission on Human Rights which was set up by the Economic and Social Council in February 1946. This Commission was set up under Article 68 of the Charter which provides "The Economic and Social Council shall set up commission in economic and social fields and for the promotion of human rights and such other commissions as may be required for the performance of its functions." The Commission on Human Rights provides overall policy guidance, studies human rights problems, develops and codifies new international norms, and monitors the observance of human rights around the world. At present the Commission comprises of representatives of 53 member states elected for a term of three years. The Commission meets for six weeks every year at Geneva to discuss ways to promote respect for human rights. The Commission also carries out studies, makes recommendations and drafts new international treaties. It can also investigate allegations of human rights violations and can take action when presented with evidence of large-scale violations.

UNIVERSAL DECLARATION OF HUMAN RIGHTS

The Commission on Human Rights set up in 1946 worked for over two and a half years and drafted a Universal Declaration of Human Rights which serves as a common standard of achievement was approved by the General Assembly on 10th December, 1948. It may be noted that the Declaration of Human Rights was merely a statement of the principles and had no legal force behind it. These principles were given a binding force only after a Covenant on Human Rights was adopted.

The Declaration affirms at the outset that all human beings are born free and equal in dignity and rights and proclaims in 30 articles a full range of civil, political, economic, social and cultural rights for which nations and individuals should strive to promote, respect and secure universal recognition. The civil and political rights enumerated in the Universal Declaration include the right to life, liberty and security of person and to freedom from slavery or torture; the right to recognition as a person before the law and to judicial remedies and fair trial; the right to leave any country, including one's own; and the right to marry, to found family, to own property. Freedom of thought, conscience, religion, opinion, expression and assembly as well as the right to take part in the government of one's country, are also cited.

The economic, social and cultural rights to which everyone is entitled as a member of society, include the right to work and to equal pay for equal work; to education, leisure, social security and adequate standard of living, as well as the right to participate in the cultural life of the community. The Declaration also emphasises the duty towards the community in which alone the free and full development of human personality is possible. Finally, the Declaration stipulates that nothing in the Declaration shall be interpreted to give any state, group or individual a basis for destroying any of the right and freedom which it defines.

Significance of the Declaration

The Universal Declaration of Human Rights was the first document of its kind in the history of international organisation. It was a sort of statement of rights considered essential for human development all over the world. Though the Declaration was not binding on the member states, still it provided a yard-stick by which the progress of the states and the people in the field of human rights could be measured. At the time of the adoption of the Declaration of Human Rights, the General Assembly observed "It is the first occasion on which the organised community of nations has made a declaration of the human rights and fundamental freedoms, and it has the authority of the body of opinion of the United Nations as a whole, a millions of men, women and children all over the world many miles from Paris and New York will turn for help, guidance and inspiration to this a document." According to Jacob Blaustin "the declaration has acquired a political and moral authority which is unequaled by any other international instrument with the exception of the Charter itself". He asserts that it is no exaggeration to say that no international instrument has received the same acceptance on all levels of society.

"Indeed the Declaration" says Prof. Eichelberger "makes one of the most remarkable developments in the law of nations. Although not to be considered binding as a threat, it has developed such authority that it not only is a source of law but is coming to have the force of law.'

The Declaration has exercised profound influence on the constitutions of new nations and regional agreements. It has proved to be a useful instrument 'm providing a readymade statement of human rights which several states have incorporated in their constitutions. The UN has tried to promote the rights enshrined in the Declaration in two ways. In the first place it has made efforts to encourage the states to bring their laws and practices in their territories in accord with the declaration. In the second place it has tried to deal with the violations of human rights through different methods.

OTHER INTERNATIONAL INSTRUMENTS ON HUMAN RIGHTS

After the adoption of the Universal Declaration of Human Rights, the task of drafting two International Covenants on Human Rights–one on economic, social, and cultural rights and the other on civil and political rights was undertaken, to give legal basis to the rights proclaimed in the Declaration. In December 1966 the General Assembly unanimously adopted the International Covenant on Economic, Social and Cultural Rights, the International on Civil and Political Rights. Although these covenants were essentially based on Universal Declaration of Human Rights, the rights covered by these Covenants were not identical to the Declaration. One right which was emphasised by the Covenants but which was missing in the Declaration of Human Rights pertained to right of people to self, determination, including their right to freely dispose of their natural wealth and resources.

The International Covenant on Economic, Social and Cultural Rights came into force on 3 January 1976. By 31 December 1994, 131 states had acceded to this Covenant. This Covenant deals with conditions of work, trade unions, social security, protection of family, standard of living and health, education and cultural life. It provides for progressive realisation of these rights without discrimination. The task of implementing the rights enshrined in the Covenant has been entrusted to an 18-member body of independent experts This body not only assists in implementing the Covenant but also discusses them with the representatives of the governments concerned. It makes recommendations to the Council to help state parties to put the rights incorporated into the Covenant into effect.

The International Covenant on Civil and Political Rights came into force on 23 March 1976 and was ratified by 129 states by December 1994. The First optional Protocol to the Covenant also came into force on 23 March 1976, and was ratified by 80 states on 31 December 1994. The Covenant lays emphasis on rights like freedom of movement, equality before law, presumption of innocence, freedom of conscience and religion, freedom of opinion and expression' peaceful assembly, freedom of association, participation in public affairs and elections. It puts a ban on arbitrary deprivation of life, torture, cruel or degrading treatment or punishment; slavery and forced labour, arbitrary arrest or detention, and arbitrary interference with privacy; war propaganda, etc.

The signatories to the above Covenant are obliged to report periodically to a committee of human rights experts on the progress they have made in fulfilling the provisions of the Covenant. In case of the Covenant on Economic, Social and Cultural Rights, the report is submitted to a group set up for that purpose by the Economic, and Social Council; while the covenant on Civil and Political Rights, the matter is reported to the Human Rights Committee. In the case of Optional Protocol the states which are member of the protocol allow the individuals to address their complaints to the Human Rights Committee, if they feel their rights under the Civil and Political Rights Covenant have been violated by that state. It is noteworthy that only claims against states parties to the Protocol can be considered. The Human Rights Committee has rendered great service to the cause of promotion of human rights by making certain recommendations on the basis of the complaiments received from various individuals and agencies. In fact several countries have made important changes in their laws on the basic of the recommendations and decisions of the Human Rights Committee. In several cases the prisoners were released and compensation paid to the victims of human rights violations.

On 15 December, 1989 the General Assembly adopted the Second Optional Protocol of the International Covenant on Civil and Political Rights Aiming at Abolition of Death Penalty. By 31 December 1994, 26 states had accepted the provisions of the Second Protocol. The Human Rights Committee is supervising the implementation of the provisions of the Second Optional Protocol.

OTHER STEPS TO PROMOTE HUMAN RIGHTS

The United Nations and its various agencies have taken several steps to promote human rights. Some of the important steps taken in this regard are listed below.

Convention on Genocide (1948)

In December 1948 the General Assembly adopted an International Convention on Genocide under which the contracting states promised to prosecute and punish all persons guilty of genocide or of incitement or conspiracy to commit it 'whether they are constitutionally responsible rulers, public officials or private individuals.' The Convention specified the crimes of genocide and made them punishable. The crimes specified by the Convention included: (i) killing members of a group because of their group affiliation; (ii) carrying bodily or mental harm to group members; (iii) deliberately inflicting conditions on the group to bring about its physical destruction; (iv) imposing measures to prevent births within the group; (v) forcibly transferring children from one group to another; and (vi) conspiracy or incitement to commit genocide as well as complicity in the crime. By June 1985-95 states had signed the Convention on the Prevention and Punishment of the crime of Genocide.

In subsequent years also the assembly continued to repeatedly express concern over the possibility of revival of Nazism or other totalitarian ideologies based on racial intolerance. In 1984 it recommended to the states to take measures to curb the activities of organisations that practice such ideologies. It called upon the states to assist each other in detecting, arresting and bringing to trial persons suspected of having committed war crimes and crimes against humanity.

Status of Women

The Charter assures status of equality to women in matter of participation in the principal and subsidiary organs of the United Nations. However, only in very few countries the women enjoy equal legal, political, economic and social status with men. In view of this in June 1946 the Economic and Social Council set up a. Commission on the Status of women which was entrusted with the responsibility of formulating recommendations and reports for promotion of women rights in political, economic, social and educational sphere.

In the political sphere the Commission favoured universal adult franchise, equal rights to vote, right to be elected and to hold office and equal participation in government. In the civil sphere the Commission recommended equality in regard to marriage, dignity of wife, monogamy, equal rights to dissolve marriage, equal rights to guardianship of children, and the right of married women to retain their own nationality if they so desire. In the economic sphere the Commission favoured grant of equal rights with men with regard to labour, wages and holidays. In fact the .Commission favoured grant of certain special privileges for the women under certain circumstances viz. before and after child birth.

In 1952 the General Assembly adopted Convention on Political Rights of Women which states that women shall be entitled to vote in all elections on equal terms with men, without any discrimination, and that they shall be eligible 'to hold public office and to exercise all public functions established by national law, on equal terms with men.

In 1957 General Assembly adopted Convention on the Nationality of Married Women was adopted under which states parties agree that neither marriage nor divorce between a citizen and an alien, nor the change of nationality of the husband, shall automatically affect the wife's nationality. In 1962 Convention on Consent to Marriage, Minimum Age for Marriage and Registration of Marriage was adopted which sought to prohibit child marriages and safeguard the principle of free consent in marriage.

In 1956 Convention on the Recovery Abroad of Maintenance was signed which was designed to make it easier for wives and children to collect from husbands or fathers who have deserted them and moved to another country. In 1956 the Supplementary Convention on abolition of Slavery was signed which included under slavery any practice whereby a woman could be given in marriage without her consent; or could be transferred to another person on payment of money or goods; or could be inherited by another person on the death of her husband. The states parties agreed to outlaw such practices and to impose criminal penalties on individuals engaging in them.

The different specialised agencies of the UN also adopted a number of instruments to assure equal status to women. These include convention concerning Equal Remuneration for Men and Women Workers for work of Equal Value (ILO 1951), the Convention and Recommendation concerning Equal Opportunities and Equal Treatment for Men and Women Workers: Workers with Family Responsibilities (ILO 1981), and the Convention against Discrimination in Education (UNESCO 1960).

Despite the above steps equality between the sexes could not be achieved. In 1967 the General Assembly acknowledged that there continued to exist 'considerable discrimination against women. In 1979 the Convention on Elimination of all Forms of Discrimination against women was adopted which defined 'discrimination against women as any distinction made on the basis of sex which impairs women's equal enjoyment of fundamental rights.' The signatory states agreed to embody the principle of equality for women and men in national legislation and to ensure advancement of women by preventing discrimination against women, eliminating prejudices and practices based on the idea of the inferiority of women and recognising men and women's joint responsibility for raising their children.

In 1993 the General Assembly adopted Declaration on Elimination of Violence against Women. The Declaration clarified that violence includes physical, sexual and psychological violence occurring in the family or the community and perpetrated or condoned by the state. It identified the measures to prevent such violence against women and the actions to be taken by the states and international organisations for this purpose.

Protection of Children

UN has also sought to provide special protection to children and to provide them necessary opportunities and facilities for full development. In 1959 the General Assembly adopted Declaration on Rights of the Child which set forth the principles for the well-being of every child. Some of the principles emphasised in the Declaration on the Rights of child include entitlement from birth to name and nationality; benefits of social security and education; and protection from neglect, cruelty and exploitation. The Economic and Social Council has insisted that persons born outside of marriage should be entitled to the same rights which are available to persons born within marriage.

The UN has expressed concern over massive exploitation of great number of children. In 1984 the Commission on Human Rights requested the Secretary General to organise a seminar in cooperation with ILO, to find out way for elimination of exploitation of child labour within the framework of human rights advisory services programme. In 1989 the General Assembly adopted Convention on Rights of the Child. BY 1994, 168 states had acceded to this convention. This Convention set up a Committee on the Rights of the Child. This Committee meets regularly to monitor the progress made by states parties to the Convention in fulfilling their obligations. The Committee can make suggestions and recommendations to the Governments of the member states as well as to the General Assembly on the way in which the objectives of the Convention may be met.

ABOLITION OF FORCED LABOUR AND PROTECTION OF MIGRANT WORKERS

The UN has also felt concerned about forced labour and ill-treatment of migrant workers. In 1957 the ILO adopted a convention concerning the Abolition of Forced Labour. Under this convention the member states agreed not to use any form of forced labour as a means of political coercion or education or as punishment for holding of expressing political views or views ideologically opposed to the established political, social or economic system; as a method of mobilising and using labour for purposes of economic development; as a means of labour discipline; as a punishment for having participated in strikes; as a means of racial, social, national or religious discrimination.

Both the Economic and Social Council as well as the General Assembly expressed concern about the illegal transportation of workers from some African countries to some European countries 'in conditions akin to slavery and forced labour'. Therefore, in 1973 the Economic and Social Council insisted on the Governments to ratify the relevant conventions of ILO and to make bilateral agreements that would protect the rights of foreign workers. To end discriminatory treatment against migrant workers, in 1977 the General Assembly insisted on the states to extend to migrant workers 'treatment equal to that enjoyed by their own nations' specially with regard to equality of opportunity and treatment in respect of employment and occupation, social security and trade union and cultural rights, as well as individual and collective freedoms. In 1990 the General Assembly adopted Convention on Protection of the Rights of All Migrant Workers and the Members of their Families. This Convention set standards for the laws and judicial and administrative procedures of states. The governments which become part of the is convention are expected to apply the provisions of the Convention and to ensure that migrant workers whose rights are violated can seek judicial remedy.

Efforts to check Prostitution

United Nations has made consistent efforts to check prostitution. In 1949 it consolidated the various international instruments which had been promulgated before and during the days of League of Nations. It formulated the Convention of 1949 for the Suppression Traffic in Persons and of the Exploitation of the Prostitution of Others. The states parties to the convention agreed to punish any person who procured or enticed another person for purpose of prostitution as well as any person who took part in the running or financing of a brothel. In 1975 the World Conference of International Women's Year described forced prostitution as 'grievous violation of the rights of women and young girls' and urged the governments to take firm action to put an end to it. In 1983 both the Economic and Social Council as well as the General Assembly recommended to the states to take measures to prevent prostitution and assist former prostitutes in re-absorption into society through education, training and employment opportunities and through efforts to eliminate discrimination against them.

Religious Freedom

The Universal Declaration of human Rights affirms faith in freedom of thought, conscience and religion. In 1981 the General Assembly adopted a Declaration on the Elimination of All Forms of Intolerance and of Discrimination based on Religion or Belief, which was the product of nearly 20 years of study and debate in the Commission on Human Rights. The Declaration asserted that everyone shall have the right to freedom of thought, conscience and religion and that no one shall be subject to coercion that would impair the freedom. It asserts that no one shall be subjected to any discrimination on grounds of religion or other beliefs and called upon all states to take measures to prevent such discrimination.

The Declaration specified the right of parents to organise family life in accordance with their religion and the right of children to have access to religious education in accordance with their parents' wishes. The Declaration specified that the term freedom of religion included freedom of worship, freedom of assembly, freedom to establish charitable institutions; to make, acquire and use ritual articles; to write, publish and disseminate religious publications; to teach a religion or belief; to solicit financial contributions; to designate religious leaders; to observe holidays and ceremonies and to communicate with others on religious matters at the national and international levels. The Declaration called upon states to enact legislation to make those rights and freedoms available to everyone in practice.

Protection of Minorities

In 1946 the Economic and Social Council set up a Sub-Commission on the Prevention of Discrimination and Protection of Minorities, to help the Commission. The Sub-Commission was expected to make recommendations to the Commission with regard to prevention of discrimination and protection of ethnic, religious, racial and linguistic minorities. In 1992 the General Assembly adopted a Declaration on the Rights of persons belonging to National or Ethnic, Religious and Linguistic Minorities. This Declaration proclaims the right or minorities to enjoy their own culture, to profess and practice their own religion, to use their own language, to establish and maintain contacts with other members of their groups and to leave any country, including their own, and to return to their country. The Convention calls upon the member states to protect the human rights and fundamental freedoms of the persons belonging to minorities, especially in the area of teaching, education, culture and information.

Protection of Indigenous People

The General Assembly has also paid attention to the problem of indigenous people.' The term 'indigenous people is used for the descendants of those who inhabited a country or a geographical region at a time when peoples of different culture or ethnic origin arrived and subsequently became dominant through conquest, occupation, settlement or other means. In 1990 the General Assembly proclaimed 1993 as the International Year of the World's Indigenous People with a view to string then international cooperation for solving problems faced by indigenous communities in the areas of human rights, the environment, development, education and health. At the end of 1993, the General Assembly proclaimed 1994-2004 as International decade of the World Indigenous People. It decided to set up a voluntary Fund to fiancée projects and programmers during the decade.

Right to Self-determination

Though the Universal Declaration of Human Rights did not make any reference about right to self-determination, but it has been accorded an important position in the international covenants since 1952 when the General Assembly took a decision that 'right of peoples and nations to self-determination is a prereuisite to the full enjoyment of fundamental rights'. In fact the right to self-determination became the cormerstone of UN's decolonization efforts.

Protection of Civilians, Prisoners and Combatants during Armed Conflicts

United Nations has also paid attention to the protection of civilians, prisoners and combatants during armed conflicts. In 1968 at the Teheran International Conference on Human Rights this point was strongly emphasised. Subsequently, the General Assembly also asserted that parties to an armed conflict must not launch attacks against civilians as such. It insisted on drawing a distinction between combatants and civilians in order to spare the latter as far as possible.

In 1970 the General Assembly asserted that fundamental rights of civilians must be protected even during times of armed conflict and neither the civilians themselves nor the civilian dwellings or other installations, such as hospitals, should be attacked. It also insisted that the civilians should not be subject to reprisals, forced transfers or other assaults. In 1974 the General Assembly approved Declaration on the Protection of Women and Children in Emergency and Armed Conflicts and condemned attacks on children population as well as the use of chemical and bacteriological weapons. It called upon states to protect women and children from the ravages of war and insisted that the civilian women and children in emergency and armed conflict situations should not be deprived of shelter, food, medical aid or other inalienable rights.

U. N and Apartheid

The United Nation has consistently worked for putting an end to Apartheid, a state-imposed system of institutionalised racial discrimination and segregation. Both the General Assembly and the Security Council have repeatedly declared that apartheid is incompatible with the Charter of the United Nations. While the General Assembly condemned apartheid as a crime against humanity, the Security Council termed it as a crime against the conscience and dignity of mankind. In fact, the apartheid issue has consistently been on the agenda of the General Assembly since early 1950's. Both the General Assembly and the Security Council made repeated appeals to the Government of South Africa to abandon its apartheid policies. However, the South African Government opposed all moves of the General Assembly and Security Council and took the view that it violated the principle of non-interference in the internal affairs of the states. In 1973 the General Assembly adopted the International Convention on the suppression and punishment of the crime of *Apartheid,* which came into force in 1976. The Convention declared apartheid as a crime against humanity and states. It asserted that inhuman acts resulting from such a policy are crimes that violate the principles of international law and the United Nations Charter. The convention included among the inhuman acts all murders, arbitrary arrests or illegal imprisonment of members of a racial group; the imposition on them of living conditions calculated to destroy the group and creation of legal and social conditions that prevent the group's development and its participation in the political, social, economic and cultural life of its country. The Convention required the states' parties to adopt legislative, judicial and administrative and other measures taken by them to give effect to the provisions of the Convention. These reports are considered by a group of three set up by the Commission on Human Rights. The members of the group of three are taken from states which are parties to the Convention.

In view of its grave concern over racial policies of the Government of South Africa, the United Nations organs agreed on a wide range of measures for action by the international community for ending apartheid. One of the important measure taken in this regard was the imposition of an arms embargo with a view to halting the build-up of arms in South Africa, some of which were being used to further government's racial policies. Initially a voluntary arms embargo was imposed in 1963 which was subsequently made mandatory by the Security Council in 1977. It is noteworthy that for the first time in the history of United Nations an action was taken against a member state under Chapter VII of the Organisation's. Charter which provides for enforcement action with respect to threats to the peace.

The UN appealed for economic and other sanctions against South Africa which produced positive results. Several Western countries prohibited further investments, stopped bank loans and transfer of technology to South Africa. Most of the oil-exporting countries prohibited supply of oil to South Africa. In the sports and cultural spheres also boycotts were imposed against South Africa. Along with these assistance was provided to the victims of apartheid by UNDP, ILO, UNHCR in South Africa.

The things improved after the resolution of Namibian question, The developments in Namibia had healthy impact on South Africa. The UN team which visited South Africa in June 1991 observed that the country had reached the threshold of a new era. After some initial difficulties the political process towards dismantling the apartheid system was initiated and gradually apartheid structure, questionable police practices, repressive laws and politically related violence were brought under control. South African Government and the African National Congress reached an understanding whereby political prisoners were released and important Apartheid laws were reapplied. The South African Government also started negotiations with the African leaders for transfer of power from the minority white regime to the majority rule and set in motion the process of democratisation. However, the process of democratisation was greatly hampered due to bickerings among the various sections of Africans. Despite this President De Klerk ordered a referendum in March 1992 and the White South Africans voted for a 'liberal' one person one vote constitution. After the referendum President De Klerk affirmed that the poll had closed the final chapter on apartheid. After prolonged negotiations between President De Klerk and ANC President Nelson Mandela, it was decided to set up a Transitional Executive Council comprising representatives from Black and White Parties. Soon after the approval of South African Parliament to the creation of Transitional Executive Council, Nelson Mandela gave a call for repealing sanctions. It may be noted, that the United Nations, specially the Security Council and the General Assembly played an important role in impressing on the parties to reach an agreement to resolve their difference and end violence In response to the two resolutions passede by the Security Council in July and August 1992, the Secretary General despatched Special Representative to South Africa to make recommendations on measures to end the violence. It also sent two special envoys to carry out fact-finding missions. The UN General Assembly exerted pressure on the white regime of South Africa to end aparthied by taking restrictive masures against the white regime. These restrictions and sanctions were lifted only after ANC President Nelson Mandla requested the Special Committee against Apartheid in September 1993 that the sanctions be lifted in view of historic advances achieved towards democracy in the form of interim Constitution and electoral bill. In April 1994 elections were held in South Africa in the presence of United Nations Observer Mission in South Africa (UNOMSA). As a result of these elections Nelson Mandella, secured 62.6 per cent votes and was proclaimed by the Parliament as the President of South Africa. This marked an end of apartheid in the country. On 15 May 1994 the Security Council lifted the embargo and other restrictions against South Africa. On 23 June 1994 South Africa one again took its place in the General Assembly after a gap of 24 years.

Bodies for Promotion of Human Rights

Several bodies and organisations have been set up for the protection and promotion of Human Rights. It shall be desirable to know about these bodies in brief.

a) *COMMISSION ON HUMAN RIGHTS.* This Commission was set up by the Economic and Social Council in 1946. The Commission submits proposals, recommendations and investigation reports on human rights to the General Assembly through the Economic and Social Council. The Commission also serves as a forum for the states, inter-governmental and non-governmental organizations to voice their concern about human rights issues. The Commission compresses of 53 members elected for a three year term. It holds its meeting for at least six weeks in a year at Geneva.

   The Commission is assisted by a sub-Commission consisting of 26 experts who are taken from all regions of the world. This Sub-Commission was set up in 1946. It makes recommendations and conducts investigations on issues dealing with the prevention of discrimination and the protection of ethnic, religious racial and linguistic minorities.

b) *WORLD CONFERENCE ON HUMAN RIGHTS.* The first World Conference on Human Rights was held at Tehran in 1968, on the occasion of twenty years of the adoption of the Universal Declaration of Human Rights. The Conference made a Proclamation and adopted a programme of action, It declared 1968 as the International Year for Human Rights.

The next important step in this direction was taken in 1993 when World Conference on Human Rights was held at Vienna. The Conference made a bid to promote and protect human rights and fundamental freedoms everywhere. The Conference tried to identify obstacles in the way of implementation of human rights and suggested ways to overcome them. The Conference at Vienna adopted a Declaration and Programme of Action which was subsequently endorsed by the General Assembly in December 1993. Some of the prominent recommendations of the Vienna Declaration included establishment of a High Commission for Human Rights; reinforcement of the universality of human rights; acceptance of right to development as an inalienable right; integration of economic, social and cultural rights with civil and political right; recognition of democracy as a human right; recognition that the acts, methods and practices of terrorism aim at the destruction of human rights; and reinforcement of policies and programmes to eliminate racism and racial discrimination. The Declaration emphasised that organisations, agencies and organs of the United Nations System as well as regional organisations and financial and development institutions should play greater role in promoting and protecting human rights.

HIGH COMMISSION FOR HUMAN RIGHTS. In December 1993 the General Assembly created the office of the High Commissioner for Human Rights who was entrusted with the responsibility of the Human Rights activities of the United Nations. He was to work under the direction and authority of the Secretary General. The first High Commissioner was appointed in February 1994.

The main responsibilities of the High Commissioner include promotion and protection of the enjoyment by all of all civil, cultural, political and social rights; promotion and protection of the right to development by enhancing support from bodies of the United Nations system for that purpose; provision of advisory services and technical and financial assistance in the field of human rights ; information programmes on human rights; to help in the removal of obstacles in the way of realization of human rights; to engage in dialogue with governments to secure respect for human rights ; and to make recommendation to the competent bodies of the United Nations system with a view to improving the promotion and protection of all human rights. The High Commission is also responsible for enhancing international cooperation for promotion and protection of all human rights and for coordinating human rights promotion and protection activities throughout the United Nations System.

Centre for Human Rights

This Center located in Geneva comprises of the office of Assistant Secretary General for Human Rights and five branches. The Centre assists the organs of the United Nations in the promotion and protection of human rights. The Centre carries out research at the request of the UN organs and disseminates information of human rights. It also provides technical assistance to 37 countries on their request. The field offices of the Centre for Human Rights are located in Guatemala, Cambodia, Burundi, Crocia, Rwande and Malawi.

How Violation of Human Rights is Curbed

The United Nations strives to curb human rights violation by focussing public attention on these violations and considering human rights violations. It also sends fact finding groups and experts to countries where human rights violations take place. On the basis of these findings and recommendations it impresses on the concerned governments to bring about necessary changes in their laws etc.

Usually the cases of human rights violations are dealt in accordance with the provisions of various treaties and conventions signed by the member states in this regard. However, every year the UN also receives thousands of letters and complaints regarding violation of human rights which are not covered by the existing conventions and mechanism provided there under. All such complaints regarding violation of human right and sent to the members of the Commission on Human Rights and its Sub-Commission. Copies of these complaints are also sent to the member states. After the response of the concerned government is received, it is first discussed in the Subcommission, and then referred to the Commission which may investigate further in the matter. The Commission in its turn submits a report on such violation of human rights to the ECOSOC (Economic and Social Council)

FURTHER READINGS

U. N. Publication — *The United Nations and Human Rights*

U. N. Publication — *Everyone's United Nations*

David P. Forsythe — *Human Rights and World Politics*

Arthur H. Robertson — *Human Rights in the World: An Introduction to International Protection of Human Rights*

Javier Perez de Cuellar — *United Nations Action in the Field of Human Rights*

Moses Moskowitz — *International Concern with Human Rights*

Chapter 14
REVIEW OF UNITED NATIONS CHARTER

Provisions in Charter

The UN Charter, like the written constitution of any country, contains provisions for effecting changes according to the requirements of the time. Necessary provisions in this regard are contained in Articles 108 and 109 of the UN Charter.

Article 108 of the Charter provides "Amendments to the present Charter shall come into force for all members of the United Nations when they have been adopted by a vote of two-thirds of the members of the General Assembly and ratified in accordance with their respective constitutional processes by two-thirds of the members of the United Nations, including all the permanent members of the Security Council." An analysis of the above article shows that (i) the amendments to the Charter may be adopted by the General Assembly without any action on the part of the Security Council; (ii) that for any amendment of the Charter approval of the five permanent members of the Security Council is essential; (iii) that once the amendment has been ratified by the requisite number of states, including the five permanent members, it is binding on all the member states; and (iv) amendments to the Charter have to be ratified by the member states in accordance with the process outlined in their respective constitutions.

Article 109 of the Charter more specifically deals with the Review of the UN Charter. It provides

1. A General Conference of the members of the United Nations for the purpose of reviewing the present Charter may be held at a date and place to be fixed by a two-thirds vote of the members of the General Assembly and by a vote of any nine members of the Security Council. Each member of the United Nations shall have one vote in the conference.
2. Any alteration of the present Charter recommended by a two-thirds vote of the conference shall take effect when ratified in accordance with their respective constitutional processes by two-thirds of the members of the United Nations, including all the permanent members of the Security Council.

3. If such a Conference has not been held before the tenth annual session of the General Assembly following the coming into force of the present Charter the proposal to call such a Conference shall be placed on the agenda of that session of the General Assembly, and the Conference shall be held if so decided by a majority vote of members of the General Assembly and by a vote of any nine members of the Security Council.

In terms of the provisions contained in Article 109 of the UN Charter, the General Assembly established a Committee, composed of all members of the United Nations, to consider fixing an appropriate time and place for a conference. However, the Assembly did not decide to convene the conference but maintained the Committee, on the understanding that any member state might request the Secretary General to convene it.

Amendments in Charter

So for only four Articles of UN Charter have been amended, one of them twice.

(1) In 1965 Article 23 of the UN Charter dealing with membership of the Security Council was amended to increase the membership from 11 to 15. It also decided to increase the number of affirmative votes needed on procedural matters from seven to nine. On all other matters it also increased the number of affirmative notes to nine, including the concurring votes of five permanent members (Art. 27).

(2) Article 61 of the UN Charter was amended twice in 1965 and 1973. By the first amendment the membership of the Economic and Social Council was increased from 18 to 27. This was further increased to 54 by the amendment carried out in 1973.

(3) In 1968, Article 109 of the Charter was amended and the number of votes required in the Security Council to convene a General Conference to Review the Charter was increased from seven to nine.

It may be observed that the Charter could not be amended more frequently, on account of political circumstances, nor review of the UN Charter could be undertaken for the same reasons. Despite this the UN Charter has undergone complete transformation. According to Wilcox and Marcy, the changes in the UN Charter have been effected in four different ways

Non-implementation of Certain Provisions

Several provisions of the UN Charter, which were considered very vital, have not been implemented either because the members deliberately disregarded them or failed to implement them. The best example of this is Article 43 dealing with collective security. In terms of this article the members of the United Nations were expected to conclude agreements, to make available to Security Council the armed forces, assistance and facilities necessary for maintaining international peace and security. But due to East-West differences the agreement envisaged in Article 43 could not be concluded due to differences among major powers. Likewise other provisions of the UN Charter viz. Articles 44, 45, 46 and 48 and major part of Article 47, which relate to the use of armed forces by the Security Council could not discharge the policing function contemplated for it under the UN Charter.

Article 106 of the Charter dealing with transitional security arrangements which stipulates that till Security Council is able to perform the peacekeeping functions under articles 42 and 43, the five permanent members of the Security Council will consult each other with a view to taking such joint action as may be necessary for the purpose of maintaining international peace and security. This provision was rendered inoperative on account of persistent differences between the eastern and western blocs.

Again the provisions of Article 23 of the UN Charter regarding the election of ten non-permanent members of the Security Council on the basis of (i) the contributions of the UN members to the maintenance of peace and security and other purposes of the Organisation; and (ii) equitable geographical distribution, could not be implemented, because the General Assembly preferred to ignore the first criteria and merely followed the second criteria viz. equitable geographical distribution. Usually five non-permanent members of the Security are taken from Africa and Asia; one from Eastern Europe; two from Latin America and two from Western Europe and other areas. Similarly, several other provisions of the Charter have been ignored.

It is noteworthy that the UN Charter does not contain any provision which can prevent the General Assembly from disregarding the provisions of the UN Charter. Nor does there exist any provision for an appeal against the action of the General Assembly. As a result, several provisions of the UN Charter have remained inoperative.

New Interpretations

The Charter does not clearly state with which authority the power of interpretation of the Charter rests. There is only a vegue reference to it in article 96 of the Charter which lays down that the General Assembly or the Security Council may request the International Court of Justice to give an advisory opinion on any legal question. It may be observed that the opinion thus rendered by the international Court is not binding on the members. Apart from the above provision the various organs of United Nations are left completely free to interpret the various articles of the Charter according to their discretion. Accordingly the various organs of the United Nations preferred to take a view which was acceptable to the majority of the members. This flexibility in interpretation of the Charter has greatly extended the scope of the United Nations. It shall be desirable to examine some of the instances how the scope of the activities of the United Nations has been expanded through new interpretations of the UN Charter.

(i) ***Voting in Security Council.*** According to 27(3) of the Charter, the decisions of the Security Council on all matters (other than procedural) shall be made by an affirmative vote of 'nine members, including the concurring votes of the permanent members. At the very early stage of the working of the Security Council a problem was posed whether the

Security Council could take a decision if a permanent member abstained from voting. The normal interpretation could have been that since abstention does not constitute an affirmative vote, the decision cannot be taken. However, the Security Council took a liberal view and asserted that an abstention or an absence of a permanent member does not constitute a negative vote. This liberal interpretation of the UN Charter by the Security Council and the absence of Soviet Union from the Security Council, made it possible for the Security Council to take action in Korea.

Similarly, the provisions of the UN Charter dealing with definition of 'procedural' and 'substantive' questions are quite vague. The General Assembly has interpreted these provisions with great elasticity and thus greatly restricted the area within which the veto can be applied. It is noteworthy that under the Charter the 'veto' can be applied only on matters of substantive nature and not on procedural questions. But for the elastic interpretation of the provisions by the Assembly there would have been more frequent use of 'veto' in the Security Council.

(ii) ***Secretary General.*** The liberal interpretation of the provisions of the UN Charter relating to Secretary General has greatly helped in redefining the role of the Secretary General. A perusal of Articles 97-100 of the Charter gives the impression that the Secretary General is merely the Chief Administrative of the United Nations who has not been assigned any important political function. But in actual practice the Secretary General has come to exercise considerable influence in the United Nations. This became possible because both the General Assembly and the Security Council have taken a broad view of the functions of Secretary General and permitted him to play an important political role. The first Secretary General (Trygve Lie) used his power under Article 99 and called the attention of the nations to the breach of peace at the 38th Parallel in Korea. He also took lead in suggesting Ten Principles of Peace to be accomplished in twenty years. These principles also included the question of Chinese representation in the United Nations.

Under Dag Hammarskjold, the second Secretary General, the office of Secretary General assumed greater importance and he played more active political role in the settlement of several disputes. He played an important role in the resolution of Middle-East crisis of 1966 because the Security Council was greatly handicapped due to use of veto by France and England. The Secretary General sent UN Emergency Force to Egypt and established peace in the Middle East. During the Lebanon crisis of 1958 the Secretary General was authorised by the General Assembly to make "such practical arrangements as would adequately help in upholding the purposes and principles of the Charter .... and there by facilitate the early withdrawal of foreign troops." Again in Laos also the Secretary General perpetuated UN presence in defiance of Soviet veto. But probably the most important political role by Hammarskjold was played in Congo where he not only carried out carried out military operations but also conducted civilian salvage. The subsequent Secretary's General also continued to play important political role in the various disputes. In short, it can be said that the Secretary General has come to assume certain important political functions which were not anticipated by the UN Charter.

(iii) ***The General Assembly.*** The role of the General Assembly with regard to peace-keeping has also undergone a change due to new interpretation of the UN Charter. Under the UN Charter the primary responsibility for the maintenance of world peace rests with the Security Council. The Charter deliberately made the Council a small body so that it could act with speed during times of crisis. On the other hand it made the Assembly merely a deliberative body and authorised it to make recommendations. But over the years the General Assembly has been assigned important role with regard to maintenance of world peace and its powers in this regard have considerably increased. This was the result of the growing estrangement between Soviet Union and the West. In view of the persistent rivalry between the two in 1950 the General Assembly adopted the Uniting for Peace Resolution, which provided that if the Security Council, because of lack of unanimity of its five permanent members fails to act on an apparent threat to peace, breach of peace or act of aggression, the Assembly itself may take up the matter within twenty-four hours and recommend collective measures, including the use of armed forces. The adoption of the Uniting for Peace Resolution virtually tantamounted to an amendment of the Charter–so extensive as to constitute a major shift of power between the organs of the UN. The resolution effected further changes in the Organisation of the United Nations by creating two important subsidiary organs viz. Collective Measures Committee to report on the methods that might be used to strengthen international peace and security; and the Peace Observation Commission, to observe and report on any situation that might endanger international peace and security.

In the subsequent years also the powers of the General Assembly continued to grow due to East-West cleavage as well as emergence of a large number of Afro-Asian countries preferred to refer their political disputes to the General Assembly rather than the Security Council, where the big five powers enjoyed veto. But gradually the Security Council again asserted its position and assumed responsibilities assigned to it under the UN Charter. Thus it played decisive role in Congo, Cyprus and in the Gulf War.

(iv) ***Non Self-Governing Territories.*** The provisions of the UN Charter with regard to Non self-governing territories have also undergone changes due to their liberal interpretation. Thus the General Assembly has come to assume certain powers regarding the non self–governing territories even though the Charter did not envisage any powers for the Assembly under Article 73(e). Under the Charter the members of the United Nations who had assumed responsibilities for the administration of non self-governing territories to transmit regularly to the Secretary General, statistical and other information of a technical nature relating to the economic, social and educational conditions in the territories for which they are respectively responsible. The Charter, however, did not accord authority to the United Nations to deal with the information furnished or to make recommendations in this regard. But the General Assembly, despite opposition from the colonial powers, went beyond this provision and created a special committee in 1949 to examine the information transmitted and to submit its reports thereon to the General Assembly. The General Assembly has frequently debated the reports submitted for its information and thus made the Colonial powers fully accountable to the United Nations for the administration of their non self-governing territories. The General Assembly also expanded its activities by prescribing standardized forms for the submission of requisite information by the Colonial powers.

In 1960 the General Assembly adopted a Declaration on the Granting of Independence to the Colonial Countries and Peoples, which not only laid emphasis on right to self-determination but also asserted that there was imminent need to grant Independence to these people in the larger interests of international peace and security. It even set up a Committee of 24 to work for the Independence of the non self-governing territories. In 1970 the General Assembly called on all the members to render all necessary moral and material assistance to the peoples of colonial territories to expedite their independence. The General Assembly even recommended sanctions against South Rhodesia, South Africa and Portugal to pressurise the regimes in these countries to grant independence to the people of non self-governing . territories by liberally interpreting the provisions of the Charter. It may be observed that the UN Charter never expected the General Assembly to play such a vital role with regard to non self-governing territories. This change in the role of the Assembly became possible because it came to be dominated by the Afro-Asian countries who were keen to see that all people under colonial powers got independence.

Conclusion of Supplementary Agreements

The conclusion of several treaties and agreements by the members to clarify certain provisions of the Charter, have also greatly contributed to the modification of the UN Charter. These treaties not only spell out the general provisions of the Charter in detail, but also outline certain obligations of the members which go much beyond those specified in the Charter. It may be noted that the UN Charter had deliberately kept certain things vague in the hope that the details could be worked out satisfactorily at a later date. Some of the agreements–concluded by the members which have greatly modified the UN Charter are as under.

(i) ***Privileges and Immunities of Members.*** The UN Charter did not specify the privileges and immunities of the members of the International Organisation and merely provided in Article 105(3) that the General Assembly may make recommendations with a view to determining the details of the application of the privileges and immunities and may propose conventions to the members of the United Nations for this purpose. In pursuance of this Article "A Convention on the Privileges and Immunities of the United Nations" was concluded in February 1946, which set forth in considerable detail the juridical personality of the United Nations, the immunity of the UN property funds, and assets, the right of the United Nations to use communication facilities, the privileges and immunities of the officials accredited to the United Nations, etc. Majority of the states have since ratified this Convention.

(ii) ***Agreement regarding Headquarters.*** Another agreement which gave substance to the general provisions of the UN Charter was the agreement signed by the United States and the United Nations in June 1947 regarding U.N. Headquarters. The agreement defined the headquarters district in New York and specified the rights and duties of the United Nations and the member states with respect to postal and radio facilities, the use of airport, the inviolability of the headquarters, police protection and other related matters.

(iii) ***Compulsory Jurisdiction of International Court of Justice.*** The decision of a number of member states to voluntarily accept the compulsory jurisdiction of the International Court of Justice has also considerably enlarged the UN Charter. The Charter merely stipulated that the member states must settle their disputes by peaceful means. It however, did not specify the actual methods to be adopted by the members for peaceful settlement. But under Article 36 of the Statute of the Court, the States were given the option to recognise the compulsory jurisdiction of the Court in all legal disputes concerning (i) interpretation of a treaty; (ii) any question of international law; (iii) the existence of any, act which if established would constitute a breach of an established obligation; (iv) the nature or extent of the reparation to be made for the breach of an international obligation. The acceptance of the optional clause of the statute by large number of member states has enhanced the competence of the United Nations.

(iv) ***Regional Pacts.*** The conclusion of various regional pacts like Brussels Treaty, the Inter-American Treaty of reciprocal Assistance, North Atlantic Treaty, Warsaw Pact, Anzus Pact, Manila Pact, South East Asian Treaty Organisation have also produced changes in the UN system. Under the UN Charter the responsibility for collective security was exclusively vested in the Security Council. However, on account of cleavage between the Soviet Union and the Western powers, the Security Council was rendered ineffective in this regard. As a result the member states were compelled to find out alternatives for security. This resulted in the conclusion of various regional defence pacts. It is noteworthy that most of these regional pacts were created under Article 51 of the UN Charter and naturally contributed to the expansion of the scope of UN Charter.

Creation of Subsidiary Organs

A number of subsidiary and special organs were also created to Supplement the United Nations which naturally contributed to the development of the International Organisation. These special organs were created under Article 22-29, which authorise the General Assembly and the Security Council to establish such organs for the performance of their respective functions. Some of the prominent commissions and committees set up by the General Assembly and the Security Council include International Law Commission, the Disarmament Commission, the Interim Committee of the General Assembly, etc. While some of these Commissions are of permanent nature, the others have an ad hoc character. Some of the ad hoc commissions set up include the Commission for India and Pakistan, the Special Committee on Balkans, the Palestine Conciliation Commission, the Commission for Unification and Rehabilitation of Korea, the Committee on Question of Defining Aggression, etc. Some of the other important subsidiary organs established since the inauguration of the UN Charter include the International Atomic Energy Agency, World Meteorological Organisation, United Nations High Commissioner for Refugees, United Nations Relief and Work Agency, United Nations International Children's Emergency Fund, etc. The chief benefit of having these subsidiary organs is that the services of experts in the various fields can be utilised. The net impact of these subsidiary organisations has been that United Nations system stands greatly modified and its functions have considerably expanded.

It is evident from the preceding account that the UN Charter at present fundamentally differs from the UN Charter adopted in 1945. These changes were effected either by permitting certain provisions to lapse through non-implementation ; or through new interpretation of the Charter; or through conclusion of supplementary agreements and creation of special organs. Despite these changes it cannot be denied that the text of the UN Charter has not undergone any substantial change.

Review of UN Charter

As noted earlier, Article 109 had envisaged revision of the UN Charter and provided that a General Conference of the members of the UN may be called for the purpose of review of present Charter at a date and place to be fixed by two-thirds vote of the members of the General Assembly. It further stipulated that if such a Conference was not held before the Tenth Annual Session of the General Assembly following the coming in force of the present Charter, the proposal to call such a conference shall be placed on the agenda of that session of the General Assembly. No wonder the question of Review of Charter evoked great interest among scholars, private organisations, foreign offices as well as the various organs of the UN for about two years before 1955 when the Review of the Charter was due.

In 1953 the United States established a special Sub-Committee on UN Charter, which collected basic documents relating to the review of the Charter and initiated a number of staff studies. The Sub-Committee favoured changes in Charter with regard to universality of membership, security, membership and voting in the Security Council, voting in the General Assembly, armaments and international law. It also favored removal of veto on questions involving pacific settlement of disputes.

But in other quarters it was felt that in view of prevailing East-West tension any diplomatic conference for revision of Charter would not help the United Nations. The General Assembly also did not take up the question of Revision Conference. Instead it appointed a Committee on Arrangements in 1955 which was expected to keep in abeyance the Conference Committee and report its recommendations to the General Assembly not later than its sixteenth session. The recommendations of the Committee were accepted by the General Assembly. However, the Assembly did not convene any conference and maintained the Committee on the understanding that any Member state might request the Secretary General to convene it.

During its 1974 session, the General Assembly established an Ad Hoc Committee to review the Charter and to consider ways, without amending the Charter, to make the Organization more effective. The following year, the Assembly decided to reconvene the Ad Hoc Committee as a 47 member Special Committee on the Charter of the U. S. United Nations and on the Strengthening of the Role of the Organization.

The Special Committee continued to meet annually after 1976 to consider the peaceful settlement of international disputes, the rationalization of existing United Nations procedures and the maintenance of international peace and security. In 1982 it succeeded in negotiating the text of the Manila Declaration on the Peaceful Settlement of International Disputes. At its 1984 session, the Special Committee reached an agreement on a number of recommendations for rationalizing the organisation's existing procedures. It recommended, for example, that the agenda of the General Assembly be simplified by grouping or merging related items and that aspects of the same question not be considered by more than one of its seven Main Committees. Approving the conclusions at its session later that year, the Assembly decided that they should be reproduced as an annex to its rules of procedure.

In 1984 the General Assembly asked the Special Committee to spend more time on the question of maintaining international peace and security in order to strengthen the role of the United Nations, particularly the Security Council. The Committee was requested to consider the prevention and removal of threats to peace, as well as situations that might lead to international friction or disputes.

PROVISIONS WHICH NEED REVISION OR IMPROVEMENT

The following provisions of the UN Charter need revision or improvement.

(i) ***Veto Provision.*** The frequent use of veto power, which was vested by the UN Charter in the permanent members of Security Council has evoked strong criticism. It has been argued that its frequent use by permanent members has given rise to doubts in the minds of smaller nations about the effectiveness of the Security Council. No wonder repeatedly a demand has been made for the elimination of veto. However, the problem cannot be solved through revision of Charter because even the proposals for amending the 'veto' provisions are subject to the vote of the permanent members and it is doubtful if the Big Powers would be willing to accept any restriction on their right of veto. The problem can be best resolved if the permanent members of the Security Council accept certain voluntary restrictions on their right to veto. Further, the veto should be used only on vital issues, and all procedural matters should be immune from it. Further, it is also desirable that veto should be eliminated with respect to admission of new members and peaceful settlement of disputes.

(ii) ***Changes in Structure of Security Council.*** Under the UN Charter the responsibility for maintenance of international peace and security was exclusively vested in the Security Council. However, due to bickerings among the major powers this responsibility was shifted to the General Assembly under the Uniting for Peace Resolution. No doubt, of late, the Security Council has once again assumed responsibility of maintenance of international peace and security, and the votes are being used less frequently, still it is desirable that the composition of the Security Council must be changed. Some of the potential powers of present times like Germany, Japan, Brazil and India must be included as permanent members of the Security Council. Further , it would be desirable to change the voting rules of the Security Council and all the decisions should be taken by a concurrent vote of the majority of the permanent members and a majority of non-permanent members.

(iii) ***Changes in General Assembly.*** Since the adoption of the UN Charter the role of General Assembly has undergone great changes. It has not only assumed responsibility for the maintenance of peace keeping but also issued instructions to the Secretary General to establish a United Nations Emergency Force for Gaza strip. It adopted the Universal Declaration of Human Rights and a Declaration for the Independence of Colonies and Colonial People. It extended the law of the Charter to the outer space and laid down that the nations will not carry any nuclear weapons on outer space vehicles. Despite these changes, certain other changes are also desirable. The General Assembly, particularly its major committees, should remain in continuous sessions. To expedite the work of the General Assembly and to effect financial savings, a number of working groups should be established at the beginning of each Assembly to prepare the resolutions. Each member state should be associated with at least one such group. The General Assembly should also set up more permanent committees to deal with specific matters during the period of its recess. Greater powers should be entrusted to the President of the General Assembly and the Chairmen of the Committees to limit discussions.

(iv) ***Changes in International Court of Justice.*** The UN Charter vested two types of functions to the International Court of Justice viz. to hear such cases which may be referred to it by the members and to render advice to the organs and specialized agencies of the UN on matters involving legal questions. It is noteworthy that the Court does not enjoy any jurisdiction with regard to cases involving the individuals. It also does not enjoy any authority to punish a state which violates the law. In other words the court has no legal authority and it enjoys only moral authority. Furthermore, the member states have not fully utilised the services of the Court to resolve their differences. The member states have preferred to take most of their disputes before the political organs rather than the court. To make the International Court of Justice more effective, it is desirable that the members should agree to submit their legal disputes to the Court. Reference of cases involving legal points to the Court would save considerable time of the political organs of the United Nations and would also ensure more satisfactory settlement of the disputes.

In view of the reluctance of the member states to accept the optional clause, the United Nations should try to broaden the scope of the jurisdiction of court on its own. Thus its organs like Security Council and the General Assembly may refuse to consider legal disputes and recommend to the parties that such disputes be taken to their Court. Such an attitude on the part of the Council or Assembly may not compel the states to take their disputes to the Courts, but it would certainly encourage them to reach some settlement outside. Again, under the provisions of UN Charter, the various organs of United Nations and its specialised agencies can seek advisory opinion from the Court on interpretation of Charter, but in actual practice only the General Assembly has made use of advisory opinion of the Court and the other organs have generally preferred to give their own interpretations. It would be desirable that the various organs of the United Nations and its specialised agencies should voluntarily accept the decisions of the court regarding interpretation of the Charter. It would also be desirable to grant authority to the Court to give binding decisions on all such political disputes which cannot be resolved by the political organs of the United Nations. Even the International Organisations, which at present cannot take their disputes to the Court, should be permitted to take their cases to the Court on terms equal to those enjoyed by the state. Even the individuals may be permitted to take certain types of cases against the states, with the consent of the latter, to the International Court of Justice.

(v) ***Independent Finances.*** For its effective working the UN must have independent finances. It is doubtful that under the 1986 agreement which insists on consensus on all budgetary matters, the financial problems of the UN can be permanently solved. In fact 'consensus' implies that each state shall have veto with regard to budget, and everything will depend on the way compromises are worked. If the developing countries try to push through proposals involving unreasonable budgetary expansions, or the developed countries try to prevent even moderate increases in the UN budget, the problem shall remain unsolved. Therefore, it is imperative that the UN should try to improve collections and raise revenues independently.

Effective measures should be adopted to collect payments from members whose capacity to pay is unquestionable. Money can also be realised from new sources like (a) exploitation of the resources of the bed of the sea beyond the limits of national jurisdiction; (b) equitable share of revenue obtained from the exploitation of the living and mineral sources of the high seas, the methods of whose exploitation have been developed with the assistance of the United Nations; (c) equitable share from the revenues from space communications; and (d) imposing nominal tax on international mail and telecommunications etc.

(vi) ***Greater Coordination of Social and Economic Activities.*** To make the United Nations more effective, it is desirable that large number of social and economic activities which at present are being carried on by different organs ofunited Nations and its specialised agencies should be coordinated by the United Nations. No doubt at present exist some coordinating bodies like ACC and ECOSOC, but they exercise only marginal influence in the operation of the UN system. The best way out would be to set up a High Powered Committee or Council which should not only be made responsible for budgetary control but should also perform overall coordination function within the UN system.

(vii) ***Enforcement Role.*** The United Nations should be assigned an effective enforcement role and be authorised to impose sanctions and take military enforcement measures, against states which act against international law. For this purpose the Military Staff Committee of the Security Council could be assigned an important role. The role of the UN peace-keeping forces should not be merely concerned with the monitoring of cease fires and other means of containing conflicts but also ensure that countries are not destabilised across frontiers. The peace keeping forces should normally be authorised and controlled by the Security Council and must play a neutral political role where they are operating. The possibility of a permanent peace-keeping fund should be explored. For the effectiveness of the peace-keeping forces, the various nations may be asked to earmark certain military units in the armed forces, for peace-keeping tasks.

In conclusion it can be said that if the United Nations is to successfully meet the challenges of tomorrow, it must undergo certain structural changes and the members of the United Nations must abide by the obligations which they accepted while joining this Organisation. Further, the United Nations must make effective use of the various regional organisations which have been evolved to secure political security and economic advancement of the member states. The UN Charter must give formal recognition to these regional organisations.

It cannot be denied that the above changes in the UN Charter are essential to make the United Nations more effective. However, it would not be easy to carry out these changes because the Permanent members of the Security council would be keen to preserve the status quo which buttresses their own dominant and special position in the world affairs. On the other hand the less developed and developing countries are in favour of arriving at some consensus regarding changes in the UN Charter. They are in favour of convening a general conference of the members of the UN for this purpose. In short there is lack of compatibility between the motivations of the affluent and powerful nations, and the developing countries. While the powerful nations want to make use of UN Security Council as an instrument for furthering their national and strategic interests, the developing countries want to strengthen the UN by making it more democratic, They also want the United Nations to be more strong to protect the sovereignty and territorial integrity of the member states. In view of the opposite interests and stands of the affluent and developing countries, it is indeed difficult to expect that desired changes would take place in the UN system.

FURTHER REAEDINGS

U.N. Publication — *Everyone's United Nations*

Benjamin V. Cohen — *The United Nations : Constitutional*

Even Luard — *Developments, Growth and Possibilities*

H.G. Nicholas — *United Nations, How it Works and What it does*

Clark M. Eichelberger — *The United Nations as a Political Institution*

Francis O Wilcox and — *U. N. the First Twenty Five Years*

Carl M. Marcy — *Proposals for Changes in the United Nations*

Inis L.Clause — *Swords into Ploughsares*

Chapter 15
ECONOMIC AND SOCIAL ACHIEVEMENTS OF UNITED NATIONS

The United Nations was established not merely to ensure international peace and security but also to promote conditions under which genuine peace could be possible. Article 1 of the UN Charter clearly states that the purpose of the United Nations also includes achievement of 'international co-operation in solving international problems of an economic, social, cultural or humanitarian character', as well as encouraging respect for human rights and for fundamental freedoms for all without distinction as to race, sex, language or religion. For the attainment of these objectives the UN is assisted by Economic and Social Council, the Councils' Commissions and specialised agencies, the Trusteeship Council and the Secretariat. We shall deal with the economic and social achievements of the United Nations in detail.

Economic Achievements

Article 55 of the UN charter enjoins upon the UN to 'promote higher standards of living, full employment and conditions of economic and social progress and development'. The United Nations realised that these goals could not be achieved without organised inter-national co-operation in the economic and financial fields. Therefore, it sought to reduce trade barriers through multilateral negotiations under the auspices of the General Agreement on Tariffs and Trade (GATT). It is a different matter that the United Nations could not achieve much success in this regard due to attitude of the developed countries. Despite this it organised International Conference and made a bid to secure interests and needs of the developing countries.

Development Decades

The United Nations tried to speed up the development of the developing countries by launching Development Decades in succession. The first Development Decade was launched by the General Assembly in 1960 in order to mobilise and sustain support for the measures required on the part of both developed and developing countries to accelerate progress towards self-sustaining growth of the economy of individual nations and their social advancement. The Assembly set the target of raising the annual rate of growth of 5 per cent in the developing countries. It urged the member states to pursue policies and adopt measures aimed at achieving this goal. However, the first Development Decade failed to achieve the desired targets due to lack of proper planning and weak implementation of UN recommendations.

The second and the third Development Decades covered the period of 1970's and 1980's. These decades were characterised by improved planning. But despite this major development goals could not be achieved. One of the main reasons for this was failure of several developing countries to carry out economic, political and social reforms . Further the developed countries failed to transfer 1 per cent of total GNP as envisaged. In fact the actual assistance during these decades fell from 0.51 per cent of GNP in 1960's to 0.40 per cent during the second and third Development Decades. During the third Development Decade the United Nations adopted a New International Development Strategy (NIDS) and established a Substantial New Programme of Action (SNPA) for the Least Developed countries. NIDS required each developed country to transfer 0.7 per cent of GNP each year to the Third World Development assistance. However, the global recession of early 1980's led to drying up of sources of capital. The growing inflation further reduced the buying power of aid funds. The SNPA urged the donor countries to contribute an additional 0.15 per cent of GNP each year for the benefit of least developed countries during the 1980's. It also recommended to the industrialised countries to convert their public loans given to the poorest countries to outright grants.

The General ' Assembly announced 1990's as the Fourth Development Decade. It called for wide ranging national and international measures to achieve rapid development of especially the least developed countries. The General Assembly, while admitting that the Third Development Decade had failed to achieve most of its objectives urged the developed nations to at least reach, if not surpass, the targets fixed for the official assistance (ODA), divert some of the funds released following disarmament to the needy countries and to recycle part of the huge surpluses built by some industrialised nations to the developing countries. It urged the developing countries to liberalise trade regimes, create trade opportunities, foster regional and sub-regional market arrangements among themselves and promote faster industrialisation, particularly by implementing the global system of trade preferences. Attention was also paid to the deteriorating debt situation in developing countries. It was stressed that the responsibility for finding solution of the debt problem was the responsibility of both debtor and creditor countries, of commercial banks and of international financial institutions. It asked the creditor countries to review their tax policies, regulations and accounting practices to make it easier for debtor nations to reduce commercial debts and debt servicing obligations. The financial institutions were asked to support schemes for this purpose by applying their guideline with flexibility.

New International Economic Order

In the early 1970's the ambitious development plans embraced by the Development Decades were jeopardized by a series of crisis that threatened the stability of world economic relations. The International Monetary System which was established in 1944 broke down. The prices of oil increased fourfold in the wake of hostilities in the Middle East. This increase in prices led to enhancement of prices of other commodities and manufactured goods. The growing debt burden, drought and famine in Africa and Indian subcontinent further aggravated the situation. In the midst of these developments the General Assembly gave call for a new economic order. In the spring of 1974 it adopted the Declaration and Programme of Action on the Establishment of New International Economic Order. In December 1974 it adopted a Charter of Economic Rights and Duties of States. The Declaration urged the member states to work together to devise an international economic order that would correct inequalities, redress injustices and ultimately eliminate the gap between developed and developing countries, irrespective of their economic and social systems. The Programme of Action included sections on raw materials and primary commodities, the international monetary system and the financing of the development; industrialisation; transfer of technology; regulation of transnational corporations; co-operation among developing countries; exercises by States of permanent sovereignty over their natural resources and a stronger role for the United Nations system in international economic cooperation.

The Charter of Economic Rights and Duties of the States affirmed the right of states to sovereignty over their natural resources and to regulate foreign investment and nationalise foreign property. The International Monetary Fund and the World Bank were asked to revise the formula that allowed the largest number of votes to countries making the largest financial contributions. It suggested that these institutions should link the distribution of Special Drawing Rights to development needs and that the transnational corporations be regulated to conform to the national development plans and objectives of the developing nations. It also suggested that measures be taken to ease the third world debts.

North-South Dialogue

The General Assembly played an important role in promoting negotiations between the developed countries (known as north because they are concentrated in the northern hemisphere), and the developing countries (as South because these countries are mostly located in the southern hemisphere). Between 1975 and 1977, 19 developing and eight developed countries held several round of talks at Paris, but could not arrive at any agreement. In December 1977 the Assembly affirmed that "all negotiations of a global nature relating to the establishment of the new international economic order should take place within the framework of the United Nations system." Two years later the General Assembly endorsed the holding of global negotiations in five areas viz. raw materials, energy, trade, development and money, and finance and called for the launching in 1980 of a round of global and sustained negotiations on international economic co-operation for development.

Development Assistance

The UN has also played an important role in stimulating and aiding technical co-operation for development. It has helped member states to establish a more effective framework for growth by helping in the preparation of comprehensive plans to ensure balanced economic and social development and making best use of available financial, natural and human resources; in modernising the expanding transport and communication facilities; and in improving national, administrative, budgetary and statistical services. In this regard the United Nations Development Programme (UNDP), which is world's largest multilateral technical grant assistance programme, plays a vital role. The UNDP was established in 1965 by merging the Expanded Programme of Technical Assistance and the Special Fund. It undertakes certain activities in partnership with the governments of the developing countries and seeks to develop in those countries a reliable inventory of natural and economic resources; a skilled workforce and effective managerial capacity; diversified technical capabilities; techniques for development planning and channels and methods for attracting development capital. The UNDP has supported thousands of projects in various countries which cover virtually the entire economic and social spectrum from agriculture, industry, power production, transport, communication and trade to health, housing, education, training, community services and public administration. Almost all the projects with UNDP funding are carried out in the field by the Department of Technical Cooperation for Development or by one or more United Nations agencies. However, some of the projects are also implemented by the governments of the concerned countries. The UNDP projects supply developing countries with high-level experts and middle level personnel. They provide equipments ranging from computers to hand tools as well as various technical services. Most of the funds for these activities of UNDP are provided by the member states through contributions. However the developing countries have to contribute 60 per cent of the cost of the project through provision of local experts, facilities, supplies and equipment.

Special Unit for Technical Co-operation among Developing Countries (TCDC)

The UNDP set up Special Unit for technical cooperation among developing countries with a view to promoting bilateral and multilateral development projects among countries in both developing and developed regions. It launched projects in countries of Africa, Asia and Pacific region; European, Latin America and Caribbean region. These projects were quite wide-ranging and covered forestry, marine science, telecommunications; research into the production and development of wheat and barley in semi-arid regions; reorganization of production, processing and marketing; organised seminars on role of public sector, human resources development, workers participation in decision making, role of women in development, etc.

United Nations Volunteers

In 1970 the General Assembly established United Nations volunteers to assist in the development projects. These volunteers work under the supervision of the UNDP Administrator and provide a broad spectrum of technical expertise from accounting, economics and business management to agriculture, forestry and irrigation. The volunteers programme has led to increased international co-operation among youth and the mobilisation of self-help efforts at the local and national levels.

Financing Technical Co-operation

For the economic and social development in the less developed countries the United Nations provides international development loans through International Bank for Reconstruction and Development (IBRD), the International Finance Corporation (IFC), the International Development Association (IDA) etc. The International Fund for Agricultural Development also provides assistance, on concessional terms, to the poorest developing countries in order to raise food production. In addition to the above, a number of other global funds have also been created which have a particular economic or social focus. Some of these funds include the Revolving Fund for Natural Resources Exploration, the Industrial Development Fund, the Special Fund for Land-locked Developing Countries, the Capital Development Fund, and Financing System for Science and Technology for Development.

Application of Science and Technology

The United Nations has tried to encourage international co-operation to promote scientific research and technological activities of the developing countries. It has tried to foster technologies which are suitable for the developing countries and fostered research on problems whose solution could have a catalytic effect in accelerating development. In 1963 the Economic and Social Council decided to set up an Advisory Committee on the Application of Science and Technology to Development, which actually came into being in 1965. In 1970 the Advisory Committee presented the world Plan of Action for the Application of Science and Technology to Development. The Plan outlined priorities for research and for the application of existing knowledge and called for the enhancement of indigenous science and technology capability in developing countries. It recommended that a special fund be set up to finance the programmes proposed by it. In 1971 the Economic and Social Council established the Intergovernmental Committee on Science and Technology for Development to recommend goals and targets for achieving the policy measures relating to science and technology in the Strategy and to examine in detail the World Plan.

In 1975 the General Assembly asked the UNIDO (United Nations Industrial Development Organization) to establish an industrial technological information bank as a component of an overall technological information exchange network. This network was to allow developing countries access to research findings of interest, as well as to project experience of other developing countries, with a view to helping to select technologies essential for their industrial growth. In 1976 the Assembly asked UNCTAD (United Nations Conference on Trade and Development) and UNIDO to intensify their efforts to assist in the establishment in developing countries of centres for the transfer of development of technology at the national, sub regional and regional levels. These centres were expected to serve as fundamental elements for an international network for the exchange of technological information. In 1979 the Conference on Science and Technology for Development held at Vienna and adopted Programme of Action which laid emphasis on the strengthening of the scientific and technological capacities of developing countries; restructuring of international scientific and technological relations; and enhancing of the role of the United Nations system in this field. The Conference in its Programme recommended the establishment of national scientific and technological information systems and a global information network; and the use of scientific and technological information for national development. It placed special emphasis on the needs of the least developed countries.

The international financial support of science and technology activities comes from a variety of sources, including bilateral and multilateral governmental arrangements, financing institutions and voluntary assistance. But generally the developed countries have preferred to extend assistance through bilateral agreements which has naturally resulted in the slow down of scientific and technological cooperation. The other factors which have contributed to the slow down of assistance is difference in perceptions of development priorities. and the deteriorating economic climate in general. If this trend persists the needs of the developing countries in the field of science and technology are not likely to be met.

Trade and Development

United Nations has tried to promote development through promotion of international trade. For this purpose it helped in the formation of the UNCTAD (United Nations Conference on Trade and Development), which became a permanent organ of the General Assembly in December 1964. UNCTAD has been holding sessions thereafter at regular intervals. The UNCTAD aims at promoting international trade, and particularly that of the developing countries with a view to accelerating their economic developement. It is also concerned with research, conceptual innovation and policy analysis; the implementation of decisions of inter-governmental bodies; technical co-operation and information exchange and consultations. It seeks to strengthen international systems, structures and arrangements in the fields of trade and finance and to make them more supportive of the national development efforts of the developing countries. During its operation of about three decades the UNCTAD has (i) emphasised the need for developing countries to expand their earnings through export of goods and services, which are their main source of external finance for development, and for the developed countries to open their markets to the third world trade; (ii) insisted on stabilization and strengthening of international commodity markets on which most developing countries remain dependent for export earnings, the enhancement of such earnings through greater participation in the processing, marketing and distribution of commodities and the reduction of that dependence through economic diversification; (iii) called for the enhancement of third world export capacity by mobilizing domestic and external resources, strengthening technological capabilities; developing merchant shipping and promoting appropriate national trade and transport policies; (iv) emphasised the need of reducing third world debt burden; (v) called for special support of world's poorest and most vulnerable countries; (vi) favoured support for expanded trade and economic cooperation among developing countries, as a complement to their traditional economic links with developed economies It is noteworthy that UNCTAD has sought to achieve this through inter-governmental consensus.

Natural Resources and Energy

The United Nations through Department of technical Cooperation for Development (DTCD) has tried to promote technical co-operation for developing countries in the fields of energy, water and mineral resources. In the field of energy DTCD implements projects in developing countries for the exploration, development and utilization of petroleum and gas, coal, electric power, new and renewable sources of energy. It also renders help to projects in the areas of energy planning, policy and conservation. It also helps the governments to strengthen their energy-related organisations through training, technical co-operation projects, direct advisory services, the publication of technical documents and international seminars.

In the field of water resources DTCD implements the projects which cover planning and management of water resources development, rural water supply, the establishment and strengthening of national water resources institutions, ground-water exploration and exploitation, and river basin development. It provides technical advisory services for programmes and project formulation and convenes training seminars on water resources related issues. It also brings out technical publications to promote state-of-the art technology transfer on specialised subjects like ground water, non-conventional water resources, computer technology for water resources development, and international river basin legislation and development.

With regard to the mineral resources development the DTCD provides technical assistance on matters relating to exploration and evaluation, mining, processing and marketing of minerals. It also provides support for training, the strengthening of government institutions and introduction of new technologies. With regard to infrastructure DTCD provides technical assistance to developing countries for public works, including road maintenance and management; cartography and remote sensing for natural resources exploration.

Protection of Environments

United Nations has also paid attention to the protection of environment. It held a Conference on the Human Environment at Stockholm in June 1972 which proclaimed the right of human beings to a healthy environment and their responsibility to protect and improve that environment for future generation. Later during the same year the General Assembly created the United Nations Environment Programme (UNEP) to monitor the environment and to encourage and co-ordinate sound environmental practices. The UNEP coordinates the environmental activities of all the UN agencies and works with governments, the scientific and business communities and non-governmental organizations. With the growing concern for environments, the UNEPs activities have greatly expanded. Now its activities include the programme of Global Environment Monitoring System (GEMS), the International Register of Potentially Toxic Chemicals (IRPTC), and world–wide data network, Inforterra. GEMS provides information in its key areas of eliminate and atmosphere, the oceans, renewable terrestrial resources, trans–boundary pollution and the health consequences of pollution. IRPTC provides vital information for decisions regarding chemical safety. It has not only developed its own data bank but also helped several developing nations to establish their own chemical information system.

UNEP through its regional seas programmes has helped in bringing countries together to protect common seas. It has been instrumental in the conclusion of several international agreements on protection of environments of regional seas. In 1987 UNEP helped in the negotiation of Montreal Protocol which seeks to reduce chemical damage to the atmospheric ozone layer, which shields life on Earth from harmful ultraviolet radiation. In 1989 UNEP negotiated the Basle Convention which provides for controls on the international movement and disposal of hazardous wastes. The UNEP, in cooperation with other LTN agencies and non-governmental organizations, is working on implementation of an Action Plan for the conservation and restoration of tropical forests whose protection is essential in limiting climate change and maintaining spices diversity. The other important activities of UNEP include desertification control, water conservation, environmental education, sustaining the productivity of the natural resources of developing countries, etc.

World Food Problem

The United Nations has also paid attention to the solution of the problem of food shortage. In 1974 the General Assembly convened a World Food Conference at Rome which focussed international attention on the scale and complexity of world food problems, and called for concerted global efforts to deal with them. On the recommendation of the Conference, the General Assembly established a World Food Council in December 1974, which is the highest UN body dealing with food and related matters. The Council has its headquarter at Rome and works through an Executive Director and a small Secretariat appointed by the United Nations Secretary General. The Council periodically reviews major problems and policy issues affecting the world food situation and recommends remedial action. It works in close cooperation with FAO, the World Food Programme (WFP), the International Fund for Agricultural Development (IFAD) and other organisations of UN system. The Council not only suggests measures to improve national and global food policies directed to the elimination of hunger and malnutrition, but also takes steps to raise the political priority of food and hunger issues and to coordinate assistance and promote co-operative actions to deal with food problems.

In recent years the Council at its Ministerial sessions undertook a comprehensive review of the world food and hunger situation and concluded that although the world now feeds one billion more people than at the time of the World Food Conference, the number of hungry and malnourished people has continued to rise to an estimated 550 million, and nutritional diseases continue to cause widespread suffering and death. The Council further noted that hunger is basically an economic problem and has become more widespread because of the combined effects of reduced economic activity in many nations, falling national incomes, reduced purchasing power, unemployment and rising food prices.

Population Question

The United Nations has also felt concerned over population question from the very beginning. In 1947 it set up a Population Commission, as one of the functional Commissions of the Economic and Social Council. This Commission arranges for studies and advises the Council on the size and structure of populations, and policies which influence them; the interplay of demography on economic and social factors; and the other demographic questions on which the United Nations and related agencies might seek advice. In addition the Commission monitors population trends and policies and reviews and appraises progress towards achieving the goals of the World Population Plan of Action, adopted in 1974. This action Plan had stressed the fundamental relationship between population factors and overall economic and social development. In the World Population Conference held at Mexico, the Conference appraised progress during the decade and approved an undated global population strategy in the form of 88 recommendations identifying areas where further action was needed. It also emphasised the need for an intersectoral approach to population and development for policies which respected individual and family rights, and for improvements in the status of women which could increase their participation in all aspects of development. In 1989 the Economic and Social Council noted the critical role of population factors in development strategies and approved convening of an international meeting on population in 1994 to *assess* the progress made in attaining the goals of the 1974 and 1984 conferences.

United Nations has felt concerned over the rapidly growing population of the world and decided to provide technical assistance in the population field. In 1967 the General Assembly established a Trust Fund for Population Activities, which was renamed as United Nations Fund for Population Activities (UNFPA) in 1969, to provide additional resources to the United Nations System for technical co-operation activities in the population field. In 1987 the name of the Fund even though the acronym UNFPA was also retained. At present UNFPA is considered as the largest internationally funded source of assistance to population programmes in developing countries. A major portion of this fund has been allocated to the family planning projects. The UNFPA assists the governments to develop population goals and programmes and provides them financial assistance to implement the same.

SOCIALACHIEVMENTS

The United Nations has also felt greatly concerned about the social questions which came to the forefront on account of economic and technological changes, growing urbanisation and growing contacts among the countries. In several developing countries economic stagnation has swelled the ranks of the poor and forced the government to effect cuts in public services. This has made UN take greater interest in the social development and it launched several programmes through its office at Vienna which seeks to help the developing countries strengthen their national and local capacity for social analysis, policy planning and design, and project implementation.

The responsibility for the social development rests with the Department of Social affairs of the UN Secretariat, ECOSOC and a number of other specialised agencies. All these bodies make bid to improve the living conditions, housing, town and country planning, community development, family, youth and child welfare, rehabilitation of the handicapped population, migration as well as the refugee questions. Some of the important achievements of the United Nations in the social field are discussed here under.

1. Improvement in Condition of Women

UN has attached great importance to the improvement of condition of women. The General Assembly declared 1975 as International Women's Year and sought to secure participation of women on equal terms with men in economic, social, political and cultural fields at the national, regional and international levels. An inter-governmental conference on women was convened in Mexico city which adopted a Declaration on the Equality of Women and their contribution to Development and Peace. It also adopted a World Plan of Action which aimed at marked increase in the literacy and civic education of women; extension of co-educational training in industry and agriculture; and equal access to education; increased employment opportunities and reduction of unemployment and discrimination in the terms and conditions of women's employment; equal eligibility to vote and seek elected office; greater participation in policy-making positions; increased welfare services; parity of civil social and political rights, and recognition of the value of women's work in the home and in other unremunerated activities.

The recommendations of the Mexico Conference were endorsed by the General Assembly which proclaimed the period 1976-1985 as United Nations Decade for Women. The Assembly established a Voluntary Fund for the Decade and approved the creation of the International Research and Training Institute for the Advancement of Women. In 1980 the second Women's Conference was convened to evaluate the progress, at Copenhagen. This conference adopted a programme of Action for the second half of the decade, in which it laid special emphasis on employment, health and education. On the recommendations of the second conference, the General Assembly convened a World Conference to review and Appraise the Achievements of the United Nations Decade for Women at Nairobi in 1985. The Conference adopted Forward-looking Strategies for the Advancement of Women to the Year 2000, a document which set forth basic strategies to be employed and measures to serve as guidelines within national priorities for implementing those strategies.

In 1982 the General Assembly adopted a Declaration on the Participation of Women in Promoting International Peace and Co-operation which states that special national and international measures are necessary to increase the level of women's participation in international relations so that women can contribute to national and international efforts to secure world peace and economic and social progress and to promote international co-operation.

Promotion of Youth Interest

Realiasing that the youth can play an important role in the development, the General Assembly adopted in 1965 the Declaration, on the Promotion among Youth of the Ideals of Peace, Mutual Respect and Understanding between Peoples. The Declaration insists that the Government should give youth an opportunity to take part in the preparation and execution of national development plans and international co-operation programmes. The UN and its members have focussed on preparation of youth, through education, for full participation in all aspects of life and development; health policies and programmes which would ensure that young people are able to take advantage of opportunities open to them; the adoption of all possible means to increase employment for youth; the opening of channels of communication between the United Nations and youth organizations; and the promotion of human rights and their enjoyment by youth.

The General Assembly named 1985 as International Youth Year with a view to bringing about widespread awareness of the situation of youth, their problems and aspirations, with a view to engaging young people in the development process. During the year 1985 the General Assembly organised a series of meetings and a World Conference for the International Youth Year. The Conference adopted guidelines for further planning and suitable follow-up in the form of global strategy for youth work beyond the year. The UN tried to implement the decisions and recommendations of the General Assembly and the Economic and Social Council regarding the youth. UN also established the United Nations Youth Fund which supports projects of catalytic or replaceable nature involving young people in the development of their countries.

Aged and Elderly Persons

United Nations has paid increasing attention to the welfare of the elderly people, who constitute the rapidly growing sector of the world population. In 1982 a World Assembly on Aging was convened in Vienna, which adopted the Vienna International Plan of Action on Aging. This plan emphasised the need for policies and plans to help the elderly persons and to deal with the long-term social and economic effects of aging populations. Some of the points emphasised in the Plan of Action included the need to help the elderly persons lead independent lives in their own families and communities; the need to give them a choice as to the kind of health care they receive; the importance of preventive health care; the need for support services to help families, particularly low income families to care for elderly relatives; and the provision of social security schemes; employment and adequate housing. The Plan of Action also insisted on meeting the needs of vulnerable groups like elderly refugees and migrant workers.

The task of reviewing the implementation of the Plan was entrusted to the Commission for Social Development. This Commission reviews the progress every four years and identifies priorities for action. The General Assembly and the Economic and Social Council have repeatedly adopted resolutions urging the governments and non-governmental organisations to give priority to the question of aging. In 1988 an International Institute on Aging was set up in Valetta (Malta).

Care of Disabled Persons

The General Assembly has sought to secure for the handicapped and disabled persons same rights which are available to normal people. In 1971 the General Assembly adopted the Declaration on the Rights of the Mentally Retarded which insisted that such individuals have, to the maximum degree feasible, the same rights as other human beings, including the right to medical care, to economic security, and to live with his or her own family or with foster parents. In case the rights of the mentally retarded persons have to be restricted or denied there must be legal safeguards against any possible abuse. In 1975 the General Assembly adopted Declaration on Rights of Disabled Persons which proclaimed that disabled persons have' the same civil and political rights as other human beings. It set out the right of disabled persons to treatment and service that would develop their capabilities to the maximum and hasten their social integration or reintegration. The other rights insisted by the Declaration included right to economic and social security and to employment or useful and remunerative occupation. In 1976 the General Assembly decided to proclaim 1981 as the International Year of Disabled Persons and called for a plan of action for the year at national, regional and international levels. It insisted that special emphasis should be laid in the plan on primary health care, rehabilitation and prevention of disability. The theme of the International Year of Disabled Persons was 'promotion of full participation and equality' of Disabled Persons in the development of their societies and enjoyment of conditions equal to those of other citizens. In 1982 the General Assembly adopted a World Programme of Action concerning Disabled Persons with a view to continuing long term programmes at the national, regional and international levels. It proclaimed the period 1983-1992 as the United Nations Decade of Disabled Persons to encourage the member states to utilize this period to carry out the programmes. In 1985 the United Nations Fund for International Year of Disabled Persons as Voluntary Fund for the United Nations Decade of Disabled Persons was set up. The Fund continued to meet requests for assistance from the developing countries for disabled persons.

Crime Prevention

United Nations has tried to reduce crimes and promote observance of international standards and norms in criminal justice. For this purpose it provides training to the personnel of the member states and renders them necessary assistance. In 1950 the General Assembly decided that a United Nations Congress on the Prevention of Crime and the Treatment of the offender, be convened every five years. These Congresses have been held at regular intervals. In these conferences criminologists, penologists, and senior police officers as well as experts in criminal law, human rights and rehabilitation, take part. The various Congresses have dealt with different problems of crime. The First Congress held in Geneva in 1955 approved. a set of Standard Minimum rules for the Treatment of Prisoners, which were formally adopted by the Economic and Social Council in 1957. The Second Congress held in London in 1960 suggested measures for preventing juvenile delinquency and considered the questions of prison labour, parole and after care. The Third Congress held at Stockholm in 1965 approved measures for crime prevention. The Fourth Congress held at Tokyo in 1970 stressed the need to take crime into account in development planning, particularly in view of the effects of urbanization, industrialisation and the technological revolution on the human environment. The Fifth Congress held in Geneva in 1975 adopted a Declaration on the Protection of all Persons from being subjected to Torture and other cruel, Inhuman and Degrading Treatment or Punishment. This was subsequently approved by the General Assembly and laid the basis for the Code of Conduct for Law Enforcement Officials approved by the Assembly in 1979. The Sixth Congress held at Caracas in 1980 dealt with problems like crime trends and Crime prevention strategies, juvenile delinquency, crime and use of power and deinstitutionalization of corrections. This declaration was endorsed by General Assembly in 1980. The Seventh Congress was held at Milan in 1985 and adopted a Plan of Action for strengthening international co-operation in crime prevention and criminal Justice, which was subsequently approved by the General Assembly. In 1985 Assembly took action on several other documents adopted by the Seventh Congress. These include Guiding Principles for Crime Prevention and Criminal justice in the Context of Development and a New International Economic Order; Basic Principles on the Independence of the Judiciary; a Model Agreement on the Transfer of Foreign Prisoners; the Declaration on the Basic Principles of Justice for Victims of Crime and abuse of Power; and Standard Minimum Rules for the Administration of Juvenile Justice.

In addition to the above measures the United Nations International Crime and Justice Research Institute has rendered valuable service to check crime by encouraging research and training activities in the field of crime prevention and control.

Control of Narcotic Drugs

United Nations has played an important role in controlling the production and distribution of narcotic drugs and psychotropic substances. It has been instrumental in conclusion of several treaties which require the government to exercise control over production distribution of narcotic drugs and psychotropic substances, combat drug abuse and illicit traffic, maintain necessary administrative machinery and report to international organs on their actions. Some of the important conventions signed in this regard include the Single Convention on Narcotic Drugs (1961), the Convention on Psychotropic Substances (1971), the Protocol Amending the Single Convention (1972). The main objective of all these treaties and conventions has been to limit the supply and demand for narcotic drugs and psychotropic substances to medical and scientific needs. In 1988 the United Nations Convention against Illicit Traffic in Narcotic Drugs and Psychotropic Substances was adopted which deals with various aspects of illicit traffic in narcotic drugs and psychotropic substances, in particular those not envisaged in the existing international drug treaties. The responsibility for the implementation of the provisions of various treaties rests with the Commission on Narcotic Drugs, one of the functional commissions of the Economic and Social Council. The Commission makes recommendations to the Economic and Social Council on the control of narcotic drugs and psychotropic substances. It is also responsible for amending the schedules annexed to the international treaties in order to bring substances under international control, delete them from control, or change the regime of control to which they are subject. The Division of Narcotic Drugs carries out various functions entrusted to the Secretary General under the international drug control treaties.

The responsibility to ensure the implementation of the drug control treaties rests with the International Narcotics Control Board. The Board reviews and confirms annual estimates of Illicit narcotic drug requirements submitted by governments which limit the manufacture and trade in narcotic drugs to medical and scientific purposes. In case of breach of treaties it asks the government to adopt remedial measures. It can also bring these violations to the notice of the Economic and Social Council and the Commission on Narcotic Drugs. In 1971 the Secretary General created the United Nations Fund for Drug Abuse Control (UNFDAC) to develop drug control programmes and to provide funds for their execution. The fund is financed entirely by voluntary contributions. In 1984 the Assembly adopted a Declaration on the Control of Drug Trafficking and Drug Abuse and called for intensification of efforts to control and eradicate complex drug problems. In 1987 the first International Conference on Drug Abuse and Illicit Trafficking was held in Vienna. The Conference adopted a document Comprehensive Multi-disciplinary Outline of Future Activities in Drug Abuse Control, which contained recommendations for practical action to be taken by the governments and organisations to prevent and reduce demand for narcotic drugs and psychotropic substances, control supply, suppress illicit trafficking and promote policies for effective treatment and rehabilitation. The Conference adopted a Declaration which committed the participants to take vigorous international action against drug abuse and illicit trafficking. It also expressed the determination of participants to strengthen action and co-operation at the national, regional and inter-regional levels towards the goal of a society free of drug abuse.

Assistance to Children

The UN has felt greatly concerned about the welfare of children. In fact the General Assembly at its first session in 1946 created the United Nations International Children's Emergency Fund (UNICEF) to meet emergency needs of children in postwar Europe and China for food, drugs and clothing. In 1950 the objective of the fund was changed to cover programme of long-range benefit to children of developing countries. In 1953 the Assembly decided that the UNICEF should continue its work indefinitely. The main function of UNICEF is to co-operate with developing countries in their efforts to protect their children and to enable them to develop their full potential. It insists that every child should be given an opportunity to enjoy the basic rights and privileges embodied in the Declaration of the Rights of the Child adopted by the General Assembly in 1959. In fact the UNICEF co-operates with the developing countries in several ways (i) it assists in the planning and extension of services benefitting children, in consultation with countries concerned, and in the exchange of experience between countries; (ii) it provides funds to strengthen the training and orientation of national personnel, including health and sanitation workers, teachers, nutritionists and child-welfare specialists; and (iii) it delivers technical supplies, equipment and other aids, ranging from paper for textbooks to equipment and medicines for health clinics, to pipes and pumps bringing clean water to villages.

In 1976 UNICEF adopted Basic Services Strategy, under which it helps governments to plan, develop and extend in both rural and urban environments low-cost community based services in the interrelated fields of material and child health, applied nutrition, clean water and sanitation, formal and non-formal education, responsible parenthood and supporting services for women and girls.

In recent years the UNICEF has brought about a virtual revolution in child survival and development by laying emphasis on immunization, breast-feeding, growth monitoring and simple oral rehydration methods.

Though the UNICEF is primarily concerned with long-range programmes for children, it also acts with great speed to meet the immediate needs of children and mothers in emergencies arising from natural disasters, civil strife or epidemics. In 1989 UNICEF launched Operation Lifeline Sudan, the most extraordinary emergency relief effort ever mounted by the international community. During this operation more than 100,000 metric tonnes of food and relief supplies were delivered over a period of three months.

Another important step taken by the UN to protect the children was taken in 1986 when the General Assembly adopted the Declaration drawn up by the Commission for Social Development. The declaration on Social and Legal Principles relating to the Protection and Welfare of Children, with special reference to Foster Placement and Adoption Nationally and Internationally sought to reconcile various juridical principles on foster placement and adoption with religious laws and practices. In view of the valuable services rendered by the UNICEF, it won Nobel Peace Prize in 1965.

Problem of Refugees

UN has played vital role in tackling the problem of refugees. In 1950 the General Assembly established the office of the United Nations High Commissioner (UNHCR) for Refugees to protect the refugees and promote durable solutions to their problems. The UNHCR extends international protection to refugees who do not enjoy the protection of their former home country. It seeks to ensure that the refugees receive asylum and are granted a favourable legal status in their asylum country. The UNHCR also helps refugees to settle on the land through the establishment of new rural communities or through strengthening the infrastructure of areas where the refugees can be absorbed spontaneously into the local population. UNHCR played a vital role in the resettlement of refugees from Latin America and Indo-China by undertaking negotiations with the governments to encourage the admission of refugees or displaced persons into their territories. UNHCR also renders advice to the refugees to find most appropriate solution to their problems. In view of the valuable services rendered by UNHCR, it was awarded Nobel Peace Prize twice in 1954 and in 1981.

Relief during Disasters

The various UN agencies have been playing an important role in providing relief during disasters from the very beginning. In 1971 the General Assembly decided to establish a central office within the United Nations to mobilize relief more rapidly; coordinate it more systematically, reduce risks of waste or duplicated efforts and improve the supply of essential items. Accordingly the office of United Nations Disaster Relief Coordination (UNDRO) was set up in Geneva. The UNDRO acts as a clearing-house for information on relief needs and what donors are doing to meet those needs. It mobilizes and coordinates the relief assistance of various organizations of the United Nations system and in turn coordinates that assistance with what is given by others. The main functions of UNDRO include (i) gathering information' from many sources on individual disaster situations and disseminating it to governments and other potential donors of aid; (ii) organizing missions to assess needs arising from natural disasters and other disaster situations; (iii) contacting potential donors, mobilizing relief contributions and ensuring the rapid transport of relief supplies; and (iv) during the post-emergency rehabilitation or reconstruction phase of disasters, advising governments on disaster-prevention concepts and disaster preparedness planning in general.

UNDRO provided secretarial assistance in the Organisation of International Decade for Natural Disaster Reduction called for by the General Assembly in 1987. The Decade to be held in the 1990's is intended to reduce, through concerted international actions, especially in developing countries, the loss of life, property damage and social and economic disruption caused by natural disaster.

The United Nations provides special assistance to countries afflicted by civil strife or other man-made disasters. UN also rendered great assistance to the countries of Sudano-Sahelian region of Africa which have been afflicted by prolonged drought, accelerating desertification and other disasters since the 1960. In 1973 the United Nations Sudano-Sahelian Office (UNSO) was established to assist in medium and long-term rehabilitation and development programmes for the drought-affected countries of the region. In 1978 the General Assembly decided to expand the functions of UNSO and included the implementation of a Plan of Action to Combat Desertification in 22 countries of the region amongst its functions. In 1985 the Secretary General established a United Nations Office for Emergency Operations in Africa which coordinated and provided assistance to help ensure broad yet concentrated international responses to the continuing drought related crisis in Sub-Saharan Africa. In 1986 the General Assembly adopted the United Nations Programme of Action for African Economic Recovery and Development (UNPAAERD) 1986-1990, whereby the international community committed its support for initiatives being undertaken by African States to promote food production, build up agricultural industries and related infrastructure, reverse the effects of drought and desertification, and develop human resources.

Human Rights and Fundamental Freedoms

The United Nations has also devoted great attention to the promotion of universal respect for human rights and fundamental freedom without distinction of race, sex, language or religion. Its first achievement in this direction was the adoption of Universal Declaration of Human Rights. This Declaration aimed at providing a common standard of rights to be achieved all over the world. After the adoption of the Universal Declaration of Human Rights, two International Covenants on Human Rights were drafted–one related to the economic, social and cultural rights and the other related to the civil and political rights. These two covenants contain some rights which do not find place in the Universal Declaration of Human Rights viz. Right to self-determination, including right of people to freely dispose of their natural wealth and resources.

In 1948 UNO adopted the Convention on Genocide which actually came into force in January 1951 after it was ratified by the requisite number of states. The Convention listed the following as genocide (i) killing members of a group because of their group affiliation; (ii) causing harm to group of members bodily or mentally; (iii) deliberately inflicting physical destruction; (iv) imposing measures to prevent births within the group; and (v) forcibly transferring children from one group to another. The ratifying states agreed to implement the convention and permit extradition of persons formally accused of genocide.

Elimination of Racial Discrimination

United Nations has also devoted attention to the protection of the interests of minorities. It has constantly pleaded for 'self-determination in non-self-governing territories' and severely condemned religious and social prosecution and discrimination. It particularly adopted strong attitude towards racial discrimination in South Africa. In 1962 the General Assembly of the United Nations established a special committee on apartheid (racial discrimination). This committee kept a continuous watch on the developments in South Africa and recommended strong measures against the South African Government.

In 1962 the General Assembly adopted the United Nations Declaration on the elimination of all Forms of Racial Discrimination. The Declaration affirmed that discrimination between human beings on the grounds of race, colour, or ethnic origin is an offence to human dignity, a denial of Charter principles, a violation of the rights proclaimed in the Universal Declaration of Human Rights and an obstacle to friendly and peaceful relations among peoples.

In 1965 the Assembly adopted International Convention on the Elimination of all Forms of Racial Discrimination. The Convention defined racial discrimination as "any distinction, exclusion, restriction or preference based on race, colour, descent or national or ethnic origin which has the purpose or effect of nullifying or impairing the recognition, enjoyment or exercise, on an equal footing of human rights and fundamental freedoms in the political economic, social, cultural or any other fields of public life." The Convention set up a Committee on the Elimination of Racial Discrimination consisting of 18 members. This committee was entrusted the responsibility of reviewing reports submitted by states parties on the measures they had taken to implement the Convention, discussed the reports with government representatives and made general recommendations.

In 1973 the General Assembly adopted the International Convention on the Suppression and Punishment of the Crime of Apartheid. The Convention provided that international responsibility for the crime of apartheid shall apply to individuals, members of organizations and institutions, and representatives of a state, whether residing in the state in which the acts are perpetrated or elsewhere. Persons charged can be tried by any state party to the Convention. The Assembly decided to celebrate 10-year period beginning from 10 December 1973 as decade for Action to Combat Racism and Racial Discrimination, and called on all states to work towards the goals of the decade by promoting human rights, especially by eradicating racism and racial discrimination; identifying and dispelling the fallacious beliefs that contribute to racism; arresting any expansion of racist policies and putting an end to racist regimes.

In 1983 the Second World Conference to Combat Racism and Racial Discrimination was held in Geneva. It found that in spite of efforts of the international community during the Decade, racial discrimination and apartheid showed no signs of diminishing. The Conference adopted a Declaration and a Programme for Action for renewed effort to end racial discrimination and apartheid. It was due to persistent pressure of United Nations that apartheid ultimately ended in South Africa.

In addition the above discussed achievements of the United Nations in the economic and social fields, it can boast of numerous other achievements which are not possible to list here. However, we can say in conclusion with Plalmer and Perkins " Overshadowing the political and security activities of the United Nations, in scope, achievement and perhaps in ultimate significance, are its operations in the economic and social fields."

However, its achievements in the social and economic field have not been that impressive because the UN had to work under several constraints. As a result of growing expenses on the peace-keeping operations, the UN was faced with the problem of paucity of funds. The problem was further complicated because of the recession and budgetary deficits in the donor countries, as well as reluctance of some of the major contributing countries to a pay their share. For example, the USA, which contributes about 25 per cent of UN budget owed nearly $ 1.4 billion to the UN as arrears towards the end of June 1994. The other major defaulters have been Russia, Germany, Great Britain, Italy, South Africa, France etc. Apart form the financial problems, the organisational and procedural shortcomings in the delivery and administration of development assistance have also hampered the process of development and enhanced the gap between the rich North and poor South over all these years.

It is true that the UN system has not come up to the expectations of the developing world in removing income disparities and alleviation of poverty, still it has played a leading role in helping the countries to accelerate their economic and social development. Its achievements may not have been spectacular in all fields, but in some respects it has done outstanding and yeomen work, which no other organisation or bilateral assistance could have done.

Chapter 16

SPECIALISED AGENCIES OF UNITED NATIONS

The United Nations Organisation is not only concerned with the establishment of peace and security in the world but also expected to promote higher standards of living, full employment and conditions of economic and social progress and development. It is charged with the duty of providing solutions for the international economic, social, health and related problems and promoting universal respect for, and observance of human rights and fundamental freedoms for all without any distinction of race, sex, language and religion. In this task the United Nations is assisted by a number of Specialised Agencies, which though not a part of the world body, play an important role in this regard.

Classification of Specialised Agencies

These specialised agencies can be broadly classified into four categories:

1. First, there are some agencies like International Civil Aviation Organisation (ICAO), World Meteorological Organisation (WMO), Inter-government Maritime Consultative Organisation (IMCO), Universal Postal Union (UPU) and International Telecommunication Union (ITU), International Maritime Organisation (IMO) which are concerned with technical matters.
2. Secondly, there are agencies like the International Labour Organisation (ILO), United Nations Educational, Scientific and Cultural Organisation (UNESCO), World Health Organisation (WHO), International Fund for Agricultural and Development (IFAD) which are concerned with social and humanitarian activities.
3. Thirdly, there are agencies like International Bank for Reconstruction and Development (IBRD) (The World Bank), International Development Association (IDA), International Finance Corporation (IFC), UNIDO, GATT, etc. which are concerned with financial and economic development.

4. Finally, there are agencies like Food and Agriculture Organisation (FAO), and International Trade Organisation which are concerned purely with economic problems.

All specialised agencies fall in one of the above noted categories. Some of these agencies like Universal Postal Union have larger membership than the United Nations. Almost all these agencies work through a Central Bureau. In addition they have general assemblies composed of representatives of the member states and a Secretariat. Let us now deal with some of the prominent agencies to fully appreciate their role in the socioeconomic field.

UNITED NATIONS EDUCATIONAL, SCIENTIFIC AND CULTURAL ORGANISATION (UNESCO)

The United Nations Educational, Scientific and Cultural Organisation came into existence in November 1946, and was recognised as a specialised agency of the United Nations in December 1946. The Organisation aims at promoting world peace by constructing defences for peace in the mind of **men.** It wants to promote greater understanding of each other's ways and lives, and remove suspicion and distrust which are responsible for the war.

Organisation

The Organisation of UNESCO consists of a General Conference, an Executive Board and the Secretariat. The General Conference which is the governing body of the Organisation consists of representatives of the member states. Each member state can send up to five delegates but possess only one vote. The General Conference decides the main line of the Organisation. It elects the members of the Executive Board and with the consent of the Board appoints the Director General of the Secretariat. The Conference convenes international conferences on education, the sciences and humanities, and dissemination of knowledge. It also considers reports submitted by the member states.

The Executive Board is composed of 51 members elected by the General Conference from amongst delegates appointed by the member states. While electing these members due consideration is given to their qualifications, experience and administrative capacity to discharge their duties. In addition the geographical factors and diversity of culture is also taken into account. The members of the Executive Board are elected for three years. The Board meets at least two times a year. The Executive Board is responsible for the execution of programmes adopted by the Conference. The Board examines the reports of the Director General and submits the same to the General Conference. The Secretariat is headed by the Director General, who is appointed by the General Conference on the recommendation of the Executive Board for a period of six years. The other members of the Secretariat are appointed by the Director General. The Director General also takes part in the meeting of the General Conference and the Executive Board without right to participate in voting.

Functions of UNESCO

The UNESCO in the main performs three types of functions. In the first place it tries to promote education among children as well as adults. It provides educational materials, books, fellowships and study grants to the war devastated countries. It helps in the promotion of education by providing advice and expert assistance on matters like teachers training, school construction, preparation of curricula and textbooks, etc. For the promotion of education the Organisation has set up a regional Research and Training Centre and an International Institute of Educational Planning at Paris.

UNESCO helps in bringing about improvement in the teaching of basic sciences at various levels. It also encourages basic Research in fields like mathematics, physics, geology, oceanography, etc. UNESCO also encourages application of science and technology to development. It has helped the developing countries by appointing advisory missions, arranging regional conferences and training scientists, technicians and technologists.

The UESCO has also attached great importance to problems of human rights and socio–economic implications of disarmament. It helps the member states in the preservation and protection of their cultural heritage and gives every possible encouragement to artistic activities. It encourages translation of the important works of different countries to make the literature available to different countries. It helps the countries with weak foreign exchange position to procure books from other countries through its scheme of book coupons. UNESCO also helps promoting international exchange of persons and plays a vital role in disseminating knowledge about the Human Rights. In short the UNESCO tries to promote a spirit of intellectual co-operation amongst the people of countries of the world with a view different to promote peace.

A serious crisis confronted UNESCO on account of withdrawal of U.S.A (w. e. f 31 December , 1984) and U.K (w.e.f 31 December 1985). These countries withdrew from the Organisation on the plea that certain tendencies had developed which were not compatible with the original aim of the Organisation. Even Singapore withdrew from this world body on account of her baby economy The withdrawal of affluent members of UNESCO created serious financial problems for the Organisation, even though other members asserted that they would be able to tide over the situation.

The working of UNESCO has been criticised on several grounds. It is alleged that it is run by the government officials. The Executive Board of UNESCO which is considered to be representative is too centralised. Further, there is lot of overlapping in the activities of UNESCO and other specialised agencies. Again UNESCO has tried to be too ambitious and held too many conferences and seminars but generally no action is taken on the outcome of these conferences and seminars. UNESCO was exected to play a significant role in promotion of development but it has failed to do so because of lack of an effective policy in this regard. As a result most of the knowledge and information available with UNESCO in the field of economic and social change has not been systematically exploited. The usefulness of UNESCO has also been reduced due to cleavage between the 'haves' and the 'havenots' and often the programmes of UNESCO do not get support from all the member-states. In other words the UNESCO has not succeeded in bridging psychological divisions between the rich and the poor nations.

THE INTERNATIONAL LABOUR ORGANISATION (ILO)

This Organisation was created in April 1919 as a part of the League of Nations. In 1946 it became the first specialised agency of the United Nations. The main task of the Organisation is to improve the living and working conditions of the workers throughout the world.

Organisation

The ILO has three organs viz., International Labour Conference, the Governing Body and the International Labour Office. The International Labour Conference is the General Conference of the member states. Each member sends four delegates to the General Conference. These delegates represent the government (2), workers (1) and employers (1). The Labour Conference lays down the minimum international standards of working and living conditions. The Labour Conference approves the annual budget of the Organisation and elects the members of the Governing Body. It also examines the reports from the member states regarding implementation of conventions, etc. adopted by the Conference.

The Governing Body of ILO consists of the 56 members-28 representing the Government, 14 representing the employers and 14 representing the workers. The Governing Body elects a Chairman and a Vice-Chairman for one year from amongst its members. The Governing Body appoints the Director General and exercises general supervision over the working of the International Labour Office. It drafts the budget proposals and determines the general policy of the Organisation. The Governing Body can constitute its own Committees to deal with particular problems.

The International Labour Office is a sort of Secretariat of the ILO. In addition it also acts as World Information Centre and Publishing House. The office is headed by the Director General appointed by the Governing Body. In addition it enjoys the service of experts drawn from different member states. The International Labour Office prepares documents and bring out periodical publications. It also undertakes research and studies on problems relating to the Labour. The International Labour Organisation brings together the government, labour and management and encourages them to accept international minimum standards and draft labour conventions on subjects like human rights, freedom of association, wages, hour of work, minimum age for employment, conditions of work for various classes of workers, workmen's compensations, social insurance, vacation with pay, industrial safety, employment services and labour inspection.

Functions of the ILO.

The ILO performs very extensive functions. Its functions include the following:

1. It tries to raise the standards of workers by setting international labour standards through international conventions. In 1962 the Labour Conference adopted a convention reducing the working hours to 48 hours a week.
2. It prevents unemployment and conducts comprehensive studies of the factors which can help in achieving the objective of full employment. ILO launched World Employment Programme in 1969 to provide jobs for the world's rapidly expanding population. In recognition of its services to the working people all over the world the ILO was awarded Nobel Peace Prize for a half century of service on behalf of working people.
3. It looks after the problem of social security of employees in industry, commerce and agriculture. It has already adopted conventions which provide for compulsory insurance against sickness, old age and death and payment of compensation for industrial accidents and occupational diseases.
4. The ILO tries to improve the working conditions of the merchant sailors. It has adopted over twenty-five conventions for this purpose. These conventions relate to the working hours, special provisions for overtime holidays, medical examinations, conditions of service, etc.
5. The ILO encourages the employees as well as employers to form their own associations.
6. It protects the industrial as well as field workers by insisting on inspection, prevention of industrial accidents etc. It has published a code of safety regulations for the industrial establishments.
7. It pays special attention to the problems of women and children. It has placed a ban on employment of women at night as well as traffic in women. Similarly, the ILO also protects the children. It has prohibited employment of children below 15 years in hazardous jobs. The other important measures taken by the ILO for the protection of women and children include employment of women before and after child birth, maternity benefits, provision of day nurseries, etc.
8. The ILO provides technical assistance to member states. It has instituted many technical assistance projects in the field of vocational guidance and training, managerial supervisory training and productivity projects. In 1965 the ILO set up the International Centre for Advanced Technical and Vocational Training in Turin (Italy), which provides programme for directors of technical and vocational institutions, training officers, managers, trade union leaders, instructors and technicians, primarily from the developing countries.

The International Labour Organisation has set over 300 international labour standards through adoption of various International Labour Conferences. Though the final authority to accept these conventions rests with the member states, but generally the states have tended to accept these conventions by ratifying them. ILO can ask the governments of member states to report how far these standards are being complied with, and the difficulties faced by them in applying these.

The Technical Assistance Programme of the ILO could not be very effective during the earlier years on account of lack of necessary financial resources. However, after large sums were made available by the United Nations under the UN Development Programmes, ILO was able to play more effective role and carried out more than 150 major projects in different parts of the world.

The ILO acts as a publishing house and brings our large number of periodicals, texts of labour law regulations, studies, technical works and manuals in different languages. It also entertains large number. of inquiries made from it every year.

The position of the ILO was greatly weakened on account of prevailing power politics in the international arena. This is evident from the fact that in 1977 United States withdrew from the Organisation on the ground that it was acting with political bias. It particularly objected that the tripartite principle (which envisaged association of governments, labour and employer) was being threatened because the delegations from Soviet Union and some other states were practically acting as representatives of the government. It was only in 1980, after ILO gave an assurance that it would act more impartially, the United States returned to the ILO.

In short the ILO through its activities seeks to create a sense of solidarity among the workers of the world. Though the ILO' s recommendations are not mandatory and their acceptance depends on the sweet will of the states, still it has made valuable contributions and tried to ensure that the benefits are extended to groups which have been less successful in obtaining improvements through national channels. Further it has sought to bring about improvements in the area where the states are reluctant to undertake improvements by themselves.

THE WORLD HEALTH ORGANISATION (WHO)

The World Health Organisation came into being on 7 April, 1948 when 26 United Nations member states ratified its Constitution. Its membership is open to all the members of the UNO. The States which are not members of UNO can become members of WHO after their application is approved by the World Health Assembly. Non sovereign states and territories can become its associate members. It aims at creating proper health conditions through international cooperation.

Organisation

The Organisation of the WHO consists of the World Health Assembly, the Executive Body, and the Secretariat. The World Health Assembly is composed of representatives of all the member states. The Assembly holds annual meetings and is responsible for laying down general policies. It approves the budget of the Organisation and adopts necessary conventions for the promotion of its objectives. The Assembly appoints the Director General, who heads the Secretariat.

The Executive Board consists of 31 members. These members are selected by the World Health Assembly from amongst persons most qualified by their technical competence in the field of health. These members are elected for three years. The Board carries out the decisions of the Assembly. It takes necessary measures to deal tied epidemics and sudden calamities.

The Secretariat under the Director General works through technical experts and committees.

Objective of WHO

The main objective of the WHO is attainment by all peoples of the highest possible level of health. This goal is to be achieved through the combined efforts of the governments and people, and involves education concerning prevailing health problems; proper food supply and nutrition; safe water and sanitation; maternal and child health, including family planning; immunisation against major infectious diseases; prevention and control of local diseases; appropriate treatment of common diseases and injuries; and provision of essential drugs.

Functions

The WHO performs following functions:

1. It tries to prevent the spread of disease by providing assistance to the states to check the disease at the source, to prevent it from spreading to other countries.
2. The WHO tries to cure the disease once it has spread, by imparting scientific knowledge about the disease by providing assistance to the states to check the diseases at the source, to prevent it from spreading to other countries and suggesting ways to combat the same. Though the actual operations for curing the disease are left to the national governments, the WHO provides necessary training to state personnel, sponsors seminars and conference for the exchange of techniques and experience.
3. The WHO provides training of personnel of different states for the prevention of diseases. It is well known that it was chiefly due to the world wide campaign by the WHO against Malaria that the disease has been checked.

4. The WHO held the member states to improve the health administration by imparting education regarding health through seminars, conferences and training projects to deal with problems like environmental hygiene, eradication of disease, control of disease etc. WHO launched a special programme, in collaboration with United Nations Development Programme(UNDP) and the World Bank, of research and training in tropical diseases like malaria, leprosy, schstosomiasis. It also launched a special programme to prevent and control AID through public information and education about the modes of its transmission.

Thus the functions of the WHO has tremendously increased since its establishment. This has further aggravated the problem of paucity of funds. As the WHO has to operate within the available resources, it has to concentrate only on some specific programmes and projects. This has greatly hampered the efficient discharge of responsibilities by WHO. However, it cannot be denied that the WHO has succeeded in securing international co-operation for solving health problems when national actions proved ineffective.

FOOD AND AGRICULTURE ORGANISATION (FAO)

The FAO was founded at a conference in Quebec on 16 October 1945 with a view to find out means for developing and maintaining an adequate food supply by encouraging use of modern tools and methods, conserving existing food supplies, searching new sources etc.

The FAO like other agencies also operates through three organs viz., the Conference, the Council and the Secretariat. The Conference consists of representatives member states with each such state enjoying only one vote. The Conference decides the policy of the Organisation. The Council consists of 49 members elected by the Conference. It discharges all the functions of the Conference during the intervening period between its sessions. The Secretariat, is headed by the Director General chosen by the Conference. The Secretariat has five Technical Divisions. In addition it has certain regional offices as well.

Functions.

The main functions of the FAO include the following

1. It collects, analyses, interprets and disseminates information relating to nutrition , food and agriculture. It has set up an International Emergency Food Council which recommends allocation of scare foodstuffs and other products among the importing countries.
2. It provides technical assistance to the member states to improve food. It provided help to Iraq regarding soil erosion. Similarly, it provided training to the Indian Mechanics for the maintenance of agricultural machinery and irrigation equipment.
3. It helps in combating various animal and plant diseases. It has done valuable work in this regard by inventing new vaccines and medicines. It also helps in controlling the locust.

4. It helps the countries in increasing production of foodstuffs by developing and introducing new seeds and methods of cultivations. It also helps in promoting fishery by suggesting new methods.
5. The FAO seeks to check diseases among children resulting from malnutrition.
6. Finally, the FAO disseminates necessary information regarding the food and other allied problems. In 1960 it launched the Freedom from Hunger Campaign to create a worldwide awareness regarding the problem of hunger and malnutrition being faced by people in certain parts of the world. Though the Organisation has not succeeded in eliminating hunger from the world its action was certainly laudable. If the different states co-operate the results can be quite rewarding.

INTERNATIONAL MONETARY FUND (IMF)

The International Monetary Fund was set up in December 1945. It aims at (i) promoting international monetary co-operation through permanent institution which provides the machinery for consultation and collaboration on international monetary problems, (ii) facilitate the expansion and balanced growth of international trade and to promote high levels of employment and real income (iii) to promote exchange stability and maintain orderly exchange arrangements among members (iv) to assist in the establishment of multilateral system of payment in respect of current transactions between members and eliminate the foreign exchange restrictions which hampers the growth of world trade, and (v) to provide Fund resources available to the members with a view to correct maladjustment in the balance of payments without resorting to measures destructive of national or international system.

The Organisation of the IMF comprises of Board of Governors, the Executive Board and the Managing Director. The Board of Governors is the highest authority and comprises of representatives of all the member states. It meets once a year. The daily business of the Fund is conducted by the Executive Board comprising of 22 Executive Directors. The Executive Board is headed by a Managing Director. The Managing Director also acts as the chief of staff of more than 1700 international civil servants.

Functions

The participants at the Bretton Woods Conference, assigned three main functions to the Fund. Firstly, a code of conduct regarding exchange rate policies and impose restrictions on payments for current account transactions. Secondly, provides the members financial resources to enable them to observe the code of conduct while correcting or avoiding payments imbalances. Thirdly, to provide a forum in which members can consult one another and collaborate on international monetary matters.

The Fund provides necessary resources to the members to overcome problem of payments. Generally, the Fund lends money to the members keeping in view two basic principles. Firstly, it expects the member states borrowing from the Fund to return the amount in the currency in which the money was borrowed, as soon as its payments problems are resolved so that the same may become available to other members of Fund. Secondly, it can ask the member states borrowing the money to indicate how they intend to solve their payment problems and assure that the money would be repaid to the Fund within normal period of repayment viz. between three to five years. However, in certain cases the Fund can extend the repayment period upto 10 years.

The IMF ensures that the states do not change the exchange rates more than 10 per cent from the initial value without its permission. Actually in the IMF the states have been accorded weightage of voting in accordance with their contributions to the fund which gives an advantage to countries like UK and USA. As a result these changes can be effected only with the consent of these two countries. The IMF keeps a watch on the domestic and international financial view to ensure genuine equilibrium in the balance of payments.

INTERNATIONAL BANK FOR RECONSTRUCTION AND DEVELOPMENT (IBRD)

The IBRD came into existence in December 1945 and was accorded the status of a special agency of the UN in November 1947. The main purpose of the IBRD is to assist in the reconstruction of capital for productive purpose; by promoting private foreign investments by means of guarantees or participation's in loans and other investments made by private investors; to promote long-range balanced growth of international trade and maintenance of equilibrium in balance of payments by encouraging international investment for development of productive sources of members; to arrange the loans made or guaranteed by it in relation to international loans through other channels; and to conduct its operations with due regard to the effect of international investments in business conditions in the territories of members.

It may be observed that IBRD while carrying out its operations keeps several things in mind viz. it lends only for productive purposes–such as agriculture and rural development, energy, education, health, family planning and nutrition, roads and railways, telecommunication, urban ports and power facilities. It has to keep in mind the prospects for repayment. The loan must be guaranteed by the government concerned toensure that loans are not available from other souses on reasonable terms. The Bank's decision to lend must be based only on economic considerations, it cannot restrict the use of loans to purchases in any particular member country or countries. It is noteworthy that since the Bank obtains loan funds from borrowing in private capital market, and not from the governments, it has to follow sound principles of international finance and take steps to protect interests of creditors.

The Organization of IBRD consists of Board of Governors, the Executive Directors and President. The real power rests with the Board of Governors which normally meets once a year. The Board appoints a body of 22 Executive Directors. The Chairman (elected by the Board of Directors every year) acts as the ex-officio Chairman of five Executive Directors. The appointment of five Executive Directors is made by the five largest stockholders and the remaining 17 Executive Directors are elected by the Governors of remaining members. The President is the Chief executive officer of the IBRD. He is selected by Board of the Governors and is assisted by other staff.

Functions

The main function of the IBRD is to raise the level of productivity. For this purpose it provides necessary loans to various countries, for development purposes. India received loan for reconstruction and development of state-owned railways from the IBRD. The Bank charges a very moderate rate of interest. After the money is made available to the country the bank ensures that the money is being used as per terms of contracts. Thus the Bank not only functions as a lender and a grarantor but also as an international brain trust for the evaluation and guidance of reconstruction and development strategy.

For quite some time the IBRD avoided social project loans (for building hospital and schools, and slum clearance, etc.), general purpose loans, and loans to resolve problems of balance of payments. However, of late it has adopted more liberal attitude and has provided loans to encourage economic growth in major debtor countries of the third world. It also provids assistance to the states in their development planning by helping them in the preparation of project proposals, providing training to senior development officials, etc. Despite this change in attitude the IBRD is not able to meet the vast capital demand of developing countries due to its limited resources and capacity.

UNITED NATIONS INTERNATIONAL CHILDREN EMERGENCY FUND (UNICEF)

The UNICEF was created in December 1946 through a resolution of the UN General Assembly with a view to help those countries with money, goods and services, who are unable to meet the needs of their children out of their own resources. UNICEF works through an Executive Board of 41 members designated by the Economic and Social Council of the UN. It also has an Executive Director who is appointed by the General Secretary of UNO in consultation with the members of the Executive Board. The necessary funds for the UNICEF are raised through voluntary contributions of governments, persons and organisations. Roughly three quarter of its income comes from Government and the remainder from general public.

The UNICEF renders assistance in providing balanced food to children and provides assistance in providing to them protective food like milk, meat, fish, fats, fish liver oil, etc. It also co-operates with other organisations for the improvement of children's health and provision of clothing. UNICEF also takes care of the interests of women and provides facilities for pregnant mothers. It has also extended support to various conventions for the suppression of traffic in women and children, crime prevention, etc. According to

Prof. Jacob and Atherton 'By its careful planning, scrupulous non-partisan administration, high operating efficiency and economy, and above all, the ever-riding sense of international responsibility for a humanitarian purpose that permeated the organisation, UNICEF vindicated the role of international organisation as agent for relief of human need and misery."

INTERNATIONAL DEVELOPMENT ASSOCIATION (IDA)

The International Development Association was established in 1960 as an affiliate of the IBRD, with a view to provide funds to the poor countries on much easier terms than the IBRD. Though legally and financially an independent body, it is administered by the same officers and staff as the IBRD. The membership of IDA is open to all the members of the Bank.

The funds of the IDA come from three sources: transfers from the Bank's net earnings; capital subscribed in convertible currencies by the members of IDA; and contributions from the richer members of IDA. A country to borrow from IDA has to meet four creterias viz. it must be very poor (the poverty ceiling was $ 796 per capita gross national product in 1981); it must have sufficient deficiency to warrant long-term development lending; it must have an unusually difficult balance of payments problem and little prospects of earning enough foreign exchange to justify borrowing all it needs on conventional terms; and it must have a genuine commitment to development as reflected in its policies.

The objectives of IDA are to promote economic development, increase productivity and raise standards of living by providing its members with finance to meet important development needs on terms which are flexible and which bear less heavily on their balance of payments.

In contrast with the IBRD loans, nearly all IDA 'credits' have been given for 50 years without interest. Only a small charge is levied to cover the administrative costs. The repayment of principal does not start till after 10 years grace period.

INTERNATIONAL FINANCE CORPORATION (IFC)

The International Finance Corporation (IFC) was established as an affiliate of the World Bank to assist the economic development of less developed member countries. The IFC promotes private sector economic growth in these countries through mobilization of domestic and foreign capital. The membership of the Corporation is open to all the government members of the IBRD.

The main objectives of the IFC are (1) to assist in financing private enterprise which could contribute to development by making investments without guarantee of repayment by the member Government concerned; (ii) to bring together investment opportunities, domestic and foreign capital, and experienced management; and (iii) to stimulate the flow of private capital, domestic and foreign, into productive investment in member countries.

It is noteworthy that IFC has mainly invested in manufacturing, but it has also made valuable investments in the field of mining and energy, tourism, utilities and projects relating to agriculture. The funds of IFC mainly come from subscriptions by its member countries and from accumulated earnings.

The organisation of IFC comprises of Board of Governors, the Board of Directors and the Chairman. The Board of Governors, in which all the powers of IFC are vested, comprises of Governors and alternates of World Bank who represent countries which are also members of IFC. The Board of Directors comprises of ex-officio Executive Directors of the World Bank who represent the countries which are also members of IFC. The Board of Directors supervise the general operations of IFC. The President of the World Bank is the ex-officio Chairman of the Board of Directors of IFC.

A perusal of the activities of IBRD and its two affiliates–International Development Association and International Finance Corporation, shows that most of the developing states have benefited from their activities. It is hoped that in future also these agencies shall continue to contribute towards the development of these countries through their lendirig operations. However, it cannot be denied that the working of these bodies has met with severe criticism at the hands of some critics.

It is alleged that these agencies are largely controlled by Western powers on account of system of weighted voting, on the basis of contributions. As a result often these bodies provide loans which are only slightly earlier than the loans provided by private banks. Despite this criticism the members of the 'World Community both developed and developing, look to these agencies as an important source of capital needs for economic development. The member states are quite optimistic that the role of these bodies will continue to grow in future.

UNIVERSAL POSTAL UNION (U.P.U)

The Universal Postal Union was established under the Berne Treaty of 1874 with a view to overcome the difficulties which the states were facing with regard to international mail. This Union formally came into being on I July, 1875 and was initially named as General Postal Union. At the second International Post Congress held in Paris in 1878, its name was changed to Universal Postal Union. It was expected to administer the services necessary for uniting the world in a single postal territory for reciprocal exchange of correspondence. Most of the states are members of the Universal Postal Union.

The Universal Postal Union has four principal organs–the Universal Postal Congress, the Executive Council, the Consultative Council for Postal Studies, and International Bureau. The Universal Postal Congress is the general body which meets once in five years to review the Acts of the Universal Postal Union, including the subsidiary agreements. The Executive Council comprises of 40 members elected by the Congress on the basis of equitable geographical distribution. The Council maintains close contact with postal administrations, exercises control over the International Bureau, ensures working relations with the United Nations and other international organisations, and promotes technical assistance. It meets annually and ensures continuity of the work of the Union between Congresses.

The Congress elects a Consultative Council for Postal Studies which comprises of 35 members. The Consultative Council meets annually at Berne. It organises studies of major technical, economic and operational problems affecting postal administration in all the member countries and examines teaching and training problems in the newly independent and developing countries.

The International Bureau is the central office of the Universal Postal Union. It coordinates, publishes and disseminates information about the international postal service. It gives opinions on disputes and acts as a clearing–house for the settlement of debts between postal administrations. It considers requests for amendments to the Acts of the Union, gives notice of changes adopted and takes part in the preparation of the work of the Congress. It also provides secretarial assistance to the Universal Postal Union bodies and promotes technical cooperation of all types.

The main functions of the UPU (Universal Postal Union) include reciprocal exchange of letter-post items; to secure improvement of the postal services; to provide technical assistance to the member countries of the Union; to promote international collaboration in postal matters; to fix rates, the maximum and minimum weight and size limits and the conditions of acceptance of letter post items; to prescribe the methods for calculating and collecting transit charges for letter-post items passing through the territories of one or more countries, etc. The Union undertakes technical projects and seeks to promote co-operation among members through planning, organisation, management, operations training and financial services. It helps the developing countries to improve their postal services by sending experts providing vocational training, awarding fellowships for individual or group courses and supplying equipment and training. The Universal Postal Union also complies useful information regarding the list of airports, air-mail lines, world map of surface communication routes, a directory of post offices, etc. It also brings out monthly journal in a number of languages to keep the members informed about the latest development. The Union has greatly contributed to the creation and maintenance of conditions for free flow of messages among the people of the world and thus contributed to the promotion of world peace and fraternity of nations.

INTERNATIONAL TELECOMMUNICATION UNION (ITU)

The first effort to secure cooperation among the members in the field of communication was made in 1865 when the International Telegraph Union was founded. It was only in 1934 that the organisation was renamed as International Telecommunication Union. In 1947 at the International conference held in United States the ITU adjusted its organizational structure and entered into an agreement with the United Nations whereby it was recognised as the specialised agency of telecommunication. Thereafter the activities of the ITU are being regulated according to various conventions which have been adopted since then.

The organisation of the ITU(International Telecommunication Union) comprises of the Plenipotentiary Conference, Administrative Council, the General Secretariat, the International Frequency Registration Board(IFRB), the International Telegraph and Telephone Consultative Committee; and the International Consultative Committee. The Plenipotentiary Conference is the supreme organ of ITU. It meets normally every five years and is responsible for laying down its basic policy. In addition it convenes administrative conference to consider specific telecommunication matters, both at world and regional levels.

The Administrative Council is elected by the Plenipotentiary Conference and comprises of 43 members. These members are elected keeping in view equitable geographical representation. The Administrative Council meets annually and coordinates the work of five permanent organs at ITU headquarters viz. the Secretariat, the International Frequency Registration Board, the International Radio Consultative Committee, the International Telegraph and Telephone Consultative Committee, and the Telecommunications Development Bureau.

The main objective of ITU is to maintain and extend international cooperation for the improvement and rational use of telecommunications of all kinds, to promote the development of technical facilities and their most efficient operation with a view to improving the efficiency of telecommunication services, increasing their usefulness and making them generally available to public and to harmonize the actions of nations in the attainment of these objectives.

For the attainment of the above objectives the ITU undertakes following functions.

(i) It allocates the frequencies on the spectrum and registers radio frequency assignments in such a way as to avoid interference between radio station of different countries.

(ii) It coordinates efforts to eliminate interference between radio stations and seeks to establish the lowest possible charges for telecommunications services.

(iii) It fosters the creation, development and improvement of telecommunications in newly independent or developing countries, principally through its participation in the United Nations programmes.

(iv) It promotes safety measures.

(v) It undertakes studies, issues recommendations and opinions, and collects and publishes information for the benefit of its members and associate members.

(vi) The International Frequency Registration Board(IFRB) keeps the Master International Frequency Registry upto date, works on technical preparations for planning conferences and organizes numerous seminars on frequency management and the use of the radio frequency spectrum.

(vii) The International Telecommunication Union carries out technical co-operation programme within the framework of the United Nations Development Programme. This programme is directed towards the technical training of local telecommunication personnel, planning regional telecommunication network, making detailed pre-investment surveys for regional networks and helping member governments establish new networks.

(viii) The ITU lays down regulations for reservation of distress frequencies for life-saving and rescue work. It also determines station identification signals, frequencies for air and marine navigational aid, and for meteorological messages and other matters relating to efficient use of radio.

In short, it can be said that the International Telecommunication Union tries to maintain conditions necessary for free flow of messages among different nations of the world.

INTERNATIONAL CIVIL AVIATION ORGANISATION (ICAO)

The International Civil Aviation Organisation(ICAO) came into existence in April 1947 in terms of the decision of International Civil Aviation Conference held at Chicago in 1944, and has its headquarter at Montreal, Canada.

The main objectives of ICAO are: (i) to ensure the safe and orderly growth of international civil aviation; (ii) to encourage the design and operation of aircraft for peaceful purposes; (iii) to support the development of airways airports and air navigation facilities for civil aviation; and (iv) to meet the needs of the international public for safe, regular, efficient and economical air transport.

For the attainment of the above objectives the ICAO has adopted a number of international standards and recommended practices which specify the design and performance of aircraft and much of their equipments. These standards also deal with the performance of airline pilots, flight crews, air traffic controllers, and ground and maintenance crews; the carriage of dangerous goods by commercial aircraft; security requirements and procedures at international airports; and the interdiction of illicit drug transportation by air.

ICAO is also responsible for the regulation of radio frequencies and security procedures. It works to facilitate the movement of aircraft passengers, crews, baggage, cargo and mail across international boundaries by reducing procedural formalities involving customs, immigration and public health authorities. It also helps the developing countries in establishing or improving air transport systems and training of aviation personnel.

Organisation

The Organisation of the ICAO comprises of an Assembly, a Council, a Secretariat and a number of commissions and committees. The Assembly is made up of all the member states of the ICAO, with each enjoying only one vote. The Assembly meets once in three years and decides the policy of ICAO, and votes on budget. It also deals with other questions which may be specifically referred to it by the Council.

The Council of ICAO comprises of 33 members elected by the Assembly. It is expected to carry out the directives of the Assembly It elects its President and appoints the Secretary General. The Council also administers the finances of the organisation. The Council creates standards for international air Invitation and safety; collects, examines and publishes information on air navigation; and also acts as a tribunal for settlement of disputes which may arise among member states relating to international civil aviation.

The Council is assisted by an Air Navigation Commission and five committees viz. air transport, legal, joint support of air navigation services, finance and unlawful interference.

WORLD METEOROLOGICAL ORGANISATION (WMO)

The World Meteorological Organisation is the successor of International Meteorological Organisation (IMO) and started its operations in 1951 even though decision for its creation was taken at the Twelfth Conference of Directors of International Meteorological Organisation. This organization was established with a view to coordinating, standardizing and improving world meteorological and related activities and to encourage an efficient exchange of meteorological and related information between countries in the aid of human activities.

The objectives of WMO include (i) to help in the establishment of networks of stations and centres to provide meteorological and hydrological observations and services; (ii) to promote the establishment and maintenance of systems for the rapid exchange of meteorological and related information; (iii) to promote standardization of meteorological and related observations; and ensure the uniform publication of observations and statistics-(iv) to further the application of meteorology to aviation, shipping, water problems, agriculture and other activities;(v) to promote activities in operational hydrology and to further close co-operation between meteorological and hydrological services; and (vi) to encourage research and training in meteorology and related fields.

Activities

The Seventh World Meteorological Congress which met in May 1975 reorganised the activities of WMO into different programmes, which deserve detailed discussion.

In the first place it has implemented the establishment of the 'World Weather Watch', using surface-based observations, meteorological satellites and a system of world and regional meteorological centres operated by national weather services or its members. In recent years, with atmospheric and oceanic data obtained from space rapidly becoming the basis of extended range-weather forecasts for the entire globe, WMO has given high priority to space-based observational systems and use of satellite communications to transmit meteorological information.

Secondly, the WMO along with Inter-governmental Oceanographic Commission of UNESCO has sponsored an international programme called the Integrated Global Ocean Station System, to produce and provide oceanographic analysis and predictions.

Thirdly, WMO has carried out the Global Atmospheric Research Programme jointly with the International Council of Scientific Unions, which increases the accuracy of meteorological forecasting and helped in obtaining a better understanding of the physical basis of climate.

Fourthly, its programme of Meteorological Application and Environment has applied meteorological knowledge to human activities such as agriculture, transport, building climatology, energy, atmospheric and marine pollution and environmental problems in general. The organisation works in close cooperation with the Food and Agriculture Organisation of UNO to increase food production in member countries.

Fifthly, under the Hydrology and Water Resources Development Programme, WMO has promoted world-wide co-operation in evaluating water resources and assisted in developing such resources through the establishment of coordinated networks and services.

Sixthly, the Technical Co-operation Programme of WMO has assisted the developing countries to improve national meteorological and hydrological service through the provision of experts, fellowships and equipment. It renders assistance to the countries to develop observational and telecommunications networks, data processing facilities, training and research institutes and to apply observational data and forecasts to other sectors of the national economy.

Seventhly, the WMO has launched the World Climate Programme which seeks to improve knowledge of natural variation in the climate and the effect of climatic changes due to natural causes or human activities.

Organisation

WMO has quite an elaborate organisation. World Meteorological Congress is the supreme body of WMO which contains representatives of all member states. Usually the states are represented by the heads of their meteorological services. The Congress meets once in four years and determines the general policy. The responsibility for the submission of the programmes approved by the Congress rests with the Executive Council comprising of 36 directors of national meteorological or hydrological services serving in individual capacity. The Executive Council holds at least one meeting every year. In addition of the above bodies, there are six regional meteorological associations which co-ordinate meteorological and related activities within their respective regions. These six regional associations are located in Africa, Asia, South America, North and Central America, Europe, and the South-West Pacific. In addition to these there exist eight technical commissions composed of experts designated by members of WMO. These commissions arc responsible for studying aeronautical, agriculture and marine meteorology, atmospheric sciences, basic systems, hydrology, instruments and methods of observation, and climatology.

INTERNATIONAL MARITIME ORGANISATION (IMO)

International Maritime Organisation, earlier known as Inter-Governmental Maritime Consultative Organisation, came into existence in March 1958 after the United Nations Maritime Conference adopted in Geneva in 1948 was accepted by requisite number of states (21). IMO has its headquarter at London.

Organisation

The Assembly is the chief policy-making body of IMO and comprises of all the member states and an associate member (Hongkong), The Assembly meets every 2 years and determines the work programme, budget and financial regulations of IMO. It also adopts recommendations on regulations concerning maritime safety, prevention of maritime pollution and other matters.

During the recess of the Assembly the Council, elected for a term of two years, acts as the governing body of the Organisation. The Council comprises of 32 members who arc elected by the Assembly. In addition to the above Organisation there are four principle committees–on maritime safety; legal matters; marine environment protection and technical co-operation. These Committees submit their reports and recommendations to the Assembly through the Council.

The IMO provides machinery for co-operation and exchange of information among governments on technical matters affecting shipping engaged in international trade. It encourages the adoption of the highest practicable standards in matters concerning maritime safety, navigational efficiency, and the prevention and control of marine pollution from ships.

The IMO provides a useful forum to member Governments and interested Organisations to exchange information and make a bid to solve problems connected with technical, legal and other questions concerning shipping and prevention of marine pollution by ships. The IMO has drafted several conventions and made recommendations which the governments have adopted. Some of the conventions adopted by the IMO in this regard include international convention for the safety of life at sea, the prevention of marine pollution by ships, the training and certification of seafarers, the prevention of collision at sea, several instruments dealing with liability and compensation, etc.

In addition to the above the IMO has adopted several hundred recommendations relating to maritime transport of dangerous goods, maritime signals, safety for fishermen and fishing vessels, and the safety of nuclear merchant ships. Though these recommendations are not binding on the members, they certainly constitute the codes and provide guidance to the governments in framing national regulations.

WORLD INTELLECTUAL PROPERTY ORGANISATION (WIPO)

The origin of the Organisation- can be traced to the Paris Convention of 1883 which set up the Organisation for the Protection of Industrial Property. Subsequently the Berne Convention of 1886 extended it to Protection of Literary and Artistic Works. However formally the World Intellectual Property Organisation came into existence as a result of convention signed in 1967, which actually came into force in 1970. In 1974 WIPO became a specialised agency of the United Nations. At present it has 155 members.

Organisation

The Organisation of WIPO comprises of a Conference and a General Assembly. The Conference comprises of all the member states, while the General Assembly is composed of those member states which are also members of the Paris or Berne Union. Generally the programmes, policy and budgets of WIPO are decided by the governing bodies of WIPO and the Unions administered by WIPO in their joint session. The Organisation has its headquarter at Geneva (Switzerland) and is headed by the Director General.

Aims and Activities

The main objectives of WIPO are to maintain and increase respect for intellectual property throughout the world, in order to favour industrial and cultural development by stimulating creative activity and facilitating the transfer of technology and the dissemination of literary and artistic works. Broadly speaking intellectual property comprises of two main branches (i) Industrial property which includes patents and other rights in technological inventions, right in trade marks, industrial designs, appellations of origin etc. (ii) copyright and neighbouring rights in literary musical and artistic works, films performances of performing artistists, phonograms etc.

The WIPO seeks to protect intellectual property by promoting wider acceptance of the existing treaties and their revision. It also encourages the conclusion of new treaties and assists in the development of national legislation. It also gives legal technical assistance to developing countries gathers and disseminates information; and maintains services for international registration or other administrative cooperation among the member states of the 'unions' which WIPO administers, and which are founded on treaties, conventions and agreements dating back to 1883.

INTERNATIONAL FUND FOR AGRICULTURAL DEVELOPOMENT (IFAD)

The International Fund for Agricultural Development (IFAD) came into force on 30 November, 1977, even though the agreement for the establishment of the Fund was taken in June 1976. IFAD has its headquarter at Rome (Italy).

Organisation

The Organisation of IFAD comprises of a Governing Council which consists of representatives of all the member states. These members fall into three categories, viz., developed countries, key contributor developing countries, and other countries, mainly recipients. These three categories of members, however, enjoy equal voting rights.

The President is the Chief Executive of the Fund. He is assisted by a Vice President and three Assistant Presidents. The President is responsible for the business of the Fund. He also acts as Chairman of the 18 member Executive Board.

Objectives

The main objective of the IFAD is to mobilize resources for improved food production and better nutrition among low-income groups in developing countries. At least 20 per cent of the people in Africa, Asia and Latin America are victims of chronic hunger and malnutrition. The fund focuses its attention on the needs of the poorest rural communities, specially small farmers, the landless, fishermen, livestock herders, and poor rural women. It pays special attention to grass-roots development and innovative approaches which build on local participation and the preservation of the natural resources base.

For the attainment of the above objectives, the IFAD lends money on highly concessional or low interest terms. It not only tries to raise agricultural production but also tries to improve local prospects for employment, nutrition and income distribution. It goes to the credit of IFAD that it has been able to mobilise the support from other external donors for its projects. It has also mopped up finances from other financial and development institutions like the World Bank and IDA, etc.

UNITED NATIONS INDUSTRIAL DEVELOPMENT ORGANISATION (UNIDO)

The United Nations Industrial Development Organisation (UNIDO) was established by the UN General Assembly in 1966 with a view to promote and accelerate the industrialisation of the developing countries, and to coordinate UN activities in this field. It was given status of a specialised agency of the United Nations in 1979 when the conference of plenipotentiaries met in Vienna and adopted a Constitution for UNIDO. The document received ratification of requisite number of states on 21 June, 1985 and an agreement between United Nations and UNIDO was signed on 17 November, 1985. On 1 January, 1986 UNIDO became a fully autonomous specialized agency.

UNIDO is the chief coordinating body for industrial development. It encourages and assists the developing countries to promote and accelerate their industrialization. For this purpose it even co-ordinates, initiates and follows up UN activities. It serves as a useful forum for promotion of contact between the industrialized and developing countries. It encourages investments and promotes transfer of technology to and between developing countries.

The usual method adopted by UNIDO to attain its objectives is to promote meetings between industrialized and developing countries with a view to accelerate industrialisation by encouraging the involvement of Governments and industry. It formulates plans in the public, cooperative and private sectors to promote industrial development. It also renders assistance in the formulation of regional industrial development plans.

UNIDO also provides technical assistance in the industrial development by organising industrial training programmes, providing advisory services, and rendering assistance to countries in obtaining fair and equitable external financing. It acts as a clearing house for industrial information. It collects, analyses, publishes and standardizes and improves industrial statistics.

Organisation

The General Conference is the principal organ of the UNIDO. It determines the guiding principles and approves the budget. It also adopts conventions and agreements. The other important organ of UNIDO is 53 member Industrial Development Board which reviews, Conference approved programmes and makes recommendations. In addition there is a 27 member Programme and Budget Committee, which as its name suggests, is concerned with the determination of Programmes and formulation of Budget.

INTERNATIONAL ATOMIC ENERGY AGENCY (IAEA)

This agency was approved by the Statute of the International Atomic Energy Agency adopted in 1956 at the International Conference held at the UN Headquarters, but actually came into existence in 1957. The same year the General Assembly approved an agreement concerning IAEA's relationship with the United States. The agency is located at Vienna (Austria) and is headed by a Director General.

The policy and programmes of the Agency are directed by the General Conference comprising of all the member states of IAFA. These members meet once a year. In addition there exists a Board of Governors comprising of 35 members, which also plays an important role in the formulation of policies and programmes.

Aims and Activities

The two main objectives of IAEA are to accelerate and enlarge the contribution of atomic energy to peace, health and prosperity through the world; and to ensure that the assistance provided by it, or at its request, or under its supervision or control, is not used to further any military purpose.

The agency fosters and guides the development of peaceful uses of atomic energy. It establishes standards for nuclear safety and environmental protection. It helps the member countries through technical cooperation and fosters the exchange of scientific and technical information.

One of the main function of IAEA is to apply safeguards to ensure that nuclear materials and equipment intended for peaceful users are not diverted to military purposes. For this purpose the IAEA can conclude various types of safeguards agreements. Over 199 safeguards agreements with over 118 states were in force on 31 December, 1994.

In the safety area, IAEA concentrated on establishing priorities for safety upgrading of various reactor types and on providing expert assistance and guidance. It also adopted an expanded safety programme covering the areas of safety of nuclear installations, radiation protection, health, radioactive waste management, nuclear power and the nuclear fuel cycle.

IAEA advises and assists the government through technical assistance programme to promote the transfer of skills and knowledge so that the recipient countries can carry out their atomic energy programmes more efficiently and safely. It provides advisers, equipment and training to member states.

IAEA formulates basic safety standards for radiation protection and issues regulations and codes of practice on specific type of operations, including the safe transport of radioactive materials. It also provides emergency assistance to the member states in the event of a radiation accident.

The IAEA through its International Nuclear Information System in Vienna collects information on all aspects of nuclear science and technology and disseminates the same. IAEA also collaborates with other UN agencies like UNESCO, FAO, and WHO etc. Thus it collaborates with FAO in research on atomic energy in food and agriculture and with WHO on radiation in medicine and biology. Likewise the Marine Environment Laboratory of IAEA in Monaco carries out worldwide marine pollution studies with UNEP and UNESCO.

Thus we find that the activities of the IAEA cover quite a wide field.

GENERAL AGREEMENT ON TARIFFS AND TRADE (GATT)

The General Agreement on Tariffs and Trade(GATT) is a multilateral instrument which came into force on I January, 1948 and laid down agreed rules for international trade. The basic aim of GATT is to liberalize world trade with a view to promote economic growth and development and welfare of the people all over the world. These objectives are to be achieved through reduction of trade barriers and other measures distort competition; to resolve the trade disputes through conciliation. The GATT not only lays down the code of rules for international trade relations but also provides a forum to the countries where they can discuss and overcome their trade problems and negotiate to enlarge world trading opportunities.

The basic principles on which GATT operates are : (i) the trade should be conducted on the basis of non-discrimination; (ii) that where protection is given to domestic industry, it should be extended essentially through the customs tariff and not through other commercial measures; (iii) that tariffs should be reduced through multilateral negotiations and be 'bound' against subsequent increase; and (iv) that Contracting Parties should consult together to overcome trade problems.

So far eight rounds of negotiations to free the international trade have been held. The first round was held at Havana in 1947 in which 23 countries took part and founded GATT. They exchanged tariff cuts for 45,000 products worth $10 billion of trade on an annual basis. The second round was held at Annecy (France) in 1949. In this round another ten countries joined and the customs duties were reduced for another 5000 items. The third round was held at Torquay (Britain) in 1951 which was attended by 38 members. These members adopted 8,700 tariff reductions. The fourth round was held at Geneva in 1956 in which 26 countries participated. They decided to further cut duties for goods worth $2.5 billion of trade. The fifth round was again held at Geneva in 1960-62. At this round a new common external tariff of the European Community was negotiated. It was decided to cut custom duties on further 4,400 items. The sixth round of talks, popularly known as Kennedy Round, were held at Geneva from 1964-67. More than 50 countries agreed to cut tariffs for industrial goods by upto 50 percent. They also assigned agreements on grains and chemical product and formalised a code on anti-dumping duties. The seventh round was held in Tokyo from 1973-79. The 99 participants cut customs duties by 20-30 percent for goods with a traded value of $300 billion. The members also negotiated improved trading framework codes covering subsidies, technical carriers to trade, public procurement and customs valuation rates. The eighth and final round was held in Uruguay from 1986 to 1993 in which originally 105 countries were involved. It covered complex new areas such as agriculture and services, including banking, insurance and telecommunications. After protracted negotiations a draft treaty popularly known as Dunkel Draft was prepared. The main objectives of the proposals were to open up the world market, particularly the developing countries to agriculture, manufactured goods and services, ; to reduce the existing tariffs by at least one-third; and to improve the productivity in the industrial as well as the farming sector by making use of the on-going improvements in technology and seeds. The Dunkel Proposals also required the member countries to open up their economics to the services like banking and insurance from other countries to make this sector more competitive and efficient.

The Dunkel Proposals evoked strong reactions among the third world countries which expressed apprehension that the proposals were drafted to serve the interests of the developed Test, particularly the United States. However, in view of the global recession the developing countries were compelled to re-orient their trade policies and they could not think of pulling out of an organisation which represented about 90 percent of the world trade. Therefore, most of the developing countries ratified the proposals after suggesting some changes to suit their local conditions and requirements. Ultimately in April 1994 an accord was approved and adopted in Marrakech(Morocco), which would come into effect in 1995 after approval by legislatures of the member countries.

The accord is expected to pave way for greater market access for all the member countries by slashing the import duties on thousands of manufactured goods by an average of about 37 per cent. This is expected to revolutionise the world trade and may boost the global income by $ 200 billion to $ 300 billion a year for over ten years after 1995. The pact has also raised hopes of higher employment, more investment and more trade. The other important features of the world treaty are that for the first time rules will govern services like banking, insurance, travel and movement of labour; for the first time agriculture has been folded into GATT and quotas converted into tariffs, which have been reduced by 36 per cent for industrialised country and 24 per cent for poor nations. These cuts will be implemented over six years by rich countries and 10 years by others. Trade distorting support for farmers has been cut by 20 per cent, over six years, in rich countries and 13.3 per cent for the developed world, while the poorest countries have been exempted from the farm reforms. Import quotas on textiles and clothing will be phased out over 10 years. Rules on imports priced below their value in the domestic market have been clarified to check dumping. The Treaty has also toughened protection for patents, copyrights, trademarks etc.

The accord is likely to immensely benefit the developing countries. According to IMF the Uruguay round will put $ 70 billion a year into the pockets of the developing countries if they rise to the challenges of the world trade. It would also lead to increased efficiency in the use of domestic resources, economies of scale in production and technology transfer. Above all, higher growth in the world economy and increased access to the markets of industrial countries will improve the external environment for developing countries.

With the establishment of World Trade Organisation (WTO) on I January 1995, the functions which were earlier being performed by GATT were taken over by the WTO and all the members of GATT became its members following acceptance of Uruguay Round Agreement and submission of commitment on trade in goods and services.

The organization of GATT comprised of a Session of Contracting Parties which met annually. It took decisions by consensus and not by vote. In between these Sessions, the Council of Representatives took action on both routine and urgent matters. The other important organs of GATT were the Committees on Trade and Development, Balance-of-Payments Restrictions and Textiles, as well as the high level Consultative Group of Eighteen.

WORLD TRADE ORGANISATION (WTO)

The World Trade Organisation was set established on I January 1995 to oversee international trade. This function was earlier being performed by the General Agreement on Tariffs and Trade (GATT). In fact all the 128 members countries of GATT automatically became members of WTO as a result of acceptance of the Uruguay Round Agreement and submission of commitments on trade in goods and services.

Organisation

The highest body of WTO is the Ministerial Conference, which meets at least once in every two years and can take decisions on all matters under any of the multilateral trade agreements. The day-to-day activities are looked after by the General Council. Its mandate includes supervision of bodies relating to dispute settlement and trade policy reviews of WTO members. The General Council can delegate its responsibilities to other committees and bodies viz. the Council for Trade in Goods, the Council for Trade in Services and the Council on Trade Related Aspects of Intellectual Property Rights. The headquarters of WTO is located at Geneva (Switzerland). It is headed by a Director General.

Aims and Activities

The WTO administers the 28 agreements on international trading relations contained in the final act of the Uruguay Round of Trade Negotiations which was approved at a meeting in Marrakesh (Morocco) in 1994. In addition to this WTO also administers a number of plurilateral agreements, notably on government procurement and civil aircraft. It may be noted that WTO is more extensive than GATT because it provides the sole legal and institutional foundation for the multilateral trading system. Whereas GATT was applied on a provisional basis, the WTO will be legally binding. It also provides principal contractual obligations determining how Governments frame and implement domestic trade legislation and regulations.

The functions of WTO include (i) the administration and implementation of multilateral and plurilateral trade agreements which make up the WTO Agreements; (ii) to act as a forum for multilateral trade negotiations among its members; (iii) to seek to resolve trade disputes among WTO members; (iv) to oversee national trade policies of its members; and (v) to cooperate with other international institutions involved in global economic policy-making.

The WTO regularly examines the trade regimes of individual members and acts as watchdog on international trade. The members are expected to notify in detail the various trade measures and statistics on the basis of which WTO maintains a large database. The trade disputes between members, which cannot be solved through bilateral talks, are adjudicated under the WTO Dispute Settlement Body

The WTO follows the code of conduct for international trade established by GATT. This includes the principle of non-discrimination between trading partners–the 'most favoured nation' clause–and equal treatment for imports and domestic goods in internal markets. WTO agreements provide for phasing out or reducing the protectionistic policies in important areas like textiles, clothing and agriculture. The WTO Secretariat helps the developing countries in the implementation of the Round through a newly established Development Division and a strengthened Technical Cooperation and Training Division.

It may be noted that far reaching reductions in tariffs and other trade barriers were brought about as a result of eight major negotiating rounds in GATT. The more significant rounds were the first round at Geneva in 1947; the Kennedy Round of 1964-67; the Tokyo Round (1973-79); and the Uruguay Rounds of 1986-1994. It may be further observed that the International Trade Centre established by GATT in 1964 is now working as a joint subsidiary organ of *WTO* and the United Nations. This Centre assists the developing countries in export promotion. It provides information and advice on export markets and marketing techniques and helps in establishing export services and training personnel.

In addition to the international agencies about which we have dealt at some length, there are numerous other agencies about which it is not possible to deal within the limited space available at our disposal, hence we have to per force skip them.

As regards the general role of these agencies they have generally contributed to the understanding and solving of the basic economic and social problems of the mankind. They have played an important role in fostering international co-operation and improving the conditions of the people all over the world. Some of the benefits which we are inclined to take for granted such as international mail service, improved standards of labour, facilities of international communication by telegraph, telephones, cable and radio, weather data from all parts of the world; reasonable foreign exchange procedure; high safety standards for international air travel; closer economic and cultural relations among the states; assistance in fighting of epidemics and plague and general improved health standards, etc. are largely due to these international agencies. They have certainly contributed to the development of more healthy and co-operative international relations.

FURTHER READINGS

UN Publication — *Everyone's United Nations*

UN Publication — *Basic Facts about the United Nations*

Jacob and Atherton — *The Dynamics of International Organisation*

Robert Cox (ed) — *International Organisation and World Politics: Studies in Economic and Social Agencies*

Elmandjra Mahdi — *The United Nations System: An Analysis*

Martin Hill — *The United Nations System: Coordinating its Economic and Social Work*

H. Spaull — *The Agencies of the UN: A Survey of Economic and Social Achievements*

Chapter 17
PEACEFUL SETTLEMENT OF INTERNATIONAL DISPUTES

U. N. CHARTER AND PEACEFUL SETTLEMENT OF DISPUTES

In modem times the war has become so costly, destructive and unpredictable in its results, that states have shown keen interest to follow peaceful methods for the settlement of their disputes. These methods interpose some delay which helps the tempers of the parties to the dispute to cool down. The Hague Conferences as well as the Covenant of the League of Nations also emphasised the importance of the pacific methods of settlement. The UN Charter also emphasises the need of peaceful settlement of disputes. Article 2 of UN Charter states "All members shall settle their international disputes by peaceful means in such a manner that peace and security, and justice are not endangered." Article 33 of the Charter outlines the various methods of pacific settlement of disputes. It provides "The parties to any dispute, the continuance of which is likely to endanger the maintenance of international peace and security, shall first of all seek a solution by negotiation, enquiry, mediation, conciliation, arbitration, judicial settlement, resort to regional agencies or arrangements or other peaceful means of their choice." It is noteworthy that the various techniques of pacific settlement of disputes enumerated by the UN Charter were known to international law and practised even before the advent of the United Nations. The UN Charter has merely recognised the existence of these methods of pacific settlement and encourages their use.

Apart from Art. 33 the UN Charter also contains provisions regarding peaceful settlement of disputes in other articles. For example Art. 36(l) provides that the Security Council may, at any stage of a dispute of the nature referred to in Article 33 or of a situation of a like manner, may recommend appropriate method of adjustment. Again Art. 36(3) enjoins upon the Council to see that legal disputes brought to its attention are referred to the International Court of Justice in accordance with the provisions of the Statute of the Court. Likewise Article 37 lays down that should the parties to a dispute, of the nature referred to in Article 33, fail to settle it by means indicated in that article, they are required to refer it to the Security Council.

Chief Methods of Pacific Settlement

Before we discuss the various methods of pacific settlement outlined by the UN Charter, it may be pointed out that most of these methods, with the exception of negotiation, involve the assistance of the third parties viz. the representatives of states or organisations which are not directly involved in the disputes. Further, most of these methods are political rather than judicial in nature insofar as the parties to the dispute are left free to accept or reject the proposed settlements, keeping inview their interests and capacities. But two methods viz. arbitration and adjudication are legal in nature because the decision is supposed to be taken on the basis of international law rather than national interest and power. Further the decisions are legally binding on the parties. The main methods of pacific settlement of dispute specified in the UN Charter are as under:

1. **Negotiation**. This is the simplest method of pacific settlement of disputes. It is the legal and orderly administrative process by which the governments, in the exercise of their unquestionable powers, conduct their relations with one another and discuss, adjust and settle their differences. Usually the negotiations are carried on either by the heads of the states or their accredited agents. The initiative in starting the negotiations is taken by the disputant states. Generally the negotiations are preceded by an exchange of correspondence to clear points of controversy. India and Pakistan resorted to this method for resolving their outstanding disputes and held negotiations at Simla after Indo-Pak War of 1971.

   The negotiations can lead to one of the following results: (i) The claims of one party may be acknowledged by the other party and the dispute may be settled, (ii) It may lead to a happy compromise to the satisfaction of both the parties, (iii) One of the party to the dispute may waive its rights and interests in the interest of general international peace, (iv) The negotiating parties may not be able to arrive at any settlement and get convinced about the inadequacy of negotiation as a method for settlement of their dispute and think of resorting to some other method of settlement of dispute.

2. **Good Offices**. This is another important method of pacific settlement of disputes, even though it does not find mention in Article 33 of the UN Charter. Under this method friendly assistance maybe rendered by a third party to bringing the disputants together so that they may seek to reach a settlement. It is noteworthy that the party which offers good offices does not participate in the negotiations. Good offices may be offered by a state, a group of states, or even by an individual of international standing such as the UN Secretary General. It is upto the parties to the dispute to accept or reject the offer of good offices. In 1951 when Australian Government offered its good offices to India and Pakistan for the settlement of their dispute, the offer was turned down by Indian Prime Minister(Jawaharlal Nehru) on the ground that the' good offices were not needed at that stage. Later on in 1965 during the Indo-

Pakistan conflict, Soviet Union offered her good offices to bring the two countries to a conference table. The offer was accepted by both the countries and a meeting between President of Pakistan (Ayub Khan) and Prime Minister of India (Lal Bahadur Shastri) took place at Tashkent which culminated in the signing of the Tashkent Declaration on 10 January 1966.

3. **Mediation.** Under this method the third party either on its own initiative or at the request of the disputant parties assumes responsibility for the settlement of the dispute. In this method the mediator acts as a middleman and tries to reconcile the opposite claims of the disputant parties. This involves the active participation of the mediator. However, the suggestions of the mediator are not binding on the parties to the dispute. This method was utilised to resolve dispute between India and Pakistan by the United Nations when it appointed Dixon, a judge of Australia, as mediator and charged him with the responsibility of helping in the preparation and supervision of the programme of demilitarization in the disputed area. It may be observed that though both in Good Offices and Mediation, the third parties are involved, but their role differs under the two. In good offices the third party tries to call negotiations into being without actually participating in the negotiations. On the other hand under mediation the mediating party takes an active part in the negotiations.

4. **Conciliation.** This is yet another method of pacific settlement of disputes and is regarded as more effective than the methods of good offices and mediation. Under this method the dispute is referred to a Commission of inquiry by the disputants themselves. The Commission investigates the facts of the dispute and makes suggestions for solution. However, these suggestions or recommendations are not binding on the disputants. Conciliation is more formal and less flexible than mediation. It involves formal submission of the dispute to a conciliation body in anticipation of final report containing the conciliators findings and recommendations for settlement. Some scholars like Prof. Ross have expressed doubts about the effectiveness of conciliation as a method for pacific settlement of disputes. He holds that the members of the UN are likely to submit the disputes to the Security Council which is a tried Organisation rather than a Committee of Conciliation. But this view is not shared by Prof. Mookerjea who holds "The Security Council and the General Assembly of the UN are troubled with so many hydro-headed problems, that Conciliation Commission are bound to relieve the congestion of business in these vital organs of the U.N." The actual experience of the UN has also shown that this method has been successfully utilised to deal with certain problems. For example this method was quite helpful in dealing with the problem of Palestine.

5. **Arbitration.** This is one of the most important methods of pacific settlement of disputes. Under this method the parties to a dispute refer their case to an individual or a small group of individuals. The parties to dispute state their case before this arbitrator and undertake to honour

the decision of the Arbitrator. This is a sort of semi-judicial method of settling a dispute.

6. **Judicial Settlement or Adjudication.** This is yet another method of pacific settlement of dispute. It differs from arbitration insofar as the judges for the settlement of the dispute are not chosen by the parties, but are members of a pre-constituted international court. They accept the authority of these judges either through voluntary acceptance through advance agreement to accept the jurisdiction of the court in special types of cases or through an agreement at the time of the submission of dispute. International Court of Justice provides the principal example of judicial settlement at the global level. It may be noted that Arbitration and adjudication fundamentally differ from each other. Arbitration is more elastic than adjudication. Through adjudication only legal disputes can be settled, while Arbitration is helpful for settlement of both legal and political disputes. Arbitration is also more simple and cheaper than adjudication. It is noteworthy that both arbitration and adjudication are legal rather than political techniques for the settlement of disputes. They are also more formal than other techniques and have proved more successful in resolving the disputes as compared to the political techniques. These methods insist on abstract justice and there is no scope for compromise.

A perusal of the various methods of pacific settlement of disputes shows that they broadly fall in two categories viz. those which are persuasive in character and lack binding force; and those which have a binding character insofar as the parties commit themselves in advance to accept the findings. While negotiations, good offices, enquiry, mediation and conciliation belong to the first category; arbitration and judicial settlement fall under the second category.

ROLE OF UNITED NATIONS IN SETTLEMENT OF DISPUTES

The United Nations has played an important role towards the settlement of disputes referred to it. According to one study, of the 123 disputes referred to the UN between 1945-1981, it helped settle 28 cases, most of them before 1970. Further, it also contributed to the reducing of intensity of conflicts, isolating the conflicts, and prevented third parties from intervening diplomatically or militarily in favour of a disputant, and helped in stopping armed hostilities. It has been asserted that the United Nations would have done still better if it had the legal right and the potentiality of enforcement. Even within the present limitations, the UN was able to prevent war of global nature and no conflict could pose a threat to the existence of system of independent states. In this respect apart from the International Court of Justice, the Security Council and the Secretary General have also played an important role.

The role of the United Nations with regard to resolution of disputes has differed with regard to various disputes. In some cases it succeeded in bringing about permanent settlement viz. Soviet Union's withdrawal of troops from Iran in 1946; the withdrawal of Soviet troops from Afghanistan in 1988; the establishment of independent state of Indonesia in 1950; establishment of independent state of Namibia in 1990; withdrawal of British and French troops from Syria, Lebanon and in the Suez crisis. In some cases like Palestine and Kashmir, the United Nations succeeded in putting a stop to hostilities and provided the basis for negotiations for settlement of outstanding issues. In some cases the United Nations failed to achieve any success viz. in Korea in 1950 and the Gulf War in 1991. In fact in both these cases the UN failed to project itself as an impartial body and identified itself with one of the parties to the dispute.

The varying success of UN was due to number of factors. In cases where the UN acted with promptness, it met with considerable success. The selection of persons to act as mediator also had an impact on the outcome of the result. For example in Kashmir, Korea, Palestine and Balkans much success could not be achieved due to indecisive nature of the members of the Commission. It is highly important that only those persons should be chosen as members of commissions who possess qualities of integrity, impartiality and discretion.

The discussion of disputes at various forums of United Nations has exercised profound influence on public mind throughout the world and has led to rational handling of the various international disputes. The rational and pragmatic approach adopted by the UN for resolution of disputes has also helped in reducing tension and encouraged the parties to dispute to adopt more realistic approach.

A noteworthy point about the role of UN in resolution of disputes is that the Security Council has been able to play more effective role than other organs. The 'veto' in the Security Council has not stood in the way of Security Council discharging its responsibilities towards peaceful settlement of disputes. In fact the 'veto' has obliged the Security Council to adopt more acceptable approach towards the resolution of disputes. Another point which deserves special attention is that the success of the United Nations in resolving international disputes has to a large extent dependent on the amount of support extended by the Great Powers. The UN has not been able to force, a solution which was not acceptable to a great power.

In conclusion it can be said that the role of United Nations in resolving international disputes through peaceful methods has been quite impressive, particularly when we keep it in mind that the disputes are referred to the United Nations only when they cannot be resolved by the disputant parties. The UN provides a forum where various possibilities of resolving the dispute peacefully can be explored.

FURTHERREADEQGS

Inis L. Claude Jr	*Swords Into Ploughshares*
Svarlien	*An Introduction to the Law of Nations*
L.M. Goodrich and A.P. Semons	*The United Nations and the Maintenance of International Peace and Security*
Y. Venkataraman	*The Ways of the Peacemaker. A Study of UN Intermediary Assistance in the Peaceful Settlement of Disputes*

Chapter 18
Collective Security And U. N.

"Collective security is not a scheme to keep some nations in check and not others. Rather, it is a plan by which any nation that uses forces illegally will be defeated."

-A. F. K. Organski

The concept of collective security was evolved with a view to check aggression and provide security to all the nations. Under this system the nations of the world pledge themselves to stand together against the aggressor nation; isolate it and overwhelm it by their superior power. Sometimes actual use of force is not made and a mere threat of action by a collectivity may oblige the aggressor to give up its proposed plans of aggression due to fear of being cut off from the markets and sources of supply all over the world. It may be observed that the device of collective security cannot be practiced by a single nation and a number of powers have to collaborate. The benefits accruing as a result of this collaboration are also shared by all the nations. According to Organski "by making themselves in advance to stand by one another in case of aggression against any nation, the nations of the world would not only be able to stop aggression in its tracks; they would prevent it from occurring in the first place."[1]

Meaning of Collective Security

The concept of collective security is quite complex and scholars have offered different definitions. According to Schwarzenberger collective security is "The machinery for joint action in order to prevent or counter any attack against the established international order." Prof. Schleicher defmes collective security as "an arrangement among states in which all promise, in the event any member of the system engages in certain prohibited acts against another member, to come to the latter's assistance." Prof, Morgenthau offers a very brief but appropriate definition of collective security. He says it is based on the principle of 'one for all and all for one'. Under this system security becomes the concern of all nations and they take care collectively of the security of each of them as though their own security were at stake.

---

1. Organski, *International Politics, p.408*

Basic Assumptions of Collective Security

According to Organski, the idea of collective security rests upon five assumptions

1. In the first place it assumes that in any armed combat all the nations will agree on which combatant is the aggressor.

2. Secondly, all the nations are equally interested in stopping aggression from whatever source it comes. Neither friendship nor economic advantage will stand in the way of action against an aggressor.

3. Thirdly, all nations are free and able to join in action against an aggressor.

4. Fourthly, the combined power of the collectivity will be great enough to overwhelm the aggressor.

5. Finally, knowing that an overwhelming power stands ready to be used against it, the agrressor nation will either sheathe its sword or go down in defeat.

Let us examine the assumptions underlying the principle of collective security and find out how far they are correct.

The first assumption that all nations agree as to which combatant is aggressor is not fully correct because in actual practice there is rarely an agreement among various nations regarding aggressor. Generally each nation denies that it started as aggressor and tries to project that it was forced to act on account of opponent's aggression. The friends of the aggressor also support this contention, while the friends of the victim protest. The ultimate decision as to who is aggressor in a particular war depends on who wins it. For example, the victorious Allies held Germany guilty of committing aggression and starting the world war. Further lack of a clear definition of aggression also makes it difficult to determine the aggression. Sometimes a mere threat of use of force can constitute an aggression. For example the taking over of Czechoslovakia by Hitler without use of force was an aggresion. Aggression can also assume ideological and economic overtones. It is well-known that Iran was brought to its knees by the Western powers by refusing to buy its oil after it nationalized the industry and threw out the British. The ideological attacks also constitute an aggression. Organski refers to the propaganda carried by Joseph Goebbels (Hitler's minister of Propoganda) and points out "how deadly such attacks can be in developing home-grown traitors and in weakening a victim's will to fight once military aggression occurs."[1] In short, it can be said that in the absence of a clear definition of aggression, aggressive acts can be disguised and even when they are committed openly, claims and counter claims can be launched as to which side started it.

The second assumption underlying collective security that all nations are interested in preventing or stopping aggression is also not quite correct History shows that the aggressors are not always alone and are generally

1. Organski, *International Politics,* p. 412

supported by their friends. Further, some nations are more interested in stopping aggressions than others. Therefore Organski says it is a mistake "to believe that peace and security are universal goals of all nations over-riding all others. When nations are immediately and severely threatened, security may fact take precedence over all other concerns, but in the normal run of events, security can be taken for granted and peace is only one of many national goals." [1]

The third assumption of collective security that the nations possess the ability to take action against the aggressor is also not correct. For example, a small country on the borders of a potential aggressor would not be willing to collaborate in any venture to stop the aggressor. Knowing it fully well that this would cause great damage as the battles to stop the aggressor are quite likely to be fought upon its territory. The states may not join in action against aggressor on account of a number of other reasons viz. their troops are committed elsewhere; they require the help of the aggressor to defend themselves against aggression from other quarters; or the aggressor happens to be their valued ally; or because of close economic links with the aggressor.

Thus we have noted that the first three assumptions underlying the collective security are wrong.

The fourth assumption underlying collective security that the collectivity is strong enough to keep peace is quite correct. No single nation, howsoever strong, is able to win victory against the combined strength of all other nations of the world. Today with the exception of USA and Soviet Union, there is no nation that can successfully resist a coalition of other powers. In fact probably even these super powers would not be able to stand against the combination of the rest of the world. Therefore, the assumption that no nation can successfully resist the combined might of all other states is quite correct,

The final assumption of collective security that peace is based on preponderant power is also correct. When a would be aggressor is faced with the certainty of a united opposition from the rest of the world, it is likely to give up its plans for aggression as hopeless. This is confirmed by history. For example during the period 1815 to 1914 the world enjoyed peace on account of preponderance of Britain which favoured maintenance of order.

According to Organski 'In a sense, the whole idea of collective security is an attempt to recreate artificially the kind of imbalance of power that guaranteed world peace in the years before world war I. The crucial difference of course is, that the earlier imbalance was caused by the power advantage of a specific group of three nations (Britain, France and the United States) who controlled the dominant positions in an international order based on their supremacy. The imbalances hoped for by the advocates of collective, on the other hand, is to be a completely artificial creation built upon the combined strength of whatever group of nation is left when aggressor is subtracted. Its unity is to be provided by principle alone, not by any common interest in any particular kind of world."[2]

1 & 2. Organski, *International Politics,* p.415

Development of Collective Security

Though President Wilson of USA is generally regarded as the enunciator of the concept of collective security in international politics, the idea is much older. We can trace its origin in the Treaty of Osnabruck concluded in the seventeenth century and William Penifs Scheme of European Order. Even the Tripple formed by Germany, Austria and Italy and the Tripple Entente formed by France, Britain and Russia in the last quarter of the nineteenth centuries were typical examples of the collective security arrangements. Both these alliances were formed to meet a probable threat to the safety and integrity of the member states. This arrangement however lasted till the first world war and ceased to exist thereafter. The concept of collective security in its modem sense was enunciated by President Wilson and it was chiefly due to his efforts that his principle was incorporated in the Covenant of the League of Nations. Wilson put forth this idea because he was convinced that the system of balance of power which had regulated the international relations all thses years had resulted in frequent wars. He therefore expressed his earnest desire to create an organisation which should be powerful enough to implement collective security and ensure durable peace.

COLLECTIVE SECURITY UNDER THE CONVENANT OF THE LEAGUE OF NATIONS

The Covenant of League of Nations made elaborate provisions for collective security in Article 10 to 16. These provisions are based on three principles–(i) the causes of war should be eliminated; (ii) if there is a dispute between two or more states efforts should be made to see that it does not lead to war, and (iii) if despite the best of efforts the war break out it should help the member states who stand by the Covenant.

For a proper understanding of the collective security arrangements envisaged under the Covenant of the League it shall be desirable to have a brief idea of the provisions made in this regard. Article 10 of the Covenant stated "The members of, the League undertake to respect and preserve as against external aggression the territorial integrity and existing political independence of all Members of the League. In case of any such aggression or case of any threat or danger of such aggression, the Council shall advise upon the means by which this obligation shall be fulfilled." Article 11 asserted that any war or threat of war is a matter of concern to the whole League and it can take any action which it deems effective and proper for the preservation of the peace. It conceded to each member of League the friendly right "to bring to the attention of the Assembly or of the Council any circumstances affecting international relations which threaten to disturb international peace or the good understanding between nations upon which peace depends."

The Covenant sought to give effect to the provisions of collective security under Article 16 which provided (1) Should any Member of the League resort to war in disregard of its Covenants under Articles 12, 13 or 15, it shall *ipso facto* be deemed to have committed an act of war against all other Members of the League, which hereby undertake immediately to subject it to the severance of all trade or financial relations, the prohibition of all intercourse between their nations and the nationals of the covenant-breaking State, and the prevention of all financial, commercial or personal intercourse between the nations of the covenant-breaking State and the nations of any other State, whether a Member of the League or not. (2) It shall be the duty of the Council in such case to recommend to the several Governments concerned what effective military, naval or air force the Members of the League shall severally contribute to the armed forces to be used to protect the covenants of the League. (3) The Members of the League agree, further, that they will mutually support one another in the financial and economic measures which are taken under this Article, in order to minimise the loss and inconvenience, resulting from the above measures and that they will mutually support one another in resisting any special measures aimed at one of their member by the covenant-breaking State, and that they will take the necessary steps to afford passage through their territory to the forces of any of the members of the League which are cooperating to protect the covenant of the League. (4) Any Member of the League winch has violated any covenant of the League may be declared to be no longer a Member of the League by a vote of the Council concurred in by the representatives of all the other members of the League represented there on."

The Covenant extended the provisions to the non-members also and provided in Article 17 that "the Council may take such measures and make such recommendations as will prevent hostilities and result in the settlement of the dispute."

Thus the Covenant made quite elaborate provisions for collective security. However, the system suffered from a number of shortcomings. Firstly, it provided very limited circumstances under which the use of force by a state was to be considered an unlawful act. Secondly, the League could not take any enforcement action until the war was actually declared in violation of the Covenant.

During its existence of less than two decades the League made at least five efforts at collective security. Under the Treaty of Mutual Assistance 1923) aggressive war was an declared international crime. Under the Geneva Protocol (1924) the signatory states agreed not to resort war except with consent of the Council or the Assembly. The Council was authorised to apply necessary sanctions against the aggressor. In 1925 the Locarno Pact collectively guaranteed the frontier between Belgium and Germany and France and the signatory states pledged to come to the rescue of the state which fell victim to aggression. In 1928 Kellogg-Briand Pact was concluded under which the member states condemned recourse to war for the solution of international controversies and renounced war as an instrument of national policy. Finally, the League was instrumental in the conclusion of the General Act of 1928 which is considered as the most important single effort of the League to establish a system of collective security.

Despite the provisions contained in the Covenant and the various measures adopted by the League for collective security in actual practice the system of collective security could not operate effectively. For example in 1923 when Italy attacked and conquered the Greek island of Corfu, the League failed to take any action against Italy and referred the dispute to a Conference of Ambassadors for the settlement. This Conference decided the case in favour of Italy. Thus League virtually protected the aggressor. Again in 1931 when Japan occupied Central Manchuria and China moved the UN for action against Japan, the League failed to take any concrete action. The League merely passed a resolution calling upon the parties to dispute to withdraw their troops, but Japan paid no heed to this resolution. The next year Japan attacked Shanghai, and the Assembly passed a resolution calling upon Japan to evacuate the same. This time Japan complied with the resolution and quitted Shanghai. But Japan refused to vacate Manchuria and established an independent kingdom of Manchukuo. This action of Japan was condemned by the League but Japan did not pay any heed to League and persisted with the violation of the Covenant. League also failed to take appropriate action against Germany for resorting to re-armament in violation of the Covenant and other treaties.

In the case of Italian attack on Abyssinia, the League however decided to apply economic sanctions against Italy. But the Member states applied these sanctions in a half-hearted manner and thus rendered this action ineffective. In short, it can be said that the system of collective security introduced by the League of Nations could not work effectively because most of the member states, specially the Great Powers, were not willing to subordinate their national interests to the interests of the world, community.

COLLECTIVE SECURITY UNDER THE U.N. CHARTER

The U.N. Charter made more elaborate provisions for collective security and avoided the shortcomings in the system of collective security provided under the Covenant. In fact the very first article of U.N. Charter emphasised that the purpose of the United Nations is to "maintain international peace and security and to that end to take effective collective measures for the presevation and removal of threats to the peace, and for the suppression of acts of aggression of other breaches of the peace." But more elaborate provisions regarding collective security are made in Chapter VII (Articles 39 to 51) of the U.N. Charter.

Under Article 39 the Security Council can "determine the existence of any threat to the peace, breach of peace or act of aggression" and suggest measures for the maintenance or restoration of international peace and security. The measures which the Security Council can recommend include complete or partial interruption of economic relations and of rail, sea, air, postal, telegraphic, radio and other means of communication as well as severance of diplomatic relations. In case, the Security Council finds the above measures inadequate it can "take such action by air, sea or land forces as may be necessary to maintain or restore international peace and security.

Such action may include demonstrations, blockade and other operations by air, sea or land force of the members of the United Nations."

Under the UN Charter all the members of the United Nations are expected to make available to the Security Council on its call and in accordance with special arrangements or agreements, armed forces, assistance and facilities including rights of passage, necessary for the purpose of maintaining international peace and security." The members of the U.N. are obliged under Article 45 of the Charter to provide to the United Nations contingents of national airforce for combined international enforcement action. The strength and the plans for action are determined by the Security Council in consultation with the Military Staff Committee consisting of the Chiefs of the permanent members of the Security Council or their representatives. But probably the most important provision relating to collective security in Article 51 of the U.N. Charter which provides that "Nothing in the present Charter shall impair the inherent right of individual of collective self-defence if an armed attack occurs against a member of the United Nations, until the Security Council has taken the measures necessary to maintain international peace and security. Measures taken by members in the exercise of this right of self-defence shall be immediately reported to the Security Council and shall not in any way affect the authority and responsibility of the Security Council under the present Charter to take at any time such action as it deems necessary in order to maintain or restore international peace and security."

It is clear from the above provisions that the U.N. Charter has avoided some of the shortcomings of the system of collective security envisaged under the Covenant of the League. It has avoided discrimination between the big and small powers and involves all the members in the collective security measures. The members are expected to give to the United Nations every assistance in any action taken by the U.N. and to accept the decision of the Security Council in this regard. Further, it authorises the members to take preventive action against the members of the U. N. as well as non-members.

Elements of Collective Security

The basic elements of Collective Security are as follows:

1. First it prohibits use of force by the states in principle even though there are two exceptions viz. the Big Five Powers can take joint action for the maintenance of world security; and the states can use force for self-defence. According to critics the right to self-defence is antithetical to collective security.
2. Secondly, it envisages collective guarantees of security by all for all states. However, this provision is greatly undermined due to provision of veto which implies that no action can be taken by the Security Council without the consent of the Permanent members.
3. Thirdly, it envisages use of collective force as a deterrence to end aggression anywhere.
4. Fourthly, it implies automatism of collective action in case of aggression anywhere. Whereas under the Covenant of the League of Nations, any

resort to war was ipso facto a war against all other members of the League, which were obliged to take immediate action against the warring state, under the UN Charter the Security Council has to determine the crisis and decide the measures. In other words automatism is not a built-in feature of the UN Security scheme.

5. Fifth, collective security implies action against any aggressor and protection of victim in any part of the world. However, in actual practice the UN cannot take any effective action against the Big Five. This renders the principle of anonymity ineffective under the UN Security system.

A look at the above features of collective security envisaged under the UN system shows that it is not fully operational. This is partly due to the failure of the framers of the UN charter who did not have a clear concept of collective security, and partly because the world is not ready for the collective security.

Collective Security and Korea

The UNO for the first time applied provisions concerning collective security during the Korean aggression of 1950. The Security Council passed a resolution by 9 to 0 votes (with Soviet Union abstaining) asserting that North Korea had committed a clear breach of peace by resorting to armed attack on South Korea. It called upon North Korea to stop hostilities and withdraw its forces to 38th parallel. As North Korea failed to comply with the resolution, the Security Council decided to go ahead with police action. It set up a unified command under UN flag and requested the member states to render necessary military assistance. Out of the sixty members of UNO sixteen nations contributed fighting forces, forty-two nations sent material aid, and two members sent hospital units. Even though almost ninety per cent of the armed forces were contributed by United States and South Korea, the enforcement action was at least nominally collective. The Korean action, according to Cohen marked "the beginning of the progressive development of an effective collective security system."

However, the things became complicated after the intervention of Chinese communist forces in Korea on the side of North Korea. The Security Council which met to decide the course of action was prevented from taking any decision on account of Soviet veto. USA sought to overcome this difficulty and suggested that the General Assembly should have authority to take over a crisis when the Security Council is unable to take any action on account of veto by one of the permanent members. It moved a resolution along with France, Philippines, Turkey, UK, Canada and Uruguay which was adopted by the General Assembly in the face of tough opposition from Soviet Union and other communist states. This resolution popularly known as Uniting for Peace Resolution, asserted that the primary responsibility for the maintenance of world peace and security rests with the Security Council. But if the Council is unable to act because of veto of one of the permanent members the General Assembly can meet in an emergency session within twenty-four hours and make necessary recommendations. Such an emergency session can be called at the request of the seven members of the Security Council or the majority of the members of the UNO. The Resolution provided for a peace observation Commission consisting of fourteen members. The Commission was authorized to report to the General Assembly about tension in any part of the world which posed a threat to world peace. The resolution asked the member states to maintain within their armed forces certain elements so trained, organized and equipped that they could be immediately made available to the United Nations for service. It suggested the establishment of Fourteen-State Collective Measure Committee to study and make report to the Security Council and the General Assembly on the methods which might be used to maintain peace and security. The members of the UNO were urged to meet and discuss collectively all those problems which posed a threat to international peace and security, and reach an agreement on the various issues in accordance with the spirit of the U.N. Charter.

The Uniting for Peace Resolution was a significant step in the direction of the development of collective security. In the worlds of Ball and Killough the resolution salvaged "collective security by reinterpreting the Charter" and greatly expanded the authority of the General Assembly. Henceforth the Assembly could determine by two-thirds majority of its members the situations which posed a threat to the peace and security and could recommend necessary measure for meeting the situation.

Other Cases of Collective Security

In the subsequent years collective security measures were applied in a number of other cases. In 1956 following invasion of Sinai peninsula by the Israelis and subsequent armed action by Britain and France in Suez a serious threat was posed to world peace. However, the Security Council failed to discharge its primary responsibility for the maintenance of international peace and security on account of lack of unanimity among the permanent members. As a result the matter came up before the General Assembly in terms of Uniting for Peace Resolution. The Assembly urged immediate ceasefire and asked the UN members to refrain from introducing military goods in the area. It also requested the Secretary General to submit a plan for setting up an emergency international UN Force to secure and supervise the cessation of hostilities.

The same year the General Assembly was called upon to consider the Hungarian question following use ofveto by Soviet Union in the Security Council. The Assembly adopted a resolution and asked Soviet Union to withdraw its troops from Hungary. It also affirmed the right of the Hungarian people to have self-government. The resolution asked the Secretary General to investigate the situation and report his findings. However, the Secretary General was not permitted to enter Hungary by Soviet Union and no further enforcement action could be taken. This proved that if an aggression was committed by a permanent member the UNO could not take any effective enforcement action.

Yet another case where collective security measures were applied is that of Congo. In 1960 the Security Council on account of the civil strife in Congo, which had assumed serious dimensions due to involvement of big powers, passed a resolution urging Belgium to withdraw its troops from Congo. It also authorised the Security General to send peace forces. Twenty-nine nations actually contributed to these forces, which stayed in Congo for about four years and succeeded in preventing Congo from becoming a seed bed of a general war.

Another recent case of collective security was action against Iraq which had annexed Kuwait in August 1990 and refused to withdraw its troops from Kuwait despite several resolutions of the UN urging her to withdraw from Kuwait. Ultimately on 29 November, 1990 the Security Council passed a resolution authorising 'all necessary means' including force to drive the invading Iraqi troops out of Kuwait if Iraq failed to act by 15 January, 1991, to comply with the UN earlier calls for withdrawal from Kuwait. As Iraq refused to comply with the deadline set by the UN, the United States launched air attacks against Iraq. Thirty countries contributed forces which fought against Iraq for 42 days and liberated Kuwait from Iraq. These forces suspended their operations only after Iraq agreed to honour all the UN resolutions.

It may be noted that collective security operations in Gulf differed from collective security operations in Korea. While in Korea, the troops of various countries fought under the UN banner, in the Gulf Operation each individual country acted on its own. In 1950 the collective action in Korea became possible due to Soviet abstention on the day of voting. In 1990 it became possible due to changed climate of cooperation between United States and Soviet Union. Even China did not use the veto due to domestic compulsions. It may be noted that in both these cases the United States Played an active role. It has been asserted that U.S. played leading role for the furtherance of its own foreign policy interests rather than in the interest of international law or *world* body.

It is clear from the above account that in comparison with the League of Nations, the UNO has been abless to make more effective use of provisions of collective security. It successfully raised a force with the contingents of the member states to deal with situation arising in Middle East and Congo. It is offten argued that the UNO could achieve success in these cases because the major powers were not directly involved. As Prof. Schwarzenberger ha observed, collective security was effective against danger to peace from the middle powers and small states backed by the world power. UNO succeeded in creating an Emergency Force for the Middle East to supervise the cessation of hostilities against the wishes of two permanent members (U.K. and France) because the two Super Powers (USA and Soviet Union) were supported by the Afro-Asian bloc in the General Assembly.

Some statesmen and commentators have tended to regard NATO (North Atlantic Treaty Organisation) as a collective security arrangement. However, Prof. Inis L. Claude does not regard NAT'O as a collective security arrangement. He says "it does not purport to be an arrangement whereby a community proposes to put down any aggressor that might rise within its ranks; rather it is a design for joint resistance to possible aggression stemming from a particular power bloc external to the community. NATO is a system of selective security, embodying the principle of some for some, whereas collective security is dedicated to the concept of all for all. Far from contributing to the collective security ideal of disarmament, NATO is fundamentally concerned with the re-armament of its members in competition with the Soviet coalition."[1]

EVALUATION OF COLLECTIVE SECURITY SYSTEM

It is evident from the foregoing discussion that despite best efforts no effective security system has developed so far due to absence of requisite subjective conditions. According to Claude "Neither peoples nor governments have undergone the transformation of view points, attitudes and values which collective security demands." The system of collective security as it exists suffers from a number of serious shortcomings.

In the first place the system is described as 'unwise and dangerous' because under it no war can be localised and there is "every possibility of every war taking the shape of a world war." According to Claude collective security tends to increase the global use of violence by universalising every local war–by organising universal opposition to local aggression. Even on moral grounds, Claude finds it difficult to justify collective security because it "contemplates the indiscriminate punishment of entire populations for the misdeeds of their governments–in short it involves resort to war rather than *police action.*"[2]

Secondly, under the system of collective security there is scope for the existence of neutral states because a state is either on the side of the aggressor or a member of the collective enforcement machinery. This has naturally given a great set back to the concept of neutrality and encouraged some of the traditional neutral countries like Switzerland to keep out of United Nations.

Thirdly, the system of collective security has been rendered quite ineffective due to cold war between USA and USSR. Quite often the effectiveness of the system was undermined because of absence of unanimity amongst the permanent members. Prof. Schwarzenberger says "until the day when the Western and Eastern worlds no longer consider each other as the potential aggressors, collective security as envisaged under the Charter of the United Nations must remain a dead letter."

Fourthly, though the system of collective security is based on the principle of equal participation of all the states in the collective security measures, in reality it operates only with the help of powerful states. As a result the big states support only those collective security measures which are in keeping with their national interests. Walter Lipmann has rightly observed that "when the issue is less than the survival of the great nations, the method of collective security will not be used because it is just as terrifying to the policeman as it is to the law-breakers. It punishes the law-enforcing States, at least until

1. Inis L. Claude Jr., *Swords into Plow Shares,* P. 275
2. Inis L. Claude Jr., *Swords into Plow Shares,* P. 290

they have paid the awful price of victory, as much as the law-breaking State. Therefore, it cannot be used as a method of enforcement, for example, as a means of ensuring the inspection of laboratories and plants working with fissionable material. There would be little surgery if the surgeon had to amputate his own arm when he was called upon to amputate the patients leg. There would be little enforcement of law in our cities if in order to arrest burglars, murderers and violators of the traffic ordinances, the police had to start a fight in which the court house, the jail and their own homes were likely to be demolished. Men will not bum down the barn in order-to roast a pig; the method of collective security is, I repeat, too crude, too expensive and too unreliable for general and regular use. It proposes to achieve peace through show by calling upon great masses of innocent people to stand ready to exterminate great masses of innocent people. No world order can be founded upon such a principle; it cannot command the support of civilized men, least of democratic men who respect the individual and consider it the very essence of justice to distinguish between the guilty and innocent, the responsible and irresponsible."

According to Claude the goal of collective security has been "pursued more ardently and consistently in words than in deeds, and statesmen have regularly turned to other objectives when confronted with concrete situation of urgency. The world is very far from the satisfaction of the essential requirements for permitting the operation of a collective security system and such a system even if feasible is in fact a less attractive ideal than it has been considered."[1]

Despite the various shortcomings and the slow progress of the system of collective security it cannot be denied that "the principles embodied in the doctrine of collective security may serve as elements contributing to the empirical development by international organisation of a more effective approach to world order than has hitherto been realized."

The real significance of the theory of collective security lies in the fact that it has "inspired the growing recognition that war anywhere is a threat to order everywhere (and) has contributed to the maintenance of the realistic awareness that it is states which are the effective components of international society ... As a doctrinaire as formula for global panacea, collective security is a snare as well as a delusion; as a formulation of the reality of global involvements and the ideal of global responsibilities, it may be a vital contribution to the evolutionary development of the conditions of peace through international organization."[2]

CONDITIONS FOR SUCCESSFUL WORKING OF COLLECTIVE SECURITY

The system of collective security, with all its faults, is highly laudable and can greatly contribute to world peace and security if certain conditions are

1. Inis L. Claude Jr., *Swords into Plow Shares,* P. 293
2. *Ibid.*, pp. 293-94

provided for its proper working. In the first place the collective system should be capable of mustering sufficient strength against the potential or actual aggressor so that it may not be able to pose a challenge to the order. Secondly, the members of collective security system must possess same conception of security and must be willing to defend the same. Thirdly, the member states should be willing to subordinate their conflicting political interests to the common good defined in terms of collective security.

Let us examine how far these conditions are able in actual practice under the present conditions. In the first place it is too much to expect that all the states will be satisfied with the existing order. On the testimony of history we can say that there are always some states which are unhappy with the existing order and wish to bring about changes in it. This is bound to come in conflict with the collective security system which stands for the preservation of the *status quo*. Secondly, the successful operation of collective security depends on common conception of security. Unfortunately at present the international atmosphere is full of distrust and suspicion and the states hold contradictory views regarding security. As a result it is not quite easy to muster overwhelming strength which could act as a deterrence. George Schwarzenberger has rightly observed "Until the day when the Western and Eastern worlds no longer consider each other as the potential aggressor, collective security as envisaged under the Charter of the United Nations must remain a dead letter."

Finally the successful working of collective security requires that the states should be willing to subordinate their conflicting political interests for the sake of common good viz. they should be willing to take collective security measures against an aggressor without discrimination. Actually, the states are always motivated by the considerations of national interest and take a stand which is likely to promote the same. As Prof. Friedmann has observed "A successful system of collective security does not necessarily presuppose a complete abandonment of national independence or individuality. It does, however, require the submission of the individual national will to collective decision."[1] The states so far have not been able to rise above selfishness and are still guided by considerations of national interests. So long the, states are not prepared to rise above national interests and give preference to the higher principles of human interests or common good, collective security cannot be an effective instrument.

1. W. Friedmann, *In Introduction to World Politics*, p. 47

Chapter 19

UNITED NATIONS AND PEACE KEEPING

Maintenance of international peace and security is one of the major objectives of the United Nations. Ever since its inception the United Nations again and again has been called upon to prevent a dangerous situation from escalating into war, to persuade the opposing parties to resolve their differences through conference rather than resort to arms, and to stop fighting when the conflict actually takes place. It is true that the UN had to frequently face frustration and setbacks, but still it has persisted with efforts at peace-keeping. This implies that the United Nations has employed various means to prevent the dispute from arising or to stabilise the situation where the conflict arose. Usually it made use of methods like mediation, truce-teams, engagement of neutral forces etc. to prevent hostilities. However, when these methods did not yield the desired results, it sent military units to keep order in the disturbed areas, while the process of peaceful settlement was also underway. This peace-keeping force of the United Nations is different from any army engaged in collective security, in so far it is not sent to fight any enemy. It is an impartial body which does not aim at victory for one side or the other. It helps to contain and resolve conflict between hostile states. According to Jack Citrin "The peace keeping operations constitute a significant innovation in the activities of the United Nations with respect to the maintenance of international peace and security, an innovation in the context of both the Organisation's formal objectives as stated in the Charter and the empirical realities of the U. N. practices in the sphere before 1956."

Provisions Of Charter

The UN Charter contains several provisions concerning maintenance of peace and security by the UN and it shall be desirable to have an idea about these provisions. Article 39 of Charter provides "The Security Council shall determine the existence of any threat to the peace, breach of peace or act of aggression and shall make recommendations, or decide what measures, shall be taken ... to restore international peace and security. For this purpose the Security Council can recommend measures, not involving use of armed forces, to give effect to its decisions (Art. 41). But if these measures prove inadequate, it can take such action by air, sea, or land forces as may be necessary to maintain or restore international peace and security. Such action can include demonstrations, blockade and other operations by air, sea or forces of members. (Art. 42). The members are expected to contribute to the Security Council, on its call and in accordance with special agreements, armed forces, assistance and facilities for the maintenance of international peace and security (Art. 43). However, the Charter limits the intervention of the UN to matters which do not fall within the domestic jurisdiction of the member states, This has been done to assure that the UN does not get involved in international security problems like political demonstrations and riots.

The Charter also makes provision for a Military Staff Committee to assist the Security Council on matters pertaining to the military requirements for the maintenance of international peace and security. This Military Staff Committee consists of the Chiefs of Staff of all the permanent members of the Security Council or their representatives.

Peace Keeping Forces

The mandate for the UN peace-keeping force is defined by the Security Council which establishes the force under the command of the Secretary General. The peace-keeping forces are composed of contingents of troops made available by member states and financed by the international community. These forces try to prevent a recurrence of fighting, to restore and maintain order, to promote a return to normal conditions and to provide humanitarian assistance. For this purpose they can verify compliance with cease-fires, supervise troop withdrawals and patrol buffer zones. They have to maintain complete impartiality at all times and avoid any action that might affect the claims or positions of the parties. These forces are lightly armed and are permitted to use their weapons only in self-defence. The UN peace-keeping force has played an important role towards the preservation of peace in Congo, Cyprus and Middle East. In recognition of the commendable work done by the UN peace-keeping force in different parts of the world the United Nations was awarded Noble Peace Prize in 1988. The growing importance of the peace-keeping operations of the United Nations in recent years is evident from the fact that as compared to 13 such operations undertaken by the UN during the first 40 years of its existence, between 1988 and 1994, 21 new peace-keeping operations were mounted by the United Nations. It is note worthy that even the character of the peace-keeping has under gone a change in recent years. Most or the 13 operations set up before 1988 were traditional operations. They were largely military in composition and were to monitor cease-fires, control buffer zones and prevent a resumption of hostilities. In other words their main objective was to maintain calm on the front line, and to create an environment which was more conducive to a negotiated settlement. On the other hand the recent peace operations have been set up to implement a settlement already negotiated by the peace makers. As such these involve not only the traditional military activities but also a range of civilian responsibilities. In addition these peace keeping operations have sought to protect civilians and provide humanitarian assistance.

PROCEDURE FOR ESTABLISHMENT OF PEACE-KEEPING OPERATIONS

The proposal for the establishment of a peace-keeping operation can be mooted by the Secretary General, or a member state or group of states who are members of UN. Usually, three conditions must be met before such a proposal is accepted. First, the consent of the country or the countries involved must be obtained. Secondly, the proposal must enjoy broad support of the international community as well as majority of the members of Security Council (including all the five Permanent Members). Thirdly, the member states must be ready to volunteer personnel for the peace-keeping force.

The expenses for the peace-keeping forces are met either on voluntary basis by the member states or through budgetary provisions in the UN Budget. In the latter case the UN General Assembly has to make necessary allocations in the budget. The commander of the peace-keeping force is named by the UN Secretary General, who is in over-all command of the peace-keeping forces. The contingents of the peace force differ from normal soldiers in so far as they are not expected to use force, except in self-defence. In fact their mission is more diplomatic than military. On account of their non-traditional military role, the UN soldiers have often found themselves in dangerous situations. Sometimes they have been taken as hostages, as in Bosnia where a number of British, French and Belgian peace-keepers wee taken as hostages: or injured in cross fire as in fight between Bosnian and Serbs

Till 1992 UN set up 20 peace-keeping operations. Half of these were peace-keeping forces, while the other half were military observer missions. In-fact it is not possible to draw a clear line of demarcation between these two categories of operations because often unarmed military observers are attached to the peace-keeping forces, while specialist military units may be attached to the observer missions. This point is best demonstrated by the UNTAG operation in Namibia which has 4462 military personnel, 1500 police monitors, 945 elections supervisors provided by the governments and 1651 U. N. employees from 124 nationalities.

Various Peace Keeping Operations

The United Nations has been involved in several peace-keeping operations since its establishment. A study of these peace-keeping operations is of great importance because these operations constitute a significant innovation in the activities of the United Nations.

(i) ***Peace Keeping in Korea.*** The Korean crisis was the first test of the United Nations to stop aggression and maintain world peace. At the end of the second world war, Korea was divided into two parts. The areas north of the 38th parallel were placed under Soviet forces and the south of this line were placed under the U.S. forces. A Joint Commission of the two powers was also set up, with a view to establishing 'provisional Korea Democratic Government.' But as the Commission could not arrive at any agreement, the Korean question was taken to the United Nations in 1947, which made an unsuccessful bid to bring about a unified Korean State through nation-wide free elections. In 1948 separate governments came into being in South Korea and in North Korea.

On 25 June 1950 the United States as well as the United Nations Commission informed the United Nations that the North Korean forces had attacked the Republic of Korea. The same day a meeting of the Security Council was held which described the attack as a clear breach of peace and called upon the parties to immediately stop hostilities. It called for the withdrawal of North Korean forces to the 38th parallel. But as the fighting continued on 27 June 1950 the Security Council called upon the members of the UN to furnish such assistance to the Republic of Korea as might be necessary to repel the armed attack and restore international peace and security in the area. On 7 July 1951 the Security Council asked the member states to provide military forces to a unified command under United States. The command, which included the military forces of republic of Korea, was authorised to fly the UN flag and constituted the United Nations Command. Sixteen member states joined the competent units and 26 states offered assistance in one form or the other. The Soviet Union as well as People's Republic of China however, considered the decision of the Security Council as illegal. The Chinese sent their volunteer forces to fight on the side of North Korea.

The fighting in Korea continued until 27 July 1953 when an Armistic Agreement was signed. Under this agreement a Military Armistic Commission was established "to supervise the implementation of the Armistic Agreement and to settle through negotiations any violations of the Armistic Agreement". The UN Commission for the Unification and Rehabilitation of Korea, which replaced the UN Commission on Korea in 1950, remained in the country until 1973 when it was dissolved by the General Assembly in deference to the wishes of North and South Korea, who issued a joint communiqué that reunification should be achieved independently, without reliance upon outside force or its interference. In 1974 the General Assembly urged North and South Korea to continue their dialogue to expedite peaceful reunification. It also expressed the hope that the Security Council would in due course give consideration to the dissolution of the United Nations Command in conjunction with appropriate arrangements to maintain the Armistic Agreement, pending negotiations and conciliation between the two Korean Governments leading to a lasting peace between them.

In 1975 United States informed the Security Council that she was prepared to terminate the United Nations Command on 1 January 1976 provided agreement was reached on arrangements for maintaining the Armistic Agreement. The matter was again debated by the General Assembly in 1975 and it adopted two resolutions., The first resolution asked all the parties directly concerned to negotiate on arrangements to replace the Armistic Agreement so that the United Nations Command may be dissolved concurrently with arrangements for maintaining the Armistic Agreement. The second resolution called for an end to 'foreign interference' in Korea and called upon 'the real parties to the Armistic Agreement 'to replace it with a peace agreement in the context of the dissolution of United Nations Command, and the withdrawal of all the foreign troops stationed in South Korea under the flag of the United Nations. However, as the issue of withdrawal of foreign forces or peaceful reunification of Korea could not be resolved, the United Nations Command continues to carry out its functions and fulfil its obligations under the mandate of the Armistic Agreement.

In the meanwhile in July 1972 Democratic People's Republic of Korea and Republic of Korea issued a joint communique stating that their common aim was to promote national unity and seek reunification through peaceful means. Though the two Koreas signed two agreements. The first agreement related to reconciliation, non-aggression, cooperation and exchange between the North and South Korea. The second was in the form of a Joint Declaration on Denuclearization of Korean Peninsula, which envisaged inter-Korean inspections.

(ii) ***Peace Keeping in Middle East.*** The United Nations has been concerned with the problem of Middle East since its early days, and has made consistent efforts to find a lasting solution to the underlying political problems there.

The Palestinian Problem

The first problem which the UN was called upon to resolve in the Middle East related to the future of Palestine. The issue was brought before the United Nations in early 1947 when Palestine was a Mandate territory under United Kingdom. In November 1947 the UN General Assembly endorsed a plan submitted by the UN Special Committee on Palestine for the partition of the territory. The plan also provided for the creation of an Arab and Jewish state with Jerusalem to be placed under international status. However the plan was not accepted by the Palestinian Arabs or the Arab states. On 14 May 1948 the Assembly appointed Count Folke Bernadotte as United Nations Mediator to promote a peaceful adjustment of the situation in Palestine. The same day the United Kingdom relinquished its Mandate over Palestine and the State of Israel was proclaimed. The following day the Palestinian Arabs, assisted by Arab states, opened hostilities against the new state. The hostilities was brought to close through a truce called for by the Security Council and supervised by the United Nations Mediator with the help of a group of military observers known as United Nations Truce Supervision Organisation (UNTSO). In 1949 under the auspices of UN Acting Mediator armistic agreements were signed by Israel and four Arab countries viz. Egypt, Jordan, Lebanon and Syria. The UNTSO through Mixed Armistic Commission continued to supervise the application and observance of the terms of the agreements.

In July 1956 in the wake of Egypt's nationalisation of Suez Canal Company, Israel as well as France and United Kingdom intervened militarily against Egypt. As this posed a threat to peace, the General Assembly held an emergency meeting and called for a cease-fire and withdrawal of forces from

Egyptian territory. It authorised the establishment of the United Nations Emergency Force (UNEF), the first United Nations peace-keeping force. This force supervised the troops withdrawals and was deployed on Egyptian territory (with the consent of Egypt), to act as a buffer between Egyptian and Israeli forces. The peace-keeping force patrolled the Egypt-Israel armistic demarcation line and the international frontier to the South of Gaza strip and succeeded in establishing calm in the area. It also cleared the Canal, blocked as a result of the hostilities. In 1967 the UNEF was withdrawn at the request of Egypt.

Fresh hostilities broke out between Israel on the one hand and Egypt, Jordan and Syria on the other hand in June 1967. The Security Council gave an immediate call for cease-fire. After six days the hostilities came to an end. However, in the meanwhile Israel occupied Sinai and the Gaza Strip, the West Bank of the Jordan, including East Jerusalem, and part of Syrian Golan Heights. As per the decision of the Security Council, the Secretary General stationed UNTSO observers in the Golan Heights and Suez Canal sectors to supervise the cease-fire. On 4 July 1967 the General Assembly in a special session, called on Israel not to take any steps to alter the status of Jerusalem.

The Security Council outlined the principles on the basis of which lasting peace could be established in the Middle East in a resolution unanimously adopted on 22 November 1967. According to these principles Israeli armed forces were to be withdrawn from the territories occupied by her in the 1967 conflict; and the sovereignty, territorial integrity and political independence of all the states in the area were to be respected. These states were assured of the right to live in peace within secure and recognized boundaries free from threats or acts of force. The Resolution affirmed the need to guarantee free navigation through international waterways in the area and insisted on just settlement of refugee problem. The Council requested the Secretary General to designate a Special Representative for Middle East help to achieve a peaceful and accepted settlement in keeping with the above resolution. Gunnar Jarring of Sweden was appointed as Special Representative for Middle East. He initiated talks with Egypt, Israel and Jordan to find a peaceful settlement. These talks continued till 1973, but no significant progress could be made due to differences among parties on the basic issues.

In October 1973 fresh hostilities broke out when Egyptian forces in Suez Canal sector and Syrian forces on the Golan Heights, attacked Israeli positions. The Security Council adopted a resolution on 22 October 1973 urging the parties to cease fire and implement the resolution of November 1967. As the cease-fire could not be achieved the Security Council decided to set-up a new United Nations Emergency Force (UNEF II) comprising 7000 men who were initially stationed in the Egypt-Israel sector. On 21 December 1973 a Peace Conference on the Middle East was held at Geneva under the auspicious of United Nations and Co-Chairmanship of Soviet Union and United States. This conference was attended by Egypt, Israel and Jordan and took a decision to make use of services of Military Working Group to achieve disengagement of forces. These discussions also paved the way for an agreement between Egypt and Isreal on 18 January 1974 whereby Israel agreed to partial withdrawal from the occupied territory in the Sinai, a buffer zone controlled by UNEF was established. The disengagement was completed on 4 March 1974 with the help of UNEF. In September 1975 Israel and Egypt signed the second disengagement agreement which provided for further Israeli withdrawals. This withdrawal was completed in February 1976 and a larger new buffer zone was set up under the control of UNEF. Thereafter the Security Council continued to extend the mandate of UNEF, which ultimately lapsed in July 1979 when the mandate was not extended. However, UNTSO observers remained stationed in Egypt in accordance with the existing decision of the Council.

An agreement regarding disengagement of Israeli and Syrian forces was signed by the two parties in May l974. The agreement provided for an area of separation and for zones of limited forces and armaments on both sides of the area. It also called for the establishment of a United Nations Observer Force to supervise its implementation. Accordingly the Security Council decided to set up United Nations Disengagement Observer Force (UNDOF) comprising 1250 men. The UNDOF completed the process of disengagement in June 1974. However, the mandate of UNDOF was repeatedly extended and is still in operation.

At the initiative of United States direct negotiations between Egypt and Israel took place in 1977-78 which culminated in the conclusion of two agreements (known as Camp David Accords). The first agreement signed in Sept. 1978 related to framework for peace in the Middle East and the second signed in March 1979 related to framework for conclusion of peace treaty between Egypt and Israel. The General Assembly condemned 'all partial agreements and separate treaties', which violated the rights of the Palestinian people, and declared that the Camp David accords and other agreements had no validity insofar as they purported to determine the future of the Palestinian people and of the Palestinian territories occupied by Israel since 1967. However, Israel withdrew its forces from the entire occupied Sinai in three stages and withdrew all her forces by 1982. Thereupon the control of the territory was taken over by the Egyptians.

The General Assembly requested the Secretary General to convene a conference of all parties to the Arab-Israeli conflict, including PLO, as well as United States, the Soviet Union and other concerned states. In 1986 the Assembly called for setting up of a preparatory committee within the framework of the Security Council and with the participation of the Council's permanent members, to take the necessary action to convene the Conference. However, the Security Council failed to comply with these recommendations of the Assembly.

In 1987 Palestinians in the occupied territories declared that the uprising would continue until Palestinian independence and statehood were achieved. Thereupon the Assembly adopted several resolutions calling upon Israel to rescind its action against detainees and imprisoned Palestinians and to release them immediately. In December 1987 the Security Council adopted a resolution requesting the Secretary General to submit a report regarding the occupied Arab territories, together with his recommendations on the means of ensuring the safety and protection of civilians in the occupied areas. The Secretary General sent Under-Secretary General for Special Political Affairs to Israel on a fact finding mission and on the basis of his findings, recommended several measures for the protection of Palestinian civilians living in the occupied areas. In November 1988 the Palestine National Council called for an international Peace Conference on the Middle East under the auspices of the United Nations with the participation of all involved and interested parties. This call was endorsed by the General Assembly on 15 December 1988. It may be noted that the Assembly has repeatedly asserted that the political question of Palestine is the core of the Middle East conflict and the peace in the region is indivisible and must be based on a comprehensive, just and lasting political solution under the auspicious of the United Nations.

Peace-keeping in Lebanon

Tension along Israel-Lebanon border increased in 1972 following Israeli attack on Palestinian camps in Lebanon to curb the Palestinian commandos operation from there. On the request of Lebanon a cease-fire observation operation was set up by UNTSO in the Israel-Lebanon sector. In 1978 fresh tension was generated in the region following Israeli invasion of Southern Lebanon in retaliation against the raids by Palestinian commandos into Israel. The Security Council called on Israel to stop military action against Lebanon and established the United Nations Interim Force in Lebanon (UNIFIL) to confirm withdrawal of Israeli forces and help the Lebanese government re-establish its effective authority in the area. It was also expected to ensure restoration of international peace and security and to prevent renewed fighting. The Israeli forces however completed their withdrawal from Lebanon on 13 June 1978 and handed over their position in the border area to Lebanese De Facto forces (Christian and associated militias) supported and supplied by them. In July 1981, a De Facto cease-five came into effect and the area generally remained quite until 1982. Though originally the UNIFI was given a mandate for only six months, but the Security Council continued to extend it. The personels for the force were contributed by Fiji, Finland, France, Ghana, Ireland, Italy, Nepal, Norway and Sweden. The UNIFIL could achieve only moderate success and failed to maintain law and order in its territory. It failed to acquire control over the whole territory assigned to it in southern Lebanon because of the opposition from the Israeli supported units. Thus the UNIFIL was able to play only very limited role in the area.

In June 1982 the Israeli forces moved into Lebanese territory, over the UNIFIL positions. and surrounded Beirut. As the hostilities continued for almost three months, the Security Council called for immediate halt to military activities and demanded that Israel withdraw all its military forces to the internationally recognized boundaries of Lebanon and immediately lift the blockade of Beirut. On 1 August 1982, the Security Council authorised the Secretary General to deploy UN military observers to monitor the situation in and around Beirut. The United Nations observers assigned to the Israel-

Lebanon Mixed Armistic Commission were constituted as the Observer Group Beirut (OGB). Ultimately a cease-fire was effected on 12 August. Towards the close of August, France, Italy and United States entered into an agreement with Lebanon for participation of their troops in a multinational force to assist Lebanese armed forces in carrying out an orderly departure from Lebanon of Palestinian armed personnel in the Beirut area. The evacuation of the Palestinian armed elements and the Arab Deterrent Force from Beirut area was completed on 1 September and the last elements of multinational force were withdrawn on 13 September. Despite this the situation in Beirut areas continued to be unstable throughout 1983-84. Therefore in November 1984 the Secretary General convened a conference of military representatives of Lebanon and Israel at UNIFIL headquarters. The conference met intermittently between November 1984 and January 1985 and considered means to expedite the orderly withdrawal of Israeli forces and to discuss related security arrangements.

The situation in the UNIFIL areas since 1985 has remained essentially unchanged with Israel maintaining its presence in Lebanon on the ground that this is necessary to ensure its security on account of Lebanese government's inability to exercise effective authority and prevents its authority from being used to launch attacks against northern Israel. The consistent efforts of the Secretary General to convince the Israeli authorities to complete withdrawal of their forces from Lebanon met with only partial success. Though Israel withdrew its forces from two positions near Yatar in October 1987, but insisted on maintaining its control in Southern Lebanon. On the other hand the Lebanese authorities insisted that Israel should withdraw its forces completely and allow UNIFIL to deploy to the international border.

In the end it can be said that though UNIFIL has not been able to implement the mandate given to it by the Security Council, it has made best efforts to keep the area free from hostilities and protect its inhabitants from worst effects of violence. It has also provided humanitarian assistance. The usefulness of UNIFIL is further evident from the fact that the Security Council has repeatedly extended the mandate of the Force at the request of the Government of Lebanon and on the recommendation of the Secretary General.

Peace-keeping In Congo

Congo (now known as Republic of Zaire), a former Belgian colony, became independent on 30 June 1960. However soon the country lapsed into chaos due to lack of personnel for management of administration. Further, the Congolese troops mutinied against their Belgian officers at Thysville and Leopoldville. In view of the Anti–Belgian riots and violence, Belgian dropped paratroopers throughout the country and encouraged Katanga, Congo's wealthiest province, to secede. Thereupon Lumumba and Kasavubu, two Congolese leaders, appealed to the United Nations and asked for aid to put an end to the Belgian aggression and the Belgian inspired secession of Katanga. On 14 July 1960 the Security Council called upon Belgium to withdraw its troops from the Congo and authorised the Secretary General to provide the

Congolese government with such military assistance as might be necessary until the national security forces might be able to meet their tasks fully.

The UN Secretary General relying heavily on the precedent of UNEF (United Nations Emergency Force) and UNOGIL (United Nations Observers Group in Lebanon) formed the United Nations Operations in the Congo (ONUC), which was to enter Congo with the agreement of the host government and was to refrain from all intervention in the internal political disputes. The members of the ONUC came from the African and Asian states who were neutral in the Congo crisis.

The Organization of ONUC consisted of an Advisor

Committee composed of one representative from each nation contributing force to the ONUC. Later on a Conciliation Committee was also formed which consisted of the African members of the Force. This Committee was directed to find out a political solution for the Congolese problem. The Special Representative of the Secretary General (who was the chief administrative officer), the Commander of the U.N. Forces, and the Head of ONUC Civilian operations were entrusted with on the spot responsibilities. It is noteworthy that the strength of the UN Forces in Congo was much larger than either of the UNEF or UNOGIL. Its strength which originally stood at 10,000 rose to more than 20,000 in 1961. The responsibilities assigned to the UN forces in Congo were also more extensive. They were not only to disarm the Congolese security forces and irregular armed groups, but also to guard the political leaders, control the airports and other major transportation and communication centres, prevent tribal warfare and take action to stop on-going tribal massacres, and to control riots etc. The other objectives of ONUC included exclusion of the Belgians, the maintenance of law and order, unification of Congo, and fair and equal treatment of all the political factions.

With the passage of time, it became clear that the ONUC will not be able to play an effective role unless it was permitted to make use of forces. Therefore in 1961 the Security Council passed a resolution authorising the ONUC to make use of force, if necessary, to avert civil war and to expel the unauthorised foreign personnel from the Congo. During 1961-62 the secessionist under the command of foreign mercenaries clashed with the UN Forces several times. In these clashes Secretary General Dag Hammarskjold lost his life in air crash while he was on way to Ndola to hold talks for cessation of hostilities. After some initial setbacks the UN forces ultimately scored a victory over Tshombe. In February 1963 Katanga was reintegrated into the national territory of Congo. Thereafter the process of phasing out of the Force began. At the request of the Congolese Government the General Assembly agreed to the stay of a reduced number of troops in Congo for a further period of six months. Ultimately the force was completely withdrawn by 30 June 1964.

In conclusion it can be said that in Congo the UN forces did a commendable job of checking foreign intervention and also greatly contributed to the establishment of law and order in the country. They greatly contributed to the restoration of the authority of the central government. All this could be possible because of the concerted efforts of all the great powers.

Peace Keeping In West Irian

United Nations also undertook between Indonesia and the Dutch on the question of West Irian. Though Indonesia achieved independence in 1949, the Dutch retained control over West Irian. It was agreed that the final fate of the territory would be settled through negotiations between the governments of Indonesia and Netherlands (Holland). In accordance with this settlement negotiations were undertaken by the two countries which continued from 1947 to 1969. However, no agreement could be reached between the two and lot of tension was generated in their relations.

In 1962 President Sukarno of Indonesia, decided to occupy the territory forcibly and organised a number of raids. However, these raids were replaced by the Dutch military forces. As this posed a threat to peace in the region the UN Acting Secretary General urged restraint. But he turned down the Dutch government request to send UN Observers on the scene. He held that such an action could be considered only if both the governments made such a request. However, the UN played an effective role in bringing the representatives of Indonesia and Netherlands on a negotiating table and an agreement was signed by the two governments on 15 August 1962. In terms of this agreement West Irian (West New Guinea) was to be transferred by the Netherlands to a United Nations Temporary Executive Authority (UNTEA) to be headed by a United Nations Administrator. The UNTEA was to have full authority after 1 October 1962 to administer the territory, maintain law and order, and protect the rights of the inhabitants and ensure uninterrupted, normal service until 1 May 1963, when the administration of the territory would be transferred to Indonesia.

The agreements further stipulated that the Secretary General would provide a United Nations Security Force (UNSF) to assist UNTEA with as many troops as the U.N. Administrator deemed necessary. Thus the United Nations was entrusted with dual responsibility of maintaining peace and monitoring the cease fire, as well as administrative responsibilities as executive authority.

In accordance with the agreement the administration of West Irian was transferred to UNTEA on 1 October 1962 and the UN flag was flown side by side with the Netherlands flag. For the next seven months the administration of territory was looked after by the United Nations Administrator appointed by the Secretary General. During this period the Administrator addressed himself to the vast economic and social problems facing the territory. It also secured the withdrawal of Dutch naval and land forces from the territory as per timetable agreed by the United Nations Administration, the Commander of UNSF and the Commander-in-Chief of the Netherlands. The UNTEA also reactivated the judiciary, which had virtually come to a standstill after the

---

1. Inis. L. *Jr. Swords into Plow Shares,* P. 275
2. Inis. L. *Jr. Swords into Plow Shares,* P. 290

departure of Netherlands personnel. The staff in the judiciary were filled through recruitment of qualified judicial officers from Indonesia.

The full administrative control of the territory was handed over by the United Nations Administrator to the representatives of Indonesian government on 1 May. In accordance with the terms of the agreement which required Indonesia to make arrangements with the assistance of the United Nations to give the people of the territory an opportunity to decide whether they wanted to retain links with Indonesia or severe their ties with Indonesia, people were given the option to indicate their preference. The people without dissent favoured the Territory remaining with Indonesia. Thus the UN forces acted as a buffer between the member states which were on the verge of an armed conflict and succeeded in preventing the conflict.

Peace-keeping In Cyprus

U. N. was involved in peace-keeping operations in a big way in Cyprus. The island state of Cyprus became independent in 1960. The island had a mixed population (80 per cent Greeks and 18 per cent Turks). In August 1960 Cyprus, Greece, Turkey and the United Kingdom entered into a treaty which guaranteed the basic provisions of the Constitution (which was designed to balance the interests of the Island's Greek Cypriots and Turkish Cypriot communities) and territorial integrity and sovereignty of Cyprus. However, in 1962 there were number of incidents of inter-communal violence which assumed serious dimensions in 1963-64. At the request of Government of Cyprus, the Security Council met to consider her complaint regarding outside intervention in her internal affairs by Turkey. Turkey, however, denied the charge of aggression and alleged that the Greek Cypriot leaders had tried to nullify the rights of Turkish Cypriot community.

In view of the desperate position in Cyprus the Security Council decided to created the United Nations Force in Cyprus (UNFICYP) with a view to prevent recurrence of fighting, help maintain law and order and promote a return to normal conditions. The expenses for the maintenance of the Forces were to be paid by voluntary contributions. The Council also appointed a Mediator who was to assist in finding out a negotiated political settlement of the dispute. The UNFICYP differed from earlier arrangements in so far as for the first time contingents from Britain, a permanent member of the Security Council, were included in the force. In addition troops were also contributed by Canada, Finland, Denmark, Sweden, Ireland and Austria. General Gyani of India, who was UN's special Representative on Cyprus, was appointed as the commander of the Forces. In addition the Secretary General also sent civilian personnel to stop hostilities and secure political agreement between the various communities as well as find a permanent peaceful solution.

As the parties to the conflict held conflicting views over the role of the mediator in 1968 the Secretary General offered his good offices. He arranged inter-communal talks between representatives of Greek Cypriot and Turkish Cypriot communities to find a just and lasting solution of the problem. These inter-communal talks were held intermittently until early 1974 when the Greek Cypriot who favoured union with Greece staged a coup d'etat. This led to military intervention by Turkey and soon the Turkish Cypriots established control over northern part of Cyprus. In view of these hostilities the Security Council unanimously called for cease-fire and laid the basis for negotiations between Greece, Turkey and United Kingdom. These negotiations continued till mid-August 1974 when they broke down. In November 1974 the General Assembly unanimously called on all states to respect the sovereignty, territorial integrity, independence and non-aligned character of Cyprus. It urged speedy withdrawal of all foreign armed forces from Cyprus, a halt to foreign interference, and safe return of all refugees to their homes. It insisted that the constitutional issues should be resolved by the Greek Cypriot and Turkish Cypriot communities with the help of the Secretary General. Despite this the Turkish Cypriot leadership unilaterally announced in February 1975 that a part of island would become the 'Turkish Federate State of Cyprus'. The Security Council expressed regret over this decision of Turkish Cypriots and asked for resumption of negotiations. The Security Council asked the Secretary General to undertake a new mission of good offices and convene talks between the representatives of the two communities under his auspicies.

The proposed talks were held by the Secretary General in Vienna in April 1975. The same year three further rounds of talks were held. In the third round of these talks an agreement was reached that Turkish Cypriots is the south of island would be allowed to proceed north with UNFICYP assistance and that a number of Greek Cypriots would be transferred to the north in order to be reunited with their families. Similarly, the Greek Cypriots in the north would be free to go south or to remain there. After the fourth round of talks held in New York , the General Assembly in November 1975 again demanded the withdrawal of all foreign armed forces from Cyprus without further delay. It also called for sessation of all foreign interference in internal affairs of Cyprus. Thereafter also efforts were continued to hold talks but the differences persisted and not much progress could be made. Therefore in 1983 the General Assembly adopted a resolution on Cyprus which was rejected by Turkish Cypriot and they decided not to attend the inter-communal talks in future. On 15 November 1983 the Turkish Cypriot authorities unilaterally proclaimed the establishment of a 'Turkish Republic of Northern Cyprus'. The Security Council considered this declaration as legally invalid and called for its withdrawal. The Security Council also requested the Secretary General to pursue his mission of good offices.

In 1984 the Secretary General reopened dialogue with the Representatives of both sides and presented a document which contained elements for a comprehensive solution to the problem through establishment of a Federal Republic of Cyprus. However, the two sides took different stands on the document which necessitated further talks between the parties during 1985-86, Ultimately on 29 March 1986 the Secretary General presented to both the sides a draft framework agreement over which agreement had been reached between the two parties during the previous two years. However, soon fresh difficulties cropped up due to differences between the two parties regarding implementation of the 1977 and 1979 high-level agreements.

As a result of persistent efforts of the Secretary General a high-level meeting took place at Geneva in August 1988, and the leaders of two sides expressed their desire to co-operate with the Secretary General. Several rounds of talks were held but the impasse remained due to two sides maintaining their respective positions.

In 1990 Security Council came forth with a proposal of one state comprising of two communities on a federal, bicommunal and bi-zonal basis. The Secretary General held discussions with the leaders of the two communities and expressed hope that an agreement could be possible if the two parties could resolve the issues of territorial adjustments and displaced persons. A number of joint meetings between the two leaders were arranged in New York in October-November, 1992. Fresh joint meeting was held in March 1993, and May 1993 where the two leaders indicated their willingness to pursue agreement on 14 proposed confidence-building measures. The most important of these measures was transfer of the vacant city of Varosha to United Nations administration and its becoming a special area for bicommunal contact and commerce; and the opening of Nicosia International Airport, under the UN administration, for unhindered traffic with both sides. But the process of improvement of relations between two Cypriot groups suffered a set back after the Turkish Cypriot leader failed to resume joint meetings.

Fresh efforts were stepped up by the Secretary General to find a solution of the problem, but he did not succeed on account of non-accommodating attitude of Turkish Cypriots. In January 1994 the Secretary General through is Special Representative sought to establish intensive contacts to achieve an agreement on the package of confidence-building measures. The representatives of two sides accepted in principle the package and agreed on an agenda for proximity talks on the modalities for implementing it. During next few months several rounds of talks were held but no agreement could be reached. Even there–after the Secretary General through his Special Representative and Special Deputy Representative maintained contact with the two parties to find out a basis for further discussion.

In the meanwhile UNFICYP continued to supervise the cease-fire and maintain close surveillance over the buffer area between the cease-fire lines. It also continued to discharge its responsibilities with regard to the security and well-being of the Greek Cypriots in the north. It is evident from the preceding account that the UNO has been making consistent efforts to secure an effective cease-fire and find out some mutually acceptable solution, even though it has not met with complete success.

Peace Keeping In Yugoslavia

The United Nations got actively involved in Yugoslavia following outbreak of fighting in that country. The Security Council adopted a resolution (713 of 1991) expressing deep concern at the fighting in that country and called on all states to implement a general and complete embargo on all deliveries of weapons and military equipment to Yugoslavia. The Security

Council invited the Secretary General to offer his assistance in promoting peace. On 15 February 1992, the Secretary General recommended the establishment of a United Nations Protection Force (UNPROFOR) in Yugoslavia to the Security Council. Accordingly the Security Council established UNPROFOR for initial period of 12 months with a view to create conditions of peace and security required for the negotiation of an overall settlement of the Yugoslav crisis. The force comprises of 14,000 personels which include the military, police and civilian components. The UNPROFOR has been deployed in the three United Nations Protected Areas (UNPA) in Croatia–Eastern Slovenia, Western Slovenia and Krajina.

It is noteworthy that in the past the United Nations has generally been sending troops to the disputed territories only after cease-fire was assured. However in Yugoslavia it sent troops even while the cease-fire could not be secured because of the complex nature of ethnic conflict. Another notable point is that in the past the United Nations maintained peacekeeping forces only as long as both the parties to the dispute wanted them. It withdrew its forces whenever any of the parties asked it to withdraw the same. In the case of UNPROFOR, the forces shall operate as long as Security Council wants them. This implies that it is only at the instance of the Security Council the forces shall be withdrawn.

It may be noted that the field of operation of UNPROFOR was expanded and enlarged in the course of time. Initially it was set up to create conditions of peace and security required for the negotiation of an overall settlement of the Yugoslav crisis, but subsequently it was entrusted with the responsibility of controlling the entry of civilians into UNPA (United Nations Protect Areas), and monitoring the demilitarisation of the Prevlake peninsula near Dubrovnik, and control of Perca dam. In June 1992, following deterioration of situation, UNPROFOR's mandate was extended to the state of Bosnia and Herzegovina. It also assumed responsibility for the security and functioning of the airport at Sarajevo, the capital of Bosnia. In September 1992 UNPROFOR's mandate was further extended and it was entrusted with the responsibility of providing humanitarian relief throughout Bosnia. It was to afford protection to the convoys of released civilian detainees, if the International Committee of Red Cross, so desired.

Peace Keeping In Iran-Iraq

Ever since inception of conflict between Iran and Iraq in September 1980 the United Nations has made efforts to secure peaceful settlement of the dispute. The Security Council at its meeting of 28 September urged Iran and Iraq to refrain from use of force and accept mediation or conciliation. The Council reiterated its support for mediation in 1982 and called for dispatch of United Nations observers to verify a cease-fire. Even the General Assembly emphasised the need for an immediate cease-fire and for the withdrawal of forces to internationally recognized boundaries. It also called upon all states to refrain from actions which could contribute to the continuation of the conflict. It even asked the Secretary General to persevere in his efforts towards peaceful settlement.

In accordance with the above directive the Secretary-General paid visit to Teheran and Baghdad and worked out a plan to bring an end to the conflict and until that goal was achieved, he tried to mitigate the effects of the conflict in areas like attacks on civilian population centres; the use of chemical weapons and treatment of prisoners of wars etc. Between March 1984 and August 1988 the Secretary-General sent seven missions to Iran-Iraq to investigate allegations concerning use of chemical weapons in the conflict. On 20 July 1987 the Security Council unanimously adopted a resolution which called for an immediate cease-fire and for the withdrawal of forces to internationally recognized boundaries without delay. It also requested the Secretary General to dispatch a team of observers to verify, confirm and supervise the cease-fire and withdrawal; urged the release and repatriation of the prisoners of war without delay and called up on Iran and Iraq to co-operate with the Secretary-General in implementing the resolution and in mediation efforts to achieve a comprehensive, just and honourable settlement of all outstanding issues. This resolution of Security Council was officially accepted by Iraq on 23 July 1987. Iran accepted the resolution on 17 July 1988. After persistent diplomatic activities the Secretary General announced on 8 August 1988 that the cease-fire would come into effect on 20 August 1988. On 9 August 1988 the Security Council set up an unarmed United Nations Iran-Iraq Military Group (UNIIMOG) for six months which was renewed on 8 February 1989 and 29 September 1989. UNIIMOG consisted of 350 military observers and necessary military and civilian staff.

As a result of a series of ministerial-level direct talks under the auspices of Secretary General and Personal Representative appointed on 1 September 1988, a Memorandum of understanding was signed by Iran and Iraq with International Committee of the Red Cross (ICRC) on 14 November 1988 concerning the release and repatriation of some sick and wounded prisoners of war. In January 1989 the Secretary General asked his Personal Representative to visit the capitals of Iran and Iraq to expedite the peace process. He himself held extensive consultations with the officials of Iran and Iraq for the implementation of resolution of July 1987. However, despite all these efforts the final peace agreement could not be signed. It was only in 1990 after Iraq got involved in war with the western powers over Kuwait that Iraq decided to withdraw its forces from the Iranian territory captured during the eight-year conflict. The two countries also agreed to set up a joint committee to oversee repatriation of all prisoners of war. In mid-October 1990 President Saddam Hussein of Iraq announced the acceptance of Iran's terms for settlement of dispute and thus the eight-year old Iran-Iraq War formally came to an end.

By November 1990 the two sides had withdrawn their troops to internationally recognized boundaries. The withdrawal was carried out under the supervision of UNIIMOG, which also tried to defuse local tension. After the completion of withdrawal of forces in February 1991 the Security Council terminated UNIIMOG's mandate. The same month a small civilian offices of the Secretary General were established in Baghdad and Tehran. In December 1991 the Secretary General asserted that no useful purpose would be served by insisting on the implementation of resolution 598, and suggested that it would be proper to continue the settlement process. By the end of 1992 the Secretary General's civilian offices in Baghdad and Teheran were phased out and the Permanent Mission of Iran and Iraq became the channel of communication between the two countries and the United Nations for matters related to resolution 598.

Peace-keeping in India and Pakistan

The United Nations has felt greatly concerned over prevailing tension between India and Pakistan over Kashmir right from the beginning. In January 1948 when Indian complained to the Security Council that tribesmen and others with Pakistan's support and participation were invading Kashmir, the Security Council established a United Nations Commission for India and Pakistan to investigate and mediate. The Council also recommended other measures such as use of observers to stop the fighting and to create proper conditions for a free and impartial plebiscite. The Commission also offered to mediate between the two countries and several proposals regarding cease-fire and withdrawal of troops. As a result of these efforts cease-fire came into effect on 1 January 1949 and the United Nations Military observers were deployed in the area to supervise it. A cease-fire line was established in Jammu and Kashmir under an agreement between the two countries reached under the auspices of the United Nations Commission. However, no agreement could be possible between the two countries regarding demilitarization of the state before plebiscite could be held. As the problem persisted for some time the matter was brought before the Security Council in 1957 and was discussed by the Security Council several times between 1957-1964.

In 1965 fresh hostilities broke out between India and Pakistan. The Security Council called for cease-fire and brought the war to a close in September 1965 with the help of United Nations Military Observer Group in India and Pakistan (UNMOGIP). The Secretary General also decided to organize the observers who would supervise the cease-fire along the India Pakistan border. The Secretary General held a series of joint meetings with the representatives of India and Pakistan and worked out a plan for ground rules and withdrawals. In the meanwhile the Prime Minister of India (Lal Bahadur Shastri) and President of Pakistan (Ayub Khan) brought the war to an end by signing Tashkent Declaration under the auspices of Soviet Union and agreed to withdraw their respective armed personnels to positions held by them before 5 August 1966. The UNMOGIP and UNIPOM military observers played an important role in supervising the withdrawal of troops.

In 1971 when hostilities broke out between India and Pakistan on the issue of penetration of large number of Bengali refugees into India, the Secretary General notified the Security Council that the situation constituted a threat to international peace and security. After the war stopped and a cease-fire was agreed, the Security Council insisted on strict observance of cease-fire until withdrawal of all armed forces to their respective territories to positions which fully respected the cease-fire line in Kashmir supervised by UNMOGIP. In July 1972 India and Pakistan signed Simla Agreement which defined line of control in Kashmir which slightly differed from the cease-fire line established under the agreement of 1949 between India and Pakistan. The Brigade Commanders of Indian and Pakistani forces tried to resolve the differences through direct talks, but failed to reach any agreement. Therefore the UNMOGIP observers continued to be deployed along both sides of the cease-fire line established under Simla Agreement. The UNMOGIP is even now trying to ensure that the two countries do not violate the accepted line of control.

Peace Keeping in Cambodia

The United Nations took keen interest in Cambodia after its peace was threatened following intervention by Vietnam in December, 1978. The General Assembly in 1979 called for the withdrawal of foreign forces, non-interference in country's internal affairs, and right of self-determination for the people of Cambodia. Subsequently in 1981 the General Assembly requested the Secretary General to exercise his good offices to establish his good offices to establish peace in the country. The Secretary General after visit to the region in 1985, listed a number of objectives on the basis of which a comprehensive political agreement could be worked out. In 1988 the Secretary General, through his Special Representative, presented to the four Cambodian parties and the States concerned a framework for settlement. In 1988 on the basis of the Secretary General's proposals the first face-to-face talks among for cambodian parties took place in Jakarta. A a result of these talks in April 1989 Viet Nam announced withdrawal of itrs trooops from Cambodia. In July-August 1989 18 Nation Conference on Cambodia was held at Paris, which was attended by the Secretary General.

In January 1990 the five permanent members of the Security Council held a series of high-level meetings on Cambodia and agreed on certain principles of political settlement. As per the plans the control over country's administrative structure was to be handed over to the United Nations, which was then to hold elections under its supervision. This plan was endorsed by the Security Council and accepted by all Cambodian parties as well as Viet Nam. In May 1991 a cease-fire was established in the country on the appeal of the Secretary General and the Foreign Ministers of France and Indonesia. In October, 1991 the Security Council established the UNITED NATIONS ADVANCE MISSION IN CAMBODIA (UNAMIC) to assist the Cambodian parties in the maintenance of cease-fire. On 23 October, 1991 all the parties signed a peace treaty to end conflict and prepare for elections.

In February 1992, the Security Council set up UNITED NATIONS TRANSITIONAL AUTHORITY IN CAMBODIA (UNTAC) to supervise the cease-fire, to end foreign military assistance and to seek withdrawal of foreign forces. The other responsibilities assigned to this organisation were disarming of all armed forces of Cambodian parties: to ensure 70 per cent level of demobilization; control and supervision of administrative structures, including the police; to ensure respect for human rights; and to organize and conduct elections in the country. Over 21,000 military and civilian personels were made available to UNTAC. In terms of Paris Agreement, in July 1992 UNTAC acquired control over foreign affairs, defence, security, finance and information with a view to establish neutral environments for the conduct of elections.

The process of elections in Cambodia started with the registration of political parties and registration of voters. By January 1993 20 parties applied for registration. By the end of January 1993 over 4.6 million Cambodian and registered themselves as voters. The elections were held in May 1993 in all the 21 provinces of Cambodia under tight security. Over 89 per cent voters made use of their franchise. FUNCINPEC polled 45 per cent of votes and emerged as the largest party with 59 seats. CPP secured 38 per cent votes and captured 51 seats KPNLF/BLDP secured only 3 per cent votes and captured 10 seats. MOLINAKA Party secured only 1 seat. The results of the election were endorsed by the Security Council and it expressed support for the newly elected Constituent Assembly.

On 24 September, 1993 the new constitution drawn up by the Constituent Assembly was promulgated and Prince Sihanouk was elected as King of Cambodia. In accordance with the constitution Sihanouk appointed the heads of new Government. On the same day UNTAC's mandate terminated. However, even thereafter UN agencies continued to assist in the development of Cambodia. Restoration of peace in Cambodia was one of the most momentous assignment of the United Nations. This involved a peace-keeping force of 22,000 military and civilian personnel. The total cost of this venture was 1.5 billion dollars. In terms of results it was most successful UN mission, which restored normalcy in the country which was war-torn since world war II.

Peace-keeping in Mozambique

Mozambique gained independence from Portuguese rule in June 1975. After enjoying peace for few years the country lapsed into civil war on account of anti-government activities of Mozambican National Resistance (RENAMO), which was supported by the minority regime in South Africa. The long drawn civil war came to an end following protracted negotiations in the Italian capital and conclusion of a General Peace Agreement at Rome in 1992 by President Joaquim Chissano of Mozambique and President of RENAMO. As per this agreement a cease-fire was to come into effect by 15 October, 1992. This was to be followed by the separation of the forces of two sides and their concentration in 49 assembly areas. All the troops which could not be absorbed in the New Mozambican Defence Force, were to be demobilized within six months of the cease-fire. In the meanwhile preparations were to be made for general election.

A major role was assigned to the United Nations with regard to the implementation of the agreement and monitoring of elections. For this purpose a special Supervisory and Monitoring Commission (CSC) was to be set up. The CSC was formally established in November 1992 to guarantee the implementation of the Agreement and settlement of disputes between the parties. The Commission on, Chaired by UN, was composed of delegations of government and RENAMO. It also contained representactives of Italy (the mediator state) France, Germany, Portugal, the United Kingdom, and OAU

(Organization of African Unity).

In December 1992 the Secretary General submitted a plan for a UNITED NATIONS OPERATION IN MOZAMBIQU (ONUMOZ) to the Security Council, which was accepted by the latter. The ONUMOZ was entrusted both military and humanitarian tasks. The military tasks of ONUMOZ included monitoring the cease-fire, the separation and assembly of forces, their demobilization, and the collection, storage and destruction of weapons ; verifying the disbanding of irregular armed groups; and providing security for United Nations and other international activities. The humanitarian task assigned to ONUMOZ included rehabilitation of 3.7 million Mozambicans displaced by the war. ONUMOZ was also expected to monitor the electoral process of legislative and presidential elections envisaged under the Peace Agreement. As there was delay in the implementation of the Peace Agreement the elections could not be held in October 1992 as originally planned. There was a stalemate among the parties regarding implementation of Peace Agreement. In October 1992 as originally planned. There was a stalemate among the parties regarding implementation of Peace Agreement. In October 1993 the Secretary General met Mozambique President Chissano and RENAMO President Dhalakama sand succeeded in achieving a breakthrough in the peace process. Agreements were reached on the assembly and demobilization of troops, the composition of the National Electoral Commission (NEC), the system and timetable for finalizing the Electoral Law etc. Several meetings were held between President Chissano and Dhalakama to sort out the differences. In March 1994 demobilization started. By August more than 76,000 soldiers from both sides were demobilized. ONUMOZ helped to combine over 10,000 of them into the new national army. ONUMOZ also collected about 155,000 weapons from the troops of both parties and from para military forces by mid-October. Considerable progress was also made in matter of resettlement of dispaced persons. By August 1994 some 75 per cent of the estimated 3.7 million people internally displaced had been resettled. Most of the refugees in the neighbourig countries also returned to Mozambique by the end of 1994.

The first multi-party elections to the 250 member National Assembly were held in October 1994, in which 90 per cent of the registered electorate voted. The elections were monitored by some 2,300 international observers. The results of the election were endorsed by the Security Council. The new National Assembly was installed on 8 December, 1994. The following day Chissano was inaugurated as President. This marked the completion of ONUMOZ'S mandate. By January 1995 ONUMOZ completed its withdrawal from Mozambique.

Peace Keeping in Somalia

UN got involved in the peace-keeping operations in Somalia in April 1992 when the Security Council decided to establish the UNITED NATIONS OPEATION IN SOMALIA (UNOSOM) in response to the request of the government of the state. However, UNOSOM became operative only in September 1992 when the first contingent of troops arrived. However, soon the ineffectiveness of UNOSOM became evident. In November 1992 the Secretary

General reported total breakdown of the law-and order in the state. It may be observed that the condition in Somalia had so much deteriorated that the various relief organisations which wanted to provide humanitarian assistance to people of Somalia were prevented from doing so. Money and relief supplies ware being extracted from donor agencies. Even the lives of donor agencies trying to distribute aid to starving people of Somalia were in danger. All this resulted in great hardship to the pople and over 3000 persons died of starvation.

In the midst of these developments the United States on 25 November 1992 offered to take lead in organising and commanding an operation to ensure the delivery of humanitarian relief. The offer was accepted by the Security Council on 3 December 1992. Accordingly the Council authorised the use of all necessary means to establish a secure environment for humanitarian relief operations. On 9 December, 1992 the Unified Task Force (UNITAF) consisting of military units from 24 countries, led by United States, was deployed. UNITAF and UNOSOM succeeded in securing free flow of humanitarian assistance and stepped up efforts to arrive at a political solution of the crisis of Somalia. In March 1993 the Security Council expanded UNSOCOM's size and mandate and authorised UNOSOM II to use force under Chapter VII of the Charter so as to enable it to establish a secure environment throughout Somalia. It also mandated UNOSOM II to assist the Somalia in rebuilding their economy and social and political life.

On the initiative of the UN Secretary General in March 1993 a Conference on National Reconciliation was held in Addis Ababa which was attended by the leaders of 15 Somali political movements. These leaders endorsed an agreement on disarmament and security, rehabilitation and reconstruction, restoration of property and settlement of disputes and the establishment of a transitional national council. Despite all these developments attacks against UNOSOM II continued and often the UNOSOM forces were involved in military action resulting in casualties among civilians as well as UNOSOM members. UNOSOM II persisted with its efforts to bring about peace in Somalia but did not succeed. Gradually UNOSOM II withdrew from Somalia and its withdrawal was completed in March 1995. The UN mission in Somalia, thus, proved to be a failure because peace enforcement in civil war situations is much more difficult than peace enforcement in inter-state wars.

Assessment of the Peace-keeping Operations.

A survey of the various peace-keeping operations undertaken by the United Nations indicates that durieng the period of cold war it could play only limited role. The success of the UN peace-keeping operations during this period greatly depended on the co-operation between the two most powerful members of the United Nations viz. United States and Soviet Union. The UN could succeed only in cases where the two powers were willing to treat the territories of dispute beyond their sphere and were willing to support the UN peace-keeping forces.

The role and effectiveness of the UN peace keeping forces underwent a great change in the post cold-war period. Between 1998 and 1991 itself the

UN brokered an agreement that brought to an end the eight year old Iran-Iraq war. It mediated a series of agreements that paved the way for the withdrawal of Soviet troops form Afghanistan. It ended civil war in El Salvador and prepared ground for Namibia's independence. It also helped in the establishment of broad based coalition government in Cambodia.

The nature of the peace-keeping operations in the post cold war period has undergone a complete change. Whereas the traditional peace keeping operations aimed at maintaining peace on a conflict-prone area in a modest way by monitoring troops movements along boundaries, or troops withdrawals with the prior agreement of the concerned parties, the peace-keeping operations in the post Cold-War period have become multi-dimensional. It is now dealing with virtually every aspect of human affairs. Some of the functions which have been assumed by the UN of late include maintenance of law and order within states; holding of elections etc. the functions which were formally performed by the states themselves functions which were formally performed by the states themselves. Thus in April 1989 UN sent a Transition Assistance Group to Namibia to prepare it for independence. It was assigned to Namibia to prepare it for independence. It was assigned the duty of planning and supervision for the conduct of 'free and fair elections'. Of late UN has come to assume that it is not only expected to help in preserving peace settlements arrived at between the sovereign nations, but also help in preserving peace within nations. As a result the United Nations has quite often tended to intervene in a series of civil war or near-civil war situations, which has often proved disastrous results. The case of Somalia is a clear example of the same. Though the UN involvement in Somalia began in the name of human rights, but it ended up in blood-letting.

Again in Bosnia, the UN decided to intervene on account of the unprecedented ethnic violence in the summer of 1992 which resulted in destruction of villages and displacement of civilian communities on a scale not seen since end of world war II. Though initially the UN was moved by the humanitarian considerations, but subsequently the peace-keeping forces were given the task of supporting efforts to deliver humanitarian relief materials to Bosnia and Herzegovina. It may be noted that both in Bosnia and Somalia the principles of consent impartiality and non-coercive action were abandoned. In Bosnia, the continuing brutality of war led to deeper UN involvement . The initial humanitarian intervention was supplemented by the enforcement action under Chapter VII. However the credibility of UN forces suffered a great set back as they were targeted by the various warring factions in Bosnia. The experience of Somalia and Bosnia clearly demonstrated that the UN cannot impose solutions on warring factions within a state. If the UN is really to play an effective role in peace-keeping and peace enforcement operations, it must be endowed with military force capable of preventing situations as developed in Somalia. Now it is generally accepted that the UN is not expected to resolve intractable conflicts within nation states and must confine its role to resolution of conflicts with the consent of involved parties

The absence of an international force has also handicapped United Nations in the discharge of its peace-keeping operations. The United Nations has to depend on the cooperation and support of the members for the raising of force. Generally the contingents to international force have been contributed by the middle and small powers, and the big powers have been reluctant to contribute troops. These big powers have, however, rendered great service in the transport of these troops and thus contributed to the success of various military operations. It is desirable that the composition of the U. N. force should be more broad-based.

The peace-keeping operations of UN have also been greatly handicapped due to reluctance of several states to make contributions for the maintenance of these forces on different pleas. It is well known that both France and Soviet Union refused to pay their contributions for the peace-keeping operations on different pleas which obliged the UN to seek advisory opinion from the International Court of Justice. The Court held that the emergency assessments for cost of peace-keeping operations in the Middle East and Congo constituted 'expenses of the organization' and the members were bound to pay for these charges. Though this opinion of the Court was accepted by the General Assembly by an overwhelming vote, both France and Soviet Union refused to make contributions.

Despite the above limitations the peace-keeping forces of United Nations have played an important role in localising the international conflicts. They kept the armed conflicts at low level while continuing efforts to secure a political settlement of the problem. The United Nations forces have prevented escalation of conflicts and promoted international peace by forming a buffer zone between the conflicting parties. The parties to conflict are always reluctant to attack the soldiers of UN force because they do not represent their country but the international community as a whole. The presence of UN forces has often encouraged the parties to dispute to settle their differences through negotiations rather than war. It is true that the UN forces did not succeed in establishing peace in all the disputes, but it cannot be denied that UNEF and UNOGIL did a commendable job. The successful role of the UN peace-keeping forces depends on the co-operation of the great powers, the supply of troops by member states. and the consent of the host states. It is well known that withdrawal of consent by the host states has often resulted in the termination of the operations of the UN peace-keeping forces. Above all the success of the UN forces depends on the availability of necessary finances for their upkeep. Unless the states are willing to contributes finances and forces, the UN cannot succeed in its mission of maintenance of peace.

How UN can play more effective role as Peace-keeper

If the UN is to play an effective role as peace-keeper certain steps must be taken. These include (i) establishment of an early warning office which should continuously monitor potential trouble spots around the world (ii) Setting up of permanent conflict resolution committees in different regions of the world to defuse tension before violence erupts (iii) Immediate deployment of peace-forces to prevent aggression (iv) Provision of a regular peace-keeping budget, with sufficient reserve funds, to meet the cost of peace-keeping operations, and to meet unforeseen expenses. As a first step in this direction, the Governments which owe money to the UN, as their contribution to peace keeping operations must clear their arrears (v) Creation of a two-tier UN peace force comprising of permanent non-combat force recruited by UN, and specially trained troops of member states which are available to the Security Council on short notice. (vi) The UN should avoid ambitious peace-keeping role, as done in the post-cold-war period. It should, as far as possible, avoid involvement in conflicts within the nation states. At the most it may act as facilitator in the resolution of such conflicts and must avoid forced settlement on recalcitrant parties.

FURTHER READINGS

Clerk M. Eicherlberger	*U.N. The First Twenty Years*
James M. Boyd	*United Nations Peace-keeping Operations: A Military and Political Appraisal*
James Alan	*The Policy of peace-keeping*
U.N. Publication	*The Blue Helmets: A Review of United Nations Peace–keeping*
Ruth B.Russel	*United Nations Experience with Military Forces: Political and Legal Aspects*

Chapter 20

UNITED NATIONS AND DISARMAMENT

The enormous destruction caused by the Second World War roused the conscience of the world statesmen. Fearing that another war may completely wipe our the human race they started making more frantic efforts to regulate the armaments. The UN Charter also laid great emphasis on the regulation of armaments. At least three of its articles were devoted to this problem. Article 11 (1) while directing the General Assembly to consider the general principles of co-operation in the maintenance of international peace and security, authorised it to make recommendations to the member states regarding the general principles governing disarmament and regulation of armaments. Article 26 likewise insisted that international peace and order should be promoted with "least diversion for armaments of the world human and economic resources." It entrusted the Security Council with the responsibility of formulating a plan for the establishment of a system for the regulation of armaments. Article 47(l) provided for the establishment of Military Staff Committee, which among other things was to assist the Security Council on the regulation of armaments and possible disarmament. However, U. N. Charter did not vest any specific authority on any of its organs to impose a system of disarmament or regulation of armaments among members. In view of this lacuna Prof. Eichelberger has asserted that the obligations under the Covenant of the League were more positive and possessed greater binding force.

1. Atomic Energy Commission

Soon after the adoption of the UN Charter the Atom Bomb was exploded on Hiroshima and Nagasaki in Japan. The untold suffering caused by the bombardment of these two towns of Japan led to a widespread demand for devising a system of control to prevent the use of atomic energy for destructive purposes, and use for humanitarian and peaceful purposes. Accordingly, on 26 January 1946 the General Assembly decided to set up an Atomic Energy Commission consisting of all the permanent members of Security Council and Canada. The Commission was expected to enquire into all aspects of the problem and make recommendations with specific proposals for "(a.) extending between all nations the exchange of basic scientific information for peaceful ends; (b) control of atomic energy to the extent necessary to ensure its use only for peaceful purposes; (c) the elimination from national armaments of atomic weapons and of all other major weapons adaptable to mass destruction; and (d) effective safeguards by way of inspection and other means to protect complying states against the hazards of violations and evasions." The Commission was subordinate to the Security Council and was expected to submit its reports and recommendations to it. It is noteworthy that in the establishment of this Commission both the superpowers offered their co-operation.

At the very first meeting of the Atomic Energy Commission on 14 June 1946 differences cropped up between the two major powers. Mr Baruch of U.S.A. presented a plan in which he insisted on managerial control or ownership of all atomic energy activities potentially dangerous to world security; power to control, inspect and license all other atomic activities; fostering beneficial use of atomic energy; and research and development of responsibilities of an affirmative nature. He also offered to destroy all atom bombs of U.S.A. and to stop their further manufacture after an adequate system of international control had been established. In short, Baruch Plan insisted on tight international control of all aspects of the use of atomic energy and a certain punishment for violations. According to Collart, The Baruch Plan was uniquely significant because 'it came from the only country which had atomic weapons at that time, it aimed at submitting the production, development and application of nuclear energy to a very extensive system of international administrations."*

As at that time Soviet Union had not tested nuclear weapons she was reluctant to support any agreement that would preclude, Soviet development of nuclear capacity. Therefore, at the second meeting of the Commission on 19 June 1946 she submitted two proposals. In her first proposal Soviet Union suggested the prohibition of the production and employment of weapons based on the use of atomic energy for the purpose of mass destruction, prohibition of production and storing of weapons based on use of atomic energy and destruction of all atomic weapons within three months of the convention. She suggested that the violation of this should be treated as an international crime. In the second proposal Soviet Union suggested the establishment of two committees concerned with exchange of scientific information and making of recommendations for the prevention of the use of atomic energy respectively.

A comparison of the proposals submitted by Soviet Union and U.S.A. shows that while U.S.A. insisted on effective international control and inspection before the abolition of atomic weapons, Soviet Union insisted on first outlawing the atomic weapons and their destruction. She argued that subsequently an appropriate inspection system could be evolved. The main plea taken by the Soviet Union against international

---

*Y. Collart, *Disarmament,* p. 17

inspection was that it violated the sovereign rights of the states. In view of this divergent stand of the two superpowers the Atomic Energy Commission could not accomplish anything.

2. Commission on Conventional Armaments

In pursuance of the General Assembly resolution of December 1946 Security Council set up a Commission on Conventional Armaments in February 1947. The Commission was expected to prepare and submit to the Council within three months proposals for "the general regulation and reduction of armaments and armed forces," and to suggest practical and effective safeguards. It may be noted that this Commission was specifically debarred from discussing issues concerning atomic weapons and their control. The Commission held its first meeting on 24 March, 1947 and finally adopted a resolution on 12 August, 1948. In this resolution the Commission recommended (a) a system for the regulation and reduction of armaments of all states, initially only those having substantial military resources; (b) measures for reduction and regulation of armaments to encourage further regulation and reduction; (c) the establishment of an adequate system of international control of atomic energy and conclusion of peace settlement with Japan and Germany; (d) regulation and reduction of armament to make possible the least diversion for armaments of the world human and economic resources and maintenance of armaments and armed forces which are indispensable for the maintenance of international peace and security; and (e) adequate method of safeguards and provision for effective enforcement action in case of violation.

When the resolution came up for discussion before the Assembly, the Soviet Union strongly opposed it. She came forward with a new proposal requiring all the permanent members of the Security Council to reduce their land, naval and air forces by one-third during one year and establishment of a control body within the framework of the Security Council to supervise the reduction of armaments and prohibition of atomic weapons. However, the Russian proposal was rejected by the Western nations. In view of the differences the Assembly adopted a resolution urging the Commission for Conventional Armaments to continue its work and formulate proposals for the receipt, checking and publication by international organ of control of full information to be supplied by members states with regard to their conventional armaments. However, Soviet Union withdrew from both the Commissions (Atomic Energy Commission and the Commission for Conventional Armaments) in 1950 on the question of the representation of Red China on it.

Disarmament Commission

The failure of these two Commissions did not deter the world leaders and they continued their efforts to regulate the armaments. On the suggestion of the American President Truman that the two Disarmament Commissions should be merged, the General Assembly set up a Committee of Twelve members (I 1 members of Security Council and Canada) to report the ways and means whereby the work of the two Commissions could be combined. The Committee recommended the merger of the two Commissions. Its recommendations were accepted by the General Assembly and a Disarmament Commission was created on 11 January 1952. It was to consist of all the members of the Security Council plus Canada. In 1957 the General Assembly increased the strength of the Disarmament Commission to 14. In 1958 all the members of the U. N. were included as its members. The Commission was requested to prepare a draft treaty for the regulation of conventional as well as atomic armaments. The Commission took up a number of issues concerning arms and their reduction but failed to make much headway because of the divergence of views amongst the superpowers. To resolve these differences in 1953 the General Assembly set up a Great Power Sub-Committee. This Committee considerably succeeded in narrowing down the area of disagreement, although the two powers continued to hold opposite views on the question of controls.

Atoms for Peace Plan (1953)

In 1953 President Eisenhower of USA came out with a new plan for peaceful use of atoms. He suggested the establishment of an international pool of fissionable materials to be used for peaceful purposes. This plan popularly known as Atoms for Peace Plan appealed to all those powers who possessed atomic energy material to contribute the same to the Atomic Energy Commission under lie United Nations. The Commission was to ensure that these materials were used for peaceful purposes and for the promotion of international peace and security. This plan was also turned down by Soviet Union who insisted on ent on prior agreements on prohibition of atomic weapons.

Anglo-French Plan (1954)

In June 1954 Britain and France took an initiative and submitted a memorandum outlining a comprehensive plan for disarmament. The memorandum outlined three phases of disarmament. During the first phase a control organ was to be set up and the military expenditure and manpower of the member states was to be frozen at specific levels. During the second phase, after the establishment of control organ, first half of the agreed reduction of armed forces, conventional weapons and military expenditure was to be carried out. Further manufacture of nuclear weapons was also to be stopped at this stage. The third and the final stage envisaged the second half of the agreed reduction and total prohibition and elimination of nuclear weapons. Though initially Soviet Union rejected the proposal but subsequently in September 1954 she communicated her willingness to the General Assembly to accept the Anglo-French Memorandum as a basis for the step by step approach to the nuclear problem. Thus it looked that the plan would be able to make much headway. However, in March-April, 1955 Soviet Union reverted to its earlier position.

Soviet Proposal of May 1955

In May 1955 Soviet Union suddenly submitted new proposal which was quite identical to the Anglo-French Memorandum in so far as it accepted the same force levels. However, this proposal was quite distasteful to U.S.A. because it insisted on dismantling of all United States overseas bases and a ban on nuclear tests. Though the proposal fell down, it certainly contributed to the spirit of detente and paved the way for the Geneva Summit of 1955.

The Geneva Summit and Open Skies Plan

In July 1955 the chiefs of state from France, U.K., USA and USSR met at Geneva to discuss among others the problem of disarmament. At this meeting U.S.A. proposed the open skies' plan. Under the plan both U.S.A. and U.S.S.R. were to exchange military information which could be verified by mutual aerial reconnaissance. Soviet Union was prepared to accept the proposal regarding exchange of military blue prints, supervision of military bases and prohibition of atomic armaments, provided her proposals regarding reduction of armaments (which she had earlier submitted) were accepted. However, Russia did not feel convinced as to how inspection of the concealed nuclear weapons shall be possible. She also insisted that all actions in this regard should be subject to Security Council's decisions and hence veto of the permanent Members of the Security Council. As these conditions were not acceptable to U.S.A. the plan fell

Six Point Plan of USA (1957)

In 1957 the U.S. representative Henry Cabbot Lodge proposed another plan before the General Assembly indicating America's willingness to take steps towards arms reduction subject to adequate inspection. The basic objective of the plan was to check the trend towards large stockpiles of nuclear weapons and reduce the further nuclear threat; provision against surprise attack, lessening of the economic burden due to armaments and utilisation of the money thus saved for the improvement of the living standards, reduction of political tension among nations and to help in settlement political issues; and devotion of research and development activities concerning propulsion of object through outer space for peaceful purposes. The plan envisaged the establishment of inspection posts at strategic points in the eastern half of United States and western border regions of Russia. After favourable initial response Soviet Union turned down the plan.

However, in November 1957 the General Assembly endorsed these proposals and insisted on (a) immediate suspension of testing of nuclear weapons with prompt installation of effective international control; (b) cession of production of fissionable materials for purpose of weapons and its future utilisation for peaceful purposes; (c) reduction of stock of nuclear weapons through a programme of transfer of stocks of fissionable material for peaceful purposes (d) reduction of armed forces and armaments with adequate safeguards; (e) progressive establishment of open inspection to guard against the possibility of surprise attack; (f) establishment of an inspection system to ensure that the sending of objects through outer space was exclusively for peaceful and scientific purposes.

The same year the General Assembly also adopted two other resolutions emphasizing the need of an accord on disarmament and enlargement of the Disarmament Commission by addition of fourteen members. Soviet Union, however, insisted that all the UN members should be included in the Disarmament Commissions. As her proposal was not accepted she announced her withdrawal from the Disarmament Commission and its sub-Committees.

Nuclear Test Ban

Encouraged by the announcement of Soviet Union n March 1958 regarding a unilateral ban on tests of atom and hydrogen bombs, three nuclear powers U.S.A., U.S.S.R. and Britain held a Conference at Geneva from October 1958 to April 1961. After long deliberations the three powers agreed to suspend forthwith all tests in the earth's atmosphere, in outer space, in ocean and underground. This was to be ensured through a worldwide detective system to be operated by a single neutral administrator and an international staff. However, Soviet Union, in violation of this agreement went ahead with the explosion of Megaton Bomb. This provoked U.S.A. to declare that she would also go ahead with similar explosion. As a result the progress made in the direction of securing nuclear test ban at the Geneva Conference was watered down.

Antarctic Treaty (1959)

In 1959 the Antarctic Treaty was signed which provided for demilitarisation of Antarctica. This treaty for the first time put in practice the concept of nuclear-weapon-free zone, in so far as it prohibited in the Antarctic region all military manoeuvres, weapon tests, building of installations or disposal at of radioactive wastes produced by military activity.

Ten Nations Disarmament Conference (1960)

In 1960 ten nations five from each block (U.S.A., U.K., Canada, France and Italy from Western bloc and Soviet Union, Yugoslavia, Poland, Rumania and Bulgaria from the Communist bloc) met at Geneva and made another serious bid to secure disarmament. As a result of prolonged deliberations the differences between the rival camps were considerably narrowed down. The Soviet Union went to the extent of announcing that she was willing to prohibit atomic weapons and even offered to destroy the atomic and hydrogen bomb, if the western powers reciprocated. She proposed a four-year plan of complete disarmament spread over three phases. During the first phase the forces of the powers were to be reduced. During the second stage the forces of all states were to be dissolved and military bases demolished. At the final stage all the nuclear weapons were to be destroyed. The Western nations did not respond favourably to the Soviet Plan and came forward with their own plan on 15 March 1960 suggesting publication of data before the release of atom bomb or missile; formation of central organisation for collection of data relating to army, navy and air force of all the countries; system of verification of information supplied by different states; assessment of military budgets of different countries; installation of the system for controlling outer space; advance notification of launching of long range missiles; prohibition of certain specified missile materials and use of the material for non-military purposes; institution of proper system of supervision to prevent production of armaments, security; and provision of adequate measure to warn against surprise attacks. The Plan was not acceptable to the Soviet Union and her allies. As a result a stalemate was reached and finally the Soviet Union and her allies walked out of the Conference. With this the Conference came to an abrupt end.

Eighteen Nations Disarmament Conference (1962)

In 1962 another conference was held at Geneva which is popularly know as Eighteen Nations Disarmament Conference. Actually in this conference only seventeen nations took part. Almost all the important powers, with the exception of France, were present in this Conference. At this Conference also separate plans were submitted by U.S.A. and Soviet Union. In its plan U.S.A. proposed a cut of thirty per cent in the nuclear delivery vehicles and major conventional armaments, within three years. It also proposed a ban on the production of the nuclear weapons. On the other hand Soviet Union insisted on general and complete disarmament within four years under strict international control. According to the Soviet Plan this was to be accomplished in three stages beginning with the destruction of all means of delivery of nuclear weapons and elimination of all foreign bases. This Conference was significant because the Neutral Nations also came forward with their own plan. They suggested the establishment of an International Commission of Scientists to process the data received form the observation posts and to report on all nuclear explosions. The Eighteen Nations Conference also could not accomplish anything and faltered over the issue of verification.

Limited Test Ban Treaty (1963)

In June 1963 President Kennedy emphasised the need for a nuclear test ban treaty. The proposal received favourable response from Soviet Union and culminated in the Test Ban Treaty of 1963. This treaty concluded at Moscow on 5 August 1963, "prohibited the states from carrying out any nuclear weapon test explosion or any other nuclear explosion at any place under their jurisdiction or control, viz., (a) in the atmosphere beyond its limits, including outer space or under water including territorial waters or high seas; (b) in any other environment if such explosion causes radioactive debris to be present outside the territorial limits of the state under whose jurisdiction or control such explosion is conducted." Though initially the treaty was concluded by the three Nuclear Powers U.S.A., U.S.S.R and U.K. it was made open to all the states.

It may be observed that the treaty made no provision for control through posts, spot inspection or international bodies. It merely prohibited those tests which could be detected and made no effort to reduce the nuclear stockpiles. In fact, both China and France (the other nuclear powers) refused to sign the treaty because it did not insist on the destruction of nuclear stockpiles of U.S.A and U.S.S.R. The decision of China and France to keep out greatly jeopardised the attempt at disarmament.

In 1964 China went ahead with her first atom bomb explosion which greatly stirred the General Assembly and it decided to convene a Conference of the five nuclear powers. In November 1965 it adopted a resolution urging all the nations to suspend all tests of nuclear and thermonuclear weapons. It even sought to extend the ban to the underground tests which were permitted under the Moscow Treaty of 1963. However, U.S.A and U.K refused to comply with the General Assembly resolution unless a guarantee was provided against similar explosions by other states.

Seven Point Plan (1966)

Seven Point Plan was presented by President Johnson of U.S.A. at the Geneva Conference in February 1966. This Plan called for a treaty to halt the spread of nuclear weapons to non-nuclear countries and demanded international safeguards over peaceful nuclear activities. It suggested the strengthening of the international security organisation and the establishment of a system of inspection. It gave a call for freezing all 'offensive and defensive" strategic bombers and missiles designed to carry nuclear weapons. However, the plan was not favourabiy received by the other powers and was abandoned. The progress of disarmament suffered a further setback following nuclear tests by France.

Outer Space Treaty of 1967

This treaty laid down the principles Governing peaceful activities of the states in outer space and prohibited nuclear weapons and their landing on the moon and other celestial bodies for military bases. The treaty was formally signed on 27 January, 1967 and came into force on 10 October 1967. Under the treaty the signatory states agreed not to place in orbit around the earth any objectives carrying nuclear weapons or other kinds of weapons of mass destruction. It also forbade the use of military personnel for scientific research for peaceful purposes. It was agreed that all stations, installations, equipment and space vehicles on the moon and other celestial bodies shall be open to the representatives of other States parties to the Treaty on the basis of reciprocity. The treaty was thrown open to other states for signatures, who could accede to it.

Treaty of Tlatelolco 1967

In 1967 the Tlatelolco Treaty was concluded by Mexico and El Salvador at Mexico, which prohibited the testing, use, manufacture, production or acquisition by any means, as well as receipt, storage, installation, development and any form of possession of nuclear weapons in Latin America. Under the Additional Protocol II, the nuclear weapon states undertook to respect the statute of military denuclearisation of Latin America and not to contribute to acts involving a violation of the Treaty, nor to use or threaten to use nuclear weapons, against the parties to the treaty. However, the treaty permitted the explosions of nuclear devices for peaceful purposes.

Conference of Non-Nuclear Weapon States (1968)

In August–September 1968 a Conference of the Non-Nuclear. Weapon States was held at Geneva at the initiative of the General Assembly. The conference was attended by 96 states, including the four nuclear powers - U.S.A., U.S.S.R. France and U.K. The Conference in all adopted fourteen resolutions and declaration concerning four subjects, viz., security of the non-nuclear weapon states establishment of nuclear weapons free zones, effective measures for prevention of proliferation of nuclear weapons and peaceful uses of nuclear energy. With regard to the security of the non-nuclear weapons states, the Conference reaffirmed the principle of non-use or threat of use of force between states. It asserted that every state had right to equality, sovereignty, territorial integrity, nonintervention in internal affairs, collective defence, etc.

With regard to the establishment of the nuclear-weapon free zones, the Conference recommended that the non-nuclear weapon states should examine the possibility and desirability of establishing military denuclearisation of their respective zones.

On the question of effective means for the prevention of the proliferation of nuclear weapons, the cessation of the nuclear arms race and nuclear disarmament, the Conference recommended to the General Assembly to urge the Eighteen Nations Disarmament Committee to undertake negotiations for prevention of further development and improvement of nuclear weapons, reduction and subsequent elimination of all stock piles of nuclear weapons; conclusion of comprehensive test-ban-treaty, etc.

On the issue of peaceful uses of energy the Conference favoured the idea of examining possibility of establishing an internationally financed *Special Nuclear Fund,* which could give grants and loans at low rates to finance such nuclear projects in the non-nuclear states. These recommendations of the Conference were accepted by the General Assembly and it requested the concerned international bodies like IAEA, IBRD and UNDP to take action for the implementation of these recommendations.

Non-Proliferation Treaty (1968)

The Treaty on Non-Proliferation of Nuclear Weapons was simultaneously signed at London, Moscow and Washington in July 1968 and actually came into force on 5 March 1970. The Treaty, based on the draft submitted by the Seventeen Nation Disarmament Committee, prohibited the transfer by nuclear weapon states to any recipient whatsoever of nuclear weapons or other nuclear explosive devices or of control over them. The signatory states were not to encourage or induce any non-nuclear weapon State to manufacture or otherwise acquire nuclear weapons or other explosive devices or control over such weapons or explosive devices. The non-nuclear states acceding to the treaty were also not to manufacture or otherwise acquire nuclear weapons or other nuclear explosive devices. However, the treaty granted the right to the member states to develop research, production and use of nuclear energy for peaceful purposes without discrimination. The signatory states were to conduct negotiations in good faith regarding effective. measures to put an end to the nuclear arms race at an early date and to make efforts to achieve general and complete nuclear disarmament under strict and effective international control.

The treaty was significant in so far it imposed an obligation on the nuclear and non-nuclear states to abstain from expanding nuclear weapons. However, it left the issue of inspection and control unresolved.

Disarmament Decade

Despite important agreements for limitation and regulation of armaments, global expenditure on arms and armies continued to mount and the limited human and material resources, which could be well utilised for development, continued to be frittered away. To check this trend in 1969 the General Assembly decided to observe 1970's as the *Disarmament Decade.* It urged the governments to intensify efforts to stop nuclear arms race and eliminate weapons of mass destruction. In 1976 the Assembly felt unhappy over the meagre achievements of the Decade and decided to hold a special session on disarmament in 1978.

Sea-Bed Treaty 1971

In February 1971 the treaty on the prohibition of the emplacement of nuclear weapons and other weapons of mass destruction on the seabed and the ocean floor and in the subsoil thereof, was concluded by U.K., U.S.A. and Soviet Union. The treaty actually came into force on 18 May 1972. The treaty provided that the signatory states would not emplant or emplace on the seabed and the ocean floor and in the sub-soil thereof beyond the outer limit of a sea-bed zone (12 miles) any nuclear weapons or any other type of weapons of mass destruction as well as structures, launching installations or any other facilities specifically designed for storing, testing or using such weapons. The member states were not to assist, encourage or participate in any actions in any other way. To ensure that the term of treaty were being complied with by all the signatory states, the members were given the right to verify through observation the activities of other states, provided such an act did not interfere with such activities. The member states also agreed to continue negotiations concerning further measures to prevent an arms race on the seabed, the ocean floor and the sub-soil.

Biological Weapons Convention 1972

An effort to check the use of bacteriological and chemical weapons was made in 1972 by signing the "Convention on the Prohibition of the Development, Production and Stockpiling of Bacteriological (Biological) and Toxin Weapons and on their Destruction." The Convention signed on 10 April 1972 at London Moscow and Washington, actually came into force on 26 March 1975. The convention impressed the need of achieving effective progress towards general and complete disarmament, including the prohibition and elimination of all types of weapons of mass destruction. It held that the prohibition of development, production and stockpiling of chemical and bacteriological weapons and their elimination will facilitate the achievement of the objective of complete disarmament under strict and effective international control. The signatory states agreed not to develop, produce, stockpile or otherwise acquire or retain microbial or other biological agents or toxins for hostile purposes or in armed conflict. They were to either destroy or divert to peaceful purpose within nine months of the enforcement of Convention, all agents, toxins, weapons, equipment and means of delivery. They were also not to encourage or assist any state or organisation of states to manufacture or otherwise acquire any of the above agents etc. If a signatory to the Convention found the other signatory state violating the provisions of the Convention it could lodge a complaint with the Security Council. Thereafter, the other members were obliged to co-operate with the Security Council in carrying out investigations. The states also agreed to continue negotiations to reach an early agreement on effective measures for the prohibition of their development, production and stockpiling.

Strategic Arms Limitation and SALT 1972

Simultaneous attention was also paid to the limitation of the starategic arms with a view to achieve disarmament. The two super powers U.S.A. and USSR held prolonged negotiations at Geneva and finally agreed to meet at Helsinki. This was indeed a significant step in the direction of disarmament because the two powers agreed in principle to restrain and put a stop to the fierce competition for the acquisition of sophisticated weapons. Though the talks did not prove fruitful, they indicated the willingness of the two super powers to reduce armament and other hazards without jeopardising their security and prestige. The negotiations continued for nearly four years before the conclusion of the Strategic Arms Limitation Treaty of 1972. It is said that the two countries held as many as 127 plenary meetings before conclusion of the above treaty.

The SALT (Strategic Arms_Limitation Treaty)

It was formally signed on 26 May 1972 with a view to curb the race in nuclear arms between the two super powers. In fact, the agreement broadly consisted of two separate treaties, viz., Treaty on the Limitations of Anti-Ballistic Missile System and the Interim Agreement on Certain Measures with respect to the Limitation of the Strategic Offensive Arms. While the former was concluded for an unlimited period, the latter was of five-year duration.

The Anti-Ballistic Missile Systems Treaty permitted the two super powers to have only two sites for ballistic missile defences, one for the protection of their national capital area and the other for the protection of the field of ICBMs. The treaty also laid down details regarding the dimensions of the ABM system the two countries were to have. Each system was to have not more than six ABM launchers and 100 ABM interceptor missiles at launching sites. The national capital area was not to have more than 133 ABM radar complexes, each with a diameter not exceeding 3 kilometres. The complex around the Missile launching region was not to have more than 18 ABM radars and two large phased ABM radars. The two powers also agreed not to develop, test or deploy ABM launchers which could launch more than one interceptor missile at a time. The treaty also prohibited the testing and development of automatic, semi–automatic or other similar systems for rapid reloading of ABM launchers. The two powers were permitted to modernise their ABM systems through replacement, but this was to be done strictly within the quantitative ceiling provided under the treaty.

The Interim Agreement with regard to the Limitation of the Strategic Offensive Arms was a very complex agreement. It covered both land based ICBMs and submarine launched ballistic missiles. The strength of ICBMs for Soviet Union and U.S.A. was fixed at 1618 and 1054, respectively, viz., on the basis of their actual strengths on 1 July 1971. The two powers undertook not to convert their land-based launches into light ICBMs. The two powers were permitted to undertake modernisation and replace their strategic Offensive Arms, but they had to scrupulously follow the numerical limits prescribed by the treaty. An agreement regarding the procedure of agreement was also reached between the two powers.

US-Soviet Accord on Limitation of Arms (1973)

A further accord for checking the armament race was reached between U.S.A. and Soviet Union in 1973 when they concluded a formal agreement regarding permanent limitation of nuclear weapons by the end of 1974. They emphasised that an effort by either of the two powers to obtain a nuclear advantage would be inconsistent with the peaceful relations between the two countries. They agreed to 'adequate verification' measures. The significance of this accord lies in the fact that it made an effort to control nuclear fission as well as research on the fundamental properties of physical matter.

The Threshold Test Ban Treaty (TTBT) 1974

This Treaty was signed by United States and USSR on 3 July 1974 and proposed a ban on carrying out of underground nuclear weapon tests having a yield of more than 150 kilotons. The two parties also pledged to limit the number of their underground weapon tests to a minimum. However, the treaty could not come into force due to non-ratification by the U.S. Senate.

US-Soviet Arms Pact 1974

Further progress in the direction of disarmament was made in July 1974 when U.S.A. and Soviet Union signed a 10 year pact, stipulating not only the limitation of the offensive nuclear weapons but also the stoppage of all underground tests of more than 150 kilotons. New limits of missile defence systems were agreed by the countries. But probably the most significant feature of this agreement was that a formal understanding was reached by the two countries to permit each observer to ensure that the terms of the agreement were being complied with. The same year in November the two countries concluded another agreement regarding limiting of nuclear arsenals. It was decided that the nuclear arsenals of the two countries shall be equal to overall number of delivery vehicles. The new treaty also incorporated the relevant provisions of the existing interim agreement which was due to expire in 1977.

The Peaceful Nuclear Explosion Treaty (PNET) 1976

This treaty was signed by United States and Soviet Union on 28 May 1976, but could not come into force due to non ratification by the U.S. Senate. Despite this both the parties pledged to observe the main provisions of the treaty. Till end of December the PNET had not formally come into force.

Final Act of the Conference of Security and Co-operation in Europe

In July-August, 1975 U.S.A., U.K., Soviet Union and a number of other European states held a conference at Helsinki with a view to find out the means of strengthening peace and security of the world. After due deliberations they signed the final act of conference of security and co-operation in Europe on I August 1975. Under this act the signatory states agreed to resist from use of force in their mutual as well as international relations. With a view to promote mutual understanding they agreed to exchange observers by invitation, at military manoeuvers. However, for such a purpose a twenty-one day notice was to be served. With a view to build mutual confidence among the states, the signatory states agreed to notify their major military movements. In order to strengthen European security, the signatory states agreed to avoid military confrontation and promote disarmament. However, complete disarmament under strict and effective international control was to be accomplished through stages.

Convention on Prohibition of Military or other Hostile Use of Environmental Modification Techniques

In May 1977 a Convention was signed at Geneva with a view to strengthen world peace and bring about complete disarmament through prohibition of military or other hostile uses of the environmental modification techniques. The signatory states agreed not to engage in military or other hostile use of environmental modification techniques. They were not to assist, encourage or induce any State, group of States or international Organisation to engage in activities contrary to the provisions of the treaty. However, the Convention did not impose any restrictions on the use of environmental modification techniques for peaceful purposes. They were to contribute individually or in cooperation with other states to the preservation, improvement and peaceful utilisation of the environments with due consideration for the needs of the developing areas of the world.

Special Session on Disarmament

The first special session on disarmament was held from 23 May to 1 July 1978 which was the largest representative meeting of nations. At this session a consensus was reached on the need for comprehensive disarmament. The Assembly adopted a final Document which stressed the central role and primary responsibility of the United Nations in the field of disarmament and outlined specific measures to strengthen the machinery available in the UN system to deal with disarmament. The final document impressed on the states the need to continue general and complete disarmament under effective control. It called for immediate action to eliminate danger of nuclear war and take measures to halt and reverse the arms race. The declaration asserted that genuine and lasting peace can only be created through effective implementation of the security system provided by the charter of United Nations and the speedy and substantial reduction of arms and armed forces..... leading ultimately to general and complete disarmament under effective international control. The declaration emphasised the urgency of revitalising existing disarmament machinery and of establishing appropriate forums for disarmament negotiations and deliberations under a more representative character.

In 1979 the general assembly declared the 1980's the Second Disarmament Decade to achieve general and complete disarmament under effective international control.

SALT II (1979)

SALT I signed by USA and USSR lapsed in October 1977. Both the powers continued to observe its provisions and continued efforts for a new agreement. After prolonged negotiations they signed at Vienna on I June 1979 the SALT II treaty to limit the strategic offensive weapons for period up to 31 December 1985. While concluding this treaty both the powers reaffirmed their desire to take further measures for further limitation and reduction of strategic arms with a view to achieve general and complete disarmament. As this agreement was in the nature of a treaty, it was sent to the US Senate for ratification, as required under the constitution. But before the Senate could ratify the same the cordial atmosphere was disturbed by the Soviet intervention in Afghanistan which jeopardised the ratification of SALT II. However, U.S.A. continued to adhere to the limits proposed by SALT II, for some time. Ultimately on 27 May 1986 President Reagan of USA announced that United States would no longer be bound by the limits set by SALT II. This evoked strong reaction in USA and the House of Representatives passed a resolution on 19 June 1986 calling upon President Reagan to stick to the limits set by the Strategic Arms Limitation Treaty Number 2. The arms services committee of the Senate also made an amendment to defence department bill and called upon the President to honour SALT II limits.

Agreement concerning Activities of States on Moon and other Celestial Bodies.

In 1979 an agreement governing the activities of states on the Moon and other Celestial bodies was worked out. The agreement amplified the relevant provisions of the Outer Space Treaty by prohibiting any threat or use of force or any other hostile acts or threat of hostile acts on the Moon as well as the use of the Moon in order to commit any such act or engage in any such threat in relation to earth, the moon-spacecraft, the personnel of spacecraft or manmade space objects.

During the year 1980 only limited contact took place between USA and Soviet Union on the question of arms control. The U.S. Government motivated by the events in Afghanistan proceeded to review and to expand its armament programme. Despite this Soviet Union repeatedly expressed its willingness to negotiate. On 18 February 1980, Soviet Foreign Minister Andrai Gromyko indicated the readiness of Soviet Union to carry on disarmament talks with the West, particularly on the reduction of nuclear arms in Europe if NATO's decision of December 1979 regarding modernisation (which involved employment of Pershing IIs and Cruise missiles) was cancelled or not implemented. In mid-August 1980 President Brezhnev wrote to western leaders expressing his willingness to engage in talks on intermediate range nuclear missiles. President Carter of USA responded favourably and agreed to hold unconditional talks on this subject. As a result Preparatory US-Soviet talks on strategic arms limitations were held in Geneva from 16 October to 17 November 1980 which resulted in greater understanding of each other's position and they agreed to resume negotiations in 1981.

After his election, President Reagan indicated on 2 February, 1981 his readiness to discuss a legitimate reduction of nuclear weapons. However, he insisted that the USA should have a military presence in the Middle East to discourage any reckless moves by the Soviet Union. On the other hand President Brezhnev also called for an active US-Soviet dialogue at all levels and proposed a moratorium on the development in Europe of new medium range nuclear missiles by NATO countries and the Soviet Union.

Soviet Proposals regarding Prohibition of Stationing of Weapons in Outer Space

In 1981, Soviet Union proposed a treaty of unlimited duration to prohibit the stationing of weapons of any kind in outer space, including stationing of 'reusable' manned space vehicle. The parties to the treaty were to undertake not to destroy, damage or disturb the normal functioning or change the flight trajectory of space objects of other states, if such objects were placed in the orbit in strict accordance with the above mentioned provisions. However, the Soviet proposal did not specify whether the development and testing of anti-satellite systems would be prohibited and whether the states would be obliged to dismantle those systems which they have already developed and tested.

In December 1981 the U.N. General Assembly taking into account the proposals of the Soviet Union, required the Committee on disarmament to embark on negotiations with a view to achieving agreement on the text of an appropriate treaty to prevent the spread of arms race to other space. Through another resolution, it requested the Committee on Disarmament to consider as a matter of priority, the question of negotiating an effective and variable agreement to prohibit anti-satellite systems. However, much progress could not be made due to the difficulties in reaching further arms control agreements relating to outer space because most of the satellites are used for military purpose. Further, the competition going on between the two super powers is bound to generate pressure for pre-emptive action and thus decrease rather than increase the sense of security of the powers in question, bringing no advantage to either side

Prohibition of Inhumane Weapons : New Small Arms Ammunition (1981)

On 10 April, 1981 the Convention on Prohibition or Restrictions on Use of certain Conventional Weapons was opened for signature at the United Nations. This convention was in the nature of an umbrella covering a number of protocols covering landmines and body-traps, incendiary weapons and fragments not detectable by X-ray.

Efforts by the UN General Assembly

During the Year 1981 the UN General Assembly also initiated a number of measures to check nuclear weapons, chemical weapons as well as to promote the disarmament. The Assembly expressed concern over continued nuclear weapons tests and urged UK, USA and USSR to resume their trilateral negotiations (which were interrupted in 1980) on a comprehensive test ban treaty and to bring them to an early conclusion. It also suggested the conclusion of an international convention on the non-use of nuclear weapons in general and declared that the use of such weapons would be a violation of the UN Charter and a crime against humanity. It also called upon the nuclear weapons states to submit their views, proposals and practical suggestions for ensuring the prevention of nuclear war. Similarly, the General Assembly while calling for continuation of negotiations on convention prohibiting chemical weapons called on all the states to refrain from any action which could impede such negotiations and to specifically refrain from the production and development of binary and other new types of chemical weapons. It also requested that chemical weapons should not be stationed in those states where there are no such weapons at present.

With a view to promote disarmament, the General Assembly recommended that a world disarmament campaign should be launched and a conference be held at the United Nations to finance the campaign. It expressed the view that a worldwide collection of signatures in support of measures to prevent the nuclear war and arms race be started, which would help in creating favourable climate for achieving progress in the field of disarmament.

However, despite its active interest to effect arms control the General Assembly could not attain much success due to an atmosphere of increased international tension. The sharp polemics between the USA and the USSR, characterised by mutual cold-war accusation of aggressiveness and bad faith negatived the effects of the international arms control endeavours.

Reagan Plan of 18 November 1981

On 18 November 1981 President Reagan of United States proposed a four point agenda suggesting (1) that the United States was prepared to cancel its deployment of Pershing II and ground launched cruise missiles if the Soviet Union would dismantle its SS-20, SS-4 and SS-5 medium and intermediate range ballistic missiles; (2) that USA would seek to negotiate substantial reduction in nuclear arms which would result in equal and verifiable levels and that to symbolise this the negotiations would be called START

(Strategic Arms Reduction Talks)- (3) that action should be taken to achieve equality at lower levels of conventional forces in Europe; and (4) that USA urged the USSR to join with it and many other nations to establish a western proposed conference on disarmament in Europe. The United States leadership expressed the hope that the acceptance of these proposals by the Soviet would benefit the people of East and West and the Third World and promote peace and security all over the world.

However, these proposals were out rightly rejected by the Soviet Union. The Soviet President Breznev said that if the United States were prepared to agree to complete reduction of all kinds of nuclear weapons in the East and West, Soviet Union would be in favour.

INF Talks at Geneva November (1981)

On 30 November, 1981 talks between U.S.A. and Soviet Union on intermediate-range nuclear force (INF) commenced at Geneva. The deliberations were held in camera. But much progress could not be made. On 3 February 1982 Brezhnev proposed that both the sides should reduce their medium range nuclear weapons by two-thirds by 1990, but the proposal was rejected by President Reagan. On 9 February 1982 Soviet Union proposed a modified plan but this was also turned down by USA the next day

USA reacted sharply and stated that it would not tolerate any stationing of nuclear missiles in Cuba. On 31 March 1982 President Reagan said 'I want an agreement on strategic nuclear weapons that reduces the risk of war, lowers the level of armament and enhances global security. We accept no less."

Brezhnev Announcement of March 1982

On 16 March 1982, the Soviet President Brezhnev announced that Soviet Union had 'decided to introduce unilaterally a moratorium on the deployment of medium range nuclear weapons in the European part of the Soviet Union' involving 'the freezing in terms both of the quantity and quality" of the weapons already in place as well as the suspension of the planned replacement of the existing SS-4 and SS-5 missiles by the new SS-20 models. He asserted the moratorium would remain in force either until the USA and the Soviet Union reached agreement on a planned reduction of nuclear weapons or on the other hand until practical preparation began for the deployment of Pershing II and ground launched cruise missile in Europe. He warned that if NATO allies went ahead with their plans to renew their nuclear strike capacity, the Soviet Union would have no choice but to take retaliatory steps.

START Negotiations

On 9 May 1982, US President suggested that formal START negotiations be held between the two countries at Geneva in June 1982. He proposed two stages. During the first stage the number of the ballistic missile war-heads was to be reduced by at least one-third below current levels. During the second stage they were to achieve equal ceilings on ballistic missiles.

The plan also insisted on effective verification procedures.But the plan was dismissed by Soviet Union 'as a hopeless attempt to ensure US superiority.' However, the plan said nothing about the programme to deploy MX missiles, strategic B - 1 bombers and Trident nuclear missile submarines.

On 18 May 1982 President Brezhnev made an offer of freeze on the nuclear missiles and proposed freeze on the modernisation and deployment of strategic weapons. He said that to begin the START talks on right note, three things should be done. (1) The talks should pursue the aim of limiting arms and reducing strategic arms rather than being a cover for the continued arms race and the breakdown of the existing parity. (2) Both sides should pay due regard to each other's legitimate security interests and acknowledge the principle of equality and equal security. (3) The positive achievements of earlier and equal talks should not be overlooked. The proposals of Brezhnev were immediately rejected by USA.

The START talks opened in Geneva on 29 June 1982 in which the delegations of USA and USSR took part. Though the talks were secret, the two delegations made certain statements regarding their respective positions, which virtually reflected the views that had already been expressed. At these talks USSR offered to make substantial cuts in the long-range missile and bomber forces in return for US agreement to forgo the deployment of new medium-range missiles in Europe and to accept stringent restrictions on all further cruise missile deployments. The Soviet Union tried to like INF and START talks. On the other hand USA was very keen to restore the credibility of its nuclear umbrella in the eyes of its friends and opponents and wanted to eliminate the enormous advantage which the Soviets had gained in land-based missle and prevent all risks of blackmail.

Second Special Session of General Assembly on Disarmament

The Second Special Session on Disarmament of the General Assembly was held in 1982 in which more than 140 states took part. Over 3000 representatives from 450 non-governmental organisations in 47 countries around the world also attended the session. After prolonged deliberations the General Assembly categorically and unanimously reaffirmed the validity of the Final Document of the First Special Session on Disarmament and urged the member states to consider as soon as possible proposals designed to secure the avoidance of war, particularly nuclear war. The Assembly also stressed the need for strengthening the central role of the United Nations in the field of disarmament and enhancing the effectiveness of the Committee on Disarmament (now known as Conference on Disarmament) as the single multilateral negotiating body.

New US Proposals on SALT

In 1983 USA proposed 'build down' whereby each side modernising its forces would effect 5 per cent reduction of its forces each year until 1992. According to this plan each new unit of ICBM fire power developed was to be matched by reduction of two old units of ICBM fire power and each new unit of submarine launched fire power was to be matched by dismantling the two old units. The proposals also envisaged the establishment of a commission to work out the details of a build down.

The Soviet Union responded to US proposals and called for reduction of strategic nuclear delivery vehicles from about 2400 to 1800 or 1850, while demanding that the US must not deploy any new intermediate range missiles in Europe whatsoever, Soviet Union also indicated its willingness to accept an overall ceiling on nuclear explosions, but did not put forward a specific number. Soviet Union also demanded that the British and the French forces be counted in INF process. However, the British and French were determined to maintain independent deterrents which were not subjected to US USSR negotiations.

On account of persistent tension between USA and Soviet Union no further progress could be made between the East and West on arms control and eventually disarmament. The Soviet Union refused to resume Geneva Disarmament talks–both negotiations on intermediate range nuclear force (INF) which were suspended in November 1983 on strategic arms reduction talks (START) which were suspended in December, 1983 on the ground that she could not resume these talks unless the policy of deployment of Perishing II and Cruise missiles in Western Europe was reversed.

Efforts for Disarmament by General Assembly after 1982

Since 1982 the General Assembly at regular intervals called for implementation of the decisions and recommendations of the first and second special sessions on disarmament. It has called for (i) cessation of test explosions of nuclear weapons including underground nuclear weapons test and called for conclusion of comprehensive. nuclear test ban treaty; (ii) negotiations for cessation of nuclear arms race and prevention of nuclear war, (iii) freeze on nuclear weapons by all nuclear weapon states; (iv) establishment of nuclear-weapon free zones in Middle East and South Asia and implementation of Declaration of the Indian Ocean as a Zone of Peace; (v) conclusion of an international convention for strengthening security of non-nuclear weapon states against use or threat of use of nuclear weapons; (vi) measures to prevent arms race in out space; (vii) conclusion of convention of prohibition of the development, production, stockpiling, and use of all chemical, radiological and nuclear neutron weapons; (viii) an agreement on the prohibition of the development and manufacture of new types of weapons of mass destruction and new systems of such weapons; and (ix) reduction of military budgets and reallocation of resources now being used for military purposes to economic and social development in developing countries.

However, these recommendations of the General Assembly, though unanimously adopted have not been faithfully implemented and much progress has not been made in the direction of disarmament.

Talks between NATO and Warsaw Pact Countries

Talks between delegations from NATO and Warsaw Pact countries on Mutual and Balanced Force Reductions in Central Europe were resumed on 16 March 1984 (which had been suspended in December 1983). On 19 April 1984 NATO members submitted a plan which envisaged first of all a reduction in combat and support troops in Central Europe by 13,000 for USA and 30,000 for the USSR and thereafter an eventual reduction of the two sides to 700,000 ground troops and 200,000 air force members for each side within four or five years. This plan was rejected by the Warsaw Pact delegation on the ground that the proposal was "neither constructive nor realistic." Despite these differences the talks continued till 19 July 1984.

Improvement of Hotline

In July, 1984 USA and Soviet Union agreed to add a facsimile transmission capability to the Direct Communication Link (DCL) popularly known as 'hotline'. The hotline was first established in August 1963 with a view to lessening of the danger of an outbreak of hostilities by accident or miscalculations. The new improvement enabled the two sides to send graphic material via the DCL

Four Continent Peace Initiative

On 22 May 1984 a plan on behalf of six political leaders form the four continents of Africa, Asia, Europe and Latin America, viz., President Raula Alfonsin on Argentian ; Prime Minister Andreas Papandreou of Greece; Prime Minister Indira Gandhi of India; President Miguel Dela Madrid of Mexico; Prime Minister Olof Palme of Sweden and President Julius Nyerere of Tanzania; was presented to the UN missions of the five nuclear-weapon powers (China, France, USSR, UK and USA). The Plan asserted "The escalating arms race, the rise in international tensions and the lack of constructive dialogue among nuclear-weapons states has increased the risk of nuclear war. The people we represent are no less threatened by nuclear war than the citizens of the nuclear-weapon states. It is primarily the responsibility of the nuclear–weapon states to prevent a nuclear catastrophe, but this problem is too important to be left to those states alone." It stated that "agreements which merely regulate an arms build up are clearly insufficient" and the leaders called on the five nuclear weapon powers "as a necessary first step to halt all testing, production and deployment of nuclear weapons and their delivery system to be immediately followed by substantial reduction in nuclear forces."

Though USA appreciated the initiative and sincerity of the leaders in taking an initiative, it asserted "we do not think that global freeze by the nuclear powers would strengthen stability or reduce the risk of war."

Initiative by India and Non-aligned Countries

In August, 1984 India and 20 other non-aligned and neutral countries suggested setting up of an ad hoc committee of the UN Disarmament Conference to negotiate measures for preventing a nuclear war. However, USA and to the Western countries did not respond favourably.

Geneva Talks (1985)

A welcome development took place in January 1985 when the foreign ministers of USSR and USA (Andrei Gromyko and George Shultz) met at Geneva on 7th and 8th January. Negotiations at Geneva could not make much progress because USSR sought to link controls of offensive missiles with the termination of Reagan's Strategic Defence Initiative (SDI), popularly known as Star Wars programme, while USA wanted to enhance the prospects of SDI by limiting the offensive missile which SDI would oppose. USA refused to link the two argued that a ban on research programme (SDI is currently a research agenda) cannot be verified. Though the two countries could not reach any accord, the resumption of talks was significant development The two sides agreed that the space weapon system and the intermediate range nuclear missiles in Europe be brought into the negotiation that originally covered strategic nuclear missiles. The delegations of Soviet Union and USA and agreed to split into three groups to negotiate on. the areas of strategic, intermediate range and space weapons with a view to "work out effective agreements aimed at preventing an arms race in space and terminating it on earth." The real significance of the Geneva talks was that it succeeded in breaking the ice. USSR had pledged not to hold any talks unless Cruise and Perishing II missiles were dismantled, but it relented on this point and agreed for talks at Geneva. Likewise USA also showed spirit of accommodation and agreed to broaden the scope of new negotiations by including within their purview the threatened arms race in space as well as existing stockpiles. The two states pledged to work for effective agreements aimed at preventing an arms race in space as well as terminating it on earth.

Six Nations Summit at New Delhi (1985)

On 28 January 1985 a six nation summit was held at New Delhi which was attended by President Raul Alfonsin of Argentina, Prime Minister Andreas Papandreou of Greece, Prime Minister Olof Palme of Sweden, President Miguel Dela Madrid of Mexico, President Julius Nyerere of Tanzania and Prime Minister Rajiv Gandhi of India. The Summit appealed to the nuclear weapon powers to halt and reverse the nuclear arms race. It urged them to immediately halt the testing of all kinds of nuclear weapons and to conclude a treaty on a nuclear weapon test ban at an early date. It called for prohibition of the development, testing, production, deployment and use of all space weapons. It warned that an arms race in the space would be enormously costly and have grave destabilising effect. The other points emphasised by the Summit were the need of strengthening of the UN System and diversion of expenditure from arms to development. The six leaders also agreed to visit nuclear powers and other capitals to impress on various powers the urgent need to put the arms race into reverse gear.

Reagan Gorbachev Summit

Disarmament suffered a serious setback in 1984-85 and two superpowers embarked on a massive programme of rearmament. This trend was reversed towards the close of 1985 when President Ronald Reagan of U.S.A. and Mikhail Gorbachev of Soviet Union met at Geneva from 19-21 November.

Though the contents of the discussion were not made public, it was quite apparent that Soviet hostility to President Reagan's Strategic Defence Initiative (popularly known as Star Wars) project proved to be the main stumbling block and no agreement could be arrived at. However, at the end of the talks the two leaders issued a joint statement in which they emphasised the desirability of intensified dialogue between the two powers through regular meetings at the highest level. They also agreed to accelerate the pace of negotiations so that early progress could be made in areas where there was a common ground such as 50 per cent cut in the overall level of armaments and the possibility of an interim INF agreement.

After the Geneva Summit the process of arriving at settlement on disarmament continued both at multi-lateral and bilateral forums. In January 1986 Gorbachev proposed a time-table for a fifteen year 'step by step' process for ridding the earth of nuclear weapons. He presented this programme at the formal talks between USA and Soviet Union on 16 January, 1986, but it was not accepted by USA.

Reykjavik Meeting (1986)

The most significant effort in the direction of disarmament was made in October 1986 when a meeting was held at Reykjavik between President Reagan and Mikhail Gorbachev. Though the meeting did not lead to any tangible agreement, it settled many of the bilateral arms-control issues which had eluded negotiations for years. There was agreement on INF and framework for 50 per cent reduction in strategic offensive weapons. But no formal agreement could be concluded on account of differences over Strategic Defence Initiative Programme (SDI). Soviet Union wanted America to cut back research and testing on the SDI programme to just the laboratory, which was not acceptable to USA.

Despite their differences fresh high level talks were held between USA and USSR at Vienna on 5-6 November 1986 in which Shutlz and Shevardnadze took part on behalf of the two countries. However, the talks were. jeopardised due to U.S. Soviet acrimony over diplomatic expulsions and counter expulsions.

In February 1987 Soviet leader Gorbachev took yet another initiative and called for the elimination of INF missiles in Europe, with a limit for each side of 100 warheads elsewhere. He also agreed to proceed without first resolving differences over SDI.

Intermediate Range Nuclear Force (INF) Treaty (1987)

This treaty, the first to abolish an entire category of nuclear weapons, was signed by President Reagan and General Secretary Gorbachev at the Washington Summit in December, 1987 and ratified by the Senate and Presidium of the two countries on the eve of the Moscow Summit in May-June, 1988. The treaty provides that during the next three years land-based missiles having a range of 500 kms to 5000kms and the launchers on which these missiles are to be mounted, will be eliminated. It also provides for the elimination of the short-range missiles within next 18 months. In accordance with this treaty USA would destroy 859 missiles based in Western Europe, while the Soviet Union would eliminate 1752 missiles based in Eastern Europe and Soviet Union. The treaty also specifies the manner in which these missiles shall be destroyed. The two parties undertook to inform each other of the type of missiles and the place where these were being destroyed. It also makes provisions for detailed on-site inspection to ensure that neither side was violating the terms of the treaty.

New Six Nation Disarmament Plan

Encouraged by the treaty between Soviet Union and the USA for the elimination of Intermediate Range Nuclear Missiles, the leaders of six nations (India, Argentina, Greece, Mexico, Sweden and Tanzania) from five continents prepared a plan for disarmament to be placed before the special session of the U.N. General Assembly on Disarmament. This Plan envisaged an important role for the United Nations in the verification of disarmament agreement. It is noteworthy that earlier in 1986 the six nations had offered to assist the two superpowers in verification of ban on nuclear tests. They proposed establishment of temporary monitoring stations at the test sites and inspection of large chemical explosions.

Third Special Session of UN General Assembly on Disarmament (June 1988)

The Third Special Session of UN General Assembly on Disarmament was held in June 1988, but it could not achieve any positive results on account of adamant attitude of the USA on the issue of shedding armaments and making commitments regarding nuclear weapons. However, the special session looked into the progress in the implementation of the first two special UN sessions on disarmament held in 1978 and 1982. It is noteworthy that while the first special session on disarmament had indicated that the final objective should be general and complete disarmament under effective international control, the immediate goal was elimination of the danger of nuclear war and the halting of arms race. The second session reaffirmed its faith in the above objectives and urged the member states to consider proposals for avoidance of war, particularly nuclear war.

Geneva Talks on Strategic Arm Reduction (June 1989)

After a gap of seven months U. S. Soviet Negotiations on reduction of long-range nuclear forces were held Geneva. However, soon it became evident that sharp differences exist between the two. While Soviet Union insisted on linking of START accord and the development of space weapons USA was opposed to it. Similarly while Soviet Union insisted on inclusion of submarine launched cruise missiles (SLCMs) in the agreement, the USA did not approve of it. Differences also existed between the two on question of mobile land based missiles, certification procedure, counting rules for warheads carried by strategic bombers etc. In view of these . differences both the sides made it clear that full agreement on strategic arms reduction treaty was not in sight.

Further Progress

Undeterred by the failure of the Geneva talks the two superpowers continued to make efforts to reach some agreement. In September the foreign ministers of USA and Soviet Union signed half a dozen agreements and announced their decision to hold a Super Power Summit in 1990 (early summer or spring). Soviet Union made a key concession and announced that Soviet Union would move ahead towards a long-range weapons agreement despite its objections to the U.S. Strategic Defence Initiative (SDI) space based antimissile programme. The two countries also reached an agreement on chemical weapons, exchange of data on chemical weapons by the end of year, visits by inspectors of other side to the stockpiles and plants by June 1990. The other accords provided for verification of missile plants and exchange of information even before a treaty to slash long-range nuclear weapons was completed etc.

US Proposes cut in Chemical Weapons

On 25 September, 1989 in the course of his address to the General Assembly President Bush of USA proposed a treaty suggesting elimination of all chemical weapons from the surface of the earth within 10 years from the date on which it is signed and indicated US readiness to destroy 98 per cent of its chemical stock-piles in 8 years provided the Soviet Union joined it in doing so. The proposal of President Bush was accepted by Soviet Union. Soviet Union offered to comply with the proposals even before the conclusion of the multilateral treaty if the United States agreed. This was a welcome development and indicates the desire of the two super powers to get rid of their it stockpiles of chemical weapons for the sake of world peace.

In short as a result of the dialogue between the two super powers since 1985 considerable progress was made and they reached substantive agreement in the areas of arms control. They ratified the 1987 INF Treaty (a focal point of controversy between the two for nearly a decade); took preliminary steps in the Strategic Arms Reduction Talks (,START) towards an agreement to reduce strategic nuclear arsenals by 50%. All these developments greatly contributed to the easing of tension between the two super powers.

Washington Summit

At the Washington Summit meeting between President Gorbachev and President Bush held in May-June 1990 further progress in the direction of disarmament was made. The two countries concluded agreements on nuclear, chemical and conventional arms. The most significant arms control agreement related to the chemical. weapons. The two sides agreed to destroy thousands of tonnes of these mass destructive weapons and reduce their stockpiles of 5,000 tonnes each. It was decided that the destruction would begin in 1992 and would last upto 2002. They also agreed to immediately stop further production of these weapons. This agreement greatly improved the prospects for a global ban on the production, possession and use of chemical weapons being negotiated by the 40-nation conference on Disarmament at Geneva.

At the Summit the two leaders also agreed on certain principles which were to govern the Strategic Arms Reduction Treaty (START), to be ready for signature by the end of the year. Another arms control agreement related to the verification protocols for the implementation of earlier treaties of mid 1970's restricting the size of underground nuclear explosions. In addition to the above agreements the two Presidents reiterated their commitment to complete the negotiations on the conventional force reductions in Europe (CFE Treaty) before the end of the year.

Treaty on Arms Cut

The next important step in the direction of disarmament was taken in September 1990 when a treaty was signed by President Bush, President Gorbachev and other European leaders at Paris which seeks to cut conventional forces in Europe. Under this treaty these leaders agreed to destroy tens of thousands of tanks, artillery and armoured combat vehicles in Europe. Each alliance was allowed a maximum of 20,000 tanks, 30,000 armoured personnel carriers, 20,000 artillery pieces, 6,800 aircraft and 2000 helicopters in four zones.

Treaty between NATO and Warsaw Pact Countries

On 19 November, 1990 the heads of states and governments of NATO and Warsaw Pact countries signed a treaty which drastically reduced their conventional arsenals for the first time since World War II. This treaty, described as the most comprehensive and far-reaching arms reduction accord ever negotiated, paved the way for new cooperation in Europe and marked the formal end of cold war.

The Strategic Arms Reduction Treaty (START)

On 31 July, 1991 the Soviet and US President George Bush signed the Strategic Arms Reduction Treaty under which the two super powers agreed to effect reduction to equal levels in defined strategic offensive arms over a period of seven years from the date the treaty came into force. Whereas Soviet Union agreed to 35' per cent cut on its strategic warheads, the United States agreed to 25 per cent cut. The Treaty provided for complex verification procedure, including on site inspections, short notice inspections and suspect site inspection. The two powers agreed to set up a joint commission on verification and inspection. The treaty was to be valid for 15 years unless superseded earlier, by a subsequent agreement. Thereafter the treaty could be extended for successive five-year period if both the sides agreed.

U. S announces Unilateral Disarmament

On 27 September 1991, President Bush of United States announced 'unilateral disarmament' to make the world a better place than ever before in the nuclear age. He asserted that this would take nuclear tactical weapons out of European soil and immediately reduce the possibility of any accidental war. He grounded all U.S. strategic bombers and took them off the alert status. He also removed from alert status all missiles covered by the Strategic Arms Reduction Treaty (START). He ordered removal of all nuclear artillery shells from overseas bases. President Bush urged Soviet Union to match the Nuclear arms cut.

President Mikhail Gorbachev responded favourably to the Bush proposals and on 5 October 1991 announced extensive cuts in tactical nuclear weapons. He announced that Soviet Union intended to eliminate nuclear artillery and nuclear warheads from tactical rockets; remove nuclear weapons from ships and submarines; take heavy bombers off battle alert and withdraw their nuclear weaponry; take 503 inter-continental ballistic missiles off battle alert; stop development of new short-range intercontinental missiles and impose one year moratorium on nuclear testing. He also offered to reduce the Soviet armed forces by 700,000 as against 500,000 offered by United States. In response to America's Star Wars research Gorbachev suggested that both the nations should mutually develop an anti-missile protection system. In short, it can be said that Soviet Union not only matched the American reduction of tactical weapons, but also announced cut of a thousand more missiles than it was required to do under the START. Above all, Soviet Union also announced one-year moratorium on nuclear testing.

It may be observed that the favourable response of the two powers to put an end to disarmament race was due both to the changed international scenario characterised by end of cold war developments in Eastern Europe and in Soviet Union, as well as domestic compulsion.

US-Russia Offer to Cut Nuclear Arms (January 1992)

A welcome development in the direction of disarmament took place in January 1992 when President Bush of USA announced bilateral reduction of nuclear arms and offered to cut nuclear arms even further if President Yeltsin reciprocated. Immediately the Russian President announced a 10-point disarmament plan with a view to liquidating all nuclear, biological and chemical mass destruction weapons. He also announced decision to cut the number of strategic nuclear missiles to the level set by the START treaty. Even proposed setting up of an international nuclear arms control agency, which should in the long run control the whole cycle of nuclear process from mining to the burial of the nuclear waste. He announced Russian decision to stop production of TU-160 and TU-95 heavy bombers as well as long-range air-based and sea-based cruise missiles.

Five Power Accord to Prevent Spread of Weapons of Mass Destruction (May 1992)

In May 1992 the five members of UN Security Council–the United States, Russia, Britain, France and China, reached an agreement to prevent the spread of weapons of mass destruction, including nuclear, chemical and biological weapons. According to-the guidelines agreed to by these powers, the states will not assist, directly or indirectly in the development, acquisition, manufacture, testing, stockpiling or development of weapons of mass destruction; promptly notify the International Atomic Energy Agency (IAEA) of the export to a non-nuclear weapons state of any nuclear materials, equipment's or facilities and place them under IAEA safeguards; exercise restraint in the transfer of sensitive nuclear facilities, technology and weapons-usable material; strictly abide by the convention on bacteriological (biological) and toxin weapons ; and not to assist in the manufacture of biological weapons. The guidelines called upon states which had not signed the nuclear non-proliferation treat as yet to sign the same. It expressed concern over the sales of ballistic missiles over 100 to 1500 km range still being made by North Korea. The states also committed to support the Missile Technology Control Regime (MTCR).

Pact on Nuclear Arms Cut (June 1992)

At the Washington summit held between President Bush and President Yeltsin in June 1992, an accord to reduce the number of nuclear warheads of the two countries from 21,000 to 7,000 by year 2003 was reached. The two countries also agreed to explore seriously the prospects of joint sponsorship of global missile defence and space cooperation.

Nuclear Arms Control Treaty (START-II)

The most significant step in the direction of nuclear arms control was taken on 3 January 1993 when President Bush of US and President Boris Yeltsin of Russia, signed the Nuclear Arms. Control Treaty which seeks to bring about two-thirds rejection in world's most terrifying weapons. Under the treaty US nuclear weapons stockpile has been limited to the position of 1960's while that of Russia has been reduced to the level of mid 1970's size. In terms of this treaty US will wind up with 1728 strategic warheads at sea and the Russians with 1600 to 1650. The land based missiles with multiple war-heads will be however dismantled by 2003 or as early as 2000 A. D. if US helps Russia get rid of its SS-18s and SS-19s.

The treaty limited the nuclear warheads with which heavy bombers of the two sides can be equipped. This limit varies form 750 to 1250 units of nuclear warheads of any type. The two countries, however, reserve the right to reorient upto 100 heavy bombers for the fulfillment of non–nuclear tasks. It may be noted that the treaty is subject to ratification by the US Senate and the Russian Parliament.

Convention on Chemical Weapons (February 1993)

On 15 February 1993 representatives of 120 countries signed Chemical Weapons Convention at Paris which placed a ban on the use, production and stockpiling of chemical weapons. Under this convention the signatory states were required to destroy stockpiles of chemical weapons within two years of ratification of treaty. The convention also contained provisions regarding international inspections of suspected violations. The Convention did not prescribe any procedure for the destruction of the chemical weapons except that it stipulated that chemical weapons should not be destroyed by sea dumping, land burial or open-pit burning. This implied that the procedure for the destruction of chemical weapons had to be environment friendly and should render such weapons unusable.

Extension of NPT (1995)

In May 1995 a global conference on the extension of Nuclear Non-Proliferation Treaty (NPT) was held at New York which decided to extend NPT indefinitely without any conditions. This permanent extension of NPT implies that only five countries the United States, the United Kingdom, Russia, China and France could legally possess nuclear weapons capability. However, to placate the non-nuclear weapons states, a list of disarmament goals was attached to the extension decision. One of these goals envisaged completion of comprehensive nuclear test ban treaty (CTBT) by next year as well as a plan for annual meetings to review the progress towards that goal. However, India refused to support the extension of NPT on account of its discriminatory nature. Pakistan also refused to sign the treaty on the ground that it would do so on if the New Delhi becomes a signatory.

Comprehensive Test Ban Treaty (CTBT) (1996)

The next important step in the direction of disarmament was the signing of CTBT in September 1996. The treaty was approved by 158-3 votes, while five countries abstained. India voted against the treaty on the ground that it was both flawed as well as discriminatory. The Treaty would however come into force only after 44 nuclear capable countries, including India sign the treaty. While opposing the treaty India's Chief Negotiator (Ms. Arundhati Ghose) told the General Assembly, that India would never sign "this unequal treaty not now, not later, until the major nuclear powers formulate a time table for eliminating their nuclear arsenal."

The treaty places a ban on all kinds of nuclear weapons test explosions. It envisages an international monitoring system to check treaty violations. A network of 20 stations would be set up which shall be able to detect underground, atmospheric or underwater explosions more powerful than the equivalent 1,000 tons of conventional explosive. Under the treaty any country would be able to request for inspection to see whether an explosion had been carried out. Such requests can be based on information collected by the international monitoring system or through surveillance, but not through spying activities. The seat of the CTBT organisation would be in Vienna (Austria). All decisions on behalf of the organisation would be made by a 51 member Executive Council to be constituted on the basis of regional representation. The Treaty would enter into force 180 days after it is ratified by 44 countries that have nuclear power or nuclear research reactors on their soil.

Chemical Weapons Treaty becomes effective

On 29 April, 1997 the Chemical Weapons Convention came into force 180 days after the 65th country (Hungary) ratified it. Subsequently more countries ratified the treaty. Thus by 1998 over 100 countries have ratified the treaty. Under the Chemical Weapons Convention (CWS), each state party undertakes never under any circumstances, to develop, produce, stockpile or retain chemical weapons or transfer directly or indirectly, chemical weapons to any one. The have undertaken not to use chemical weapons; engage in any military preparation to use chemical weapons and assist, encourage or induce, in any way anyone to engage in any activity prohibited by the Convention. The signatories to the Convention are also expected to destroy the chemical weapons which they own or possess, or which are located in any place under their jurisdiction or control. They are also expected to destroy the chemical weapons abandoned on a foreign territory. This treaty is different form other treaties on arms control in so far as it requires total elimination of the chemical weapons, while the other treaties have generally been limited arms control treaties.

Evaluation of UN's role in Field of Disarmament

It is evident form the preceding account that United Nations, since its inception, has accorded top priority to disarmament, even though its approach towards this problem has continued to change according to political realities and international conditions. In the 1950's the UN's main objective was the regulation, limitation and balanced reduction of all armed forces and armaments through a coordinated, comprehensive programme. In the 1960's the UN objective changed to general and complete disarmament, with immediate concentration on partial disarmament. The UN objective underwent further change inthe 1970's when multilateral disarmament efforts were stepped up. In 1978 the General Assembly held a special session devoted to disarmament. The General Assembly adopted a Final Document which stipulated the agreed goals, principles and priorities in arms limitation and disarmament. It also suggested measures to strengthen the multilateral machinery to deal with disarmament issues within the UN system. In 1982 and 1988 the General Assembly held further sessions on disarmament, but could not reach any agreement regarding the programme of actions. However it succeeded in establishing the United Nations Disarmament Information Programme.

The UN efforts towards arms limitation and disarmament underwent further changes after 1990, as a result of dissolution of the Soviet Union and end of cold war. A significant success in the field of reduction of nuclear weapons was achieved in 1991 and 1993 when the two major nuclear power arms (START I and START II). Another notable change which took place in 1990's was that the various powers concluded treaties on reduction of their strategic offensive agreed to exchange objective information on military matters and maintain transparency in military expenditures and arms transfers, The other issues taken up during 1990s include safe and cost-effective destruction of weapons; verification in accordance with the existing agreements etc.

It may be observed that the United Nations has played a theee-fold role in the promotion of disarmament. In the first place, it has taken initiative to start negotiations for disarmament and has been primarily responsible for keeping these negotiations going. Secondly, the United Nations established procedures for consultation which enabled the concerned sates to meet and exchange proposals regarding disarmament. Thirdly, the United Nations has greatly contributed to making disarmament the business of all states. It has enabled the smaller and less powerful states to fully appreciate the problem and encouraged them to exert increasing influence and pressure to ensure success of disarmament.

UN Machineey for dealing with Disarmaemnt

The UN charter itself provided for machinery for dealing with disarmament and related international security issues. This was further elaborated through the decisions of of the General Assembly and the Security Council, in the light of prevailing conditions.

The General Assembly is the chief deliberative organ of the United Nations in the field of disarmament. It works through two subsidiary bodies – the Disarmament and International Security Committee (popularly known as first Committee), and the United Nations Disarmament Commission. The membership of these bodies is open to all the members of the United Nations. The Disarmament and the International Security Committee meets while the Assembly is in session and deals with all disarmament items on the agenda of the Assembly. The United Nations Disarmament Commission is a specialized body which meets outside the Assembly and focuses on specific issues.

Another notable body concerned with global disarmament is Conference on Disarmament. The Conference has a limited number of members. This is the single global disarmament negotiating forum of the international community. It considers matters relating to nuclear and other weapons of mass destruction. Of late it has also been discussing matters relating to transparency in convention weapons. The conference has a unique relationship with the UN. It takes into account the recommendations of the General Assembly and reports to the Assembly annually.

United Nations Institute for Disarmament Research (UNIDIR)

This autonomous institution within the framework of the United Nations was established by the General Assembly in 1980 to undertake independent research on disarmament and related problems, particularly international security. The institutes is financed through voluntary contributions from states, private organizations and public. The main objectives of UNIDIR are (i) to provide the international community with more diversified and complete data on problems relating to international security, the arms race and disarmament, particularly in the nuclear field, so as to facilitate progress, through negotiations, towards greater security and economic and social development; (ii) to promote informed participation by all States in disarmament efforts; (iii) to assist negotiations on disarmament efforts and efforts to ensure greater international security at a progressively lower level of armament, particular nuclear armaments, by means of objective and factual studies and analysis; and (iv) to carry out research on disarmament so as to provide insight into the problems involved and stimulate initiatives for new negotiations.

For the attainment of the above objectives UNIDIR organizes conferences, publishes papers and implements projects. It provides fellowships to the scholars of developing countries for research.

Implications of Arms Race and Suggestions for Future

The implications of arms race have been beautifully brought out by UN Report thus : "The Arms race represents a waste of resources, a diversion of the economy away form humanitarian purposes, a hindrance to national development effort and threat to democratic process. But its most important feature is that in effect it undermines national, regional and international security, It involves the constant risk fo war engaging the larger Powers, including nuclear war and it is accompanied by an endless series of wars at lower levels. It raises an even greater barrier against the development of an atmosphere in which the role of the force in international relations may be downgraded. In addition, it impedes relations between countries affecting the volume and direction of exchanges, diminishing the role of cooperation among States and obstructing effort towards establishing the role of co-operation among States and obstruction effort towards establishing a new international economic order on a more equitable basis."

In the international sphere the arms race has threefold consequences. In the military sphere it increases the possibility of war, rather even the possibility of nuclear conflagration, In the economic sphere it has for reaching effects. Lot of money is spent not only on arms race and military preparations, but vast resources are also diverted away form production and growth which contributes to assume serious dimensions. Generally the security consideration comes to occupy prominent position in the policy formulation. Most of the states try to create spheres of influence in which even local conflicts become linked to regional or even global confrontations.

The Committee of experts appointed by the Secretary General under directive of General Assembly in 1976 to look into the social and economy consequences of arms race while emphasising the need of disarmament observed that "the most important goals of international community are disarmament and development, which the members of UN are committed to pursue vigorously. In fact these goals are intimately linked. Development both at an acceptable rate would be hard, if not impossible to reach with a continuation of the arms race. Research and development is one area where the misdirection of efforts is glaring. In this, as other respect, vast resources, badly needed for development are being consumed as countries make even greater sacrifices for military purposes. The Committee argued that "Progress towards disarmament would release internal material, financial and human resources, both in developed and in developing countries and would permit their redeployment to purpose of development. The relaxation of the climate of fear, hostility and confrontation which progress towards disarmament would remove some of the barriers now hampering international exchanges in general and free circulation of raw materials and advanced technology in particular, and would greatly facilitate the free choice by each country of its particular path towards development. As a result of disarmament the industrially developed countries would save a lot in their military expenditure which could easily be passed on to the developing nations in the shape of aid.. This aid shall go a long way in improving the living standard of the people in these countries.

The Committee made certain suggestions to achieve the objective of complete disarmament. It proposed that a comprehensive disarmament scheme should be prepared in which partial measures would no doubt find a place. However, in this context it would be imperative that negotiations on general and complete disarmament should receive greater and more urgent attention than they have received in the past. With a view to impart new momentum to disarmament efforts, it insisted on the need of involving all countries on the basis of equality; simultaneous curtailment of the qualitative arms race and reduction of military budgets. It emphasized that nuclear disarmament must be given highest priority partly because of the intolerable threat posed by the nuclear weapons and partly because of the possibility of their proliferation of new states which would enhance the threat and make disarmament more difficult in future.

Finally, the committee also emphasised the need of expert advice. It recommended "There is always a need for expert advice and assistance on a more continuous basis to follow developments closely to advise the General Assembly, the Secretary General and member states on questions of disarmament and to assist in the elaboration, specification and adjustment of targets and programmes". Improvement of the machinery of the United Nations in this direction appears to be necessary if the world organisation is to fulfill its task in the field of disarmament.

FURTHER READINGS

Charles A. Becker (Ed) — *Problems of World Disarmament*
Avi Beker — *Disarmament Without Order*
Myrdal Alva — *The Game of Disarmament*
U. N. Publication — *Everyone's United Nations*
U. N. Publication — *Basic Facts About the United Nations*

Chapter 21
UNITED NATIONS AND COLONIALISM

Colonialism was one of the dominant features of international politics during the past three centuries. Its origin can be traced back to the discovery of India by Vasco-da-Gama. The Portuguese and the Spanish were the first to establish their domination's overseas. Soon they were joined by other European powers like English, French, Dutch etc. However, Britain because of her mastery over the seas and industrial head-start emerged as the most powerful colonial power. The British steadily extended the sway over India, while France made encroachments in Algeria and Indo-China. The other European power like the Dutch and the Spaniards also set up some colonies. In the last quarter of the nineteenth century the imperialist powers embarked on ruthless colonialisation and divided the whole world between them. They not only consolidated their hold over the existing colonies but also carved out new colonies in Africa and Asia. Germany, Italy, Japan and U.S.A. also joined the fray for colonies. Thus colonialism reached its height in the closing years of the nineteenth century and the first decade of the present century.

Before we examine the process of Decolonisation it shall be desirable to know about the meaning of colonialism and policies followed by some of the colonial powers.

Meaning of Colonialism

Various definitions of colonialism based on the value and emotions, have been offered. According to the Western concept Colonialism is the establishment and maintenance for an extended time, of rule over an alien people that is separate and subordinate to the ruling power. It implies rule over people of different race inhabiting lands separated by salt waters from the imperial centre. More particularly it signifies direct political control of European States or state settled by Europeans, over people of other race notably over Asian and Africans. The main features of colonialism according to the Western concept include domination of an alien minority asserting racial and cultural superiority over a materially inferior native majority, contact between a machine oriented civilization with Christian civilization, that lacks machine and is marked by the backward economy and a slow rhythm of life, and the imposition of the first civilization upon the second

The leftist scholars, who consider colonialism as an evil, define it as "the military or economic enslavement of any dependent country" and see it as accompanied by bestial expatiation and extermination of the indigenous.

The African and Asian scholars also ten to agree with the leftist definition of Colonialism. For example, President Sukarno of Indonesia defined colonialism in the course of his opening address to the Bandung Conference of 1955 thus: "I beg of you not to think of colonialism in the classic form which we know. Colonialism has also its modern dress in the form of economic control, intellectual control and actual physical control by a small but alien community within the nation." Another definition of colonialism, which was accepted for long time was offered by J.A. Hobson in his book *Imperialism: A study.* He says "Colonialism, in its best sense is natural overflow of nationality: its test is the power of colonialists to transplant the civilization they represent to the new natural and social environments in which they find themselves."

Varying Colonial Policies

There has been a wide variation in the policy pursued by various colonial powers towards their colonies. It is not possible to deal with the policies of all the colonial powers here. However, we may deal with the policies of some of the major colonial powers, viz., Britain, France, Belgium and Portugal, to form an idea about the attitude of the colonial powers towards the colonies.

British Policy

Great Britain adopted a very flexible policy towards her colonies. She did not treat the colonies merely as integral part of the mother country but as countries with their own distinctive ways of life and facilitated their autonomous development. She provided increasing share to the people of the land in the governing councils, civil services and judiciary to give them training in self-government and to prepare them for ultimate independence. Starting with India in 1947 and West Indies, the British transformed most of the colonies into independent states in-keeping with their long-established policy. However she had to face some difficulties in colonies liked Rhodesia, Kenya and British Guinea because of presence of large number of white settlers in these colonies.

French Policy

France followed quite a different colonial policy. Though she extended enormous aid to her colonies and introduced a number of reforms after Second World War, she was not willing to grant independence to these colonies. As a result of this policy the French colonies of Indo-China and Algeria had to wage violent struggle for their independence. In case of Guinea also the French leadership did not approve of its decision to opt out in 1958 and treated her as an outlaw. However, in subsequent years the French leaders effected certain changes in their attitude. They granted freedom to a number of African colonies and tried to cultivate intimate relations with them after grant of independence.

Belgian Policy

The colonial policy of Belgium was quite at variance with the policy pursued by Britain and France. She did not associate the people of her colony (Congo) either with the local administration (as was done by the British) nor with imperial centre (as was done by the French.).She took no steps to create an elite class, which could take over the reins of power once she decided to withdraw. As a result, when in 1959 in wake of riots in Leopoldville Belgium hastily severed her ties with Congo and left the country, the people were in lurch because they neither possessed trained leaders and officials nor an army manned by the African officer.

Portuguese Policy

The Portuguese, the oldest colonial power, followed a colonial policy which was quite different form the one followed by Britain, France and Belgium. She did not provide education to the people in her colonies and kept them away from modernity. In the wake of Angolan rising, the Portuguese government introduced a number of reforms and provided the colonial people an equal status witting the Portuguese domain. She deliberately encouraged the Portuguese peasants and workers to emigrate to Portuguese Africa to solve the problem of poverty and to strengthen her hold on the African territory. In fact because of her own backwardness she had hardly any capacity to secure the advancement of millions of people overseas.

DECOLONISATION

It is commonly held that the idea of decolonisation is the product of the twentieth century and particularly of the post World War II period. However, this is not correct. The feeling of anti-colonialism first manifested itself in the eighteenth century when the thirteen American colonies revolted against the colonial rule of Britain and set themselves as an independent country. Subsequently, the Latin American countries also waged anti colonial struggle and attained independence. Philosophers like Benth also strongly pleaded that Britain and France should rid themselves of their dependencies. But it was only after the First World War that the problem of colonies received serious attention. The peace-makers at Versailles, who were confronted with the problem of the territories of the defeated powers, thought it proper to pay due attention to the well-being and development of these territories. Accordingly, they incorporated certain provisions in the Covenant of the League of Nations to deal with this problem. The Covenant laid down that "the well-being and development" of the people of these territories was "a sacred trust of civilization" and entrusted these territories to various Allied and Associated powers as mandatory on behalf of the League. However, these powers were not genuinely concerned with the welfare of the people of these territories and treated these territories merely as a status symbol.

In the post-World War I period the spread of nationalism in the colonial areas of Asia and elsewhere posed a serious challenge to the colonial rule. Though the process of decolonisation did not start during this period but no further colonies were established. The only notable exceptions were the seizure of Ethiopia by Italy and drive of Japan on China and South East Asia. It was only in the post World War II period that the process of Decolonisation was greatly speeded up. According to Rupert Emerson "After 1945 the flood-tide of anti-colonialism swept away the colonial system with a speed and thoroughness that matched colonialism's advance at the close of the 19th century. The possession of colonies, so long a matter of pride and prestige, now became a sin to be expiated only, if at all, by the granting of immediate independence. The League of Nations' indifference to the problem was replaced by the profound involvement of the United Nations in the process of decolonisation."*

UN Charter and the Colonial People

In view of the rising tide of nationalism in the colonial areas the delegates to the San Francisco Conference made elaborate provisions concerning the colonial people which constituted an advance over the League Covenant. They incorporated a Declaration Regarding Non-Self Governing Territories in the UN charter which imposed an obligation on the members regarding the administration of territories whose people had not yet reached a full measure of self-government. The Declaration, contained in Article 73, is of great significance and deserves to be quoted in full. It states:

"Members of the United Nations which have to assume responsibilities for the administration of territories whose people have not yet attained a full measure of self-government recognize the principle that the interests of inhabitants of these territories are paramount, and accept, as a sacred trust the obligation to promote to the utmost within the system of international peace and security established by the Present Charter, the well-being of the inhabitants of these territories and to this end:

a. to ensure with due respect for the culture of the people concerned, their political, economic, social and educational advancement, their just treatment, and their protection against abuses;

b. to develop self-government, to take up due account of the political aspirations of the people, and to assist them in the progressive development of their free political institutions according to the particular circumstances of each territory and its peoples and their varying stages, of development;

c. to further international peace and security;

d. to promote constructive measures of development, to encourage research and to co-operate with one another and, when and where appropriate, with specialized international bodies with a view to the practical achievement of the social, economic, and scientific purposes set forth in the Article; and

e. to transmit regularly to the Secretary General for information purposes, subject to such limitations as security and constitutional considerations may require statistical and other information of a technical nature relating to economic, social and educational conditions in the territories for which they are respectively responsible.

---

* *International Encyclopaedia of Social Sciences,* Vol. 3, p.3

Article 74 of the Charter asserted that the other members of the UN have interests in the colonial territories. If the administering powers adopt arbitrary policies with regard to immigration, trade and commerce etc. the non-administering countries can complain. In short the UN Charter held out hopes of self-government for the colonial areas.

Commenting on the significance of the Declaration Regarding Non Self-Governing Territories of UN Charter, Ball and Killough say "it represents perhaps a great advance in international responsibility for the welfare of the dependent people than does the trusteeship system. In the Declaration on Non-Self-Governing Territories the ...powers recognized for the first time as international instrument that the welfare of the dependent peoples was the paramount consideration in the adminstratin of all dependent areas. The declaration in the Charter goes further and carries with it an obligation also undertaken for the fist time for all dependencies to report to an international agency on the steps taken to implement the basic principles."[1]

In is true that the provisions of the UN charter provided a new impetus to the decolonization movement but it would certainly be wrong to assert that all decolonisation in the post World War II period has been solely due to the UN efforts. David W. Wainhouse who has made a special study of the role of the United Nations in ending colonialism, says, "Whereas the Charter enshrined the principle of self-government and the U.N. bodies have provided the main arena of the colonial debate, the direct role of the Organization itself in the process of decolonisation has been a limited one. In some countries such as India, Burma and Syria the nationalistic movements had developed before it was founded. In others such as Indo-China, Morocco and Algeria, decisions were deliberately kept outside of United Nations by the states concerned notably France." The United Nations did play an important role, however in the ending of colonial rule in Indonesia and in certain African trust territories, and it was very much involved in the disposition of the former mandated territory of Palestine. A special case in which the Organization had a decisive role was that of the Italian colonies of Libya, Eritrea and Somaliland, for which the General Assembly provided a solution when the four foreign Minster of the Allied Powers were unable to settle the problem after several years of efforts."

However, he asserts that the most important contribution of the U.N. has been "the creation of a climate of opinion which has given the decolonisation movement a considerable impetus. This it has done merely by being a world forum where claims demands and protests inevitably have had a hearing and by providing organized channels for the making of resolutions and decisions berring the stamp of the world organization. Throughout the Trusteeship Council and the subsidiary organs of the General Assembly, The United Nations has spurred the Colonial power to improve the lot of their dependent peoples. The widespread concern for their welfare it has helped to arouse and has in turn served as forum of pressure on the imperial powers to speed up the process of decolonisation."[2]

1. Ball and Killough, *International Relations* p.297

From the very beginning the United Nations started playing an important role in speeding up the process of decolonisation. Though in the first few years the discussion on Non-Self-Governing Territories were mainly concerned with establishing procedure for the transmission and examination of information, but the basic issue underlying this whole discussion was the question of the competence of the General Assembly regarding the political and constitutional progress in the non-self governing territories. Soon the General Assembly was able to assert its right to examine the information transmitted by the administering powers and to make recommendations on the conditions in the territories. It also asserted its competence to determine whether a territory should be classified as Non-self government or not. In 1946 the General Assembly listed 74 territories in respect of which the administering powers were to transmit information. Subsequently it added some more territories, which were under the administration of Spain and Portugal to this list.

In 1947 the General Assembly set up a Committee of 16 members equal–representation being given to the colonial and non-colonial powers. This Committee was to assist the Assembly in dealing with the reports submitted by the administering power. The colonial powers objected to the setting up of the Committee on the plea that they were merely expected to send report for the information of the General Assembly. They further contended that they were expected to send reports only with regard to the areas which had not yet become self-governing in the social, economic and educational fields, and that the right to determine whether a territory was self-governing or not rested with them. The non-colonial powers on the other hand asserted that the administering powers were expected to send reports until the territory attained political self-government. As regards the question whether a territory was a self-governing or not the decision should rest with the General Assembly. In view of the rigid stand taken by the colonial and non-colonial powers on these issues lot of tensions was generated. Ultimately, the non-colonial powers succeeded in pushing through the General Assembly a number of resolutions, in the face of protest from colonial powers, asserting that the non-self governing territories were a matter of international concern.

Despite this tension the U.N. was able to secure independence for a number of colonies during the first fifteen years of its life. It laid down the conditions for the eventual independence of Libya, Eritrea and Somaliland and secured their independence. On the surrender of mandate over Palestine by Great Britain, United Nations took a decision regarding the partition of the territory and created the independent state of Israel. It also played an important role in securing independence of Indonesia from the Dutch rule. It may be noted that the independence of the colonies was not solely due to the policy and efforts of the UN, it was also largely due to the liberal policy adopted by some of the colonial powers. For example, Britain granted independence to India, Pakistan, Burma, Ceylon, Malaya etc., on her own. Similarly, France voluntarily granted independence to most of her colonies except Algeria. U.S.A. also granted independence to Philippines on her own.

2. David W. Wainhouse, *Remnants of Empire : The United Nations and the Colonialism,* p.4

Banding Conference

The countries which gained independence from the colonial rule organized themselves and tried to exert pressure for speeding up the process of decolonisation. At the Bandung Conference of 1955 they mounted a diplomatic offensive for ending the colonialism. They declared that "colonialism in all its manifestations is an evil which should speedily be brought to an end." They argued that the subjection of people to alien subjugation, domination and exploitation constitutes a denial of fundamental human rights, is contrary to the Charter of the United Nations and is an impediment to the promotion of world peace and co-operation." What is more significant is that they tried to cover all the colonial territories regardless of the degree of enlightenment with which the people were ruled or of their readiness for independence.

Declaration on the granting of independence to colonial countries and people

A new era of decolonisation set in with the adoption of the Declaration on the Granting of Independence to the colonial countries and people. By 1960 a number of Afro-Asian countries had again gained independence and were admitted as members to the United Nations. Their strength had increased so much that they came to acquire virtually a two thirds majority in the General Assembly. Fully aware of their strength these Afro-Asian countries sought to take more effective steps to speed up the process of decolonisation and ensure emancipation of the rest of the colonies. After prolonged negotiations forty-three African and Asian delegates introduced a draft which was adopted after a long and momentous debate by the General Assembly on 14 December 1960. This resolution was adopted by a vote of ninety to zero with nine abstentions. The members who abstained were all important colonial powers. This resolution was in the shape of a Declaration, which has been described as Charter of Independence for dependent people. The Declaration stated;

1. The subjection of peoples to alien subjugation, domination and exploitation constitutes a denial of fundamentals human rights is contrary to the Charter of the United Nations and is an impediment to the promotion of world peace and co-operation.
2. All peoples have the right to self-determination; by virtue of that right they freely determine their political status and freely pursue their economic, social and cultural development.
3. Inadequacy of political, economic, social or educational preparedness should never serve as a pretext for delaying independence.
4. All armed actin or repressive measures of all kinds directed against dependent people shall cease in order to enable them to exercise peacefully and freely their right to complete independence, and the integrity of other national territory shall be respected.
5. Immediate steps shall be taken, in trust and non-self-governing territories or all other territories which have not yet attained independence to

transfer all powers to the people of those territories, without any conditions or reservations, in accordance with their freely expressed will and desire, without any distinction as to race, creed or colour, in order to enable them to enjoy complete independence to freedom.

6. Any attempt aimed at the partial or total disruption of the National unity and the territorial integrity of a country is incompatible with the purposes and principles of the charter of the United Nations.
7. All states shall observe faithfully and strictly the provisions of the Charter of the United nations, the Universal Declaration of Human Rights and the present Declaration on the basis of equality, non-interference in the internal affairs of all states and respect for the sovereign rights of all people and their territorial integrity.

Follow-up Action

Ever since the adoption of the Declaration on decolonisation the General Assembly has repeatedly called upon the administering powers to implement the Declaration and to take all necessary steps to enable the dependent peoples of the territories concerned to exercise without further delay their right to self determination and independence. It has asserted that the continuation of colonialism in all its forms and manifestations, including raclism, *apartheid,* the exploitation by foreign and other interests of economic and human resources and the waging of the colonial wars to suppress the national liberation movement of the colonial territories in Africa, is incompatible with the Charter, the Universal Declaration of Human Rights and the Declaration on decolonisation and poses a serious threat to the international peace and security. While recognising the legitimacy of the struggle of the colonial people by all the means at their disposal, it has urged the other states to render moral and material assistance to the people. It also impressed on the specialist agencies and international institutions to withhold assistance from South Africa and Southern Rhodesia till they renounce their policy of colonial domination and recial discrimination. Above all it condemned the practice of using mercenaries in these territories and has prohibited the nationals from serving as mercenaries. It has appealed to the colonial powers to withdraw their military bases and installations from the colonial territories and to refrain form establishing new ones. Above all the Assembly has repeatedly reaffirmed the importance of ensuring the widest possible dissemination of information on colonialism on the efforts of the colonial people to achieve liberation and on the assistance being provided by the international community to eliminate the remaining vestiges of colonialism.

Special Committee on Decolonisation

With a view to ensure the implementation of the Declaration on the Granting of Independence to Colonial Countries and people, the General Assembly set up a Special Committee on Decolonisation in 1961. While adopting the resolution for the creation of Special Committee in November 1961 the General Assembly noted with regret that with few exceptions, the provisions of the Declaration had not been carried out and in particular that armed action and repressive measures continued to be taken against dependent peoples. The Assembly called on all the concerned states to take action without further delay with a view to faithful application and implementation of the Declaration. It set up a Special Committee consisting of 17 members (it was enlarged to 24 at the end of 1962). These members were to be appointed by the President of the Assembly and were expected to examine the application of the Declaration as well as to make suggestions and recommendation on the progress and extent of its application. The Special Committee was also entrusted with the functions of three other Committees before it started working in 1962. Thereafter, it has remained the main United Nations body cerned with the matter relating to the progress towards self-determination and independence, of peoples in the dependent Territories.

In 1962 the Genial Assembly requested the Special Committee to propose specific measures for expediting the process of decolonisation. It also requested the Committee to appraise the Security Council of developments in the Territories covered by the Declaration which posed a threat to international peace. In 1965 the General Assembly made a request to the Special Committee to pay special attention to the small Territories and to recommend necessary steps to enable the people of these Territories to exercise fully their rights to self-determination and independence. It asked the Special Committee to recommend, wherever appropriate, deadline for independence in each Territory in accordance with the wishes of the people. Thus the Special Committed continued to work actively, in co-operation with the General Assembly and the Security Council to expedite the process of decolonisation.

In addition the Special Committee also sought to secure the co-operation of the administering powers. It despatched a number of visiting missions to some of the non-self-governing territories to obtain first information on the situation in these territories as well as to ascertain the wishes of the inhabitants regarding their future. Some of the territories which were visited by these missions included Aden (1967), Niue (1972), Cocos (Keeling) Islands and Gilbert the Elise Islands (1974), Cape Verde, Montserrat and Spanish Sahara–now Western Sahara (1975); the British Virgin Islands and Tokelan Islands (1976); and the Cayman islands and the United States Virgin Islands (1977). In 1972 a Special Mission visited the Liberated areas of the independent State of Guinea-Bissau. The Special Committee also held meetings at the African capitals in 1966, 1967, 1969 and 1972 and in Portugal in 1975 in connection with the examination of the colonial territories in Southern Africa. The Special Committee set up a sub-committee on petitions for looking into complaints of the people from the non-self-governing territories and on the basis of these petitions made necessary recommendations to the General Assembly. The Committee in its recommendations to the Assembly impressed that the "colonial conflicts constitute a serious threat to the world peace" and "all the peoples have an inalienable right to complete freedom".

Probably the most outstanding accomplishment of the Special Committee was that it succeeded in getting a special resolution adopted by the General Assembly in 1970 concerning the "programme of Action for the Full Implementation of the Declaration of the granting of independence to colonial countries and people." By virtue of this resolution, the General Assembly acknowledged the right of self-determination of the colonial people as well as the right to carry struggle against colonial powers with all the means at their disposal. For effective implementation of the objectives laid down in the Declaration it impressed on the members states to render every possible moral and material assistance to the people in their struggle. It asked the Security Council to impose sanctions against South Africa and Portugal and to widen the scope of sanctions against the illegal regime of Southern Rhodesia.

In subsequent years also the General Assembly adopted a number of resolutions on the recommendation of the Special Committee in which it asserted that foreign economic, financial and other interests operating in Colonial territories constitute a major obstacle to the political independence and to the enjoyment of the natural resources of those territories by the indigenous inhabitants. It asserted that this constituted a violation of the obligations under the UN Charter. It called upon the administering powers to abolish all discriminatory and unjust practice applied to the inhabitants of the territories under the administration and in all other territories under colonial and racial regimes notably in Southern Africa.

It appealed to the Colonial Powers and other concerned states to prevail upon those nationals who were operating enterprises in the colonial territories to abandon such activities which were detrimental to the interests of the inhabitants of the territories. It further requested them to stop supply of funds and other forms of assistance to colonial regimes which used such assistance for the suppression of liberation movement.

Both the Special Committee and the General Assembly have felt concerned over the growing military activities of the Powers in the colonial territories which greatly impeded the implementation of the Declaration. In 1975 the Special Committe reported to the General Assembly that the colonial powers and minority racist regimes had continued to defy Assembly resolution calling for immediate and unconditional withdrawals of all military base and installations from colonial territories. The Committee expressed the view that such activities were aimed at subjugating the colonial peoples and repressing three liberation movement. It considered that starategic military considerations were an important factor in prolonging the colonial rule in many parts of the world, particularly in smaller territories. According in 1976 and 1977 the General Assembly renewed its call to the Colonial Powers to withdraw immediately and unconditionally their bases and installations from colonial territories and to refrain form establishing new ones.

In 1978 the UN General Assembly adopted a declaration of Namibia containing programme of action in support of self–determination and national independence for Namibia. The Declaration stressed the commitment to end South Africa's illegal occupation and right of self-determination and independence for the Namibian people. It appealed to the member states to render increased and sustain support and assistance to SWAPO and to resist from all kinds of direct and indirect com-operation or collaboration with South Africa.

In April 1979 the Special Committee of 24 on Decolonistaion met in Yugoslavia and adopted a final Document on the Decolonisation of Zimbabwe and Namibia, in which it called for extended sanctions against Southern Rhodesia and mandatory sanctions against South Africa. It also condemned the "Wanton and increasing resort to violence and intimidation against the African peoples under the domination and their cynical defiance of United Nations in its efforts to bring about the genuine and completed decolonisation of Southern Rhodesia and Namibia.

In subsequent years also the General Assembly continued to adopt resolutions condemning colonialism and reiterate its determination to eliminate colonialism.

The General Assembly at its Thirty-Ninth Session held in 1984-85 adopted a series of resolutions on decolonisation. These resolutions were largely identical to resolutions approved during the earlier sessions, and reiterated Assembly's condemnation of activities of foreign economic and other interests which are impeding the implementation of the Declaration on Granting of Independence of Colonial countries and Peoples. It called for full implementation of the 1960 Declaration by the specialized agencies and international institutions of the U.N. System. It deplored military activities and arrangements by colonial powers (i.e. south Africa) in territories under their administration which might be impeding implementation of the 1960 Declaration.

The Assembly also adopted a series of resolutions reaffirming "the inalienable right to self-determination and independence of the peoples U.S. Pacific dependencies of American Somoa, Guam, the U.S. Virgin Islands in Caribbean; and the British dependencies of Bermuda, British Virginia Island, the Cayman Islands, all in the Caribbean. The Assembly also adopted a similar resolution in respect of the U.K. dependency of Anguilla, consideration of which had been deferred at its Thirty-Eighth session. Through another resolution the U.N. Assembly adopted an extensive programme of activities for 1985 to mark the 25th Anniversary of the adoption of the 1960 Declaration on the Granting of Independence to Colonical 'Countries and People.

Some time back the UN General Assembly adopted a resolutions forwarded by the Non-Aligned Movement declaring 1990-2000 as the International decade for the Eradication of Colonialism. The resolution urged the UN Secretary General to submit a report to the 44th session of the General Assembly leading to the adoption of an action plan aimed at ushering in the 21st century a world free from colonialism.

The above discussion shows that the United Nations has made significant contribution towards the process of decolonisation by creating a climate of opinion, which provided a new impetus to the decolonisation movement. "This it has done merely by being a world forum where claims, demands and protests inevitably have had a hearing and by providing organized channels for the making of resolutions and decisions bearing the stamp of the world organizations. Through the Trusteeship Council and the subsidiary organ of the General Assembly' the United Nations has spurred the colonial powers. The widespread concern for their welfare has helped to arouse and has in turn served as form of pressure on the imperial powers to speed up the process of declination."[1]

According to Jacobson the most important contribution of the United Nations has been that it prevented the use of the violence in the settlement of colonial issues. He says "On balance, the colonial revolution has probably been more peaceful because of United Nations involvement. A case can be made to the effect that the United Nations has contributed to International stability through its activities at the time of the accession of dependent territories of self government or independence."[2]

It is evident from the above discussions that the United Nations (including its various agencies and committees has played a commendable role in the process of decolonisation. As one writer has observed it has acted as a catalyst in the process of decolonisation. It has provided impetus, cohesion and direction to the forces of anti-colonialism. Even Perez de Cuellar, the Secretary General of United Nations, greatly lauded the achievements of the United Nations in the field of decolonisation. He told the Special Committee of Decolonisation "The Achievements of the United Nations in the historic process of decolonisation are among the origination's most extraordinary achievement." However he warned that "our satisfaction with those achievements should not halt or diminish our efforts. On the contrary we must focus our efforts on what remains to be done. There are many complex and difficult problems that must still be solved. It is important to maintain the impetus achieved in the past two decades until we have achieved the final goal of complete decolonisation."

Even Secretary General U. Thant greatly admired the role of United Nations in bringing about independence of colonial people. He observed "..in the field in which the United Nations has been engaged to accelerate the emergence of the dependent countries into independent ones, the United Nations record has been most impressive. The United Nations has been the sole agency, which has been responsible for the creation of many independent states, particularly in Asia and Africa ... This in my view, is the most impressive and remarkable achievement of the United Nations."

Expansion of International Community

As a result of the process of decolonisation, large number of territories which were formerly under the control of various colonial powers have since gained independence and the size of the international community has greatly expanded. This is evident form the fact that whereas UNO in 1945 consisted of only 51 members, its membership has arisen to 185 in 1996. We can form an idea about the steady growth of the international community from the following Table:

1. David W. Wainhouse, *op. cit,* p. 4
2. Harold K. Jacobson, *The United Nations and Colonialism : A Tentative Appraisal in International Organisation,* Vol. XVI No. 1, Winter 1962, p. 55.

GROWTH OF MEMBERSHIP OF UNO BETWEEN 1945-1998

Years	Number of Members
1945	51
1946	55
1947	57
1948	58
1949	59
1950	60
1955	76
1956	80
1957	82
1958	83
1960	100
1961	104
1962	110
1963	112
1964	115
1965	118‘
1966	122
1967	123
1968	126
1970	127
1971	132
1973	132
1974	138
1975	144
1976	147
1977	149
1978	151
1979	152
1980	154
1981	157
1983	158
1984	159
1985	159
1986	159
1987	159
1988	159

1989	159
1991	166
1992	175
1993	183
1994	185

The emergence of large number of new countries and their entry into the UNO has exercised profound influence on the international relations.

FURTHER READINGS

U. N. Publication — *Everyone's United Nations*

Even Luard — *The United Nations : How it Works and What it does*

David W. Wainhouse — *Remnants of Empire; The United Nations and Colonialism*

Ball and Killough — *International Relations*

Chapter 22
INTERNATIONAL CIVIL SERVICE

The identity of organization–be it a giant industrial corporation, a community welfare agency, a labor union, a national government or an international organization – is lodged in its professional staff. Members, stockholders, or citizens may control the organization, but they cannot be it; the staff is the organization. For the effective working of the international organization the international civil service' plays a vital role. In fact the 'international administration civil service "with its growing experience and techniques of international administration, its relative permanence and continuity and its sense of direct responsibility for the various agencies operations, knits the organization together and furnishes constant impetus, to accomplishment of their objectives." The term civil service with respect to the United Nations includes all the civil servants engaged by the United Nations right from the Secretary General to the lowest clerk who undertakes to serve the international agency. The UN charter clearly states that the responsibilities of its civil services are not national but exclusively international, Obviously the civil servants engaged by the United Nations perform different functions than those performed by the national civil services.

HISTORY OF INTERNATIONAL CIVIL SERCVICES

The idea of regular International Civil Services originated with the League of Nations and the International Labour Organisation after the First World War. The initiative in establishing a truly international civil service was taken by the first Secretary General of the League of Nations (Sir Eric Drummond). He recruited staff from several nations to serve as individual members of the international body rather than as contingents of national representatives. In fact before Sir Eric Drummond took this step, doubts had been expressed in various quarters that it would indeed be difficult to create a workable team out of the diverse multi-national recruits. However, Sir Eric Drummond succeeded admirably in his mission. Walters has described his action of the Secretary General as one of the most important events in the history of international politics.

INTERNATIONAL CIVIL SERVICE UNDER UN

The International Civil Service created by the League of Nations was retained by the United Nations. UN Charter kept all the features of international civil service viz. unitary staff, multinational composition but strictly international character, in tact. However, the UN Charter permitted the specialised agencies of the United Nations to have independent civil service directly responsible to them. Thus it encouraged decentralisation of the international civil services. In fat a number of international civil services came into being with different specialised agencies of United Nations processing independent civil services. It is noteworthy that each employee of the International Organization, before assuming office, has to swear that he would perform his functions with full loyalty and conscientiousness. Such employees are not expected to receive any instructions from any government or other authority external to the Organisation. They have to faithfully carry out the functions assigned to them by the United Nations or the respective agencies and carry out their orders.

The UN charter has tried to ensure international character of the civil services, and provided in Article 101 of the Charter that "Due regard shall be paid to the importance of recruiting the staff on as wide a geographical basis as possible." However, while making the recruitment the principle of securing highest standards of efficiency, competence and integrity' is also to be observed. As almost all the states are keen to secure maximum quota of posts for their citizens, usually the jobs are allotted to citizens of various countries in approximately the same ratio as their budgetary contribution. Due consideration is also given to the claims is of the big and small states.

PRIVILEGES AND IMMUNITIES

The international civil servants are granted certain special privileges and immunities to enable them to discharge their dutie honestly and sincerely. Sufficient care is taken to protect them from undue pressure of influence of home government so that they may be able to discharge their duties and responsibilities impartially.

FUNCTIONS AND ROLE

The civil servants discharge only service functions and have nothing to do with the formulation of policy. They merely collect the necessary information on behalf of various United Nations agencies; plan for the sessions of various organs, make reports, keep records, translate documents and publicise the work done by the organisation. Some civil servants are also assigned technical functions. Thus the WHO engages medical experts who are sent to various developing contries to render assistance in health programmes. Likewise the International Monetary Fund requisitions the services of financial experts who advise the various governments on fiscal policies.

As the international civil servants provide the basic facts on the basis of which the policy is determined they indirectly exercise considerable influence on the determination of the policy. Usually the international civil servants with their long experience and expert knowledge, are also able to servants with which are quite helpful in handling the various problems confronting the Organisation. In short, it can be said that the international civil servants do not merely act as clerks of the United Nations and its other agencies, but actually act as their real custodians.

Jacob and Atherton have high lighted the important role of the international civil services in the working of the international Organisation thus "the international civil service, with its growing experience in the techniques of techniques of international administration, its relative permanence and continuity and its sense of direct respobilitiy for the various agencies operations, knits the organizations together and furnishes constant impetus to accomplishment of their objectives."

FURTHER READINGS

Inis L. Claude, Jr.	*Swords Into Plowshares*
Walters	*A History of the League of Nations*
Jacob and Atherton	*The Dynamics of International Organisation*

Chapter 23

UNITED NATIONS AND REGIONAL ORGANISATIONS

The security minded governments, despite their professions of support for the United Nations, have really not put their faith in the collective security system envisaged under the UN Charter, and have continued to concoct defence alliances with states sharing common fears of specific enemies. Some of these alliances of expedience, however, are now considered to have introduced a new, more promising approach to security by establishing commitments and procedures for mutual defence on a regional basis.

Broadly speaking there are two types of international organisations for security purpose. First, the organisations which have global basis. Second the organisations which are organised exclusively in regional compartments. It has been contended by certain scholars that the two types of organisations cannot co-exist and the regional organisations are bound to detract from the effectiveness of the global organisations. Further, the supporters of regional Organisations hold that the regional organisations are superior to universal organisations because the sense of involvement and joint responsibility which exists among the members of regional organisations is difficult to develop amongst the peoples living in different parts of the world. However, this view is erroneous because the regional organisations do not cover only the states in a particular geographical region. Quite often regional pacts are also concluded by states widely scattered over the globe. It is not essential that the states which enter into regional pacts must have a kind of 'persistent cultural, economic or political affinity among people'. These alliances generally spring from a sense of expediency. The member states of regional organisations promise to extend military or other support to the allies in the event of attack. It is noteworthy that all these alliances are made by the member states without surrender of their sovereignty.

The emergence of regional organisations has made some people express the fear that this would reduce the effectiveness of the International Organisation. This view rests on the wrong assumption that the regional arrangements are also concerned with the problems which are the concern of the United Nations. It is true that both the regional organisations and the United Nations are concerned with the problem of collective security, but still they differ from each other. While the regional organisations assist only in the solution of the problems which are essentially regional in character, the international problems can be tackled only by the global organisations like the United Nations. For example the problem of disarmament, which is essentially an international problem can be tackled only by the United Nations. However, it would be wrong to assume that the regional organisations and United Nations are contradictory and that the regional organisations have in any way reduced the importance of the United Nations. Actually, viewed on practical plane, the regional organisations are an essential prelude to any kind of an international or universal Organisation.

Un Charter and Regional Organisations

The UN Charter attaches great importance to the regional organisations and expects them to serve as adjuncts to the United Nations. In fact the United Nations exercises considerable control over these regional organisations and can issue them directions. Article 52 of the UN Charter provides:

1. Nothing in the present Charter precludes the existence of regional arrangements or agencies for dealing with such matters relating to the maintenance of international peace and security as are appropriate for regional action, provided that such arrangements or agencies and their activities are consistent with the purposes and principles of the United Nations.
2. The members of the United Nations entering into such arrangements or constituting such agencies shall make every effort to achieve pacific settlement of local disputes through such regional arrangement or by such regional agencies before referring them to the Security Council.
3. The Security Council shall encourage the development of pacific settlement of local disputes through such regional arrangements or by such regional agencies either on the initiative of the states concerned or by reference from the Security Council.

It will be observed from the above provisions of article 52 that the UN Charter specially authorizes the use of regional arrangements and gives them a degree of priority as media for peaceful settlement of disputes.

The regional organisations are expected to work only under the authority of the Security Council and have an obligation to keep the Security Council informed ,f all activities undertaken by them. Thus Article 53 of the UN provides:

1. The Security Council shall, where appropriate, utilise such regional arrangements or agencies for enforcement action under its authority. But no enforcement action shall be taken under regional arrangements or by regional agencies without the authorization of the Security Council, with the exception of measures against any enemy state ... or in regional arrangements directed against renewal of aggressive policy on the part of any such state, until such time as the Organisation may, on request of the Governments concerned, be charged with the responsibility for preventing further aggression by such a state.

2. The term enemy state, as used in paragraph 1 of this Article applies to any state which during the Second World War has been an enemy of any signatory of the present Charter."

Article 54 of the Charter stipulates "The Security Council shall at all times be kept fully informed of activities undertaken, or in contemplation under regional arrangements or by regional agencies for the maintenance of international peace and security."

Thus the UN Charter contains clear provisions for the formation of the regional organisations and no wonder a large number of regional organisations made appearance over all these years. Most of these regional organisations were in the nature of Security Arrangements which were made in accordance with the provisions of art. 51 of the UN Charter which states noting in the present Charter shall impair the inherent right of individual or collective self-defence if an armed attack occurs against a Member of the United Nations, until the Security Council has taken measures necessary to maintain international peace and security. Measures taken by members in exercise of this right of self-defence shall be immediately reported to the Security Council and shall not in any way affect the authority and responsibility of the Security Council under the present Charter to take at any time such action as it deems necessary in order to maintain or restore international peace and security." Some of the important Regional Security Arrangements made in pursuance of the above article include the North Atlantic Treaty Organisation (NATO), Brussels Treaty, Rio Pact, the Anzus Pact, Manila Pact, Balkan Pact, Warsaw Treaty etc. Some of these pacts contain a clear reference to articles 51 in their respective constitutions. It is noteworthy that these regional organisations were formed mainly to resist aggression from outside the region. For example, the NATO was set up mainly to meet the aggression contemplated from Eastern Europe. Its constitution makes very little provision for setting up machinery for adjusting difficulties and promoting co-operation among its members. It mainly concentrates on the problem of security economic an military co-operation of the members. Likewise the Rio Pact was also mainly designed to repell outside aggression or foreign interference.

The above discussion, however, should not give an impression that the regional organisations cannot be formed for purposes other than security. Several organisations have been formed for other purposes as well. For example, the Colombo Plan with India, Pakistan, Burma. Ceylon (Sri Lanka) and Indonesia was formed to secure economic co-operation of the members. The other organisations which were formed for non-security purposes include the Benelux Organisation for European Economic Cooperation, Organisation of American States, Organisation of Petroleum Exporting Countries etc. It shall be desirable to know about some of the important regional organisations in detail to fully appreciate the scope of their operation.

Regional Organisations

The regional Organisation is a sort of formal association of sovereign states of a particular region with permanent Organisation. It is not essential that all the States of a particular region must be member of the Organisation. For example the Arab League, a regional Organisation of the Middle Eastern States does not contain all the states of the Middle East. Similarly, the Organisation of American States does not contain Canada or other European dependencies of the Western Hemisphere. Again North Atlantic Treaty Organisation contains Italy, Greece and Turkey as members, even though they are not North Atlantic countries.

Organisation of American States (OAS)

This Organisation is the oldest and one of the largest regional organisation. The-origin of OAS can be traced back to 1889 when the first Pan-American Conference was held. Since then it has gradually grown and developed. It was given the shape of a comprehensive regional arrangement in 1948. The Constitution of the Organisation of American States is found in three basic documents thc OAS Charter which provides the general framework of the Organisation; the Rio Treaty (also known as Inter-American Treaty of Reciprocal Assistance) which provides for regional collective security; and the Pact of Bagota (1948) which relates to the pacific settlement of disputes among the members.

The OAS Charter came into force on 13 December 1951 and was reformed in 1967. The membership of the organisation is open to all the American states, including Canada. Any member can withdraw from the organisation by giving two years notice.

It consists of following organs:

1. ***The General Assembly***, which was known as Inter-American Conference before 1970 is the supreme organ of the OAS. It consists of representatives of all the member states. It meets once in five years at different places by rotation. It determines policy, structure and functions of other organs. The Conference takes all the decisions by majority. As a matter of practice, however the members try to arrive at unanimous decisions.
2. ***Foreign Ministers Meeting.*** This body meets on the request of the majority of the members and deals with pressing security and related problems of common interest to the American states. This body acts as the enforcement agency of the OAS and can order the member statesto take collective measures or impose sanctions in particular cases.
3. ***Permanent Council,*** which contains delegates of all the member states. The Council elects a Chairman and a Vice-Chairman from amongst its members every year. The Council is responsible for the smooth working of the OAS and is responsible for convening the conferences and meetings of the members. It prepares the agenda for these conferences in consultation with the concerned Governments.
4. ***The Pan American Union,*** which works as the Secretariat of the O. A. S. It coordinates the social and economic activities and promotes welfare of members.

5. ***The Specialised Organisation,*** which carries on co-operative programmes in the fields of health, child welfare, education, agriculture, etc.

6. ***The Specialised Conferences,*** which are called to encourage joint efforts to solve technical problems.

Inaddition to the above organisations OAS has certain specialised and subsidiary organisations. The specialised Organisation include Inter American Institute of Agriculture Sciences, Inter-American Children's Institute, Inter-American Commission of Women, Inter-American Commission of Human Rights, Inter-American Indian Institute, Pan-American Health Organisations and Pan-American Institute of Geography and History. These agencies look after their allotted specialised functions. The Specialised institutions of OAS include three Councils viz. Inter-American Economic and Social Council, the Inter-American Cultural Council and Inter-American Council of Jurists.

The members of the O. A. S. hold faith in settling their disputes through peaceful methods. Before referring their disputes to the Security Council they submit these disputes to the regional organization. Generally these disputes are resolved through conciliation or investigation. The members of O. A. S. are pledged to assist each other in case of armed attack against any American State and collectively deal with aggression. An attack against any state is taken as an attack against all American states.

The members are pledged to resolve amicably the political, juridical and economic problems arising among them, and to cooperate in the economic, social and cultural development.

The Organisation of American States has played an effective role in checking the threat of Communism in the hemisphere. The Organisation played an effective role in the Dominican Republic in 1965. It also checked the guerilla warfare in several states. In the Organisation of American States, the United States has played a dominant role, specially in the matters relating to security. Similarly, in the field of economic development also USA has played a dominant role and provided necessary finances.

Organisation of African Union (O. A. U.)

The Organisation of African Union was formed by the independent African States in May 1963 with a view to resolve the economic and Political problems confronting the African States. Originally 32 members joined their Organisation but their strength has been steadily increasing with the attainment of independence by several African countries. In fact all the African states are members of O. A. U. The main objectives of the Organisation were stated in Article II of the Charter, which included (i) promotion of unity and solidarity of African states; (ii) coordination and intensification of co-operation and efforts to achieve a better life for the people of Africa; (iii) defence of the sovereignty, integrity and independence of the African states; (iv) eradication of all forms of colonialism from Africa; and (v) promotion of international co-operation while having due regard to the U. N. Charter and the Universal

Declaration of Human Rights.

The organisation of O. A. U. consists of an Assembly of Heads of States and Governments, the Council of Ministers, the General Secretariat and the Commission of Mediation, Conciliation and Arbitration.

The Assembly of Heads of States and Governments is the supreme organ of O. A. U. It meets annually and discusses matters of common concern to Africa with a view to coordinate and harmonise the general policy of the Organisation. Each member has one vote and all decisions are taken by two-third majority of the members.

The Council of Ministers consists of Foreign Ministers or such other ministers as are designated by the Member states, The Council meets at least twice a year. In addition, extraordinary sessions of the Council can be held on the request of the two-thirds of the members. The Council is responsible to the Assembly of Heads of State and is responsible for making all preparations for the Conferences of Assembly It Is also responsible for the implementation of the decisions of the Assembly and coordinates the activities of the African States in accordance with instructions of Assembly Each state has only one vote in the Council.

The General Secretariat is headed by the Administrative Secretary General, who is appointed by the Assembly of the Heads of States and Governments. The Secretary General and other members of the Secretariat do not receive any instructions from their government and are expected to follow the directions of the Organisation.

The Commission of Mediation, Conciliation and Arbitration was set up by the Assembly of the Heads of the State and Government by a separate protocol. This body tries to resolve the disputes among the members through peaceful means in addition to the above organs the Assembly is authorised to set up Specialised Commissions like Economic and Social Commission; Educational and Cultural Commission; Health, Sanitation and Nutrition Commission; Defence Commission; and Scientific, 'Technical and Research Commission. These Commissions work according to the regulations framed by the Council of Ministers.

The Budget of the Organisation is prepared by the Administrative Secretary General and approved by the Council of Ministers. The funds are contributed by the member states in accordance with the scale of assessment of the United Nations with the conditions that no single country can be required to contribute more than twenty per cent of the yearly regular budget oi the organisations.

Though the broad objectives of the O. A. U. are generally accepted by the members, it has remained a loose association of sovereign states. The Organisation has made many joint pronouncements, but taken very little concerted action. The internal political rivalries, ideological differences, conflicting ties with major powers and an overriding concern with the presentation of personal power and sovereignty have further stood in the way of the effective working of the Organisation. The members have not been able to create a common force to fight African colonial regimes as envisaged in the Charter. Similarly, they have not been able to achieve any success in the direction of launching co-operative programmes for aid to members in the economic development due to paucity of funds. However, it cannot be denied that the O. A. U. has succeeded in creating a spirit of extensive co-operation among the African States. An African Development Bank has been established and discus- ions for setting up a Common Market have been undertaken. Above all, in the United Nations, the O. A. U. functions as an effective caucusing group when issues of common interest to the members come for discussion.

The Arab League

The Arab League was formed in March 194S when Egypt, Iraq, Jordan, Lebanon, Saudi Arabia, Syria and Yemen signed the pact for its creation in Cairo. Subsequently other countries like Algeria, Kuwait, Libya, Morocco, Sudan and Tunisia also joined it. In 1980 the strength of the League rose to 21. The League was created to encourage close collaboration between the member states and to safeguard the independence and sovereignty of the Arab states.

The objectives of the League have been outlined in Article 2 of the Charter which include the following. First, to strengthen relations between the member states. Secondly, to coordinate the policies of the member states with a view to encourage co-operation among them and to safeguard their independence and sovereignty. Thirdly, to have general concern with the affairs and interests of the Arab countries. Fourthly, to promote close co-operation among the member states, with due regard to their Organisation and circumstances, on the matters relating to (a) economic and financial affairs including commercial relations, customs currency and questions of agriculture and industry-(b) communication, including rail-roads. roads, aviation, navigation, telegraphs and posts; (c) cultural extra affairs;(d) nationality, passports, visas, execution of judgements and extradition of criminals;(c) social affairs; and (o human problems.

In addition to this the member states are expected to respect the systems of governments existing in other member states and are pledged to abstain from any action calculated to change established system of government.

The Council or the Majlis is the principal organ of the League. It consists of all the members, who are represented equally on it. The Council meets twice a year. Special sessions of the Council can be convened at the request of at least two states. The Council supervises the execution of the multilateral agreements concluded by the members of the League. It also enjoys important powers with regard to settlement of disputes among member states. The Council is assisted in its task by a Political Committee and other permanent Committees formed to secure co-operation among the member states in the economic, social and cultural spheres.

The Secretary General of the League is the administrative officer. He is appointed by the ***Majlis*** (Council).

The Arab League has played significant role in the-resolution of disputes among the member states. It also played an important role in the conclusion of agreement between England and Egypt in July 1954. It played commendable role in the Lebanon and Libya. However, the League could not succeed in protecting the Arab interests against Israel although it inflicted a defeat on Israel in 1973. It has also functioned effectively as a caucusing group at the United -Nations. Despite the growing compatibility among the members of the League, the rivalries among the Arab states and struggle for leadership among the member states still persists.

In the social, economic and cultural sphere also the League has played an important role. It secured the conclusion of a number of agreements regarding economic co-operation among the member states, on the basis of preferential trade. In the cultural sphere it has tried to bring the states closer to each other. A Cultural Committee has been formed which meets once a year and works for Promotion of closer cultural relations. A permanent Bureau and Cultural Department for mutual co-operation has also been created.

However, despite these achievements, it has to be admitted that the Arab League has not been able to achieve its professed goal of unifying the Arab world and this goal is still far from realisation.

Organisation of Petroleum Exporting Countries (OPEC)

This Organisation was formed in Baghdad (Iraq) ;In 1960 with Iran, Iraq, Kuwait, Saudi Arabia and Venezuela as founder members. Subsequently Algeria, Ecuador, Gabon, Indonesia, Libya, Nigeria, Qatar, United Arab Emirates also became its members. The membership of this Organisation is open to any other country having substantial net exports of crude petroleum, which has fundamentally similar interests to those of the member countries.

The main objectives of the OPEC are(i)to make efforts to restore price of crude oil to the level existing before reductions of 1958-60;(ii)to effect stability in oil prices and avoid unnecessary fluctuations in prices;(iil)to carry out consultations among companies of concerned countries before making modifications in prices of oil;(iv)to control production with a view to ensure stability of prices;(v)to ensure regular supply of petroleum to consumers and equitable remuneration to investors and regular revenues to oil producing states,(vi)hold regular consultations among the member states to safeguard their common interest.

Arab Common Market. This Market was set up on I January 1965 in terms of an agreement signed by Iran, Jordan, Syria, and Egypt on 13 August 1964. The membership of the Market is open to all the Arab League states. The agreement for creation of Arab Common Market provided for the abolition of customs duties on agricultural products and natural resources within five years by reducing tariff at an annual rate of 20 per cent. It envisaged reduction of custom duties on industrial products by 10% annually It also provided for free movement of capital and labour between the member states and provided for establishment of common external tariffs and framing of a common foreign economic policy

The ASEAN (Association of South-East Asian Nations)

The ASEAN was created in 1967 through Bangkok Declaration by Indonesia, Malaysia, the Philippines, Singapore and Thailand. The leaders of these countries felt the need of the Organisation because the situation in Vietnam, as a result of US imperialist action, political crisis in Cambodia, Indonesia, Laos and Burma convinced them that their interest could be best served only if they united. The end of confrontation between Indonesia and Malaysia and the strong anti-Chinese stance of the Military regime of Indonesia also facilitated the creation of this organisation. However, Burma and Cambodia did not join the Organisation on account of its anti-Chinese stance.

The main objectives of the ASEAN are (i)to accelerate the economic growth, social progress and cultural development in the region;(ii) to promote regional peace and stability;(iii)to promote active collaboration and mutual assistance on matters of common interest in the economic, social, cultural, technical, scientific and administrative fields;(iv)to provide assistance to each other in the form of training and research facilities in educational, technical and administrative sphere; (v) to promote South East Asian Studies; and (vi) to collaborate for greater utilisation of their agriculture and industries and expansion of trade etc; (vii) to maintain close and beneficial co-operation with existing international and regional Organisation with similar aim and purposes.

The Organisation of the ASEAN consists of Ministerial Conference, Standing Committee, the Secretariat and a number of Permanent and Ad hoc committees. The Minister's Conference is composed of the Foreign Ministers of the member states. The Conference holds periodical consultations with regard to military and other matters relating to the area. Generally its meetings are held annually in each country by rotation. The Standing Committee meets when necessary between Ministerial meetings for consultation., The meetings arc held in the five countries by rotation. The Committee consists of the Foreign Minister of the host country and Ambassadors of the other four countries. The ASEAN also has a permanent Secretariat with its headquarter at Jakarta(Indonesia). The Secretariat was set up in 1976. In addition to these organs the ASEAN has one permanent committee with headquarters in Singapore and ten special committees, viz., Navigation, Trade and Tourism; Industrial Minerals and Energy; Food, Agriculture and Forestry; Transportation and Communications; Finance and Banking; Science and Technology-Social Development; Culture and Information and Budget. In addition there are eight adhoc committees.

During the first few years of its existence the ASFAN made little progress towards any substantial regional co-operation beyond laying down the framework for the five member countries to work out their consensus through periodic consultation. However, after 1975 ASEAN underwent a transformation and it really began to move. It Pot only enlarged its administrative machinery but also made serious proposals in respect of economic co-operation and took unified stand on extra regional affairs. As one writer has put it 'without doubt the machinery has been refined, the framework strengthened, and the momentum created, for a more serious approach to regionalism. The strength of the Association rose to nine in 1997. These nine members include Brunei, Indonesia, Laos, Malaysia, Myanmar, Philippines, Singapore, Thailand and Vietnam.

The significance of ASEAN in international affairs lies in the fact that it represents an effort to develop Asian solution to the Asian problems in a co-operative arrangement consisting wholly of nations in the region. Although, it is mainly concerned with the economic and social problems, it has also tried to reduce the foreign influence in the region and assert that all foreign bases in the region arc temporary. The Association has also undertaken projects with a view to improve tourism, shipping, fishing, trade, etc.

Towards the close of 1997 ASEAN countries were faced with a serious financial crisis. They made a bid to resolve the crisis at a summit held at Kuala Lumpur in December 1997. At this summit the ASEAN leaders called for greater national, regional and international efforts, including the major economics and international financial institutions to overcome the financial turmoil. They appealed to the IMF to expedite measures for the stabilization of the currencies. In March 1998 the Finance Ministers of ASEAN countries met at Singapore and made a bid to arrive at an agreement regarding implementation of regional currency payment for intra-regional trade. However, they could not achieve much success in this regard. But it cannot be denied that the leaders of ASEAN are aware of the importance of co-operation on economic and financial issues. Despite these problems, it cannot be denied that ASEAN, over the years, has emerged as a viable regional Organisation.

The European Economic Community

The European Economic Community was formed in 1958 by six countries of Europe, viz., France, Italy, West Germany, Belgium, Netherlands and Luxemburg. However, subsequently England, Ireland, Denmark, Greece, Spain and Portugal were also admitted as its members, and the strength of the Community rose to 12. The Community was further expanded in January 1995 with the admission of Austria, Finland and Sweden. Thus at present the European Union has 15 members and is regarded as world's biggest and richest supranational bloc. The chief objectives of the European Community include (i) consolidation of the tariff schedules of the members into a single system applicable to imports from Third World countries;(ii) progressive reduction and removal of all fiscal and physical restrictions on the free movement of goods, capital and labour, between member countries;(iii) harmonisation of economic politics of the member states. With a view to eliminate competition the members concentrate on the production of commodities for the entire community and as such each member concentrates on the production of a limited number of items and produces them in bulk. The Organisation of the EEC consists of European Commission, the Council of Ministers, the European Parliament, Economic and Social Committee and the Court of justice. The Commission consisting of members, who are appointed with the unanimous consent of the member governments, for a period of four years, enjoys super-national powers in many respects. It performs executive functions, and takes important decisions regarding policy. It also ensures that the decisions taken by the Council of Ministers are carried out and that the basic text and subsequent Community legislation are correctly observed.

The Council of Ministers consists of one minister from each state. The Council meets at least once a month and takes all major decisions. The Council works in complete co-operation with the Commission, and the members of the Commission also take active part in the deliberations of the Council.

The Parliament or Assembly is a large body consisting of representatives of all the member states. These members arc elected by the legislatures of the respective states from amongst themselves. Representation has been accorded to the various member states in the Parliament on the basis of their population and economic potentials. These members are not expected to work according to the instructions of their governments but to take independent decisions. The Parliament exercises general supervision over the working of the Commission and the Council through debates and annual reports. The Parliament can make formal recommendations to the Council on its own, although these recommendations are not binding on the Council.

The Economic and Social Committee consists of representatives drawn from economic and social life of various countries. These members are appointed by the Council for a term of four years by unanimous vote. Usually one-third on these members represent the trade union, one-third represent the employers and the rest represent the general interest. The recommendations of the Economic and Social Committee are treated with due deference by the Commission, even though they lack binding character.

Then there is a Court of Justice. Its members are appointed for a term of six years The Court ensures the observance of rule of law in the countries of the community. The decisions of the Court are binding on all the parties, including the government and there cannot be any appeal against them.

The necessary finances to meet the expenses of the Community are contributed by the member states in agreed proportions.

The European Economic Community has proved quite effective as a regional Organisation. It has not only been able to solve the problems of tariff adjustments among the members and ensure greater co-operation among them, but also exercise influence over other regions of the world in the sphere of economic development. To a large extent the idea of evolving regional organisations for greater economic co-operation in different regions of the world drew inspiration from the success of the European Economic Community.

Single EC Market

Effort to achieve greater unification among members of EC were stepped up in December 1992 when the Edinburgh Summit evolved a formula for the creation of a single market within the barriers and amending various rules and laws across the countries of the community. The creation of a new border-free single market within the Community has resulted in tearing down the barriers to trade in goods and services among all EC countries. Even the travelers can move freely over the new single market and the bankers are free to open new branches anywhere. The workers and professionals can also move about freely from one country to another. It is hoped that this single market would ultimately lead to thc, emergence of 'unified Europe' even though the task is not likely to be an smooth.

Border less European Union

A further step in the direction of European unity was taken in March 1995 when Schengen agreement was signed to enable some 370 million citizens to move freely within the union. Initially seven countries viz. Germany, France, Spain, Portugal, Belgium, Luxembourg, and Netherlands decided to abolish their border controls. Subsequently eight other member states also signed the agreement. As a result now the European citizens can travel without passport restrictions from Iceland to Greece in the Mediterranean. Of late the exodus of Kurds from Turkey, Iraq and Iran to European Union countries, has posed a serious threat to the open border policy and apprehensions have been expressed in certain quarters that the member states may not be able to practice 'open border' policy for long. It may be noted that England and Ireland have not accepted the Schengen agreement.

Economic and Monetary Union

In March 1998, eleven of the 15 members of the European Union, announced their decision to create a monetary union and merge their currencies at the beginning of 1999. These eleven countries include Germany, France, Belgium, the Netherlands, Luxembourg, Ireland, Italy, Finland, Spain, Portugal and Austria. Three members-Britain, Denmark and Sweden, refused to join the monetary Union, while Greece could not quality for membership in terms of the Maastricht Treaty of 1992, which had laid down the criterias to be fulfilled by the countries seeking membership of the Monetary Union. This is a significant development and is expected to effect a historical change in the international monetary order since the collapse of the Bretton Wood System.

Impact and Importance of Regional Organisations

It has been argued in certain quarters that the formation of regional organisations has greatly undermined the position of the United Nations and poses a serious threat to the existence of the international organisations. For example Carlos Romulo of Philippines observed that the United Nations is dying because the states are more and more taking the great political issues outside the framework of the Organisation. Similarly Edgar S. Furniss also holds that "The United Nations has been placed in a position of inferiority, that now the links between the regional arrangements and the world Organisation exist at the practical pleasure of the former." However, the above view is not universally accepted and majority of the scholars hold it as erroneous. This erroneous view largely exists because of the assumption that the regional organisations are also concerned with all the problems which are the concern of the United Nations and operate at- cross purposes with the world body Actually the regional organisations serve as adjunct to the U. N. and are subordinate and harmonious with the United Nations. They have proved immensely useful in many ways. In the first place, it is proper and natural for the neighbors in any region to organise to meet their common problems. The members of regional organisations are able to deal with their problems more effectively. Thus they relieve the United Nations of some burden of handling the local problems and concentrate its attention on global problems.

Secondly, the regional Organisation are able to meet threat to peace more effectively by guaranteeing regional collective security. The UN Secretary - General Trygve Lie also admitted that the regional arrangements can be very useful element in the preservation of world peace, provided they recognise the supremacy of the Charter.

Thirdly, the regional organisations have played an important role in promoting social and economic co-operation among the member states and encouraged them to rise above narrow nationalism. In this respect they constitute an important step towards universalism. As Prof. Palmer and Perkins have observed "If international regionalism is properly developed and is closely integrated into a more universal framework ... it can fill a real gap in the existing pattern of international society."

Finally, the regional organisations are also able to operate more freely without ideological obstructions. In short, we can say that regional organisations have played significant role in the international sphere without undermining the authority of the United Nations because by and large these organisations have accepted the overall authority of the United Nations.

Chapter 24

Assessment of working of the United Nations and its Future

The United Nations, which was created to ensure peace and harmony all over the world, has failed to achieve its basic objectives and the world continued to witness various conflicts which have jeopardised international peace. It is true that the United Nations has succeeded in preventing large-scale wars, but could not prevent the wars as such. In fact there have been more than 2000 large and small conflicts since the establishment of the United Nations in 1945. In these wars though nuclear weapons were not used but liberal use of conventional weapons was made. Under the UN Charter the great powers were assigned special responsibility for the maintenance of peace and security, as is evident from the veto power granted to the great powers in the Security Council. But within a few years of the creation of United Nations cold war set in, which prevented the great powers from taking joint action for the maintenance of world peace. On most of the issues these great powers took opposite stands and made use of their veto power. This often prevented the Security Council to take decision and also deterred the UN to act and check aggression through use of 'collective force', as envisaged under the UN Charter.

An effort was made to overcome these obstacles either through 'informal' amendments in the Charter, or by granting greater responsibility to the General Assembly to deal with threats to peace and security, through the adoption of Uniting for Peace Resolution. Even the Secretary General was granted more powers to enable him to play a more effective role during the various crisis.

The United Nations also made use of Peacekeeping force to maintain peace between the parties to the conflict. Peacekeeping force was for the first time instituted in 1956 during the Suez Crisis. It was entrusted with responsibility of keeping the opposing forces on the Arab-Israeli border disengaged and thus reduce tension. Similar peacekeeping forces were also set up in subsequent years to defuse tension and contain conflicts in various parts of the world.

Despite its various limitations the United Nations during the first two decades, continued to be at the centre of international stage and the member states looked towards it for an effective role during the various conflicts.

UN in Sixties and Seventies

The Western nations in general and the United States in particular, got disillusioned with the United Nations in the mid 1960's because they could not count on the support of the Afro-Asian countries which had majority in the Assembly. Therefore, United States preferred to deal with the issues outside the United Nations. In the 1970's even Soviet Union also got somewhat disillusioned with the role of the United Nations. In the 1970's the two Superpowers preferred to deal with each other directly on all bilateral issues such as negotiations on strategic arms or regional conflicts. As a result of this approach the role of the United Nations in maintenance of world peace was considerably undermined.

UN in Eighties and Nineties

In the 1980's as a result of improved relations between the two Superpowers and their joint interest in making the UN work in solving regional conflicts the United Nations once again started playing an important role. One of the reasons which prompted United States to rely increasingly on the United Nations was that as a result of the reforms undertaken in the late 1980's United States was given greater voice in UN decision–making bodies.

As a result of sudden invasion of Kuwait by Iraq in August 190, a new life was injected into United Nations. On account of co-operation between the two Superpowers the United Nations took the drastic step of asking Iraq to withdraw its forces from Kuwait. It passed a resolution (No.678) stating that if its directive was not complied with by the fixed date, the UN member-states could use all necessary measures to make Iraq pull out its forces from the illegally occupied territory. This virtually tantamounted to an ultimatum to Iraq to quit Kuwait. It also cleared the way for a war against Iraq. It is noteworthy that though the Security Council permitted only minimum use of force and that too for the limited purpose of enforcing mandatory sanctions approved by the Security Council, but USA went full steam ahead and threatened the use of force to starve the people of food. USA interpreted the Security Council Resolution as a mandate for mounting full scale offensive against Iraq. Likewise, though the Security Council did not sanction naval blockade and merely directed the member-states not to have trade relations with Iraq, the United States exceeded the limits of the resolution and mounted naval blockade and deployed ships to physically prevent imports or exports of commodities. It even did not care for the objections raised by the Soviet Union that the UN mandate was for the liberation of Kuwait and not for the liberation of Iraq from Saddam Hussein. USA even did not care for the objection of President Mitterant of France that the UN mandate had terminated with the liberation of Kuwait and did not extend to the internal affairs of Iraq. In fact USA repeatedly interfered in the internal affairs of Iraq in defiance of UN resolutions.

Later on in April 1991 when United Nations proposed to hold a conference on peace in West Asia, United States did not favour any major role for the United Nations and insisted that peace in West Asia can be assured only by the countries of the Gulf region under the aegis of USA and USSR. The dominant role played by the United States in the Gulf War made critics skeptical about the effectiveness of UN regarding maintenance of world peace and settlement of international diputes through negotiations. In fact after the collapse of the Soviet Union, and Moscow's pursuit of non-ideological foreign policy, United States has tried to cloth its foreign policy goals in the garb of collective world consensus and tried to persuade other countries to toe its line in the United Nations. This has not been favoured by the countries of the third world, who have suggested that certain structural reforms must be carried out to make the United Nations an effective guardian of peace, and to ensure that the Secretary General and the Security Council do not succumb to the pressure of United States.

Achievements of United Nations

Despite its alleged failure and shortcomings the United Nations has left a permanent imprint on almost all major political, economic, social and humanitarian problems. The United Nations has served as an important meeting and debating forum for nations where the different members have putforth their viewpoints and understood the views of others. This has promoted a spirit of understanding and accommodation among the member states. It was chiefly due to United Nations that East-West détente became possible because it provided them an opportunity to settle their differences through discussion and dialogue. Again United Nations was instrumental in focussing on the problems of racism, colonialism and new international economic order. The United Nations contributed towards decolonisation by implementing the provisions of UN Charter concerning trusteeship an non-self governing territories. Through trusteeship it ensured accountability of the Trusteeship Powers for the transformation of the colonial states into independent states. Once these states gained independence the United Naions provided them a forum where they could stand on terms of equality with their former colonial masters.

The various agencies of the United Nations have also rendered valuable service in the field of health, transportation, communication, science, education, reduction of trade barriers to promote international trade, etc. They have also done commendable work in the field of protection and settlement of refugees, and promotion of the interests of children. United Nations system also contributed to the flow of aid and technical assistance to the less developed countries, which has helped in the development of these countries. Through its activities the United Nations has been able to impress that the development of the backward countries is an international responsibility. It has also rendered great service to the cause of promotion of human rights through discussions, declarations and international covenants.

It is true that the United Nations has not been able to achieve all its objects. This has largely been due to differing ideologies, cultures, material interests and levels of development prevailing in different, parts of the world which rendered multilateral co-operation difficult. The lack of necessary force at the command of the United Nations also prevented it from playing an effective role because it could not enforce its decisions on states reluctant to conform to them. Above all, the reluctance of the member states to compromise with their sovereignty for the sake of international good, also rendered the United Nations ineffective.

Though the United Nations has achieved only limited success, it connot be denied it has set certain norms for the conduct of international relations. In the first place, it has formulated procedures for legitimate political activities of the individual states. It has provided opportunities for multilateral contracts and acted as catalyst of change in the international system. It has provided a forum where the various members of the United Nations meet, express their respective views and try to arrive at some sort of consensus. In other words, it has provided a forum for communication among states where the member states can freely meet and discuss problems.

Secondly, the United Nations has tried to bring about some sort of stability in the international system by keeping the conflicts within reasonable limit by imposing restrictions on the contestants.

Thirdly, United Nations has sought to bring about political changes without disrupting the system. For example it has played a significant role in the liquidation of colonialial relationship and was instrumental in bringing about political change in Congo after the death of UN Secretary General Hamarskjold. In recent years also the United Nations has played an important role in international politics specially with regard to problems of South Africa and distribution of economic resources between North and South.

U. N. at Present

The ideological differences and Superpower rivalry, which earlier rendered the United Nations ineffective, has now disappeared. As a result of the disintegration of the Soviet Union, United States has emerged as the only Superpower, which is now dominating the international system. Howerver, some scholars have contended that due to decline in the economic power of United States and the rise of new economic powers like Germany, Japan and Europe, the political rivalry in international politics has given way to economic power confrontation.

For successful working of the United Nations, it is absolutely esential that the members of the United Nations, must be willing to accept the decisions of the United Nations even if they do not coincide with their immediate desires and interests. This can be achieved by negotiations and diplomacy. In recent years the emphasis has shifted to economic and social relations and issues like human rights and economic co-operation have assumed great importance and the United Nations would have to play a more effective role in the resolution of these problems.

Suggested Changes in United Nations

The effective role expected of United Nations in the present context demands certain changes in the United Nations. Some of the important improvements which can go a long way in improving the working of the United Nations, include the following:

1. In the first instance there is imperative need to broad-base the organisation and functioning of the United Nations. The international organisation which originally had only 50 members in 1945 has now more than 180 members. If the UN is to function as representative of our world today, there is an urgent need for broadbasing its functioning and organisation. The five permanent seats allotted to five countries (USA, UK, China, France and Russia) can better be allotted to five important continents viz. Europe, Asia, Africa, North America and Latin America. Their representation can be decided either on the basis of rotation among the local powers or by an agreed process of election.
2. Secondly, the value of votes of different members in various agencies of the United Nations, which at present is decided on the basis of their financial contributions, can be elaborated and greater weightage can be given to the size of country and its population. Further, countries with bad human right record or unproportionate military build-up could be given negative points. This would ensure greater political support for the United Nations.
3. In the field of non-proliferation also there is need for change. At present the North, especially the US and Britain, have determined the structures and norms or control. The Nuclear Non-Proliferation Treaty (NPT) and Missile Technology Control Regime (MTCR) have been devised by the advanced countries and are hegemonic, restrictive and discriminatory in approach, organisation and aim. They do not aim at controlling weapons proliferation but at securing the sole possession of these weapons for the countries that have already manufactured and proliferated them. Their main aim is to prevent the developing countries from acquiring capability to build the weapons. They certainly do not aim at achievement of genuine disarmament.

FURTHER READINGS

James Barros (ed)	*The United Nations, Past, Present and Future*
Evan Luard	*The United Nations in a New Era*
Robert Adams and Kingsbury Benedict	*UN, Divided World – the UN's Role in International Relations*
Kenneth J. Twitchett	*The Evolving United Nations: A Prospect for Peace*

Appendix – 1
COVENANT OF THE LEAGUE OF NATIONS

The Covenant entered into force on January 10, 1920.

The texts printed in italics indicates amendments.

The High Contracting Parties,

in order to promote international cooperation and to achieve international peace and security

by the acceptance of obligations not to resort to war,

by the prescription of open, just and honorable relations between nations,

by the firm establishment of the understandings of international law as the actual rule of conduct among Governments, and

by the maintenance of justice and a scrupulous respect of all treaty obligations in the dealings of organized peoples with one another.

agree to this covenant of the League of Nations.

ARTICLE 1
Membership and Withdrawal

1. The original members of the League of Nations shall be those of the Signatories which are named in the Annex to this Covenant and also such of those other States named in the Annex as shall accede without reservation to this Covenant. Such accessions shall be effected by a declaration deposited with the Secretariat within two months of the coming into force of the Covenant. Notice thereof shall be sent to all other Members of the League.
2. Any fully self-governing State, Dominion or Colony not named in the Annex may become a Member of the League if its admission is agreed to by two-thirds of the Assembly, provided that it shall give effective guarantees of its sincere intention to observe international obligations, and shall accept such regulations as may be prescribed by the League in regard to its military, naval and air forces and armaments.

3. Any Member of the League may, after two years' notice of its intention so to do, withdraw from the League, provided that all its international obligations and all its obligations under this Covenant shall have been fulfilled at the time of its withdrawal.

Entered into force on January 10, 1920. The texts printed in Italics indicate the amendments. Article 6 as amended has been in force since August 13, 1924. Articles 12, 13 and 15 as amended since September, 26, 1924, and Article 4 as amended since July 29, 1926.

ARTICLE 2

Executive Organs

The action of the League under this Covenant shall be effected through the instrumentality of an Assembly and of a Council, with a permanent Secretariat.

ARTICLE 3

Assembly

The Assembly shall consist of representatives of the Members of the League.

The Assembly shall meet at stated intervals and from time to time, as occasion may require, at the Seat of the League or at such other place as may be decided upon.

The Assembly may deal at its meetings with any matter within the sphere of action of the League or affecting the peace of the world.

At meetings of the Assembly each Member of the League shall have one vote and may have not more than three Representatives.

ARTICLE 4

Council

1. The Council shall consist of representatives of the Principal Allied and Associated Powers [the United States of America, the British Empire, France, Italy and Japan], together with Representatives of four other Members of the League. These four Members of the League shall be selected by the Assembly from time to time on its discretion. Until the appointment of the Representatives of the four Members of the League first selected by the Assembly, Representatives of Belgium, Brazil, Greece and Spain shall be Members of the Council.
2. With the approval of the majority of the Assembly, the Council may name additional Members of the League, whose Representatives shall always be Members of the Council; the Council with like approval may increase the number of Member of the League to be Selected by the Assembly for representation on the Council.

2. *bis. The Assembly shall fix by a two-thirds' majority the rules dealing with theelection of non-permanent Members of the Council, and particularly such regulations as relate to their term of office and conditions of re-eligibility.*

3. The Council shall meet from time to time as occasion may require, and at least once a year, at the Seat of the League, or at such other place as may by decided upon.

4. The Council may deal at its meetings with any matter within the sphere of action of the League or affecting the peace of the world.

5. Any Member of the League not represented on the Council shall be invited to send a Representative to sit as a member at any meeting of the Council during the consideration of matters specially affecting the interests of that Member of the League.

6. At meetings of the Council, each Member of the League represented on the Council shall have one vote, and may have not more than one Representative.

ARTICLE 5

Voting and Procedure

Except where otherwise expressly provided in the Covenant or by the terms of the present Treaty, decisions at any meeting of the Assembly or of the Council shall require the agreement of all the Members of the League represented at the meeting.

All matters of procedure at meetings of the Assembly or of the Council, including the appointment of Committees to investigate particular matters, shall be regulated by the Assembly or by the Council and may be decided by a majority of the Members of the League represented at the meeting.

The first meeting of the Assembly and the first meeting or the Council shall be summoned by the President of the United States of America.

ARTICLE 6

Secretariat and Expenses

1. The permanent Secretariat shall be established at the seat of the League. The Secretariat shall comprise a Secretary-General and such secretaries and staff as may be required.

2. The first Secretary-General shall be the person named in the Annex: thereafter the Secretary-General shall be appointed by the Council with the approval of the majority of the Assembly.

3. The secretaries and the staff of the Secretariat shall be appointed by the Secretary-General with the approval of the Council.

4. The Secretary-General shall act in that capacity at all meetings of the Assembly and of the Council.

5. *The Expenses of the League shall be borne by the Members of the League in the proportin decided by the Assembly.*

Article 7

Seat, Qualifications of Officials, Immunities

1. The Seat of the League is established at Geneva.
2. The Council may at any time decide that the Seat of the League shall be established elsewhere.
3. All positions under or in connection with the League, including the Secretarial, shall be open equally to men and women.
4. Representatives of the Members of the League and officials of the League when engaged on the business of the League shall enjoy diplomatic privileges and immunities.
5. The buildings and other property occupied by the League or its officials or by Representatives attending its meetings shall be inviolable.

Article 8

Reduction of Armaments

1. The Members of the League recognize that the maintenance of peace requires the reduction of national armaments to the lowest point consistent with national safety and the enforcement by common action of international obligations.
2. The Council, taking account of the geographical situation and circumstances of each State, shall formulate plans for such reduction for the consideration and action of the several Governments.
3. Such plans shall be subject to reconsideration and revision at least every ten years.
4. After these plans shall have been adopted by the several Governments, the limits of armaments therein fixed shall not be exceeded without the concurrence of the Council.
5. The Members of the League agree that the manufacture by private enterprise of munitions and implements of war is open to grave objections. The Council shall advise how the evil effects attendant upon such manufacture can be prevented, due regard being paid to the necessities of those Members of the League which are not able to manufacture the munitions and implements of war necessary for their safety.
6. The Members of the League undertake to interchange full and frank information as to the scale of their armaments, their military, naval and air programmes and the condition of such of their industries as are adaptable to warlike purposes.

ARTICLE 9

Permanent Military, Naval and Air Commission

A permanent Commission shall be constituted to advise the Council on the execution of the provisions of Articles 1 and 8 and on military, naval and air questions generally.

ARTICLE 10

Guarantees against Aggression

The Members of the League undertake to respect and preserve as against external aggression the territorial integrity and existing political independence of all Members of the League. In case of any such aggression in case of any threat or danger of such aggression the Council shall advise upon the means by which this obligation shall be fulfilled.

ARTICLE 11

Action in Case of War or Threat of War

1. Any war or threat of war, whether immediately affecting any of the Members of the League or not, is hereby declared a matter of concern to the whole League, and the League shall take any action that may be deemed wise and effectual to safeguared the peace of nations. In case any such emergency should arise the Secreatary-General shall on the request of any Member of the League forthwith summon a meeting of the Council.
2. It is also declared to be the friendly right of each Member of the League to bring to the attention of the Assembly or the Council any circumstance whatever affecting international relations which threatens to disturb international peace or the good understanding between nations upon which peace depends.

Article 12

Disputes to be Submitted for Settlement

1. The Members of the League agree that, if there should arise between them any dispute likely to lead to a rupture, they will submit the matter either to arbitration *or judicial settlement* or to inquiry by the Council, and they agree in no case to resort to war unitl three months after the award by the arbitrators or the judicial decision, or the report by the Council.
2. In any case under this Article the award the arbitrators of the *judicial decision* shall be made within a reasonable time, and the report of the Council shall be made within six months after the submission of the dispute

ARTICLE 13

Arbitration or Judicial Settlement

1. The members of the League agree that, whenever any dispute shall arise between them which they recognize to be suitable for submission to arbitration or *judicial settlement,* and which can not be satisfactorily settled by diplomacy, they will submit the whole subject-matter to arbitration or *judicial settlement.*
2. Disputes as to the interpretation of a treaty, as to any question of international law, as to the existence of any fact which, if established, would constitue a breach of any international obligation, or as to the extent and nature of the reparation to be made for any such breach, are declared to be among those which are generally suitable for submission to arbitration or judicial settlement.
3. *For the consideration of any such dipute, the court to which the case is referred shall be the Permanent Court of International Justice, established in accordance with Article 14, or any tribunal agreed on by the parties to the dispute or stipulated in any convention existing between them.*
4. The Members of League agree that they will carry out in full good faith any award *or decision* that may be rendered, and that they will not resort to war against a Member of the League which complies therewith. In the event of any failure to carry out such an award or decision, the Council shall propose what steps should be taken to give effect there to

ARTICLE 14

Permanent Court of International Justice

The Council shall formulate and submit to the Members of the League for adoption plans for the establishment of a Permanent Court of International Justice. The Court shall be competent to hear and determine any dispute of an international character which the parties thereto submit to it. The Court may also give an advisory opinion upon any dispute or question referred to it by the Council or by Assembly.

ARTICLE 15

Disputes Not Submitted to Arbitration or Judicial Settlement

1. If those should arise between members of the League any dispute likely to lead to a rupture, which is not submitted to arbitration or judicial settlement in accordance with Article 13, the Members of the League agree that they will submit the matter to the Council. Any party to the dispute may effect such submission by giving notice of the existence of the dispute to the Secretary-General, who will make all necessary arrangements for a full investigation and consideration thereof.

2. For this purpose the parties to the dispute will communicate to the Secretary-General, as promptly as possible, statements or their case with all the relevant fact and papers, and the Council may forthwith direct the publication thereof.

3. The Council shall endeavour to effect a settlement of the dispute, and, if such efforts are successful, a statement shall be made public giving such facts and explanations regarding the dispute and the terms of settlement thereof as the Council may deem appropritate.

4. If the dispute is not thus settled, the Council either unanimously or by a majority vote shall make and publish a report containing a statement of the facts of the dispute and the recommendations which are deemed just and proper in regard thereto.

5. Any Member of the League represented on the Council may make public a statement of the facts of the dispute and of its conclusions regarding the same.

6. If a report by the Council is unanimously agreed to by the Members thereof other than the Representatives of one or more of the parties to the dispute, the Members of the League agree that they will not got to war with any party to the dispute which complies with the recommendations of the report.

7. If the Council fails to reach a report which is unanimously agreed to by the members there–of, other than the Representatives of one or more of the parties to the dispute, the Members of the League reserve to themselves the right to take such action as they shall consider necessary for the maintenance of right and justice.

8. If the dispute between the parties is claimed by one of them, and is found by the Council, to arise out of a matter which by international law is solely within the domestic jurisdiction of that party, the Council shall so report, and shall made no recommendation as to its settlement.

9. The Council may in any case under this Article refer the dispute to the Assembly. The dispute shall be so referred at the request of either party to the dispute, provided that such request be made within 14 days after the submission of the dispute to the Council.

10. In any case referred to the Assembly, all the provisions of this Article and of Article 12 relating to the actions and powers of the Council shall apply to the actions and powers of the Assembly, provided that a report made by the Assembly, if concurred in by the Representatives of those Members of the League represented on the Council and of a majority of the other Members of the League, exclusive in each case of the Representatives of the parties to the dispute, shall have the same force as a report by the Council concurred in by all the members thereof other than of Representatives of one or more of the parties to the dipsute.

ARTICLE 16

Sanctions of Pacific Settlement

1. Should any Member of the League resort to war in disregard of its covenants under Articles 12, 13 or 15, shall *ipso facto* be deemed to have committed an act of war against all other Members of the League, which hereby undertake immediately to subject it to the severance of all trade or financial relations, the prohibition of all intercourse between their nationals and the nationals of the covenant-breaking State, and the prevention of all financial, commercial or personal intercourse between the nationals of the covenant–breaking State and the nationals of any other State, whether a Member of the League or not.
2. It shall be the duty of the Council in such case to recommend to the several Governments concerned what effective military, naval or air force the Members of the League shall severally contribute to the armed forces to be used to protect the covenants of the League.
3. The Members of he League agree, further, that they will mutually support one another in the financial and economic measures which are taken under this Article, in order to minimize the loss and inconvenience resulting from the above measures, and that they will mutually support one another in resisting any special measure aimed at one of their member by the covenant-breaking State, and that they will take the necessary steps to afford passage through their territory to the forces of any of the Members of the League which are cooperating to protect the covenants of the League.
4. Any Member of the League which has violated any covenant of the League may be declared to be no longer a Member of the League by a vote of the Council concurred in by the Representatives of all the other members of the League represented thereon.

ARTICLE 17

Disputes involving Non-Members

1. In the event of a dispute between a member of the League and a State which is not a Member of the League, or between States not Members of the League, the State or States not Members of the League shall be invited to accept the obligations of membership in the League for the purposes of such dispute, upon such conditions as the Council may deem just. If such invitation is accepted, the provisions of Articles 12 to 16, inclusive, shall be applied with such modifications as may be deemed necessary by the Council.
2. Upon such invitation being given the Council shall immediately institute an inquiry into the circumstances of the dispute and recommend such action as may seem best and most effectual in the circumstances.

3. If a State so invited shall refuse to accept the obligations of membership in the League for the purposes of such dispute and shall resort to war against a Member of the League, the provisions of Article 16 shall be applicable as against the State taking such action.
4. If both parties to the dispute when so invited refuse to accept the obligations of membership in the League for the purposes of such dispute, the Council may take such measures and make such recommendations as will prevent hostilities and will result in the settlement of the dispute.

ARTICLE 18

Registration and Publication of Treaties

Every treaty or international engagement entered into hereafter by any Member of the League shall be forthwith registered with the Secretariat and shall as soon as possible be published by it. No Such treaty or international engagement shall be binding until so registered.

ARTICLE 19

Review of Treaties

The Assembly may from time to time advise the reconsideration by Members of the League of treaties which have become inapplicable, and the consideration of international conditions whose continuance might endanger the peace of the world.

ARTICLE 20

Abrogation of Inconsistent Obligations

1. The Members of the league severally agree that this Covenant is accepted as abrogating all obligations or understandings *inter se* which are inconsistent with the terms thereof, and solemnly undertake that they will not hereafter enter into any engagements inconsistent with the terms therof.
2. In case any Member of the League shall, before becoming a Member of the League, have undertaken any obligations inconsistent with the terms of this Covenant, it shall be the duty of such Member to take immediate steps to procure its release from such obligations.

ARTICLE 21

Engagements That Remain Valid

Nothing in this Covenant shall be deemed to affect the validity of international engagements, such as treaties of arbitration or regional understandings like the Monroe doctrine, for securing the maintenance of peace.

Article 22

Mandatory System

1. To those colonies and territories which as a consequence of the later war have ceased to be under the sovereignty of the States which formerly governed them and which are inhabited by peoples not yet above to stand by themselves under the strenuous conditions of the modern world, there should be applied the principle that the well being and development of such peoples form a sacred trust of civilization and that securites for the preformance of this trust should be embodied in this Covenant.

2. The best method of giving practical effect to this principle is that the tutelage of such peoples should be entrusted to advanced nations who by reason of their resources, their experience or their geographical position can best undertake this responsibility, and who are willing to accept it, and that this tutelage shloud be exercised by them as Mandatories on behalf of the League.

3. The character of the mandate must differ according to the stage of the development of the people, the geographical situation of the territory, its economic conditions and other similar circumstances.

4. Certain communities formerly belonging to the Turkish Empire have reached a stage of development where their existence as independent nations can be provisionally recognized subject to the rendering of administrative advice and assistance by a Mandatory unitil such time as they are able to stand alone. The wishes of these communities must be a principal consideration in the selection of the Mandatory.

5. Other peoples, especially those of Central Africa, are at such a stage that the Mandatory must be responsible for the administration of the territory under conditions which will guarantee freedom of conscience and religion, subject only to the maintenance of public order and morals, the prohibition of abuses such as the slave trade, the arms traffic and the liquor traffic, and the prevention of the establishment of fortifications of military and naval bases and of military training of the natives for other than police purposes and the defence of territory and will also secure equal opportunities for the trade and commerce of other Members of the League.

6. There are territories, such as Southwest Africa and certain of the South Pacific Islands, which owing to the sparseness of their population, or their small size, or their remoteness from the centres of civilization, or their geographical contiguity to the territory of the Mandatory, and other circumstances, can be best administered under the laws of the Mandatory as integral portions of its territory, subject to the safeguards above mentioned in the interests or the indigenous population.

7. In every case of mandate, the Mandatory shall render to the Council an annual report in reference to the territory committed to its charge.

8. The degree of authority, control or administration to be exercised by the Mandatory shall, if not previously agreed upon by the Members of the League, be explicitly defined in each case by the Council.

9. A permanent Commission shall be constituted to receive and examine the annual reports of the Mandatories and to advise the Council on all matters relating to the observance of the mandates.

ARTICLE 23

Social and Other Activities

Subject to and in accordance with the provisions of international conventions existing or hereafter to be agreed upon, the Members of the League :

a. Will endeavour to secure and maintain fair and humane conditions of labour for men, women and children, both in their own countries and in all countries to which their commercial and industrial relations extend, and for that purpose will establish and maintain the necessary international organizations;

b. Undertake to secure just treatment of the native inhabitants of territories under their control;

c. Will entrust the League with the general supervision over the execution of agreements with regard to traffic in women and children, and the traffic in opium and other dangerous drugs;

d. Will entrust the League with the general supervision of the trade in arms and ammunition with the countries in which the control of this traffic is necessary in the common interest;

e. Will make provision to secure and maintain freedom of communications and to transit an equitable treatment for the commerce of all members of the League. In this conneection, the special necessites of the regions devastated during the war of 1914-1918 shall be borne in mind;

f. Will endeavour to take steps in matters of international concern for the prevention and control of disease.

ARTICLE 24

International Bureaus

1. There shall be placed under the direction of the League all international bureaus already established by general treaties if the parties to such treaties consent. All such international bureaus and all commissions for the regulation of matters of international interest

hereafter constituted shall be placed under the direction of the League.

2. In all matters of international interest which are regulated by general conventions but which are not placed under the control of international bureaus or commissions, the Secretariat of the League shall, subject to the consent of the Council and if desired by the parties, collect and distribute all relevant information and shall render any other assistance which may be necessary or desirable.

3. The Council may include as part of the expenses of the Secretariat the expenses of any bureau or commission which is placed under the direction of the League.

ARTICLE 25

Promotion of Red Cross and Health

The Members of the League agree to encourage and promote the establishment and cooperation of duly authorized voluntary national Red Cross organizations having as purposes the improvement of health, the prevention of disease and the mitigation of suffering throughout the world.

ARTICLE 26

Amendments

1. Amendments to this Covenant will take effect when ratified by the Members of the League whose Representatives compose the Council and by a majority of the Members of the League whose Representatives compose the Assembly.

2. No such amendment shall bind any Member of the League which signifies its dissent there from, but in that case it shall cease to be a Member of the League.

Appendix –2

CHARTER OF THE UNITED NATIONS

We the People of the United Nations determined

To save succeeding generations from the scourge of war, which twice in our lifetime has brought untold sorrow to mankind, and

To reaffirm faith in fundamental human rights, in the dignity and worth of the human person, in the equal rights of men and women and of nations large and small, and

To establish conditions under which justice and respect for the obligations arising from treaties and other sources of international law can be maintained, and

To promote social progress and better standards of life in larger freedom,

And for these ends

To practice tolerance and live together in peace with one another as good neighbors, and

To unite our strength to maintain international peace and security, and

To ensure, by the acceptance of principles and the institution of methods, that armed force shall not be used, save in the common interest, and

To employ international machinery for the promotion of the economic and social advancement of all peoples,

Have Resolved to combine our efforts to Accomplish these Aims

Accordingly, our respective Governments, through representatives assembled in the city of San Francisco, who have exhibited their full powers found to be in good and due form, have agreed to the present Charter of the United Nations and do hereby establish an international organization to be known as the United Nations.

CHAPTER I

PURPOSE AND PRINCIPLES

ARTICLE I

The Purposes of the United Nations are:

1. To maintain international peace and security, and to that end: to take effective collective measures for the prevention and removal of threats to the peace, and for the suppression of acts of aggression or other breaches of the peace, and to bring about by peaceful means, and in conformity with the principles of justice and international law, adjustment or settlement of international disputes or situations which might lead to a breach of the peace ;
2. To develop friendly relations among nations based on respect for the principle of equal rights and self-determination of peoples, and to take other appropriate measures to strengthen universal peace;
3. To achieve international co-operation in solving international problems of an economic, social cultural, or humanitarian character, and in promoting and encouraging respect for human rights and for fundamental freedoms for all without distinction as to race, sex, language, or religion; and
4. To be a centre for harmonizing the actions of nations in the attainment of these common ends.

ARTICLE 2

The Organization and its Members, in pursuit of the purposes stated in Article 1, shall act in accordance with the following principles.

1. The Organization is based on the principle of the sovereign equality of all its Members.
2. All Members, in order to ensure to all of them the rights and benefits resulting form membership, shall fulfill in good faith the obligations assumed by them in accordance with the present Charter.
3. All Members shall settle their international disputes by peaceful means in such a manner that international peace and security, and justice are not endangered.
4. All Members shall refrain in their international relations from the threat or use of force against the territorial integrity or political independence of any state, or in any other manner inconsistent with the Purposes of the United Nations.
5. All Members shall give the United Nations every assistance in any action it takes in accordance with the present Charter, and shall refrain from giving assistance to any state against which the United Nations is taking preventive or enforcement action.

6. The Organization shall ensure that states which are not Members of the United Nations act in accordance with these Principles so far as may be necessary for the maintenance of international peace and security.
7. Nothing contained in the present Charter shall authorize the United Nations to intervene in matters which are essentially within the domestic jurisdiction of any state or shall require the Members to submit such matters to settlement under the present Charter; but this principle shall not prejudice the application of enforcement measures under Chapter VII.

CHAPTER II

MEMBERSHIP

ARTICLE 3

The original Members of the United Nations shall be the states which, having participated in the United Nations Conference on International Organization at San Francisco, or having previously signed the Declaration by United Nations of 1 January 1942, sign the present Charter and ratify it in accordance with Article 110.

ARTICLE 4

1. Membership in the United Nations is open to all other peace-loving states which accept the obligations contained in the present Charter and, in the judgement of the Organization, are able and willing to carry out these obligations.
2. The admission of any such state to membership in the United Nations will be effected by a decision of the General Assembly upon the recommendation of the Security Council.

ARTICLE 5

A Member of the United Nations against which preventive or enforcement action has been taken by the Security Council may by suspended from the exercise of the rights and privileges of membership by the General Assembly upon the recommendation of the Security Council. The exercise of these rights and privileges may be restored by the Security Council.

ARTICLE 6

A Member of the United Nations which has persistently violated the Principles contained in the present Charter may by expelled from the Organization by the General Assembly upon the recommendation of the Security Council.

CHAPTER III

ORGANS

ARTICLE 7

1. There are established as the principal organs of the United Nations: a General Assembly, a Security Council, an Economic and Social Council, a Trusteeship Council, an International Court of Justice, and a Secretariat.
2. Such subsidiary organs as may be found necessary may be established in accordance with the present Charter.

ARTICLE 8

The United Nations shall place no restrictions on the eligibility of men and women to participate in any capacity and under conditions of equality in its principal and subsidiary organs.

CHAPTER IV

THE GENERAL ASSEMBLY

Composition

ARTICLE 9

1. The General Assembly shall consist of all the Members of the United Nations.
2. Each Member shall have not more than five representatives in the General Assembly.

Functions and Powers

ARTICLE 10

The General Assembly may discuss any questions or any matters within the scope of the present Charter or relating to the powers and functions of any organs provided for in the present Charter, and except as provided in Article 12, may make recommendations to the Members of the United Nations or to the Security Council or to both on any such questions or matters.

ARTICLE 11

1. The General Assembly may consider the general principles of co-operation in the maintenance of international peace and security, including the principles governing disarmament and the regulation of armaments, and may make recommendations with regard to such principles to the members or the Security Council or to both.

2. The General Assembly may discuss any questions relating to the maintenance of international peace and security brought before it by any Member of the United Nations, or by the Security Council, or by a state which is not a Member of the United Nations in accordance with Article 35, paragraph 2, and, except as provided in Article 12, may make recommendations with regard to any such questions to the state or states concerned or to the Security Council or both. Any such question on which action is necessary shall be referred to the Security Council by the General Assembly either before or after discussion.

3. The General Assembly may call the attention of the Security Council to situations, which are likely to endanger international peace and security.

4. The power of the General Assembly set forth in this Article shall not limit the general scope of Article 10.

ARTICLE 12

1. While the Security Council is exercising in respect of any dispute or situation the function assigned to it in the present Charter, the General Assembly shall not make any recommendation with regard to that dispute or situation unless the Security Council so requests.

2. The Secretary-General, with the consent of the Security Council, shall notify the General Assembly at each session of any matters relative to the maintenance of international peace and security which are being dealt with by the Security Council and shall similarly notify the General Assembly, or the Members of the United Nations if the General Assembly is not in session, immediately the Security Council ceases to deal with such matters.

ARTICLE 13

1. The General Assembly shall initiate studies to make recommendations for the purpose of:
   a. promoting international co-operation in the political field and encouraging the progressive development of international law and its codification;
   b. promoting international co-operation in the economic, social, cultural, educational, and health fields, and assisting in the realization of human rights and fundamental freedoms for all without distinction as to race, sex, language, or religion.

2. The further responsibilities, functions and powers of the General Assembly with respect of matters mentioned in paragraph 1(b) above are set forth in Chapter IX and X.

ARTICLE 14

Subject to the provisions of Article 12, the General Assembly may recommend measures for the peaceful adjustment of any situation, regardless or origin, which it deems likely to impair the general welfare of friendly relations among nations, including situations resulting from the violation of the provisions of the present Charter setting forth the Purposes and Principles of the United Nations.

ARTICLE 15

1. The General Assembly shall receive and consider annual and special reports from the Security Council; these reports shall include an account of the measures that the Security Council has decided upon or taken to maintain international peace and security.
2. The General Assembly shall receive and consider reports from the other organs of the United Nations.

ARTICLE 16

The General Assembly shall perform such functions with respect to the international trusteeship system as are assigned to it under Chapters XII and XIII, including the approval of the trusteeship agreements for areas not designated as strategic.

ARTICLE 17

1. The General Assembly shall consider and approve the budget of the Organization.
2. The expenses of the Organization shall be borne by the Members as apportioned by the General Assembly.
3. The General Assembly shall consider and approve any financial and budgetary arrangements with specialized agencies referred to in Article 57 and shall examine the administrative budgets of such specialized agencies with a view to making recommendations to the agencies concerned.

Voting

ARTICLE 18

1. Each Member of the General Assembly shall have one vote.
2. Decisions of the General Assembly on important questions shall be made by a two-thirds majority of the members present and voting. These questions shall include ; recommendations with respect of the maintenance of the international peace and security, the election of the non-permanent members of the Security Council, the election of the members of the Economic and Social Council, the election of members of the Trusteeship Council in accord-

ance with paragraph 1(c) of Article 86, the admission of new Members to the United Nations, the suspension of the rights and privileges of membership, the expulsion of Members, questions relating to the operation of the trusteeship system, and budgetary questions.

3. Decision other questions, including the determination of additional categories of questions to be decided by a two-thirds majority, shall be made by a majority of the members present and voting.

ARTICLE 19

A Member of the United Nations which is in arrears in the payment of its financial contributions to the Organization shall have no vote in the General Assembly if the amount of its arrears equals or exceeds the amount of the contributions due from it for the preceding two full years. The General Assembly may, nevertheless, permit such a Member to vote if it is satisfied that the failure to pay is due to conditions beyond the control of the Member.

Procedure

ARTICLE 20

The General Assembly shall meet in regular annual sessions and in such special sessions as occasion may require. Special sessions shall be convoked by the Secretary General at the request of the Security Council or of a majority of the Members of the United Nations.

ARTICLE 21

The General Assembly shall adopt its own rules of procedure. It shall elect its President for each session.

ARTICLE 22

The General Assembly may establish such organs as it deems necessary for the performance of functions.

CHAPTER V

THE SECURITY COUNCIL

Composition

ARTICLE 23

1. The Security Council shall consist of fifteen Members of the United Nations. The Republic of China, France, the Union of Soviet Socialist Republics, the United Kingdom of Great Britain and Northern Ireland and the United States of America shall be permanent members of the Security Council. The General Assembly shall

elect ten other Members of the United Nations to be non-permanent members of the Security Council, due regard being specially paid in the first instance to the contribution of Members of the United Nations to the maintenance of international peace and security and to the other purposes of the Organization, and also to equitable geographical distribution.

2. The non-permanent members of the Security Council shall be elected foraterm of two years. In the first election of the non-permanent members after the increase of the membership of the Security Council from eleven to fifteen, two of the four additional members shall be chosen for a term of one year. A retiring member shall not be eligible for immediate re-election.

3. Each member of the Security Council shall have one representative.

Functions and Powers

Article 24

1. In order to ensure prompt effective action by the United Nations, its Members confer on the Security Council primary responsibility for the maintenance of international peace and security, and agree that in carrying out its duties under its responsibility the Security Council acts on their behalf.

2. In discharging these duties the Security Council shall act in accordance with the Purposes and Principles of the United Nations. The specific powers granted to the Security Council for the discharge of these duties are laid down in Chapters VI, VII, VIII, and XII.

3. Th Security Council shall submit annual and, when necessary, special reports to the General Assembly for its consideration.

Article 25

The Members of the United Nations agree to accept and carry out the decisions of the Security Council in accordance with the present Charter.

Article 26

In order to promote the establishment and maintenance of international peace and security with the least diversion for armaments of the world's human and economic resources, the Security Council shall be responsible for formulating, with the assistance of the Military Staff Committee referred to in Article 47, plans to be submitted to the Members of the United Nations for the establishment of a system for the regulation of armaments.

Voting

ARTICLE 27

1. Each Member of the Security Council shall have one vote.
2. Decisions of the Security Council on procedural matters shall be made by an affirmative vote of nine members.
3. Decisions of the Security Council on all other matters shall be made by an affirmative vote of nine members including the concurring votes of the permanent members; provided that, in decisions under Chapter VI, and under paragraphs 3 of Article 52, a party to a dispute shall abstain form voting.

Procedure

ARTICLE 28

1. The Security Council shall be so organized as to be able to function continuously. Each member of the Security Council shall for this purpose be represented at all time at the seat of the Organization.
2. The Security Council shall hold periodic meetings at which each of its members may, if it so desires, be represented by a member of the government of by some other specially designated representative.
3. The Security Council may hold meetings at such places other than the seat of the Organization as in its judgement will best facilitate its work.

ARTICLE 29

The Security Council may establish such subsidiary organs as it deems necessary for the performance of its functions.

ARTICLE 30

The Security Council shall adopt its own rules of procedure, including the method of selecting its President.

ARTICLE 31

Any Member of the United Nations which is not a member of the Security Council may participate, without vote, in the discussion of any question brought before the Security Council whenever the latter considers that the interests of that Member are specially affected.

ARTICLE 32

Any Member of the United Nations which is not member of the Security Council or any state which is not a Member of the United Nations, if it is party to a dispute under consideration by the Security Council shall be invited to participate, without vote, in the discussion relating to the dispute. The Security Council shall lay down such conditions as it deems just for the participation of a state which is not a Member of the United Nations.

CHAPTER VI

PACIFIC SETTLEMENT OF DISPUTES

ARTICLE 33

1. The parties to any dispute, the continuance of which is likely to endanger the maintenance of international peace and security, shall first of all seek a solution by negotiation, enquiry, mediation, conciliation, arbitration, judicial settlement, resort to regional agencies or arrangements, or other peaceful means of their own choice.
2. The Security Council shall, when it deems necessary, call upon the parties to settle their dispute by such means.

ARTICLE 34

The Security Council may investigate any dispute, or any situation which might lead to international friction or give rise to a dispute, in order to determine whether the continuance of the dispute or situation is likely to endanger the maintenance of international peace and security.

ARTICLE 35

1. Any Member of the United Nations may bring any dispute or any situation of the nature referred to in Article 34, to the attention of Security Council or of the General Assembly.
2. A state which is not a Member of the United Nations may bring to the attention of the Security Council or of the General Assembly any dispute to which it is a party if it accepts in advance, for the purposes of the dispute, the obligations of pacific settlement provided in the present Charter.
3. The proceedings of the General Assembly in respect of matters brought to its attention under this Article will be subject to the provisions of Articles 11 and 12

ARTICLE 36

1. The Security Council may, at any stage of a dispute of the nature referred to in Article 33 or of a situation of like nature, recommend appropriate procedures or methods of adjustment.
2. The Security Council should take into consideration any procedures for the settlement of the dispute which have already been adopted by the parties.

3. In making recommendations under this Article the Security Council should also take into consideration that legal disputes should as a general rule be referred by the parties to the International Court of Justice in accordance with the provisions of the Statute of the Court.

ARTICLE 37

1. Should the parties to a dispute of the nature referred to in Article 33 fail to settle it by the means indicated in that Article, they shall refer it to the Security Council.
2. If the Security Council deems that the continuance of the disputes is in fact likely to endanger the maintenance of international peace and security, it shall decide whether to take action under Article 36 or to recommend such terms of settlement as it may consider appropriate.

ARTICLE 38

Without prejudice to the provisions of Articles 33 to 37, the Security Council may, if all the parties to any dispute so request, make recommendations to the parties with a view to a pacific settlement of the dispute

CHAPTER VII

ACTION WITH RESPECT TO THREATS TO THE PEACE, BREACHES OF THE PEACE, AND ACTS OF AGGRESSION

ARTICLE 39

The Security Council Shall determine the existence of any threat to the peace, breach of peace, or act of aggression and shall make recommendations, or decide what measures shall be taken in accordance with Articles 41 and 42 to maintain or restore international peace and security.

ARTICLE 40

In order to prevent an aggravation of the situation, the Security Council may, before making the recommendations or deciding upon the measures provided for in Article 39, call upon the parties concerned to comply with such provisional measures as it deems necessary or desirable. Such provisional measures shall be without prejudice to the rights, claims, or position of the parties concerned, the Security Council shall duly take account of failure to comply with such provisional measures.

ARTICLE 41

The Security Council may decide what measures not involving the use of armed force are to be employed to give effect to its decisions, and it may call upon the Members of the United Nations to apply such measures. These may include complete or partial interruption of economic relations and of rail, sea, air, postal, telegraphic, radio, and other means of communication, and the severance of diplomatic relations.

ARTICLE 42

Should the Security Council consider that measures provided for in Article 41 would be inadequate or have proved to be inadequate, it may take such action by air, sea, or land forces as may be necessary to maintain or restore international peace and security. Such action may include demonstrations, blockade, and other operations by air, sea, or land forces of Members of the United Nations.

ARTICLE 43

1. All Members of the United Nations, in order to contribute to the maintenance of international peace and security, undertake to make available to the Security Council, on its call and in accordance with a special agreement of agreements, armed forces, assistance, and facilities, including rights or passage, necessary for the purpose of maintaining international peace and security.
2. Such agreement or agreements shall govern the numbers and types of forces, their degree of readiness and general location, and the nature of the facilities and assistance to be provided.
3. The agreement of agreements shall be negotiated as soon as possible on the initiative of the Security Council. They shall be concluded between the Security Council and Members and shall be subject to ratification by the signatory states in accordance with their receptive constitutional processes.

ARTICLE 44

When the Security Council has decided to use force it shall, before calling upon a member not represented on it to provide armed forces in fulfillment of the obligations assumed under Article 43, invite that Member, if the Member so desires, to participate in the decisions of the Security Council concerning the employment of contingents of that Member's armed forces.

ARTICLE 45

In order to enable the United Nations to take urgent military measures, Members shall hold immediately available national airforce contingents for combined international enforcement action. The strength and degree of readiness of these contingents and plans for their combined action shall be determined, within the limits laid down in the special agreement or agreements referred to in Article 43, by the Security Council with the Assistance of the Military Staff Committee.

Article 46

Plans for the application of armed force shall be made by the Security Council with the assistance of the Military Staff Committee.

Article 47

1. There shall be established a Military Staff Committee to advise and assist the Security Council on all questions relating to the Security Council's military requirements for the maintenance of international peace and security, the employment and command of forces placed at its disposal, the regulation of armaments, and possible disarmament.
2. The Military Staff Committee shall consist of the Chiefs of Staff of the permanent members of the Security Council or their representatives. Any Member of the United Nations not permanently represented on the committee shall be invited by the committee to be associated with it when the efficient discharge of the committee's responsibilities requires the participation of that Member in its work.
3. The Military Staff Committee shall be responsible under the Security Council for the strategic direction of any armed forces placed at the disposal of the Security Council. Questions relating to the command of such forces shall be worked out subsequently.
4. The Military Staff Committee, with the authorization of the Security Council and after consultation with appropriate regional agencies, may establish regional sub-committees.

Article 48

1. The action required to carry out the decision of the Security Council for the maintenance of international peace and security shall be taken by all the Members of the United Nations or by some of them, as the Security Council may determine.
2. Such decisions shall be carried out by the Members of the United Nations directly and through their action in the appropriate international agencies of which they are members.

Article 49

The Members of the United Nations shall join in affording mutual assistance in carrying out the measures decided upon by the Security Council.

ARTICLE 50

If preventive or enforcement measures against any state are taken by the Security Council, any other state, whether a Member or the United Nations or not, which finds itself confronted with special economic problems arising from the carrying out of those measures shall have the right to consult the Security Council with regard to a solution of those problems.

ARTICLE 51

Nothing in the present Charter shall impair the inherent right of individual or collective self-defence if anarmed attack occurs against a Member of the United Nations, until the Security Council has taken measures necessary to maintain international peace and security. Measures taken by Members in the exercice of this right of self-defense shall be immediately reported to the Security Council and shall not in any way affect the authority and responsibility of the Security Council under the present Charter to take at any time such action as it deems necessary in order to maintain or restore international peace and security.

CHAPTER VIII

REGIONAL ARRANGEMENTS

ARTICLE 52

1. Nothing in the present Charter precludes the existence of regional arrangements or agencies for dealing with such matters relating to the maintenance of international peace and security as are appropriate for regional action, provided that such arrangements or agencies and their activities are consistent with the Purposes and Principles of the United Nations.
2. The Members of the United Nations entering into such arrangements or constituting such agencies shall make every effort to achieve pacific settlement of local disputes through such regional arrangements or by such regional agencies before referring them to the Security Council.
3. The Security Council shall encourage the development of pacific settlement of local disputes through such regional arrangements or by such regional agencies either on the initiative of the states concerned or by reference from the Security Council.
4. This Article in no way impairs the application of Articles 34 and 35

ARTICLE 53

1. The Security Council shall, where appropriate, utilize such regional arrangements or agencies for enforcement action under its authority. But no enforcement action shall be taken under regional ar-

rangements or by regional agencies without the authorization of the Security Council, with the exception of measures against any enemy state, as defined in paragraph 2 of this Article, provided for pursuant to Article 107 or in regional arrangements directed against renewal of aggressive policy on the part of any such state, until such time as the Organization may, on request of the Governments concerned, be charged with the responsibility for preventing further aggression by such a state.

2. The term enemy state as used in paragraph 1 of this Article applies to any state which during the Second World War has been an enemy of any signatory of the present Charter.

Article 54

The Security Council shall at all times be kept fully informed of activities undertaken or in contemplation under regional arrangements or by regional agencies for the maintenance of international peace and security.

CHAPTER IX

INTERNATIONAL ECONOMIC AND SOCIAL CO-OPERATION

Article 55

With a view to the creation of conditions of stability and well-being which are necessary for peaceful and friendly relations among nations based on respect for the principle of equal rights and self-determination of peoples, the United Nations shall promote;

a. higher standard of living, full employment, and conditions of economic and social progress and development;

b. solutions of international economic, social, health, and related problems; and international cultural and educational co-operation; and

c. universal respect for, and observance of, human rights and fundamental freedoms for all without distinction as to race, sex, language, or religion.

Article 56

All Members pledge themselves to take joint and separate action in co-operation with the Organization for the achievement of purposes set forth in Article 55.

Article 57

1. The various specialized agencies, established by intergovernmental agreement and having wide international responsibilities, as

defined in their basic instruments, in economic, social, cultural, educational, health, and related fields, shall be brought into relationship with the United Nations in accordance with the provisions of Article 63.

2. Such agencies thus brought into relationship with the United Nations are herein after refereed to as specialized agencies.

ARTICLE 58

The organization shall make recommendations for the coordination of the policies and activities of the specialized agencies.

ARTICLE 59

The organization shall, where appropriate, initiate negotiations among the states concerned for the creation of any new specialized agencies required for the accomplishment of the purposes set forth in Article 55.

ARTICLE 60

Responsibility for the discharge of the functions of the Organization set forth in this Chapter shall be vested in the General Assembly and, under the authority of the General Assembly, in the Economic and Social Council, which shall have for this purpose the powers set forth in Chapter X.

CHAPTER X

THE ECONOMIC AND SOCIAL COUNCIL

Composition

ARTICLE 61

1. The Economic and Social Council shall consist of fifty-four Members of the United Nations elected by the General Assembly.
2. Subject to the provisions of paragraph 3, eighteen members of the Economic and Social Council shall be elected each year for a term of three years. A retiring member shall be eligible for immediate reelection.
3. At the first election after the increase in the membership of the Economic and Social Council from twenty-seven to fifty-four members whose term of office expires at the end of that year, twenty-seven additional members shall be elected. Of these twenty-seven additional members, the term of office of nine members so elected shall expire at the end of one year, and of nine other members at the end of two years, in accordance with arrangements made by the General Assembly.
4. Each member of the Economic and Social Council shall have one representative.

Functions and Powers

ARTICLE 62

1. The Economic and Social Council may make or initiate studies and reports with respect to international economic, social, cultural, educational, health, and related matters and may make recommendations with respect to any such matters to the General Assembly, to the Members of the United Nations, and to the specialized agencies concerned.
2. It may make recommendations for the purpose of promoting respect for, and observance of human rights and fundamental freedoms for all.
3. It may prepare draft conventions for submission to the General Assembly, with respect to matters falling within its competence.
4. It may call, in accordance with the rules prescribed by the United Nations, international conferences on matters falling within its competence.

ARTICLE 63

1. The Economic and Social Council may enter into agreements with any of the agencies referred to in Article 57, defining the terms on which the agency concerned shall be brought into relationship with the United Nations. Such agreements shall be subject to approval by the General Assembly
2. It may co-ordinate the activities of the specialized agencies through recommendations to the General Assembly and to the Members of the United Nations.

Article 64

1. The Economic and Social Council may take appropriate steps to obtain regular reports from the specialized agencies. It may make arrangements with the Members of the United Nations and with the specialized agencies to obtain reports on the steps taken to give effect to its own recommendations and to recommendations on matters falling within its competence made by the General Assembly.
2. It may communicate its observations on these reports to the General Assembly.

ARTICLE 65

The Economic and Social Council shall furnish information to the Security Council and shall assist the Security Council upon its request.

ARTICLE 66

1. The Economic and Social Council shall perform such functions as fall within its competence in connection with the carrying out of the recommendations of the General Assembly.
2. It may, with the approval of the General Assembly, perform services at the request of Members of the United Nations and at the request of specialized agencies.
3. It shall perform such other functions as are specified elsewhere in the present Charter or as may be assigned to it by the General Assembly.

Voting

ARTICLE 67

1. Each member of the Economic and Social Council shall have one vote.
2. Decisions of the Economic and Social Council shall be made by a majority of the members present and voting.

Procedure

ARTICLE 68

The Economic and Social Council shall set up commission in economic and social fields and for the promotion of human rights, and such other commissions as may be required for the performance of its functions.

ARTICLE 69

The Economic and Social Council shall invite any Member of the United Nations to participate, without vote, in its deliberations on any matter of particular concern to that Member.

ARTICLE 70

The Economic and Social Council may make arrangements for representatives of the specialized agencies to participate, without vote, in its deliberations and in those of the commissions established by it, and for tis representatives to participate in the deliberations of the specialized agencies.

ARTICLE 71

The Economic and social Council may make suitable arrangements for consultation with non-governmental organizations which are concerned with matters within its competence. Such arrangements may be mead with international organizations and, where appropriate, with national organizations after consultation with the Member of the United Nations concerned.

ARTICLE 72

1. The Economic and Social Council shall adopt its won rules of procedure, including the method of selecting its president.
2. The Economic and Social Council shall meet as required in accordance with its rules, which shall include provision for the convening of meetings on the request of a majority of its members.

CHAPTER XI

DECLARATION REGARDING NON-SELF-GOVERNING TERRITORIES

ARTICLE 73

Members of the United Nations which have or assume responsibilities for the administration of territories whose people have not yet attained a full measure of self-government recognize the principle that the interests of the inhabitants of these territories are paramount, and accept as a sacred trust the obligation to promote to the utmost, within the system of international peace and security established by the present Charter, the well-being of the inhabitants of these territories of these territories, and, to this end:

a. to ensure, with due respect for the culture of the people concerned, their political, economic, social and educational advancement, their just treatment, and their protection against abuses;

b. to develop self-government, to take due account of the political aspirations of the peoples, and to assist them in the progressive development of their free political institutions, according to the particular circumstances of each territory and its peoples and their varying stages of advancement;

c. to further international peace and security;

d. to promote constructive measures of development, to encourage research, and to co-operate with one another and, when and where appropriate, with specialized international bodies with a view to the practical achievement of the social, economic, and scientific purposes set forth in this Article; and

e. to transmit regularly to the Secretary General for information purposes, subject tp such limitation as security and constitutional considerations may require, statistical and other information of a technical nature relating to economic, social, and educational conditions in the territories for which they are respectively responsible other than those territories to which Chapters XII and XIII apply.

ARTICLE 74

Members of the United Nations also agree that their policy in respect of the territories to which this Chapter applies, no less than in respect of their metropolitan areas, must be based on the general principle of good-neighbourliness, due account being taken of the interests and well-being of the rest of the world, in social, economic, and commercial matters,

CHAPTER XII

INTERNATIONAL TRUSTEESHIP SYSTEM

ARTICLE 75

The United Nations shall establish under its authority an international trusteeship system for the administration and supervision of such territories as may be placed thereunder by subsequent individual agreements. These territories are hereinafter referred to as trust territories.

ARTICLE 76

The basic objectives of the trusteeship system, in accordance with the Purposes of the United Nations laid down in Article 1 of the present charter, shall be:

a. to further international peace and security;

b. to promote the political, economic, social, and educational advancement of the inhabitants of the trust territories, and their progressive development towards self-government or independence as may be appropriate to the particular circumstances of each territory and its people and the freely expressed wishes of the peoples concerned, and as may be provided by the terms of each trusteeship agreement;

c. to encourage respect for human rights and for fundamental freedoms for all without distinction as to race, sex, language, or religion, and to encourage recognition of the interdependence of the peoples of the world; and

d. to ensure equal treatment in social, economic, and commercial matter for all Members of the United Nations and their nationals, and also equal treatment for the latter in the administration of justice, without prejudice to the attainment of the foregoing objectives and subject to the provisions of Article 80.

ARTICLE 77

1. The trusteeship system shall apply to such territories in the following categories as may be placed thereunder by means of trusteeship agreements:

   a. territories now held under mandate;

b. territories which may be detached from enemy states as a result of the Second World War; and

c. territories voluntarily placed under the system by states responsible for their administration.

2. It will be a matter for subsequent agreement as to which territories in the foregoing categories will be brought under the trusteeship system and upon what terms.

Article 78

The trusteeship system shall not apply to territories which have become Members of the United Nations, relationship among which shall be based on respect for the principle of sovereign equality.

Article 79

The terms of trusteeship for each territory to be placed under the trusteeship system, including any alteration or amendment, shall be agreed upon by the states directly concerned, including the mandatory power in the case of territories held under mandate by a Member of the United Nations, and shall be approved as provided for in Articles 83 and 85.

Article 80

1. Except as may be agreed upon in individual trusteeship agreements, made under Articles 77,79 and 81 placing each territory under the trusteeship system, and until such agreements have been concluded nothing in this Chapter shall be construed in or of itself to alter in any manner the right whatsoever of any states or any peoples or the terms of existing international instruments to which Members of the United Nations may respectivley by parties.
2. Paragraph 1 of this Article shall not be interpreted as giving grounds for delay or postponement of the negotiation and conclusion of agreements for placing mandated and other territories under the trusteeship system as provided for in Article 77.

Article 81

The trusteeship agreement shall in each case include the terms under which the trust territory will be administered and designate the authority which will exercise the administration of the trust territory. Such authority, hereinafter callled the administering authority, may be one or more states or the Organization itself.

Article 82

There may be designated, in any trusteeship agreement, a strategic area or areas which may include part or all the trust territory to which the agreement applies, without prejudice to any special agreement or agreements made under Article 43.

ARTICLE 83

1. All functions of the United Nations relating to strategic areas, including the approval of the terms of the trusteeship agreements and of their alteration or amendment, shall be exercised by the Security Council.
2. The basic objectives set forth in Article 76 shall be applicable to the people of each strategic area.
3. The Security Council shall, subject to the provisions of the trusteeship agreements and without prejudice to security considerations, avail itself of the assistance of the Trusteeship Council to perform those functions of the United Nations under the trusteeship system relating to political, ecoonomic, social, and educational matters in the strategic areas.

ARTICLE 84

It shall be duty of the administering authority to ensure that the trust territory shall play its part in the maintenance of international peace and security. To this end the administering authority may make use of volunteer forces, facilities, and assistance from the trust territory in carrying out the obligations towards the Security Council undertaken in this regard by the administering authority, as well as for local defence and the maintenance of law and order within the trust territory.

ARTICLE 85

1. The functions of the United Nations with regard to trusteeship agreements for all areas not designated as strategic, including the approval of the terms of the trusteeship agreements and of their alteration or amendment, shall be exercised by the General Assembly.
2. The Trusteeship Council, operating under the authority of the General Assembly, shall assist the General Assembly in carrying out these functions

CHAPTER XIII

THE TRUSTEESHIP COUNCIL

Composition

ARTICLE 86

1. The trusteeship Council shall consist of the following Members of the United Nations:
   a. those Members administering trust territories;
   b. such of those Members mentioned by name in Article 23 as

are not administering trust territories; and

c. as many other Members elected for three-year terms by the General Assembly as may be necessary to ensure that the total number of members of the Trusteeship Council is equally divided between those Members of the United Nations which administer trust territories and those which do not.

3. Each member of the Trusteeship Council shall desingate one specially qualified person to represent it therein.

Functions and Powers

Article 87

The General Assembly and, under its authority, the Trusteeship Council, in carrying out their functions, may:

a. consider reports submitted by the administering authority;

b. accept petitions and examine them in consultation with the administering authority;

c. provide for periodic visits to the respective trust territories at times agreed upon with the administering authority; and

d. take these and other actions in conformity with the terms trusteeship agreements.

Article 88

The Trusteeship Council shall formulate a questionnaire on the political, economic, social, and educational advancement of the inhabitants of each trust territory, and the administering authority for each trust territory within the competence of the General Assembly shall make an annual report to the General Assembly upon the basis of such questionnaire

Voting

Article 89

1. Each member of the Trusteeship Council shall have one vote.

2. Decisions of the Trusteeship Council shall be made by a majority of the members present and voting.

Procedure

Article 90

1. The Trusteeship Council shall adopt its own rule of procedure, including the method of selecting its President.

2. The Trusteeship Council shall meet as required in accordance with its rules, which shall include provision ofr the convening of meetings on the request of majority of its memebrs.

ARTICLE 91

The Trusteeship Council shall, when appropriate, avail itself of the assistance of the Economic and Social Council and of the specialized agencies in regard to matters with which they are respectively concerned.

CHAPTER XIV

THE INTERNATIONAL COURT OF JUSTICE

ARTICLE 92

The International Court of Justice shall be the principal judicial organ of the United Natins. It shall function in accordance with the annexed Statute, which is based upon the Statute of the Permanent Court of International Justice and forms and integral part of the Present Charter.

ARTICLE 93

1. All Members of the United Nations are *ipso facto* parties to the Statute of the International Court of Justice.
2. A state which in not a Member of the United Nations may become a party to the Statute of the International Court of Justice on conditions to be determined in each case by the General Assembly upon the recommendation of the Security Council.

ARTICLE 94

1. Each Member of the United Nations undertakes to comply with the decision of the International Court of Justice in any case to which it is a party
2. If any party to a case fails to perform the obligations incumbent upon it under a judgement rendered by the Court, the other party may have recourse to the Security Council, which may, if it deems necessary, make recommendations or decide upon measures to be taken to give effect to the judgement.

ARTICLE 95

Nothing in the present Charter shall prevent Members of the United Nations from entrusting the solution of their differences to other tribunals by virtue of agreements already in existence or which may be concluded in the future.

ARTICLE 96

1. The General Assembly or the Security Council may request the International Court of Justice to give an advisory opinion on any legal question.
2. Other organs of the United Nations and specialized agencies, which

may at any time be so authorized by the General Assembly, may also request advisory opinions of the Court on legal questions arising within the scope of their activities.

CHAPTER XV

THE SECRETARIAT

ARTICLE 97

The Secretariat shall comprise a Secretary General and such staff as the Organization may require. The Secretary General shall be appointed by the General Assembly upon the recommendation of the Security Council. He shall be the chief administrative officer of the Organization.

ARTICLE 98

The Secretary General shall act in that capacity in all meetings of the General Assembly, of the Security Council, of the Economic and Social Council, and of the Trusteeship Council, and shall perform such other functions as are entrusted to him by these organs. The Secretary General shall make an annual report to the General Assembly on the work of the Organization.

ARTICLE 99

The Secretary General may bring to the attention of the Security Council any matter which in his opinion may threaten the maintenance of international peace and security.

ARTICLE 100

1. In the performance of their duties the Secretary General and the staff shall not seek or receive instructions from any government or from any other authority external to the Organization They shall refrain from any action which might reflect on their position as international officials responsible only to the Organization.
2. Each Member of the United Nations undertakes to respect the exclusively international character of the responsibilities of the Secretary General and the staff and not to seek to influence them in the discharge of their responsibilities.

ARTICLE 101

1. The Staff shall be appointed by the Secretary General under regulations established by the General Assembly.
2. Appropriate staffs shall be permanently assigned to the Economic and Social Council, the Trusteeship council, and, as required, to other organs of the United Nations. These staffs shall form a part of the Secretariat.

3. The paramount consideration in the employment of the staff and in the determination of the conditions of service shall be the necessity of securing the highest standards of efficiency, competence, and integrity. Due regard shall be paid to the importance of recruiting the staff on as wide a geographical basis as possible.

CHAPTER XVI

MISCELLANEOUS PROVISIONS

ARTICLE 102

1. Every treaty and every international agreement entered into by any Member of the United Nations after the present Charter comes into force shall as soon as possible be registered with the Secretariat and published by it.

2. No party to any such treaty or international agreement which has not been registered in accordance with the provisions of paragraph I of this Article may invoke that treaty or agreement before any organ of the United Nations.

ARTICLE 103

In the event of a conflict between the obligations of the Members of the United Nations under the present Charter and their obligations under any other international agreement, their obligatins under the present Charter shall prevail.

ARTICLE 104

The Organization shall enjoy in the territory of each of its Members such legal capacity as may be necessary for the exercise of its functions and the fulfilment of its purposes.

ARTICLE 105

1. The Organization shall enjoy in the territory of each of its Members such privileges and immunities as are necessary for the fulfilment of its pruposes.

2. Representatives of the Members of the United Nations and officials of the Organization shall similarly enjoy such privileges and immunities as are necessary for the independent exercise of their funcitons in connection with the Organization.

3. The General Assembly may make recommendations with a view to determining the details of the application of paragraph 1 and 2 of this Article or may propose conventions to the Members of the United Nations for this purpose.

CHAPTER XVII

TRANSITIONAL SECURITY ARRANGEMENTS

ARTICLE 106

Pending the coming into force of such special agreements referred to in Article 43 as in the opinion of the Security Council enable it to begin the exercise of its responsibilities under Article 42, the parties to the Four-Nation Declaration, signed at Moscow, 30 October 1943, and France, shall in accordance with the provisions of paragraph 5 of that Declaration consult with one another and as occasion requires with other Members of the United Nations with a view to such joint actin on behalf of the Organization as may be necessary for the purpose of maintaining international peace and security.

ARTICLE 107

Nothing in the present Charter shall invalidate or preclude action, in relation to any state which during the Second World War has been an enemy of any signatory to the present Charter, taken or authorized as a result of that war by the Governments having responsibility for such action.

CHAPTER XVIII

AMENDMENTS

ARTICLE 108

Amendments to the present Charter shall come into force for all Members of the United Nations when they have been adopted by a vote of two thirds of the members of the General Assembly and ratified in accordance with their respective constitutional processes by two thirds of the Members of the United Nations icluding all the permanent members of the Security Council.

ARTICLE 109

1. A General Conference of the Members of the United Nations for the purpose of reviewing the present Charter may be held at a date and place to be fixed by a two-thirds vote of the members of the General Assembly and by a vote of any nine members of the Security Council. Each Member of the United Nations shall have one vote in the conference.
2. Any alteration of the present Charter recommended by a two-thirds vote of the conference shall take effect when ratified in accordance with their respective constitutional processes by two thirds of the

Members of the United Nations including all the permanent members of the Security Council.

3. If such a conference has not been held before the tenth annual session of the General Assembly following the coming into force of the present Charter, the proposal to call such a conference shall be placed on the agenda of that session of the General Assembly, and the conference shall be held if so decided by a majority vote of the members of the General Assembly and by a vote of any seven members of the Security Council.

CHAPTER XIX

RATIFICATION AND SIGNATURE

ARTICLE 110

1. The present Charter shall be ratified by the signatory states in accordance with their respective constitutional processes.
2. The ratifications shall be deposited with the Government of the United States of America, which shall notify all the signatory states of each deposit as well as the Secretary General of the Organization when the has been appointed.
3. The present Charter shall come into force upon the deposit of ratifications by the Republic of China, France, the Union of Soviet Socialist Republics, the United kingdom of Great Britain and Northern Ireland, and the United States of America, and by a majority of the other signatory states. A protocol of the ratifications deposited shall thereupon be drawn up by the Government of the United States of America which shall communicate copies thereof to all the signatory states.
4. The States Signatory to the present Charter which ratify it after it has come into force will become original Members of the United Nations on the date of the deposit of their respective ratifications.

ARTICLE 111

The present Charter, of which the Chinese, French, Russian, English and Spanish texts are equally authentic, shall remain deposited in the archives of the Government of the United States of America. Duly certified copies thereof shall be transmitted by that Government to the Governments of the other signatory states.

In Faith Whereof the representatives of the Governments of the United Nations have signed the present Charter.

Done at the city of San Francisco the twenty-sixth day of June, one thousand nine hundred and forth-five.

Appendix – 3

Statute of the International Court of Justice

Article 1

The International Court of Justice established by the Charter of the United Nations as the principal judicial organ of the United Nations shall be constituted and shall function in accordance with the provisions of the present Statute.

CHAPTER I

ORGANTATINS OF THE COURT

Article 2

The Court shall be composed of a body of independent judges, elected regardless of their nationality from among persons of high moral character, who possess the qualifications required in their respective countries for appointment to the highest judicial offices, or are juries consults of recognized competence in international law.

Article 3

1. The Court shall consist of fifteen members, no two of whom may be nationals of the same state.
2. A person who for the purposes of membership in the Court could be regarded as a national of more than one state shall be deemed to be a national of one the in which he ordinarily exercises civil and political rights.

Article 4

1. The members of the Court shall be elected by the General Assembly and by the Security Council form a list of persons nominated by the national groups in the Permanent Court of Arbitration, in accordance with the following provisions.

2. In the case of Members of the United Nations not represented in the Permanent Court of Arbitration, candidates shall be nominated by national groups appointed for this purpose by their governments under the same conditions those prescribed for members of the Permanent Court of Arbitration by Article 44 of the Convention of The Hague of 1907 for the pacific settlement of international disputes.

3. The conditions under which a state which is a party to the present Statute but is not a member of the United Nations may participate in electing the members of the Court shall, in the absence of a special agreement, be laid down by the General Assembly upon recommendation of the Security Council.

Article 5

1. At least three months before the date of the election, the Secretary-General of the United Nations shall address a written request to the members of the Permanent Court of Arbitration belonging to the states which are parties to the present Statute, and to members of the national groups appointed under Article 4, paragraph 2, inviting them to undertake, within a given time, by national groups, the nomination of persons in a position to accept the duties of member of the Court.

2. No group may nominate more than four persons, not more than two of whom shall be of their own nationality. In no case may the number of candidates nominated by a group by more than double the number of seats to be filled.

Article 6

Before making these nominations, each national group is recommended to consult its highest court of justice, its legal faculties and schools of law and its national academies and national sections of international academies devoted to the study of law.

Article 7

1. The Secretary General shall prepare a list in alphabetical order or all the persons thus nominated. Save as provided in Article 12, paragraph 2, these shall be the only persons eligible.

2. The Secretary General shall submit this list to the General Assembly and to the Security Council.

Article 8

The General Assembly and the Security Council shall proceed independently of one another to elect the members of the Court.

ARTICLE 9

At every election, the electors shall bear in mind not only that the persons to be elected should individually possess the qualification required, but also that in the body as whole the representation of the main forms of civilization and of the principal legal systems of the world should be assured.

ARTICLE 10

1. Those candidates who obtain an absolute majority of votes in the General Assembly and in the Security Council shall be considered as elected.
2. Any vote of the Security Council, whether for the election of judges or for the appointment of members of the conference envisaged in Article 12, shall be taken without distinction between permanent and non-permanent members of the Security Council.
3. In the event of more then one national of the same state obtaining an absolute majority of the votes both of the General Assembly and of the Security Council, the eldest of these only shall be considered as elected.

ARTICLE 11

If, after the first meeting held for the purpose of the election, one or more seats remain to be filled, a second and, if necessary, a third meeting shall take place.

ARTICLE 12

1. If, after the third meeting, one or more seats still remain unfilled, a joint conference consisting of six members, three appointed by the General Assembly and three by the Security Council, may be formed at any time at the request of either the General Assembly or the Security Council, for the purpose of choosing by the vote of an absolute majority one name for seat still vacant, to submit to the General Assembly and the Security Council for their respective acceptance.
2. If the joint conference is unanimously agreed upon any person who fulfils the required conditions, he may be included in its list, even though he was not included in the list of nominations referred to in Article 7.
3. If the joint conference is satisfied that it will not be successful in procuring an election, those members of the Court who have already been elected shall, within a period to be fixed by the Security Council, proceed to fill the vacant seats by selection from among those candidates who have obtained votes either in the General Assembly or in the Security Council.

4. In the event of an equality of votes among the judges, the eldest judge shall have a casting vote.

Article 13

1. The members of the Court shall be elected for nine years and may be re-elected; provided, however, that of the judges elected at the first election, the terms of five judges shall expire at the end of three years and the terms of five more judges shall expire at the end of six years.
2. The judges whose terms are to expire at the end of the above-mentioned initial periods of there and six years shall be chosen by lot to be drawn by the Secretary General immediately after the first election has been completed.
3. The members of the Court shall continue to discharge their duties until their places have been filled. Though replaced, they shall finish any cases which they may have begun.
4. In the case of the resignation of a member of the Court, resignation shall be addressed to the President of the Court for transmissions to the Secretary General. This last notification makes the place vacant.

Article 14

Vacancies shall be filled by the same method as that laid down for the first election, subject to the following provision: the Secretary General shall, within one month of the occurrence of the vacancy, proceed to issue the invitations provided for in Article 5, and the date of the election shall be fixed by the Security Council.

Article 15

A member of the Court elected to replace a member whose term of office has not expired shall hold office for the remainder of his predecessor's term.

Article 16

1. No member of the Court may exercise any political or administrative function, or engage in other occupation of professional nature.
2. Any doubt on this point shall be settled by the decision of the Court.

Article 17

1. No member of the Court may act as agent, Counsel or advocate in any case.
2. No member may participate in the decision of any case in which he has previously taken part as agent, counsel, or advocate for one of the parties, or as a member of a national or international court or of a commission of enquiry, or in any other capacity.

3. Any doubt on this point shall be settled by the decision of the Court.

Article 18

1. No member of the Court can be dismissed unless, in the unanimous opinion of the other members, he has ceased to fulfil the required conditions.
2. Formal notification thereof shall be made to the Secretary General by the Registrar.
3. This notification makes the place vacant.

Article 19

The members of the Court, when engaged on the business of the Court, shall enjoy diplomatic privileges and immunities.

Article 20

Every member of the Court shall, before taking up his duties, make a solemn declaration in open court that will exercise his powers impartially and conscientiously.

Article 21

1. The Court shall elect its President and Vice-President for three years; they may be re-elected.
2. The Court shall appoint its Registrar and may provide for the appointment of such other officers as may be necessary.

Article 22

1. The seat of the Court shall be established at The Hague. This, however, shall not prevent the Court from sitting and exercising its functions elsewhere whenever the Court considers it desirable.
2. The President and the Registrar shall reside at the seat of the Court.

Article 23

1. The Court shall remain permanently in session, except during the judicial vacations, the dates and duration of which shall be fixed by the Court.
2. Members of the Court are entitled to periodic leave, the dates and duration of which shall be fixed by the Court, having in mind the distance between The Hague and the home of each judge.
3. Members of the Court shall be bound, unless they are on leave or prevented from attending by illness or other serious reasons duly explained to the President, to hold themselves permanently at the disposal of the Court.

Article 24

1. If, for some special reason, a member of the Court considers that he should not take part in the decision of particular case, he shall so inform the President.
2. If the President considers that for some special reason one of the members of the Court should not sit in a particular case, he shall give him notice accordingly.
3. If in any such case the member of the Court and the President disagree, the matter shall be settled by the decision of the Court.

Article 25

1. The full court shall sit except when it is expressly provided otherwise in the present Statute.
2. Subject to the condition that the number of judges available to constitute the court is not thereby reduced below eleven, the rules of the Court may provide for allowing one or more judges, according to circumstance and in rotation, to be dispensed from sitting
3. A quorum of nine judges shall suffice to constitute the Court.

Article 26

1. The Court may form time to time from one or more chambers, composed of three or more judges as the court may determine, for dealing with particular categories of cases; for example, labour cases and cases relating to transit and communications.
2. The Court may at any time form a chamber for dealing with a particular case. The number of judges to constitute such a chamber shall be determined by the Court with the approval of the parties.
3. Cases shall be heard and determined by the chambers provided for in this article if the parties so request.

Article 27

A judgement given by any of the chambers provided for in Articles 26 and 29 shall be considered as rendered by the Court.

Article 28

The chambers provided for in Articles 26 and 29 may, with the consent of the parties, sit and exercise their functions elsewhere than at The Hague.

Article 29

With a view to the speedy dispatch of business, the Court shall form annually a chamber composed of five judges which, at the request of the parties, may hear and determine cases by summary procedure. In addition, two judges shall be selected for the purpose of replacing judges who find it impossible to sit.

Article 30

1. The court shall frame rules for carrying out its functions. In particular, it shall lay down rules of procedure.
2. The Rules of the Court may provide for assessors to sit with the Court or with any of its chambers, without the right to vote.

Article 31

1. Judges of the nationality of each of the parties shall retain their right to sit in the case before the Court
2. If the Court includes upon the bench a judge of the nationality of one of the parties, any other party may choose a person to sit as judge, such person shall be chosen preferably from among those persons who have been nominated as candidates as provided in Articles 4 and 5.
3. If the Court includes upon the Bench no judge of the nationality of the parties, each of these parties may proceed to choose a judge as provided in paragraph 2 of this Article.
4. The provisions of this Article shall apply to the case of Articles 26 and 29. In such cases, the President shall request one or, if necessary, two of the members of the Court forming the chamber to give place to the members of the court of the nationality of the parties concerned, and failing such, or if they are unable to be present, to the judges specially chosen by the parties.
5. Should there be several parties in the same interest, they shall, for the purpose of the preceding provisions, be reckoned as one party only. Any doubt upon this point shall be settled by the decision of the Court.
6. Judges chosen as laid down in paragraphs 2,3 and 4 of this Article shall fulfil the conditions required by Articles 2, 17 (paragraph 2), 20 and 24 of the present Statute. They shall take part in the decision on terms of complete equality with their colleagues.

Article 32

1. Each member of the Court shall receive an annual salary.
2. The President shall receive a special annual allowance.
3. The Vice-President shall receive a special allowance for every day on which he acts as President.
4. The judges chosen under Article 31, other than members of the Court, shall receive compensation for each day on which they exercise their functions.
5. These salaries, allowances, and compensation shall be fixed by the General Assembly. They may not be decreased during the term of office.

6. The salary of the Registrar shall be fixed by the General Assembly on the proposal of the Court.
7. Regulations made by the General Assembly shall fix the conditions under which retirement pensions may by given to members of the Court and to the Registrar and the conditions under which members of the Court and the Registrar shall have their travelling expenses refunded.
8. The above salaries, allowances, and compensation shall be free of all taxation.

Article 33

The expenses of the Court shall be borne by the United Nations is such a manner as shall be decided by the General Assembly.

CHAPTER II

COMETENCE OF THE COURT

Article 34

1. Only states may be parties in cases before the Court.
2. The Court, subject to and in conformity with its Rules, may request of public international organizations information relevant to cases before it, and shall receive such information presented by such organizations on, their own initiative.
3. Whenever the construction of the constituent instrument of public international organization or of an international convention adopted there–under is in question in a case before the Court, the Registrar shall so notify the public international organization concerned and shall communicate to it copies of all the written proceedings.

Article 35

1. The Court shall be open to the states parties to the present Statute.
2. The conditions under which the court shall be open to other states shall, subject to the special provisions contained in the treaties in force, be laid down by the Security Council, but in no case shall such conditions place the parties in a position of inequality before the Court.
3. When a state which is not a Member of the United Nations is a party to a case, the Court shall fix the amount which that party is to contribute towards the expenses of the Court. This provision shall not apply if such state is bearing a share of the expenses of the Court.

ARTICLE 36

1. The jurisdiction of the Court comprises all cases which parties refer to it and all matter specially provided for in Charter of the United Nations or in treaties and convention in force.
2. The states parties to the present Statute may at any time declare that they recognize as compulsory *ipso facto* and without special agreement, in relation to any other state accepting the same obligation, the jurisdiction of the Court in all legal disputes concerning:
   a. the interpretation of a treaty;
   b. any question of international law;
   c. the existence of any fact which, if established, would constitute a breach of an international obligation;
   d. the nature of extent of the reparation to be made for the breach of an international obligation.
3. The declarations referred to above may be made unconditionally or on condition of reciprocity on the part of several or certain states, or for a certain time.
4. Such declarations shall be deposited with the Secretary General of the United Nations, who shall transmit copies thereof to the parties to the Statute and to the Registrar of the Court.
5. Declarations made under Article 36 of the Statute of the Permanent Court of International Justice and which are still in force shall be deemed, as between the parties to the present Statute, to be acceptances of the compulsory jurisdiction of the International Court of Justice for the period which they still have to run and in accordance with their terms.
6. In the event of a dispute as to whether the Court has jurisdiction, the matter shall be settled by the decision of the Court.

ARTICLE 37

Whenever a treaty or convention in force provides for reference of a matter to a tribunal to have been instituted by the League of Nations, or to the Permanent Court of International Justice, the matter shall, as between the parties to the present Statute, be referred to the International Court of Justice.

ARTICLE 38

1. The Court, whose function is to decide in accordance with international law such disputes as are submitted to it, shall apply:
   a. international conventions, whether general or particular, establishing rules expressly recognized by the contesting state;

b. international custom, as evidence of general practice accepted as law;

c. the general principles of law recognized by civilized nations;

d. subject to the processions of Article 59, judicial decisions and the teachings of the most highly qualified publicists of the various nations, as subsidiary means for the determination of rules of law.

2. This provision shall not prejudice the power of the Court to decide a case ex aequo et bono, if the parties agree thereto.

CHAPTER III

PROCEDURE

Article 39

1. The official languages of the Court shall be French and English. If the parties agree that case shall be conducted in French, the judgment shall be delivered in French. If the parties agree that the case shall be conducted in English, the judgement shall be delivered in English.

2. In the absence of an agreement as to which language shall be employed, each party may, in the pleadings, use the language which it prefers; the decision of the Court shall be given in French and English. In this case the Court shall at the same time determine which of the two texts shall be considered as authoritative.

3. The Court shall, at the request of any party, authorize a language other than French or English to be used by that party.

Article 40

1. Cases are brought before the Court, as the case may be, either by the notification of the special agreement or by a written application addressed to the Registrar. In either case the subjects of the dispute and the parties shall be indicated.

2. The Registrar shall forthwith communicate the application to all concerned.

3. He shall also notify the Members of the United Nations through the Secretary General, and also any other states entitled to appear before the Court

Article 41

1. The Court shall have to power the indicate, if it considers that circumstances so require, any provisional measures which ought to be taken to preserve the respective rights of either party.

2. Pending the final decision, notice of the measures suggested shall forth– with be given to the parties and to the Security Council.

ARTICLE 42

1. The Parties shall be represented by agents.
2. They may have the assistance of counsel or advocates before the Court
3. The agents, counsel, and advocates of parties before the Court shall enjoy the privileges and immunities necessary to the independent exercise of their duties.

ARTICLE 43

1. The procedure shall consist of two parts: written and oral.
2. The written proceedings shall consists of the communication to the Court and to the parties of memorials, counter-memorials and necessary replies; also all papers and documents in support.
3. These communications shall be made through the Registrar, in the order and within the time fixed by the Court.
4. A certified copy of every document produced by one party shall be communicated to the other party.
5. The oral proceedings shall consist of the hearing by the Court witnesses, experts, agents, counsel, and advocates.

ARTICLE 44

1. For the service of all notices upon person other than the agents, counsel, and advocates, the court shall apply direct to the government of the state upon whose territory the notice has to be served.
2. The same provision shall apply whenever steps are to be taken to procure evidence on the spot.

ARTICLE 45

The hearing shall be under the control of the President or, if he is unable to preside, of the Vice-President; if neither is able to preside, the senior judge present shall preside

ARTICLE 46

The hearing in Court shall be public, unless the Court shall decide otherwise, or unless the parties demand that the public be not admitted.

ARTICLE 47

1. Minutes shall be made at each hearing and signed by the Registrar and the President
2. These minutes alone shall be authentic

ARTICLE 48

The Court shall make orders for the conduct of the case, shall decide the form and time in which each party must conclude its arguments, and make all arrangements connected with the taking of evidence.

ARTICLE 49

The Court may even before the hearing begins, call upon the agents to produce any document or to supply any explanations. Formal note shall be taken of any refusal.

ARTICLE 50

The Court may, at any time, entrust any individual, body, bureau, commission, or other organization that it may select, with the task of carrying out an enquiry or giving an expert opinion.

ARTICLE 51

During the hearing any relevant questions are to be put to the witnesse and experts under the conditions laid down by the Court in the rules of procedure referred to in Article 30

ARTICLE 52

After the Court has received the proofs and evidence within the time specified for the prupose. It may refuse to accept any further oral or written evidence that one party may desire to present unless the other side consents.

ARTICLE 53

1. Whenever one of the parties does not appear before the Court, or fails to defend its case, the other party may call upon the Court to decide in favour of its claim.
2. The Court must, before doing so, satisfy itself not only that it has jurisdictiton in accordance with Articles 36 and 37, but also that the claim is well founded in fact and law.

ARTICLE 54

1. When, subject to the control of the Court the agents, counsel, and advocates have completed their presentation of the case, the President shall declare the hearing closed,
2. The Court shall withdraw to consider the judgement
3. The deliberations of the Court shall take place in private and remain secret.

ARTICLE 55

1. All questions shall be decided by a majority of the judges present.
2. In the event of an equality of votes, the President or the judge who acts in his place shall have a casting vote.

ARTICLE 56

1. The judgement shall state the reasons on which it is based
2. It shall contain the names of the judges who have taken part in the decision.

ARTICLE 57

If the judgement does not represent in whole or in part the unaimous opinion of the judges, any judge shall be entitled to deliver a separate opinion.

ARTICLE 58

The judgement shall be signed by the President and by the Registrar. It shall be read in open court, due notice having been given to the agents.

ARTICLE 59

The decision of the Court has no binding force except between the parties and in respect of that particular case.

ARTICLE 60

The judgement is final and without appeal. In the event of dipsute as to the meaning or scope or the judgement, the court shall construe it upon the request of any party

ARTICLE 61

1. An application for revision of a judgement may be made only when it is based upon the discovery of some fact of such a nature as to be a decisive factor, which fact was, when the judgement was given, unknown to the Court and also to the part claming revison, always provided that such ignoracne was not due to negligence.
2. The proceedings for revision shall be opened by a judgement of the Court expressly recording the existence of the new fact, recognizing that it has such a character as to lay the case open to recession, and declaring the application admissible on this ground.
3. The court may require previous compliance with the terms of the judgement before it admits proceedings in revison.
4. The application for revision must be made at latest within six months of the discovery of the new fact

5. No application for revision may be made after the lapse of ten years from the date of the judgement

ARTICLE 62

1. Should a state consider that it has an interest of legal nature which may be affected by the decision in the case, it may submit a request to the Court to be permitted to intervene.
2. It shall be for the court to decide upon this request.

ARTICLE 63

1. Whenever the construction of a convention to which states other than those concerned in the case are parties in question, the Registrar shall notify all such states forth with.
2. Every state so notified has the right to intervene in the proceedings; but if it uses this right, the construction given by the judgement will be equally binding upon it.

ARTICLE 64

Unless otherwise decided by the Court, each party shall bear its own costs.

CHAPTER IV
ADVISORY OPINIONS

ARTICLE 65

1. The Court may give an advisory opinion on any legal question at the request of whatever body may be authorized by or in accordance with the Charter of the United Naions to make such a request.
2. Questions upon which the advisory opinion of the Court is asked shall be laid before the court by means of written request containing an exact statement of the question upon which an opinion is required, and accompanied by all documents likely to throw light upon the question.

ARTICLE 66

1. The Registrar shall forth–with give notice of the request for an advisory opinion to all states entitled to appear before the Court.
2. The Registrar shall also, by means of special and direct communication notify any state entitled to appear before the Court or international organization considered by the Court, or, should it not be sitting, the questin. that the Court will be prepared to receive, within a time limit to be fixed by the President, written statements, or to

hear, at a public sitting to be held for the purpose, oral statements relating to the question.

3. Should any such state entitled to appear before the Court have failed to receive the special communication referred to in paragraph 2 of this Article, such state may express a desire to submit a written statement or to be heard, and the Court will decide.

4. States and organization having presented written or oral statements or both shall be permitted to comment on the statements made by other states or organization in the form, to the extent and within the time limits which the Court, or, should it not be sitting the President, shall decide in each particular case. Accordingly, the Register shall in due time communicate any such written statements to states and organizations having submitted similar statements.

ARTICLE 67

The Court shall deliver its advisory opinions in open Court, notice having been given to the Secretary General and to the representatives of Members of the United Nations, of other states and of international organizations immediately concerned.

ARTICLE 68

In the exercise of its advisory functions the Court shall further be guided by the provisions of the present Statute which apply in contentious case to the extent to which it recognizes them to be applicable

CHAPTER V

AMENDMENT

ARTICLE 69

Amendments to the present Staute shall be effected by the same procedure as is provided by the charter of the United Nations for amendments to that Charter, subject however to any provisions which the General Assembly upon recommendation of the Security Council may adopt concerning the participation of states which are parties to the present Statute but are not Members of the United Nations.

ARTICLE 70

The Court shall have power to propose such amendments to the present statute as it may deem necessary, through written communications to the Secretary General, for consideration in conformity with the provisions of Article 69.

Appendix –4
UNIVERSAL DECLARATION OF HUMAN RIGHTS

Adopted and Proclaimed by the General Assembly of the United Nations on 10 December 1948

Whereas recognition of the inherent dignity and of the equal and inalienable rights of all members of the human family is the foundation of freedom, justice and peace in the world,

Whereas disregard and contempt for human rights have resulted in barbarous acts which have outraged the conscience of mankind, and the advent of a world in which human beings shall enjoy freedom of speech and belief and freedom from fear and wat has been proclaimed as the highest aspiration of the common people.

Whereas it is essential, if man is not to be compelled to have recourse, as a last resort, to rebellion against tyranny and oppression, that human rights should be protected by the rule of law.

Whereas it is essential to promote the development of friendly relations between nations.

Whereas the peoples of the United Nations have in the Charter reaffirmed their faith in fundamental human rights, in the dignity and worth of the human person and in the equal rights of men and women and have determined to promote social progress and better standards of life in larger freedom.

Whereas Member States have pledged themselves to achieve in co-operation with the United Nations, the promotion of universal respect for and observance of human rights and fundamental freedoms,

Whereas a common understanding of these rights and freedoms is the greatest importance for the full realization of this pledge.

The General Assembly proclaims

This Universal Declaration of Human Rights as a common standard of achievement for all peoples and all nations to the end that every individual and every organ of society, keeping this Declaration constantly in mind, shall strive by teaching and education to promote respect for these rights and freedoms and by progressive measures, national and international, to secure their universal and effective recognition and observance, both among the people of Member States themselves and among the peoples of territories under their jurisdiction.

Article 1

All human beings are born free and equal in dignity and rights. They are endowed with reason and conscience and should act towards one another in a spirit of brotherhood.

Article 2

Everyone is entitled to all the rights and freedoms set fourth in this Declaration, without distinction of any kind, such as race, colour, sex language, religion, political or other opinion, national or social origin, property, birth or other status.

Furthermore, no distinction shall be made on the basis of the political, jurisdictional or international status of country or territory to which a person belongs, whether it be independent, trust, non-self-governing or under any other limitation of sovereignty.

Article 3

Everyone has the right to life, liberty and security of person.

Article 4

No one shall be held in slavery or servitude; slavery and the slave trade shall be prohibited in all their forms.

Article 5

No one shall be subjected to torture or to cruel, inhuman or degrading treatment or punishment.

Article 6

Everyone has the right to recognition everywhere as person before the law.

Article 7

All are equal before the law and are entitled without any discrimination to equal protection of the law. All are entitled to equal protection against any discrimination in violation of this Declaration and against any incitement to such discrimination.

Article 8

Everyone has the right to an effective remedy by the competent national tribunals for acts violating the fundamental rights granted to him by the constitution or by law.

Article 9

No one shall be subjected to arbitrary arrest, detention or exile.

Article 10

Everyone is entitled in full equality to a fair and public hearing by an independent and impartial tribunal, in the determination of his rights and obligations and of any criminal charge against him.

Article 11

1. Everyone charged with a penal offence has the right to be presumed innocent until proved guilty according to law in a public trial at which he has had all the guarantees necessary for his defence.
2. No one shall be held guilty of any penal offence on account of any act or omission which did not constitute a penal offence, under national or international law, at the time when it was committed. Nor shall a heavier penalty be imposed than the one that was applicable at the time the penal offence was committed.

Article 12

No one shall be subjected to arbitrary interference with his privacy family, home or correspondence nor to attacks upon his honour and reputation. Everyone has the right to the protection of the law against such interference or attacks.

Article 13

1. Everyone has the right to freedom of movement and residence within the borders of each State.
2. Everyone has the right to leave any country, including his own, and to return to his country.

Article 14

1. Everyone has the right to seek and to enjoy in other countries asylums form persecution.
2. This right may not be invoked in the case of prosecutions genuinely arising from non-political crimes or from acts contrary to the purposes and principles of the United Nations.

Article 15

1. Everyone has the right to a nationality.
2. No one shall be arbitrarily deprived of his nationality nor denied the right to change his nationality.

ARTICLE 16

1. Men and women of full age, without any limitation due to race, nationality or religion, have the right to marry and to found a family. They are entitled to equal rights as to marriage, during marriage and at its dissolution.
2. Marriage shall be entered into only with the free and full consent of the intending spouses.
3. The family is the natural and fundamental group unit of society and the State.

ARTICLE 17

1. Everyone has the right to own property alone as well as in association with other.
2. No one shall be arbitrarily deprived of his property.

ARTICLE 18

Everyone has the right to freedom of thought, conscience and religion; this right includes freedom to change his religion or belief, and freedom, either alone or in community with others and in public or private, to manifest his religion or belief in teaching, practice, worship and observance.

ARTICLE 19

Everyone has the right to freedom of opinion and expression; this right includes freedom to hold opinions without interference and to seek, receive and impart information and ideas through any media and regardless of frontiers.

ARTICLE 20

1. Everyone has the right to freedom of peaceful assembly and association.
2. No one may be compelled to belong to an association.

ARTICLE 21

1. Everyone has the right to take part in the government of his country, directly or through freely chosen representatives.
2. Everyone has the right of equal access to public service in his country.
3. The will of the people shall be the basis of the authority of government; this will shall be expressed in periodic and genuine elections which shall be by universal and equal suffrage and shall be held by secret vote or by equivalent free voting procedures.

Article 22

Everyone, as a member of society, has the right to social security and is entitled to realization, through national effort and international co-operation and in accordance with the organization and resources of each State, of the economic, social and cultural rights indispensable for his dignity and the free development of his personality.

Article 23

1. Everyone has the right to work, to free choice of employment , to just and favourable conditions of work and to protection against unemployment
2. Everyone, without any discrimination, has the right to equal pay for equal work.
3. Everyone who works has the right to just and favourable remuneration ensuring for himself and his family an existence worthy of human dignity, and supplemented, if necessary, by other means of social protection.

Article 24

Everyone has the right to rest and leisure, including reasonable limitations of working hours and periodic holidays with pay.

Article 25

1. Everyone has the right to a standard of living adequate for the health and well-being of himself and of his family, including food, clothing, housing and medical care and necessary social services, and the right to security in the event of unemployment, sickness, disability, widowhood, old age or other lack of livelihood in circumstances beyond his control
2. Motherhood and childhood are entitled to special care and assistance. All children, whether born in or out of wedlock, shall enjoy the same social protection

Article 26

1. Everyone has the right to education. Education shall be free, at least in the elementary and fundamental stages. Elementary education shall be compulsory. Technical and professional education shall be made generally available and higher education shall be equally accessible to all on the basis of merit.
2. Education shall be directed to the full development of the human personality and to the strengthening of respect for human rights and fundamental freedoms. It shall promote understanding, tolerance and friendship among all nations racial or religious groups, and shall further the activities of the United Nations for the maintenance of peace.

3. Parents have a prior right to choose the kind of education that shall be given to their children.

ARTICLE 27

1. Everyone has the right freely to participate in the cultural life of the community, to enjoy the arts and to share in scientific advancement and its benefits.

2. Everyone has the right to the protection of the moral and material interests resulting from any scientific or artistic production of which he is the author.

ARTICLE 28

Everyone is entitled to a social and international order in which the rights and freedoms set forth in this Declaration can be fully realized.

ARTICLE 29

1. Everyone has duties to the community in which alone the free and full development of his personality is possible.

2. In the exercise of his rights and freedoms, everyone shall be subject to such limitations as are determined by law solely for the purpose of securing due recognition and respect for the rights and freedoms of others and of meeting the just requirements of morality, public order and the general welfare in a democratic society.

3. These rights and freedoms may in no case by exercised contrary to the purposes and principles of the United Nations.

ARTICLE 30

Nothing in this Declaration may be interpreted as implying for nay State, group or person any right to engage in any activity or to perform any act aimed at the destruction of any of the rights and freedoms set forth herein.

LATEST DEVELOPMENTS

Chapter 1
UNO: A Brief Overview

Introduction

League of Nations was created by Treaty of Versailles (1919) and disbanded in 1946. UN succeeded the League of Nations. On January 1, 1942, 26 countries signed the Declaration by UN, which delineated the war aims of Allied Powers.

The first major step towards the formation of UNO was initiated during August 21 to October 7 1944, at the Dumbarton Oaks Conference (Washington). There was a meeting of Big Three powers plus China (Big Four). United Nations Organization, also called UN, was set up on October 24, 1945. UN has headquarters in New York City and offices in Geneva, Vienna and the Hague. Its official languages are Arabic, Chinese, English, French, Russian and Spanish. First session of UN General Assembly was organized on January 10, 1946 at Central Hall.

According to its Charter, UN aims to save posterity from war. It wants to establish faith in fundamental human rights and establish conditions under which justice and respect for obligations arising from international treaties can be maintained. It stands for social progress and fine life standards. It intends to maintain peace and security. It promotes friendly relationships among nations. UN aims to resolve global economic, social, cultural and humanitarian issues. It stands for human rights. It is a hub from which countries can coordinate their actions to achieve the aforementioned goals.

Influence of Superpowers

US and Soviet Union affected UN functions during its first 45 years. Decolonization in Africa, Asia and Middle East increased the actions in political, economic and social matters. Cold War ended in 1991. In the beginning of 21st century, UN struggled to supply humanitarian support and material to war-ravaged areas of the world. It handled refugees, terrorists, nations at war and Somali pirates during the last 20 years. It fought against AIDS, leprosy, polio and small pox. It succeeded on many fronts but on some others, it acted as a spectator.

US, UK and Soviet Union built UNO. Roosevelt, Churchill and Joseph Stalin were the pioneers of UN. Soviet Union demanded individual membership and voting rights for its constituent republics. Britain wanted its colonies not to be placed under UN control.

At the Yalta Conference, a meeting of the **Big Three** was organized in February 1945. Roosevelt, Churchill and Stalin laid the bedrock for Charter provisions. They delimited the authority of Security Council. They reached a tentative agreement on the number of Soviet republics to be granted independent memberships in UN. Three leaders agreed that the new organization would include a trusteeship system to succeed League of Nations mandate system. Dumbarton Oaks proposals, with modifications from the Yalta Conference, formed the bedrock of negotiations at the UN Conference on International Organization (UNCIO); it was arranged in San Francisco on April 25, 1945. It delivered the final Charter. San Francisco conference was attended by representatives of 50 countries (9 from Europe, 21 from Americas, 7 from the Middle East, 2 from East Asia, 3 from Africa, 1 each from the Ukrainian Soviet Socialist Republic and the Belorussian Soviet Socialist Republic (plus Soviet Union) and 5 from British Commonwealth countries). Poland was allowed to become an original member of UN. Security Council veto power (among the permanent members) was affirmed, although any member of General Assembly was able to raise issues for discussion. Other political issues resolved by compromise were: role of UN in promotion of economic and social welfare; status of colonial areas and distribution of trusteeships; status of regional and defense arrangements; and Great Power dominance versus the equality of States. UN Charter was unanimously adopted and signed on June 26. It was promulgated on October 24, 1945. The purposes, principles and organization of UN are outlined in the Charter. The tenets active behind purposes and functions of UN are in Article 2. They encompass the following: (1) UN is based on the sovereign equality of members. (2) Disputes to be settled by peaceful means (3) Members are to avoid using threat or force. (4) Every State must assist UN in any enforcement actions it takes under the Charter (5) Non-member States must act as per these tenets principles to maintain international peace and security.

Article 2 clarifies that UN will not intervene in matters considered within the domestic jurisdiction of any country. The arenas of international and domestic jurisdiction overlapped later. We can see that the domestic issues of Syria have been addressed by UN in May-June 2012. New members are admitted to UN on the recommendation of UN Security Council (UNSC) and by a two third vote of General Assembly. The P-5 group—comprising China, France, Russia (since 1991), UK and USA—discusses the admission of new members. By 1950, only 9 of 31 applicants were told to join UN. In 1955, the 10th Assembly proposed a draft. The draft was modified by UNSC and led to admission of 16 new States (4 eastern European and 12 noncommunists). The case for China was placed before General Assembly and blocked by US at every session from 1950 to 1971. In 1971, US did not block Assembly's vote. Thus, China was admitted to UN. UN expelled Taiwan (ROC); there were 76 votes in favour of expulsion, 35 votes opposed and 17 States were absent. West Germany and German Democratic Republic (East Germany) were divided states; so were North and South Korea and North and South Vietnam. German states were admitted as members (1973); these two seats were made one after German unification (1990). Vietnam was admitted (1977) after the defeat of South Vietnam and the reunification of the country (1975). Two Koreas were admitted separately (1991). From 1955 to 1960, 40 new members were admitted. By the end of 1970s, there were 150 members. Currently, it has 190 member States.

UN has 6 principal organs--**General Assembly, Security Council, Economic and Social Council, Trusteeship Council, International Court of Justice, and Secretariat**.

Conclusion

UN has been able to make this world much saner and peaceful, despite its limitations. The dominance of P-5 has overshadowed all the limitations of UN and its organs. These five nations have used arm-twisting measures on many an occasion to get decisions passed in their favour. Today, the world is facing serious economic and political crises. UN can play better roles to diffuse them if it is given more powers and resources. The US, the largest contributor to the funds of UN, is not keen to give more, given that its own economy is in shambles. Other countries are also reeling under the pangs of economic recession. Thus, UN is at cross-roads. It has to handle pirates, terror elements, and poorest nations and sparks the fly between superpowers many times. It does not have enough powers; even if it has, it is limited to P-5 block. This status quo must be changed. It cannot be changed so soon, though.

Chapter 2

FDI: India Third Most Favoured Destination

Introduction

US President Barack Obama's called for lifting of foreign investment curbs by India. India said that Washington not to meddle with its internal affairs. It stated that US should lead the fight against protectionism.

The UNCTAD World Investment Report (July 2012) stated (we quote): "India is the third most desirable destination for Foreign Direct Investment (FDI)." It further added that China and India had inflows rising by 8% and 31%, respectively (this data pertains to 2011-12). When the UNCTAD report was released, it went largely unnoticed. But facts would remain facts. India is a hot destination for growth, investment and industrial experimentation.

President Obama had said that that India was prohibiting foreign investment in sectors such as retail. He wanted another series of economic reforms. However, PMO condemned Obama for his peculiar stand on FDI (in July 2012). India is a hot spot for investment. The government, which has been pushing for allowing retail chains to set up multi-brand stores, did not state anything on the issue. It, however asked Uncle Sam to focus on removing barriers to trade such as a hike in visa fees.

Conclusion

This is good news that India has come up as a favourite destination for investment. In the era marked by recession and economic chaos, this seems to be good news. However, India must look into the areas that urgently need investment and technology. Retail already has big investors. But there is no investment in agriculture, roads, infrastructure, power generation and other key areas of economy. We must set the priorities as per the needs of our country, not as per the needs of other countries. Investment norms and needs differ from country to country. Even within India, they would differ from region to region. The government must have a look at the investment scene of today. Then, it can change the policies regarding investment to get the best possible output for its organs and the private sector players operating in various parts of the country.

Chapter 3

Congo Peace Mission Successful

Introduction

The term MONUSCO stands for **United Nations Organization Stabilization Mission in the Democratic Republic of the Congo**. Following the 1994 genocide in Rwanda and the establishment of a new government there, 1.2 million Rwandese Hutus — including elements who had taken part in the genocide — fled to the neighbouring Kivu regions of eastern DRC (formerly Zaïre) an area inhabited by ethnic Tutsis. A rebellion began in 1996. The forces led by Laurent Désiré Kabila fought against the army of President Mobutu Sese Seko. Kabila's forces, supported by Rwanda and Uganda, took the capital city of Kinshasa (1997) and renamed the country the Democratic Republic of the Congo (DRC).

In 1998, a rebellion against the Kabila government started in the Kivu regions. Rebels seized large areas of the country. Angola, Chad, Namibia and Zimbabwe promised President Kabila military support but rebels maintained their hold on eastern regions. Rwanda and Uganda supported the rebel movement, Congolese Rally for Democracy (RCD). The Security Council called for a ceasefire and the withdrawal of foreign forces.

Following the signing of the Lusaka Ceasefire Agreement in July 1999 between the Democratic Republic of the Congo (DRC) and five regional States (Angola, Namibia, Rwanda, Uganda and Zimbabwe) in July 1999, the Security Council established the United Nations Organization Mission in the Democratic Republic of the Congo (MONUC) by its resolution 1279 of November 30 1999, initially to plan for the observation of the ceasefire and disengagement of forces and maintain liaison with all parties to the Ceasefire Agreement. Later in a series of resolutions, the Council expanded the mandate of MONUC to the supervision of the implementation of the Ceasefire Agreement and assigned multiple related additional tasks.

Mr. M'Hand Ladjouzi, Ituri head of office of the MONUSCO,

welcomed the surrender, on June 16 2012, of Lieutenant Colonel Brice Bady Kasima. He is one of the leaders of the Front de Résistance Patriotique de l'Ituri (FRPI). Note that MONUSCO supports the Congolese Government to restore peace and security in the country. Mr. Roger Meece of MUNSUCO presented to the UN Security Council on June 12 2012 the last Secretary General's report on the situation in Congo.

Initial authorization for this vital mission has the following data:

1. 22,016 total uniformed personnel. 2. 19,815 military personnel. 3. 760 military observers. 4. 391 police. 5. 1,050 personnel of police units. 6. Civilian, judiciary and correction component.

Strength on May 31 2012: 1. 19,171 total uniformed personnel. 2. 17,042 military personnel. 3. 730 military observers. 4. 3,126 police (including formed units). 5. 954 international civilian personnel. 6. 2,864 local civilian staff. 7. 614 United Nations Volunteers.

Police and military personnel from many countries (nearly 100) took part in this mission and operation. The total number of fatalities was 43 during the mission. The mission had an approved budget of $1,489,390,500. Its duration was from July 1 2011 to June 30 2012.

The country's first free and fair elections in 46 years were held on July 30 2006. Voters elected a 500-seat National Assembly. President Joseph Kabila was declared winner. MONUC remained on the ground and continued to implement multiple political, military, rule of law and other tasks as mandated by Security Council resolutions. On July 1 2010, the Security Council, by its resolution 1925, renamed the mission as MONUSCO. The new mission has been authorized to use all necessary means to carry out its mandate relating to the protection of civilians, humanitarian staff and human rights defenders under threat of physical violence and to support the Government of DRC in its stabilization and peace consolidation procedures.

Council decided that MONUSCO would comprise a maximum of 19,815 military personnel, 760 military observers, 391 police personnel and 1,050 members of formed police units. Future reconfigurations of MONUSCO would be determined as the situation evolved on the ground, including: the completion of ongoing military operations in North and South Kivu as well as the Orientale provinces; improved government capacity to protect the population effectively; and the consolidation of state authority throughout the territory.

Conclusion

The success of MONUSCO in Congo has proved that UN and the groups sponsored by it can help the world maintain peace and order.

The surrender by a rebel army man in Congo proves that UN has the powers to alter strategic and social scenarios around the globe. This is one feather in the UN cap that would be viewed with respect by all peace=-loving citizens of the world.

Chapter 4
Tremseh Massacre in Syria and UN Efforts

Introduction

Secretary-General Ban Ki-moon and Joint Special Envoy for United Nations and League of Arab States for Syria (Kofi Annan) strongly condemned attacks on Tremseh (Syria), which reportedly resulted in over 220 deaths. The incident took place on June 12 2012. Mr. Moon said UN was outraged by the reports of mass murders in Tremseh in the province of Hama because civilians, including children and those running away from armed Shabiha cadres, were among those killed.

UNSC Briefed by Annan

Mr. Annan briefed the Security Council by video-conference on his visit to Damascus, where he met with President Bashar Al-Assad. He also met Iranian and Iraqi leaders during a visit to the region in June-July 2012. He also concurred on the results of the UN-backed Action Group on Syria, which had met in July 2012. Addressing reporters in Geneva (Switzerland), Mr. Annan said that during his meeting with Mr. Al-Assad, they had agreed to take immediate action in places experiencing severe violence, while still working to implement the six-point peace plan put forward by the Joint Special Envoy earlier this year. The UN-Arab League envoy is trying to implement a six-point peace plan to end hostilities in Syria. The warring factions are not paying much attention to this effort of UN, though.

Under resolution 2043 adopted in April 212, Council established UNSMIS – for three months and with up to 300 unarmed military observers – to monitor cessation of violence in Syria, support full implementation of six-point plan. In the middle of June 2012, UNSMIS suspended its monitoring activities due to gory clashes. UNSMIS' three-month mandate ended on July 20 2012. Nearly 10,000 people, mostly civilians, were killed in Syria and thousands were displaced since the uprising against Bashar Al-Assad began in 2011.

Gory and Grim Scenario at Tremseh

This village is in Hama province in Syria. Opposition activists and witnesses say army tanks bombarded the village in June 2012 for several hours before pro-government militiamen swept in. They shot at and stabbed victims at close range. Nearly 220 people were killed, including a number of rebel fighters. The Syrian government says at least 50 people were killed in Tremseh. It blamed many armed terrorist organisations. On July 19 2012 fresh violence had erupted in Syria. The death toll at Tremseh could be even 350. The exact figures are not being disclosed by Syrian authorities. Violence has been going on in this war-ravaged nation for the past 17 months.

Shia Sunni Row Is Very old

Since the beginning of the uprising against President Bashar al-Assad in March 2011, this was the goriest incident in Syria. Tremseh is a predominantly Sunni Muslim village about 35 km due north-west of the city of Hama. It is flanked by villages dominated by the Alawites, the Shia heterodox sect. President Assad belongs to this sect.

What Actually Happened

A convoy of vehicles, containing uniformed soldiers and members of a pro-government militia (Shabiha), tanks and artillery surrounded Tremseh at about 06:00 (03:00 GMT), searching for members of the rebel Free Syrian Army (FSA). Soldiers and tanks were used due east of the village; from there, they opened fire with heavy weapons and machine guns. Shabiha soldiers went along the western edge of Tremseh and fired at anyone whom they saw. River Orontes provided a barrier in the south.

Electricity and telephone lines were severed. People were not able to flee due to blockade. The cadres of Free Syrian Army were in the village, hence this reprisal by Shabiha. After the bombardment, in the afternoon, Shabiha cadres entered Tremseh and shot people one by one. Many were shot or stabbed. Dozens of bodies were burned or dumped in the streets. The UN Stabilisation Mission in Syria (UNSMIS) told that there was continuous fighting in the Tremseh area.

Diary of violence is as follows: **(1) 3 February:** At least 55 killed in Homs in month-long bombardment by military. (2) **3 April:** Military attack on Taftanaz in Idlib. Mass graves said to hold 57 people. (3) **25 May:** Some 108 killed in Taldou, in Houla region, many of them women and children. (4) **6 June:** At least 79 people, many of them women and children, killed in village in Hama province.

Later, some people went into the village and saw bodies in fields, on streets and in homes. Nearly 50 bodies were pulled out of River Orontes. Most of the victims were farmers. The names of 100 victims were documented before they were buried. Many bodies were yet to be recovered till the reports last came in.

Local Co-ordination Committee (an opposition activist network) stated that more than 220 people had been killed in Tremseh. The same methodology, tools and means as previous massacres was used. The forces of regime's army bombed. Then, evil cadres of Shabiha entered and killed individuals. They burned the wounded and bodies of the dead. Sana, the state news agency reported the massacre and stated that Syria was facing the worst ever crisis since the start of uprising. The agency did not publish photos or videos to support details.

Bashar's Forces versus Rebels

The forces of Bashar al-Assad are strong as of now. But rebels would take no time in taking bloody revenge. They are adamant upon making Syria a democratic nation. They can do a Tremseh to the forces of government and supporters of Al-Assad. The struggle for acquiring a democratic regime has taken a bloody turn in Syria. Forces loyal to al-Assad should give power to the rebels and sow the foundations of democracy there. After all, they are part of one nation. The modern era should look forward to creating peace, since a lot of blood has already been shed. West Asia must start peaceful negotiations and solve its conflicts in an amicable manner.

India's Vote at UN about Syria

Voting in favour of the UNSC resolution that called on Syrian President Bashar al-Assad to step down, India supported the effort of Arab League for a peaceful resolution of the 11-month-old Syrian crisis. "Our support for the Resolution is in accordance with our support for the efforts by the Arab League for a peaceful resolution of the crisis through a Syrian-led inclusive political process," said Hardeep Singh Puri, the Indian Ambassador to the UN.

Russia and China vetoed the Arab League-backed resolution aimed at putting pressure on Syria to end its crackdown on anti-government protests that has killed more than 200 people in one of the bloodiest episodes of the uprising against Assad's regime. This is the second time that Russia and China have carried out their double veto after the first one on October 5 2011. India, the US and 11 other nations backed the move. France, Britain and Pakistan also voted in favour of the resolution.

Explaining the reasons for India's position on Syria, Puri told the powerful 15-member body that New Delhi believes that the leadership of Syria is a matter of the Syrian peoples. They would decide about the leader they invest their trust in.

Conclusion

Syria is at cross-roads today. Russia supports Syria's former regime that was under the control of Bashar al-Assad. The rebels are hell bent upon ousting the forces of al-Assad and want a new democratic system to be initiated in the country. This gory massacre has taken sectarian tinge; this was a show of hostility between Shias and Sunnis. This is a bad trend by any norm. Syria must come to the realm of normalcy because in all parts of the world, democracy is being touted as the elixir for human race. Communal and sectarian classes (within a religious group) can complicate the world scene even further. We are already facing problems in Libya, Chad, Congo, Kenya, Pakistan, Afghanistan, the two Koreas and Iran. Violence is not solution of these problems. Negotiations, a keen sense of giving and professional implementation of contracts must be done. India must lend a helping hand by supplying medicines, doctors, blankets, clothes and other things to the victims of Tremseh. Syria is a friendly country for India.

Chapter 5

UN Working Group on Enforced or Involuntary Disappearances: Locating Missing/Lost Persons

Introduction

At the end of 2010, an estimated 27.5 million people were internally displaced due to conflict. Further, millions more have asked for refuge abroad. Ten United Nations agencies and their partners have urged Members States to place humanitarian concerns at the forefront of their discussions aimed at reaching agreement on a comprehensive and robust arms trade treaty.

UN Conference on Arms Trade Treaty, a gathering that started at UN Headquarters in New York on July 2 2012, has united UN's 193 Member States. Assistant Secretary-General delivered the statement on behalf of the **FAO**, Office of the Coordination for Humanitarian Affairs (**OCHA**), Office of the High Commissioner for Human Rights (**OHCHR**), **UNICEF**, **UNDP**, **UNHCR**, **UNFPA**, **WFP**, **WHO** and the UN Special Rapporteur on the human rights of Internally Displaced Persons.

Review of Cases

On July 13 2012, independent UN human rights experts reviewed more than 200 cases concerning over 30 countries during the session that **ended** today. The five-member UN Working Group on Enforced or Involuntary Disappearances also reviewed responses from various governments to prompt intervention letters, urgent appeals and general allegations during the session. The panel held meetings with representatives of the governments of Algeria, Japan and Republic of Korea. Views were exchanged. It also met with non-governmental organizations and family members of disappeared individuals. Members of the Working Group also held informal bilateral meetings with States to exchange information with a view to enhancing cooperation. During the session, the Group's official mission to Pakistan was confirmed for September 2012.

Two Draft General Comments

In the session, the Working Group discussed two draft general comments on the provisions of the Declaration on the Protection of All Persons from Enforced Disappearance with regard to the impact of enforced disappearance on women and children. The Group examined cases concerning Afghanistan, Albania, Algeria, Argentina, Bangladesh, Belarus, Bhutan, Central African Republic, Colombia, Democratic People's Republic of Korea, Egypt, Georgia, Kenya, Kuwait, Laos, Libya, Mexico, Morocco, Myanmar, Pakistan, Peru, Russia, Saudi Arabia, Spain, Sri Lanka, Switzerland, Syria, Tajikistan, Thailand, Turkey, Uzbekistan and Yemen.

Created in 1980, the Working Group currently comprises Chair-Rapporteur Olivier de Frouville (France); Ariel Dulitzky (Argentina); Jasminka Dzumhur (Bosnia and Herzegovina); Osman El-Hajjé (Lebanon), and Jeremy Sarkin (South Africa). Its members are independent and report to the UN Human Rights Council in Geneva.

Conclusion

Displaced and lost persons during combat and noncombat operations are needed by concerned countries and families. UN has taken the initiative to trace those persons and restore them to their families. This is being done by UN on humanitarian grounds. We appreciate and fully support this move of UN officials.

Chapter 6

UNESCO: New Biosphere Reserves

Introduction

On July 11, 2012, UNESCO has added 20 new sites to global network of biosphere reserves. Now, there are 599 biosphere reserves. They are located in 117 countries of the world and are being monitored by the UNESCO through its officials and environmentalists. The meeting was held in Paris. Our valued readers may recall that a biosphere reserves is a habitat recognized by Man and the Biosphere Programme (**MAB**) where local communities are actively involved in governance and management, research, education, training and monitoring at the service of both socio-economic development and biodiversity conservation.

List of Reserves

The new reserves added by UNESCO to the existing list are as follows: (1) Sheka Reserve Ethiopia. (2) La Selle, Haiti. (3) Korgalzhyn, Kazakhstan. (4) Sao Tome and Principe. (5) West Polesie Transboundary Biosphere Reserve (which crosses Belarus, Poland and Ukraine). (6) Four islands that make up the Wakatobi reserve (Indonesia); (7) Ferlo reserve in Senegal (threatened by drought and human actions). (8) Salzburger Lungau and Kärntner Nockberge, Austria. (9) Jinggangshan, China. (10) Niubeiliang, China. (11) Mura-Drava-Danube, Croatia/Hungary. (12) Bassin de la Dordogne, France. (13) Achanakmar-Amarkantak, India. (14) Aya, Japan. (15) Tehuacán-Cuicatlán, Mexico, (16) Ferlo, Senegal. (17) La Gomera, Spain. (18) Las Ubiñas-La Mesa, Spain. (19) East Vättern Scarp landscape, Sweden. (20) Galloway and Southern Ayrshire Biosphere, UK.

There were also extensions to four reserves as follows: (1) Fray Jorge Biosphere Reserve in Chile. (2) Réserve de biosphère des Iles et de la Mer d'Iroise in France. (3) Doñana in Spain. (4) Sierra Nevada Biosphere Reserve in Spain.

Goodwill Ambassador Supports Biodversity Protection

On June 21 2012, Ed Norton, UN Goodwill Ambassador for Biodiversity, gave frank answers to all questions at the UN New Centre. He discussed about the importance of learning how biodiversity affects our daily lives, why local initiatives are key to making progress on sustainable development issues, and why he remains optimistic about the world's chances to make a positive impact in the environment.

UN Conference on Sustainable Development (**Rio+20**) has brought together thousands of people from all walks of life to Rio de Janeiro (Brazil) to help delineate new policies to promote prosperity, reduce poverty and enhance social equity and environmental protection. Mr. Norton appreciated Convention of Biological Diversity (CBD) and the way in which it relates to the larger macro-strategies been implemented by **UNDP**, UN Environment Programme (**UNEP**) and Global Environmental Facility (GEF). UNESCO officials are keen to unite global audiences on a very specific critical agenda. They have to create rules, protocols, agendas and agreements. Goals would be set and then, they would be achieved, said Mr. Norton.

Mr. Norton also said that global warming and biodiversity were complex things for ordinary people of the world. But they do affect all of us, said he. He answered the questions of the people present at the Centre. CBD must do a job of connecting concepts and issues for people. Note that forests have 80 per cent of our terrestrial biodiversity. Afforestation and felling of trees were discussed. Programme projects for the GEF are on in Kenya and Rwanda.

Retain and Sustain Biodiversity

Biodiversity affects the fundamental pillars of global economy that are integrated with biodiversity health. But progress on biodiversity on events like Rio+20 is slow. People are not aware of real issues. They waste fuels and wood. Eco-friendly citizens are dwindling in terms of number. Every family has more cars than it can afford to drive. If it has less number of cars, it aims to buy more.

Convention on Biodiversity and UNDP are interlinked. Today, sustained development is the name of the game. UNDP has invested millions of dollars to support biodiversity projects around the globe.

A Background of CBD

Convention on Biological Diversity (CBD) was signed by 150 government leaders at the Rio Earth Summit (1992). It aims to develop national strategies for conservation and sustainable use of biological diversity. It emphasizes upon the glaring fact that biological diversity is about more than plants, animals and microorganisms and their ecosystems. Thus, it involves people in its programmes. It addresses issues like food security, medicines, fresh air, potable water, shelter and a healthy environment.

NGOs, government organs, private players and individuals must make agreements and execute them in letter and spirit to maintain biodiversity. The protection of ecosystems must be balanced with better investments returns and sustainable development, aver UN experts who are handling the issues at CBD. The idea is to work together in this segment and deliver concrete results.

CBD's Partners from UN

CBD has a lot of partnerships with UNDP, UNEP and GEF. The Equator Prize for UNDP has also been announced. It would be given to those people from very poor communities and traditional cultures all over the globe who have made an extraordinary difference with very little resources.

Conclusion

The expansion of the list of biodiversity reserves has been welcomed by all quarters of the globe. UNESCO is doing a commendable job.

Chapter 7

Rio Plus 20

Introduction

World leaders, along with thousands of participants from governments, the private sector, non-governmental organizations (NGOs) and other groups will come together from June 20-22 2012 in Rio de Janeiro (Brazil) to participate in UN Sustainable Development Conference (**Rio+20**). The idea is to make our planet more sustainable, hence this top-level meet.

Global Food Scenario

Poverty, agriculture, social policies and environmental dimensions because are related to one another. Food situation around the globe is that countries have rapidly growing populations, growing incomes, changing consumption patterns and finally, people eating more animal products, vegetables, fruits and oils. The total quantities of food needed are much higher than they were nearly a decade ago. The industrial and economic growth rates were also good during the early years of this century. Today, they are hovering between 1.0 to 6.0 percent (we are considering all countries in this percentage bracket). International Fund for Agricultural Development (IFAD) is addressing the problem of global food security. There are no solutions as on date.

The resources of world are finite. Fuel prices have sky-rocketed. So, food is costly. Food has become a critical issue. The drought of 2012 has not augured well for India. We are trying our hands on at renewable energy sources. Renewable energy source can be bio-ethanol produced from corn. The food market and energy market are intertwined. If we produce fuels, we lack food and vice versa. The same is the case with sugarcane (sugar and rum or gasohol). Self-sufficiency in food is better than having the money to buy food. Money is less important today. Its value has gone down. Food is scarce. It has become gold.

Food Shortage along with Faulty Food Consumption

In developed countries, basic food and calories are very cheap. People there are consuming those types of empty calories. This trend is leading to obesity. Now, high-density energy food is also being usurped by the middle classes of developing countries. Fast food intake has increased over the past two decades. Malnutrition goes along with fast food consumption. Rich people eat burgers and submarines. Poor people are unable to get enough vitamins and calories. Malnutrition and poverty go hand in hand. Food price volatility is bad for the poor, for they spend a major chunk of their income on food products.

Role of Agriculture in Eliminating Food Scarcity

Agriculture is the single largest employer in the world, providing livelihoods for 40 per cent of today's global population. It is the largest source of income and jobs for poor rural households. Nearly 500 million small farms worldwide, most still rain-fed, provide up to 80 per cent of food consumed in a large part of the developing world. Investing in smallholder women and men is an important way to increase food security and nutrition for the poorest, as well as food production for local and global markets.

Since 1900s, nearly 75 per cent of crop diversity has been lost from farmers' fields. Better use of agricultural biodiversity can contribute to more nutritious diets, enhanced livelihoods for farming communities and more resilient and sustainable farming systems.

Further, nearly 1.3 billion people have no access to electricity worldwide - most of which live in rural areas of the developing world. Energy poverty in many regions is a fundamental barrier to reducing hunger and ensuring that the world can produce enough food to meet future demand.

Food Security and Sustainable Agriculture: Goal for Rio+20

Discussion sessions in Rio would search for solutions on food. The importance of small land farmers is vital in this debate. They control a very significant part of the land, water and labour in developing countries. They were part of Rio Plus agenda.

Main Challenge during Rio+20

Agriculture, social policies, environment, political issues and economic hassles must be addressed in complex partnership scenes. No country is big or small. Someone has oil. Someone else has food grains. We need all of them. We must also take care of the deprived people; they are getting nothing and starving as a result. We must function across various sectors. Countries must sink their political differences. They must strengthen UN, for it is the only solution for the problems related to food and poverty.

While discussing United Nations Decade on Biodiversity, UN Secretary-General Ban Ki-moon stated (we quote), "It is essential for all the world's peoples to understand not only the value of biodiversity, but what they can do to protect it. The global rate of biodiversity loss is unmatched in human history. Many ecosystems are verging on tipping points beyond which they will not recover. These trends are being compounded by climate change. In 2012, global population reached 7 billion people. Ensuring truly sustainable development for our growing human family depends on biological diversity and the vital goods and services it offers. While the poor suffer first and worst from biodiversity loss, all of society stands to lose from this mass extinction."

"I call on all the parties to the Convention on Biological Diversity and to all the biodiversity-related conventions, as well as all members of the United Nations system, the private sector, civil society groups and individual citizens and consumers worldwide, to rally to the call of the United Nations Decade on Biodiversity. Let us work together to live in harmony with nature. Let us preserve and wisely manage nature's riches for prosperity today and for the future we want."

Rio+ Centre

Brazilian Government announced the creation of Rio+ Centre, the World Centre for Sustainable Development, at a ceremony. The ceremony was attended by Izabella Teixeira, Brazil's Minister for the Environment and Helen Clark, UNDP Administrator. The Rio+ Centre will facilitate research, knowledge exchange and promote international debate about sustainable development. It will bring together a broad international union of partners, consisting of government agencies, UN organs, local governments, NGOs, universities, elite thinkers and private sector players.

The objective behind the creation of the *Rio+ Centre* is to build on new and innovative mechanisms for engaging the participation of local governments, civil society, business and academia in knowledge exchange and discussions around the subject.

From the outset, the *Rio+ Centre* will provide continuity to the discussions launched by the Rio Dialogues for Sustainable Development (www.riodialogues.com). The Dialogues were launched by the Government of Brazil with the support of UNDP in the lead-up to Rio+20 as a way of actively ensuring inputs of civil society and experts worldwide.

The new centre will build on the successful existing partnership between the Government of Brazil and UNDP: the International Policy Centre for Inclusive Growth (IPC-IG), established in 2004, in Brasilia. Since its founding, IPC-IG has been playing a key role in the dialogue between countries of the South on policies for social protection and inclusion, development innovation as well as rural and sustainable development issues.

The establishment of the *Rio+ Centre* has received support from the following institutions:

- United Nations Development Programme (UNDP)
- United Nations Environment Programme (UNEP)
- International Policy Centre for Inclusive Growth (IPC-IG)
- United Nations Programme for Human Settlements (UN-HABITAT)
- International Labour Organisation (ILO)
- Institute of Advanced Studies,
- United Nations University (UNU-IAS)
- Regional Centre of Expertise in Education for Sustainable Development (RCE)
- Government of the Federative Republic of Brazil
- State Government of Rio de Janeiro
- Municipality of Rio de Janeiro
- Financier of Studies and Projects (FINEP)
- Banco Nacional de Desenvolvimento Economico e Social (BNDES)
- Center for Strategic Studies and Management (CGEE)
- Global Institute for Green Technologies and Employment (GIGTech, COPPE / UFRJ)
- Center for Sustainable Development at the University of Brasilia (UNB-CDS)
- FGV Network of Technology and Innovation of Rio de Janeiro (REDETEC)
- Technological Information Network Latin America (RITLA / UNESCO)
- National Confederation of Industry Brazil (CNI)
- Brazilian Service to Support Micro and Small Enterprises (Sebrae)
- Brazilian Business Council for Development (CEBDS)
- Brazilian Foundation for Sustainable Development (FBDS)
- BVRio (Bolsa Verde Rio)
- Reverurbano

- Pro-Natura Foundation

Conclusion

The problems of inflation, fuel price rise, biodiversity decay, pollution, global warming and nations at war with their own people are very much intertwined, if we carefully analyse the current socio-economic-political scenario. Food security is the major burning issue. Rio Plus 20 has tried to address the issue. But we have a long way to go, for we have not been able to unite as humans.

On July 13 2012, A UN expert stated that resettlement and land reform were two of the main challenges for the consolidation of peace and stability in Rwanda. Basic human rights issues were being addressed by UN, she added. A scheme called **Villagization** (*Imidugudu*) was launched (1994) by the government to give housing to thousands of returnees after the genocide. The programme focuses on rural people; the idea is to bring scattered households closer in villages. Government has also made efforts to reach out to communities in the most remote areas. But these efforts must not exclude any Rwandan.

Ms. Rolnik also visited inhabitants of several neighbourhoods in Kigali and villages in the countryside that are being set up in the context of the villagization policy and discussed with inhabitants the impacts of this policy on their housing and living conditions.

In the UN Human Rights Council in Geneva, the reports on the state of Rwanda would be presented. The Council shall rope in connoisseurs, who would work to examine and report back on the Ground Zero situation.

Chapter 8

UN Global Pulse: Era of Big Data Is Here

Introduction

The era of 'Big Data' presents the United Nations with an historic opportunity to offer better support to and protect populations through the analysis of digital information, according to a report launched on July 10 2012 at UN Headquarters in New York.

Produced by UN Global Pulse, the report is titled ***Big Data for Development: Opportunities and Challenges***. It was released on July 10 2012. It explores how data from social media and various sources can generate information about population' basic features, including responses to job loss, changing food prices and various other economic indicators. The idea is to combat hunger, poverty and disease. But these positive actions need awareness in big data community and development community. The organizations must form strategic partnerships, develop innovative approaches and show their potential to the results of change processes. Big Data is now front-page news, much to the delight of world's globally active communities.

Statement of an Official

Global Pulse's research proved that (we quote) "social media chat can be an early indicator of spikes in unemployment in countries such as United States and Ireland and that price of food commodities mined from websites closely matches the official Consumer Price Index in six Latin American countries." This output was generated after the collaboration with several data research companies and institutions (including Jana, the SAS and Crimson Hexagon).

Conclusion

The implementation strategy of this organization includes working with member countries to establish a network of Pulse Labs to find out the potential of new data sources of data and delineate successful techniques. Indonesia and Uganda are setting up first two labs in Jakarta and Kampala Funds for Jakarta lab shall be provided by Australia; the lab would be started in September 2012.

Chapter 9

UNSC: Ending Hostilities in Mali

Introduction

On July 5 2012, UNSC condemned the seizure of power in Mali earlier this year. It also called for immediate stoppage of hostilities by rebels in the country's north and showed its willingness to consider the deployment of a stabilization force in Mali.

In the adopted resolution and acting under Chapter VII of UN Charter, the 15-member body also expressed concern about the deteriorating humanitarian conditions and terrorist threat due to the presence of members of Al-Qaeda in Islamic Maghreb (AQIM) in many parts of the country.

It urged member nations to "undertake measures to prevent the proliferation of all arms and related material of all types in the Sahel region." It all rebel groups in Mali to refrain from any form of association with AQIM.

Conflict had started in northern Mali between government troops and Tuareg rebels in January 2012. The insecurity due to these clashes. This led to swarming of armed groups in the region. Then, a coup d'état occurred in March 2012. It has uprooted nearly 3,20,000 people. Many of them went to neighbouring countries.

On the humanitarian front, the UN and its partners have appealed for $1.6 billion to provide aid to people in Africa's Sahel region, which includes Mali. The UN Office for the Coordination of Humanitarian Affairs (**OCHA**) stated that the conditions in Sahel region had deteriorated in 2012 primarily due to drought, less rainfall, poor harvest, rising food prices, displacement and insecurity. Council called on all concerned groups to ensure access for the timely delivery of humanitarian aid. It also requested the factions at war to ensure the safety and security of personnel who would supply this aid for war victims.

ECOWAS Asks for UNSC Resolution

In June 2012, Economic Community of West African States (ECOWAS) and the African Union (AU) requested for a Security Council mandate. This mandate would authorize the deployment of an ECOWAS stabilization force to protect Malian state institutions. It would also assist in upholding the territorial integrity of Mali. Further, it would provide all types of assistance to challenge and fight against the menace of terrorism. In the resolution that was passed, the Council expressed its readiness to examine this request. It also encouraged close cooperation between the Malian Transitional authorities, ECOWAS, African Union and other nations that were affected by the conflict.

The Council called on all national stakeholders to "create the necessary conditions for enabling the transitional authorities to fully exercise their primary responsibilities and to ensure the full restoration and preservation of constitutional order." Its statement was received well by participants and global audiences. The Council strongly condemned the damage and destruction of sites of holy, historic and cultural significance. Timbuktu, a city connected with fables, was also affected by the violence.

In June 2012, the World Heritage Committee–it is a prestigious organ of **UNESCO**– placed Timbuktu and the Tomb of Askia on its **List of World Heritage in Danger**. Since then, UN officials have been incessantly calling for protection of this city of dreams.

Conclusion

As per UNESCO, Timbuktu was an intellectual and spiritual capital and a centre for the propagation of Islam throughout Africa in the 15th and 16th centuries. The 17-metre-high pyramidal structure of the Tomb of Askia was built by the Emperor of Songhai in 1495. It gives testimony for the power and wealth of an empire that had survived during the Fifteenth and Sixteenth centuries. It did control the trans-Saharan trade during its hey days.

Chapter 10

UN General Assembly: West Africa in Doldrums

Introduction

Recently, Kenyan churches were subjected to bomb blasts. Several people had died in those blasts and several hundreds were hurt or maimed by the same. Kenya is a peace-loving country. In such a nation, the emergence of the terror dragon is a matter of serious debate. Let us scan the situation in nutshell.

On July 3 2012, the President of the United Nations General Assembly, Nassir Abdulaziz Al-Nasser, censured deadly attacks carried out on two churches in Kenya in a crowded weekend in 2012. The attacks, which took place in the town of Garissa near Kenya's border with Somalia, resulted in the killing of 17 persons. They also inflicted serious injuries on many more individuals. A spokesperson said on behalf of the President of UNGA that the UNGA had expressed anguish at the death of those victims. He also added that the families of the victims deserved the soothing support of the world. The people of Kenya were also with the families of victims, the statement said.

Secretary-General Ban Ki-moon condemned the attacks. He also called for the punishment of perpetrators of attacks. He said that the recent terrorist attacks imposed on Kenya must be held accountable. The attackers may have hatched the plans in Somalia. The pirates of Somalia are also known for their ruthless behaviour and merciless killing sprees. Kenya and Somalia share borders by they have different cultures or ideologies. At least these massacres indicate this new trend.

Although progress was made over the past years to promote peace in West Africa, the attention and support of the UN remains critical. This area is a hotspot for a major war, which can be trigger hostilities between and among the hungry masses or rebels of various countries of that region. The head of the UN Office for West Africa (**UNOWA**) informed the UNSC that the security situation in the region was precarious and reversible as the root causes of instability ought to be addressed. Secretary-General Ban Ki-moon's latest report on the region covered the period from January to 1 to June 30 2012. It gave an overall view of national and cross-border developments in West Africa. The actions done by UNOWA were also highlighted and discussed. In the report, the review period was marked by unconstitutional changes of power in Guinea-Bissau and Mali, conflict in northern Mali and the lethal situation in the Sahel, where lakhs of people were starving due to food insecurity.

Mr. Djinnit reported that besides the crises in Mali and the Sahel, West Africa continued to face piracy and armed robbery at sea in the Gulf of Guinea. The coastal countries and their landlocked neighbours are especially at the risk of being exploited by sea pirates. The recent upsurge of violence between Liberia and Côte d'Ivoire led to the death of seven UN peacekeeper officials. Several civilians also died, said Mr. Djinnnit.

Conclusion

UN alone cannot resolve the burning crises in West Africa, a region marked by piracy, poverty and the lack of industrial activities. Regional players need to enhance their efforts to tackle the problem of drug trafficking and organized crime. It may be noted that the rising levels of poverty in West Africa have directly contributed to the ailments like clashes between nations, clashes between armed groups within a nation and high-sea piracy. Drug cartels and other criminal networks are active in West Africa. This has made the situation even more volatile. UN agencies are finding it hard to tackle the many small armies that have mushroomed in that region over the past one decade or so. The Executive Director of the UN Office on Drugs and Crime (**UNODC**), Mr. Yury Fedotov, informed the UN that the drugs scenario was worsening in West Africa. People of that region have taken to drugs like fish does to water. Organised crime has one basic reason behind it--*people are consumers of drugs because food is nowhere to be scene.*

Chapter 11

IMF: Euro Blues

Introduction

The euro crisis continues to weigh down the global economy, the International Monetary Fund said on July 16 2012. It exerted pressure on the European Central Bank to lower its interest rate even further and issue more cheap loans to the banks. Note that the countries that had adopted Euro as their de facto monetary standard are reeling under the pangs of the worst economic recession of the region. Seventeen countries are in the grip of hardcore recession. Three countries (Spain, Italy and Greece) are at the verge of bankruptcy. They are getting dole from EU to sustain their peoples. Germany, France and England are on a solid ground, insofar as economic stability and industrial production are concerned. Thus, these three nations are dictating their terms at EU forums.

"There is room for monetary policy in the euro area to ease further. In addition, the ECB should ensure that its monetary support is transmitted effectively across the region and should continue to provide ample liquidity support to banks under sufficiently lenient conditions," the IMF said in its annual World Economic Outlook. This finance organ of the UNO cut its global economic growth forecast to 3.9 percent from 4.1 percent in April 2012. That was due to the continued stress in the euro zone and weaker-than-expected economic activity in emerging countries. "The utmost priority is to resolve the crisis in the euro area," the IMF official said. Overall, the 17 euro countries will contract by 0.3 percent this year and return to a 0.7 percent growth rate next year, the key finance organization of the world prophesized.

The specific reference to ECB is meant to increase pressure for this body to turn on the printing presses via cheap loans, low interest rates and "some form of quantitative easing", meaning direct or indirect bond purchasing aimed at lowering government borrowing costs. The ECB had bought some Italian and Spanish bonds in 2011 on the secondary markets, where they are traded after being purchased from governments (primary markets). But ECB chief (Mario Draghi) ruled out the revival of this programme.

Another interest rate cut in September and further easing of collateral rules for banks (when they seek ECB loans) could be the two measures taken by the organization in the immediate future. It is not unusual for the IMF to come up with "provocative" ideas which originate from a different central bank culture. Unlike the US Federal Reserve, the ECB has been prohibited from buying bonds directly from governments.

German Delay on Bailout Fund

The IMF report praised euro-leaders for their "step in the right direction" at a June 28 2012 summit where they agreed to create a single supervision for euro zone banks and to re-capitalise banks in distress directly from the bailout funds, rather than going through governments balance sheets. But the German constitutional court announced that it would wait until September 12 2012 before ruling on the constitutionality of the new euro zone bailout fund, the European Stability Mechanism and also, on the treaty on fiscal discipline. This treaty was signed by 25 EU states. The ESM should have come into being on July 9 2012. Delayed or no policy action would be the biggest risks to global economic recovery. The IMF stated that this could worsen the euro crisis.

Conclusion

“Simply put, the euro periphery countries have to succeed,” IMF chief economist Olivier Blanchard said. But it is easier said than done. The February 2008 massacre of stock markets has triggered a wave of global recession. Europe has not been able to come out of it. War-ravaged West Asia and inflation-ravaged India are unable to come out of the pangs of this recession. Europe stands at a very slippery path today. It would not be able to come out of the dole era so quickly, experts aver.

Chapter 12
UN Activities on Social Front and Human Rights

Introduction

The promotion and protection of all human rights is among the main objectives of the UN. The UNO has set up many organizations to deal with human rights, including the Commission on Human Rights. It has drafted various human rights instruments, encouraged countries to accede to them, adopted resolutions requesting that states should improve their human rights situations and organized a number of conferences.

Plethora of Useful Activities

In June 1993, World Conference on Human Rights adopted the Vienna Declaration and Programme of Action. The post of the United Nations High commissioner for Human Rights was created (1993). Mrs. Mary Robinson, former Irish President, was appointed as the second High Commissioner in (June 1997). She coordinated UN activities and international cooperation efforts after assuming the office.

Japanese Cooperation

Japan firmly supports High Commissioner's activities including human rights field operations and advisory services and technical assistance. This nation from the Pacific Rim has been actively taking part in the U.N. Commission on Human Rights as its member since 1982. It has increased its contribution to the Voluntary Fund for Advisory Services and Technical Assistance. Japanese experts have contributed to these activities as members of the sub-commissions and committees. It has also concluded a number of human rights instruments.

Partnership for Democratic Development (PDD)

Japan gives impetus to institutional building in various fields like legislative, administrative and electoral systems to promote democratic development and protect human rights in developing countries. Japan announced at the Lyon Summit an initiative named "Partnership for Democratic Development (PDD)." Its aim is to strengthen cooperative activities in human rights field. This initiative is based on the understanding that there are many nations which have the political will to promote democracy and human rights but lack the systems, institutions and human resources to achieve those pious aims. Japan supports activities of the Voluntary Fund for Advisory Services and Technical Assistance in the field of human rights. The U.N. Crime Prevention and Criminal Justice Programme are also being supported. NGOs. The press of various countries and other organizations are also being involved in these change-oriented programmes.

UN and Social Issues: Women

In September 1995, ten years after the Nairobi World Conference, the Fourth World Conference on Women adopted the Beijing Declaration and Platform for Action. At this conference, Japan announced its intention to promote the Initiative on Women in Development (WID). Japan submitted to the Third Committee of the 50th UN General Assembly a resolution on the Role of the United Nations Development Fund for Women in Eliminating Violence against Women. It was adopted by consensus. It had 46 co-sponsors. Thus, on the basis of this resolution, Trust Fund in Support of Actions to Eliminate Violence against Women was established within the United Nations Development Fund for Women (UNIFEM). Japan gives hefty financial contribution to this Fund. It remained a member of the Commission on the Status of Women and has an expert participate in the Committee on the Elimination of All Forms of Discrimination against Women. Japan has been providing funds to UNIFEM and International Research and Training Institute for the Advancement of Women (INSTRAW).

UN and Social Issues: Children

In order to respect and protect the rights of all children of the world, the U.N. adopted the Convention on the Rights of the Child in 1989, 10 years after the International Year of the Child, 1979. In September 1990, the World Summit for Children was convened with the attendance of 71 Heads of States and Governments, and adopted the World Declaration and the Plan of Action for implementing the World Declaration on the

Survival, Protection and Development of Children. As of February 1998, the Convention on the Rights of the Child has been ratified by 191 countries. This fact shows its distinguished universality among the U.N. human rights instruments. Japan ratified it in April 1994 and submitted the initial report on this convention in May 1996.

The United Nations Children's Fund (UNICEF) has implemented development activities in the field of health, sanitation, basic education and emergency assistance. Japan is a member of the Executive Board. It has been making contributions from the government (7.83% of the whole donation, as of 1997) and from private sector.

UN and Social Development

Social problems likes poverty, unemployment and social exclusion of vulnerable people were discussed and debated at the World Summit for Social Development. It was held in Copenhagen (Denmark) in March 1995. The summit adopted the Copenhagen Declaration on Social Development and Programme of Action, which showed the international commitment to social development. Prime Minister Tomiichi Murayama attended this summit and made a speech. He stressed to give the key role to the realization of social justice. He also said that Japan would place special emphasis on social development in the field of ODA, promote technical assistance in such areas as education and vocational training and increase assistance for women in developing countries.

Conclusion

In recent years, too Japan has contributed immensely to the social causes and women's development the world over. Its Tsunami tragedy (2011) also could not stop it from giving adequate funds and making high-quality contributions to the Un and its organs. Other countries must learn a lesson from the Japanese example. They must also understand that social transformation alone can lead to economic upliftment. Women and children must be given adequate opportunities to learn, earn and live with dignity. Therefore, we conclude that on the social front, the contribution of various oragnisations of the UNO is commendable and worthy of giving support of all genres.

Chapter 13
United Nations Decade for Human Rights Education

Introduction

In order to raise international awareness for human rights, the 10-year period beginning from 1995 was declared as the UN Decade for Human Rights Education. Under the Decade, UN organizations, governments, human rights institutions in different parts of the world are expected to head towards the goal by promoting human rights education. To accomplish this task, in December 1995, the Government of Japan established the Headquarters for the Promotion of the Plan of Action of the UN Decade for Human Rights Education, with the Prime Minister as its chair. The Headquarters finalized a National Plan of Action in July 1997.

Symposium on Human Rights

In January 1998, the Ministry of Foreign Affairs of Japan and United Nations University co-sponsored the Third Symposium on Human Rights in the Asia-Pacific Region. It provided the opportunity for experts on human rights in this region to exchange their views. Japan expected the discussion on human rights to be deepened and developed in the symposium.

Japan's annual contributions to the UN Funds on human rights totaled about US$1 million. In addition, Japan has contributed $700,000 and $800,000 to the Human Rights Field Operations in Rwanda (HRFOR) and the former Yugoslavia, respectively.

ODA for the Project

Guided by the belief that human rights are universal, Japan has expressed its concerns upon human rights violations, calling on countries of concern to improve the human rights situation. Japan pays full attention to the human rights situations and efforts for promoting democratization as proclaimed in the ODA Charter. When any improvement in human rights situations or any trace of democratization is recognized, Japan helps these changes through aids. On the contrary, when the situation is clearly accusable, Japan reviews its ODA projects to the country concerned.

Conclusion

The Human Rights issue is a major concern area for UN. After the completion of UN Rights decade, the process should not be deemed over. Human rights abuse is going on in Somalia, Kenya, Syria, India, Libya, China, North Korea and other countries of the world. UN must take adequate steps to eliminate the menace of human rights abuse. Concrete steps must be taken in this context. Defaulters must be fined or punished. All countries must contribute towards this noble objective.

Chapter 14

UNDP: Achieve Millennium Development Goals by 2015

Introduction

In 2000, 189 nations promised to liberate people from extreme poverty and deprivations. This vow was the **Eight Millennium Development Goals.** They must be achieved by 2015. The idea seems to be Utopian by any norm.

The MDGs

They are as follows: 1. Eradicate Extreme Hunger and Poverty. 2. Achieve Universal Primary Education. 3. Promote Gender Equality and Empower Women. 4. Reduce Child Mortality. 5. Improve Maternal Health. 6. Combat HIV/AIDS, Malaria and Other Diseases. 7. Ensure Environmental Sustainability. 8. Develop a Global Partnership For Development

India's Report Card

ECOSOC published a report (February 2012) and stated in it that there were obstructions on the way to achieving MDG in the Asia-Pacific. The Indian nation may not be able to eliminate poverty because it is a deep-rooted and pretty old disease. Other goals would be achieved to a moderate extent. India's report card is as follows:

- Population **1.21 billion**
- Poverty Rate **37.2%**
- Per capita income **$1,330** (2011)
- Human Development Index **0.547**

Read **Table 1-I** in the context of the achievement of MDGs (by India).

Table 1-I: MDGs Not Achieved in Toto by India

Serial No.	Details of Goals to be Achieved	Progress Report
1.	Halve, between 1990 and 2015, the part of population below national poverty line.	**Slow**
2.	Cut down to 1/2, between 1990 and 2015, proportion of hungry people.	Almost Off-track
3.	By 2015 children everywhere, boys and girls alike, will be able to complete a full course of primary education.	On Track
4.	Remove gender disparity in primary and secondary education by 2005 and in all levels of education, not beyond 2015.	Moderate yet Slow
5.	Cut down by two third, between 1990 and 2015, the under-five mortality rate.	**Slow**
6.	Reduce by three quarters, between 1990 and 2015, the maternal mortality ratio.	**Slow**
7.	Get stopped by 2015 and start reversing the spread of HIV/AIDS.	**Nearly on Track**
8.	Get stopped (by 2015) and start the reversal of the incidence of malaria and other major diseases.	**Nearly On Track or Slow**
9.	Integrate the tenets of sustainable development into country policies and programmes and reverse the loss of environmental resources.	**On Track**
10.	Halve, by 2015, the proportion of people without sustainable access to safe drinking water and basic sanitation.	**Nearly On Track**
11.	By 2020, to have achieved, a significant improvement in the lives of at least 100 million slum dwellers.	**Almost Off-track**
12.	With the private sector, make available the benefits of new technologies, information and communication.	**On Track**

UN Millennium Campaign

It is an inter-agency initiative of UN. It was created (2002) to support citizens' efforts to hold their governments accountable for the achievement of MDGs. In India, the campaign focused on MDGs 1-7 and on developing partnerships and strengthening capacities of 6 key constituencies to achieve the Goals.

Developing Strategies

The 12th Five-Year Plan aimed at getting faster, sustainable and inclusive growth. UNDP India has shared the MDG Acceleration Framework (MAF) which was ratified as a potential framework for prioritizing action towards achieving MDGs.

Working with Government

UNDP and UN partners have developed a set of indicators that can be used to track MDGs at the district level. A community monitoring tool for quantitative and qualitative assessment by people of health-, education- and livelihood-related outcomes was piloted in seven districts. People's Audit of Health, Education and Livelihoods (PAHELI) was conceived as a result of a discussion between UNDP and Pratham to develop a people-friendly approach to District Human Development report cards.

Role Played by UNDP

UNDP supports local capacity development initiatives. It works directly with more than 15 central ministries and several states, elected representatives and government officials at state, district and local levels. It takes part in government development programmes that would help India get to MDGs. **UNDP is working in these areas: (1)** Poverty Reduction. (2) Democratic Governance. (3) Crisis Prevention and Recovery. (4) Environment and Energy (5) Women's Empowerment and Inclusion. (6) Human Development. (7) HIV and Development.

UNDP, in collaboration with the UNDG and the Inter Agency Expert Group (IAEG) on Targets and Indicators, is providing technical and financial support to countries in reporting progress on their national MDG targets and developing MDG National Report Guidelines. Nearly 400 nationally owned reports have been published. Data and lessons generated in these reports helped make a strong case for the UNDG endorsed and UNDP field-tested MDG Acceleration Framework (MAF). Last round of national MDG reports will provide a collective review and key lessons for MDG achievement. Then, the development agenda beyond 2015 would be designed.

Conclusion

Three important targets on poverty, slums and water have been met three years ahead of 2015, says this year's Report on the Millennium Development Goals (MDGs). Meeting the remaining targets is possible but only if Governments do not waiver from their commitments made over a decade ago. India's report card is not very much impressive. That is because nearly 23 percent of India's populace lives below poverty line. Monsoon is erratic. Food grain prices and commodity rates are rising. The poorest masses cannot have access to proper sanitation, health care facilities and potable water. The global wars and battles may not allow us to achieve MDGs by 2015. In any case, the targets are too gargantuan to be achieved in such a small time frame.

Chapter 15

IMF: Forecast for Global Economy

Introduction

On June 16 2012, International Monetary Fund (IMF) slashed its growth forecast for world economy. The signs of weakness in the global recovery due to European debt crisis and a slowdown in emerging economies were the two reasons cited by the UN agency. Let us have a look at facts and figures.

Unhealthy Figures

IMF cut the growth forecast for 2013 to 3.9 percent from 4.1 percent (delineated in April 2012). The projection for this year was left unchanged at 3.5 percent. Advanced economies are now expected to expand at 1.4 percent this year, in tune with the April projection. The forecast for next year was lowered to 1.9 percent from 2 percent.

The 2012 growth outlook for the U.S. was cut to 2 percent from 2.1 percent, while the 2013 projection was lowered to 2.3 percent from 2.4 percent. The crisis-plagued Eurozone is still expected to shrink 0.3 percent this year. The 2013 growth forecast for the currency-bloc was cut to 0.7 percent from 0.9 percent.

Within the Eurozone, Germany is expected to grow 1.0 percent this year, better than 0.6 percent seen in April. Next year, the largest economy in the euro area is seen expanding 1.4 percent, which is less than the 1.5 percent forecast earlier.

France is expected to log 0.3 percent growth this year, below April's projection of 0.4 percent. The forecast for 2013 was slashed to 0.8 percent from 1 percent.

Among the big four, Italy and Spain are expected to contract. Italy is seen shrinking 1.9 percent this year and 0.3 percent in 2013, unchanged from the previous forecasts.

Meanwhile, Spain's 2012 projection was upwardly revised to show a 1.5 percent contraction this year compared to the 1.9 percent contraction expected earlier. However, the country's outlook for 2013 was slashed and IMF now sees a 0.6 percent contraction versus the 0.1 percent growth expected in April.

The U.K. had the most severe downgrade in growth projections. The 2012 forecast was slashed to 0.2 percent from 0.8 percent, while the 2013 outlook was cut to 1.4 percent from 2 percent.

In Asia, Japan's growth forecast for this year was raised to 2.4 percent from 2 percent. However, the outlook for growth next year was cut to 1.5 percent from 1.7 percent.

The emerging economies also saw downgrades to their growth forecasts. China, which was earlier expected to grow 8.2 percent this year, is now seen expanding 8 percent. The projection for growth next year was cut to 8.5 percent from 8.8 percent.

Global Economic Indicators

Dollar Continued to weaken after disappointing in June 2012. New York Manufacturing Activity expands at fast rate in July 2012. US retail sales unexpectedly dropped by 0.5 percent in June 2012. Euro selling spree continues on in June-July 2012. Industry reeled under inflationary pressures in March-July 2012 around the world. In India the IIP was 0.1 percent (growth) in May-June 2012. A US Dollar was equivalent to Rs. 56 (July 2012). Europe has not come out of the vortex of recession. EU leaders are trying to be harsh towards Spain and Greece. However a dole package would be decided soon for the troubled nations of Europe. In Africa, South Africa is doing pretty well. Australian economy is looking up but there are no signs of full recovery from global recession. Russian economy is oil-based. It is supplying oil and gas to Europe and other parts of the world. The situation of 2012 is not very rosy, given that monsoons are weak and delayed and industrial production is down around the world. The most immediate risk to the global recovery is that delayed or insufficient policy action will further escalate euro area crisis, said one IMF official.

On June 16 2012, India's growth forecast for 2012 was cut sharply to 6.1 percent from 6.8 percent. Next year, the economy is expected to grow only 6.5 percent, much less than April's prediction of a 7.3 percent expansion. Canada is still expected to grow 2.1 percent this year and 2.2 percent next year.

It has based the latest projections on three assumptions. Firstly, policymakers are expected to take enough action to ease the financial conditions in the euro area, including Greece and Spain, through 2013. Secondly, the IMF does not expect the U.S. fiscal policy to tighten sharply next year. Thirdly, it expects emerging markets to take steps to boost growth pace.

On June 28 2012, a deal was struck by euro area leaders. IMF welcomed that move. It released its update to Global Financial Stability Report, which said the risks to financial stability increased in the second quarter of 2012. The reasons were continued slow global recovery and fears about the quality of bank assets in Europe.

An update to the IMF's Fiscal Monitor released today indicated that fiscal adjustment in both advanced and emerging economies is proceeding as expected. Advanced economy budget deficits are forecast to decline by about 0.75 percent of GDP this year and about 1 percent of GDP in 2012, the report said.

While Spain and Italy are implementing sizable deficit reductions in the next two years, the adjustment is proceeding in Greece, Ireland and Portugal.

The recent deterioration in the political and economic climate in Greece serves as a warning about the potential onset of "adjustment fatigue," which remains a threat to continued reforms, the Fiscal Monitor added.

China's economic recovery is yet to gain momentum and the economic strains may continue for some more time, Premier Wen Jiabao has warned, the official Xinhua news agency reported. The country's economic recovery is not yet stable and economic hardships may continue for a period of time, said Jiabao. The Chinese economy expanded 7.6 percent in the second quarter, marking the weakest growth rate since the first quarter of 2009. In the second half of the year, the government will increase efforts to fine-tune its policies and make policies more targeted and effective, Wen Jiabao averred. The State Council had earlier warned the economy is currently facing "increasing downward pressure."

The Premier noted that the economy is running at a slower, but more stable pace. The economic growth rate is still within the government target range set early this year and the stabilization policies taken by the government are working, he added. China's economic fundamentals remain sound and the country still enjoys huge growth potential, Wen Jiabao finally said.

However, concerns remain over the economy's ability to sustain its growth momentum. On July 5, the People's Bank of China unexpectedly reduced the interest rate for a second time in less than a month. The bank has cut the reserve requirement rate three times since November 2011.

The Asian Development Bank last week cut China's growth forecast for 2012 to 8.2 percent from 8.5 percent citing a fall in exports, industrial output and investment. The lender also lowered the 2013 growth projection to 8.5 percent from 8.7 percent.

Conclusion

IMF has not painted a rosy picture of the global economic scenario. War, recession and financial uncertainty have taken their toll around the world. People are investing more in gold and less in stocks. That is why ten grams of gold sold for 31,700 rupees in New Delhi in July 2012. People do not trust industry or stock markets to increase their earnings. They are using banks, land investment and gold to enhance their earnings. World trade has taken a serious beating due to wars and West Asia, the North Korea crisis and US-Iran standoff on nuclear weapons. The world must change this status quo. A meeting of IMF must be arranged. All countries must find ways and means o end the four-year-old era of recession. Fuel prices must be slashed. Bank interest rates must be cut down. Loan should be disbursed in a more liberal manner. Food commodity prices must be slashed so that poor people may be able to survive. These recessionary trends can be reversed only if humans check their greed and try to be more humane.

Chapter 16

UNDF: A Fund for Democracies

Introduction

On July 4 2005, the then UN Secretary-General, Mr. Kofi Annan, announced the creation of the UN Democracy Fund at the African Union summit. The World Summit (2005) reaffirmed democracy as "a universal value." So, there is no single model of democracy. It does not belong to any country or region. On August 31 2006, Mr. Annan called on all Members States to support Fund and use it as an innovative mechanism for advancing the UN democracy agenda. In April 2007, at the UN Democracy Fund's fourth Advisory Board meeting, Secretary-General Ban Ki-moon averred that promotion of democracy is inseparable for UN's broader work for security, development and human rights. In 2012, the Fund has assumed more importance, given that countries are painfully inching towards democracy through means that are violent or peaceful.

Hoe UNDF Works

The Secretary-General's Advisory Board is UNDEF's main governing mechanism. It comprises 19 members. They include: 13 Member States (seven largest contributors to UNDEF, Australia, France, Germany, India, Japan, Qatar and USA; and six countries that represent the balance of UN Members, Mali, Mozambique, Peru, Philippines, Romania and Vanuatu); four personal representatives of the Secretary-General (Ms. Aye Aye Thant, President of U Thant Institute; Professor Adebayo Olukoshi, Executive Secretary of Council for the Development of Social Science in Africa; and Professor Michael Doyle of Columbia University; and Mr. Amir A. Dossal, Executive Director of United Nations Office of Partnerships); and two representatives of non-governmental organizations (Mr. Ziad Abdel Samad, Executive Director of Arab NGO Network for Development; and Mr. Nicholas Howen, Secretary-General of the International

Commission of Jurists). The 2008 Advisory Board was appointed by the Secretary-General in January 2008. The next meeting was organized on July 15 2008.

The PCG

The Programme Consultative Group (PCG) serves as UN inter-agency mechanism that provides expert advice and is comprised of DPA, DPKO, OHCHR, UNDGO, UNDP, UNIFEM, and UNODC. The Peace building Support Office also participates in its meetings. Fund's office has an Executive Head, two professional staff, one Junior Professional Officer, interns and support staff. Fund launched its first call for proposals on April 15 2006 and its second call on November 15 2007.

UNDEF launched its second round of projects in November 2007 and received 1,873 applications. After having consultations with PCG, UN Resident Coordinators and the Expert Groups, UNDEF produced a list that had 86 projects. In mid-May 2008, 86 projects were approved by the Secretary-General. Currently, UNDEF is in the process of negotiating project documents with project implementing agencies. Grants were given later.

UNDEF also participated in a meeting on world movement for democracy in Kiev (April 2008). It did take part in a round-table meet on the issue of role of multilateral organizations in supporting democracy in Stockholm (April 2008). Finally, its representatives attended a NGO meeting organized by the UN Office for the High Commissioner for Human Rights in Geneva in April 2008.

International Day of Democracy

On September 15 2008, the first International Day of Democracy was organized following the proclamation of this date in the General Assembly Resolution 62/7. UNDEF hosted an "Information Event" at Dag Hammarskjöld Library Auditorium on September 15 2008.

Supply of Funds for UNDF

Thirty-five Member States have contributed to the Fund, which has received approximately US$96 million to till 2008.

Conclusion

This organ of the UN is basically focusing on the democratization of those States that are heading towards democratic regime system. Many countries have democracy for namesake. They are being persuaded by the UN to become truly democratic by the UNDF. Funds for the campaigns and seminars are generated by UN itself. Eventually dictator countries would realize that democracy is the only elixir left for the human race. Teething troubles are there but UNDF is going great guns at the global democratic front.

Chapter 17

ECOSOC: Elections of 2011-12

Introduction

The Economic and Social Council has an election system that helps it appoints members. It has 54 members and 18 seats are either renewed or newly elected every year according to geographical representation.

Distribution of Seats

The scheme is as follows:

Table 1-II: Regional Distribution of Seats

Region of World	Total	Open in 2011
1. African States	14 seats	5 seats
2. Asian States	11 seats	3 seats
3. Eastern European States	6 seats	1 seat
4. Latin American and Caribbean States	10 seats	4 seats
5. Western European and other States	13 seats	5 seats

Some Member States also serve on ECOSOC's various commissions; they are elected by ECOSOC for three or four years.

Member Status in 2012

The most recent election of 18 new members to the UN Economic and Social Council was completed on October 24 2011. The member states were elected to fill the open seats. The details are as follows:

(A) African States: Burkina Faso, Lesotho, Libya, Nigeria, and Ethiopia

(B) Asian States: Indonesia, India, and Japan

(C) Eastern Europe: Belarus

(D) Latin America: Brazil, Cuba, Dominican Republic, and El Salvador

(E) Western European and Other States: France, Germany, Spain, Ireland, and Turkey

These eighteen new members joined ECOSOC on 1 January 2012 to replace the states whose terms expire at the end of 2011. The Netherlands and Switzerland were also elected in the place of Belgium and Norway. Hungary relinquished its seat in favor of Bulgaria.

Germany and France have been serving on the ECOSOC council for more than 60 years and Japan is entering its 30th year.

Next Election Spree

The next elections will likely be held in October 2012. Therefore, 18 seats will be open, as terms of some States would end on December 31 2012. These States are as follows: Argentina, Bahamas, Bangladesh, Belgium, Canada, Chile, Comoros, Egypt, Ghana, Iraq, Italy, Mongolia, Philippines, Rwanda, Slovakia, Ukraine, the United States and Zambia.

Conclusion

The ECOSOC has a democratic election system. Its 18 seats are renewed as per a preset programme and schedule. It is an important economic think tank of the UNO. We shall keep our valued readers apprised of the latest developments in ECOSOC.

Chapter 18

UNSC: Pakistan against Granting India Permanent Seat

Introduction

On January 27 2012, Pakistan opposed a key proposal by India, Japan, Germany and Brazil to expand the powerful UNSC, describing it as "zero-sum" that was likely to help only G-4 nations. The G4's draft resolution was the focus of the first day of the eighth round of inter-governmental negotiations on UNSC reforms. Since it is a roadblock on the way to India's seat in UNSC, India has taken Pak view quite seriously. Note that Pakistan has always been spoiling India's apple-cart at the UNSC.

Four Nations Unite

The four nations had issued a joint statement that said their proposal focuses on two aspects of Security Council reform that were: (a) expansion in membership in both categories, permanent and non-permanent; and (b) the working methods of the 15-member Council should be improved.

Pakistan joined the UNSC as a non-permanent member for a two-year term. It called the decision of four nations a "short resolution."

Haroon's Tough Stand

Pakistani envoy, Mr. Haroon, said that if this scheme were accepted, there would be 4 winners and 188 losers in UN. Now, UN has 193 members but excluding the five veto-holding permanent members, the tally comes to 188. Pak envoy said that G-was never able to get significant support for its draft resolution.

He sought to undermine the support for this G-4 proposal. Pak envoy said the group claims that it has the support of 80 member states, but "the same number keeps being repeated ever since. This is not even a simple majority."

Given the idea of limited expansion, adding four to six new permanent members will create imbalance between the elected and non-elected members, thereby impacting working methods and relationship of the Security Council, he said. He said such proposals will only help enlarge the "club of the privileged" who will have a vested interest in addressing most issues in the Council, "further draining the oxygen out of the Assembly, and enhancing the domination of the Security Council." "It will increase divisions and tensions, not only within the United Nations, but within various regions, contradicting the objective of promoting peace and security," Haroon underlined. He said on the issue of Council reform, Africa united the entire membership while the G-4 is seen to divide it. It is evident from the ongoing negotiations that a number of member states favour a "compromise solution". Pakistan, along with its partners in the Uniting for Consensus Group (UfG), has emphasized the value of a fair compromise, the envoy said.

India's Stand

India has said the 15-nation UN Security Council should be expanded to include about 10 more members. So, the total number of members in UNSC can be 25.

Participating in the 8th round of intergovernmental negotiations on UN Security Council reforms, India's Permanent Representative to the UN Ambassador (Mr. Hardeep Singh Puri) said that India thought that reform and expansion of the UNSC were mandatory if realities were taken in full view. A reformed SC, with expansion in the permanent and non-permanent categories, shall increase the Council's credibility and effectiveness in dealing with global issues. Puri said that an expanded Council should have a total of 25-26 members.

He said structural reform of the Council should respond to the pressing need for credible improvements in the global governance architecture.

"Concrete developments are being witnessed in other international institutions such as the IMF, World Bank," he said.

Conclusion

It seems that despite heavy support to India from the corners of the West, it may not be able to secure a seat in the UNSC as a permanent member. India has always been overambitious in this context but its desire has not been fulfilled. We suggest that India take a neutral stance on this issue. It must not hanker after the permanent seat. It can contribute a lot to UN and world even as an ordinary member.

Chapter 19

UNSC: Resolution on Nuclear Disarmament

Introduction

Nuclear disarmament is the process of removing nuclear weapons from States under the Un so that they are not able to use them to the detriment of others and also, the weapons are used for the production of energy or for research in the field of medicine or are disposed of in a scientific manner so that they do not pose a threat to ecology or humanity or both.

Commendable Efforts of UN

In September, 2009, The UNSC summit was chaired by US President Barack Obama to pass a comprehensive resolution on nuclear non-proliferation and disarmament. This was the fifth summit-level meeting of the UNSC and the first time an American president will chair it. "Our goal in this regard is to underscore the global reach of proliferation threats, the broadly shared obligation to respond to these threats, and the positive steps that have been taken to reduce nuclear dangers and the essential role of the Security Council in addressing growing and pressing nuclear threats," Susan Rice (UN Ambassador to UN) said.

The focus was on three areas: (1) "The US and other international efforts, particularly among the permanent five members of the Security Council, the nuclear powers, to move in a direction that is reinforcing of the goal that the President articulated of a world without nuclear weapons. So there is a significant disarmament aspect of this. (2) The resolution emphasised on the means to strengthen the global nuclear non-proliferation regime. (3) The third area relates to securing loose nuclear materials, a very important goal that the US President Barack Obama has long articulated.

Current Scene

Russia, US, UK, India, Pakistan, France, China, Israel and Russia have n-bombs. Further, Iran, North Korea, South Korea, militant groups operating in West Asia and groups operating in Pakistan have either the access to fissile material or crude nuclear weapons of their own. The reports received by the author do not indicate whether they certainly have such weapons or weapon-grade material. Iran has denied the charges of possessing n-weapons or n-grade fissile material. The IAEA frisked the country but could not find any fissile material at any of Iran's nuclear research facilities. The threat remains, though. The militants can use the nuclear option against the US or its allies. Nuclear technology is sophisticated as well as dangerous.

Conclusion

Countries can be told to shed n-weapons but we would have to snatch n-bombs from terror elements through bloody battles, even wars. This is an issue UN his been trying to address for the past 40 years. No solutions are in sight, though.

Chapter 20

UNSC: Palestinians Warned over Key Resolution

Introduction

On January 20, 2011, Palestinian envoys stepped up lobbying for a UN Security Council resolution condemning Israeli settlement building but the United States spoke out strongly against the initiative.

The USA warned at the UNO that putting the resolution to a Security Council vote would complicate peace efforts. It has still not said though whether it would veto the measure.

The Palestinian resolution against Israel's building in the occupied territories and East Jerusalem was formally put to the 15-member council; Lebanon, Brazil and South Africa were the council sponsors.

Palestinian Standpoint on Israeli Settlement

Palestinian Ambassador to the UN, Mr. Ryad Mansour, said the resolution would help revive direct talks. Palestinians refused to take part in talks since Israel ended a moratorium on settlements at the end of September 2010.

"There are a lot of political activities in all corners of the globe, in all capitals," Mansour told reporters. "Our objective is to remove this obstacle from the process of negotiations."

"We are working very hard with all Security Council members, including the United States of America, to succeed in having the council adopt this draft resolution," he said. "That would send a very powerful message to the occupying power, to Israel, to listen."

No vote is expected for several days, possibly weeks. And the United States warned the Palestinians against pressing for a vote.

A council resolution "would only complicate efforts to achieve that goal," said an expert on the issue. He was supporting the objections raised by the US ambassador to UNO.

The United States was alone among the five permanent veto-wielding members of the Security Council in opposing the resolution. The other four -- Britain, China, France and Russia -- have all indicated they would probably vote for the resolution, diplomats said.

The resolution was one tool of a new diplomatic offensive by the Palestinian Authority. It got recognition from 107 countries. Mansour said he was confident that two thirds of the 192 UN members would be signed up. Israeli diplomats missed the Security Council debate because of a strike by Israeli Foreign Ministry staff.

Conclusion

Israel is building settlement colonies in the disputed territory and Palestinians are opposing the move. Due to American intervention, Palestine is not able to get its land. Israel is hostile towards Palestinian demands and Hezbullah is after the blood of Israelis. This complicated situation in West Asia has catapulted the world to the brink of a major war, which may be triggered at any point of time (due to the lack of patience of the Palestinian peoples). UNSC must intervene to find out amicable solutions of the problem. In our view, construction should not be done by Israel on the disputed land pieces. When issues are settled between Israel and Palestine, Israel should go ahead with construction.

Chapter 21

New International Economic Order

Introduction

The **New International Economic Order** (NIEO) was a set of proposals put forward during the 1970s by some developing countries through the United Nations Conference on Trade and Development to promote their interests by improving their terms of trade, increasing development assistance, developed-country tariff reductions and other modes. This system was supposed to support Third World countries. It was due to replace the Bretton Woods system. The USA and other developed nations are the beneficiaries of the Bretton Woods system. The basic gist of NIEO is "zero-sum game." It means that no party gains in the parlance of world trade. At the most, the rich countries may gain, at the expense of the poor ones. Politics always interferes in the formation and implementation of any global economic mechanism and this fact is true about NIEO as well. The Declaration for the Establishment of a New International Economic Order, adopted by the United Nations General Assembly in 1974, is the source of NIEO. The trade, financial, commodity and debt-related issues are considered in the gamut of NIEO.

NIEO Vital for World

NIEO led to the initiation of "North-South Dialogue; it is a series of discussions between developed and developing countries to enhance the economic cooperation and bring about transformation of global economy. Besides the Declaration, a Programme of Action and a Charter of Economic Rights and Duties of States were adopted. During 1970s and 1980s, developing nations supported NIEO. They wanted its documents to be adopted by the UN General Assembly. However, political upheavals and conflict between east and the West did not allow NIEO to take concrete shape. Non-legal, non-binding Restrictive Business Practice Code was adopted in 1980. Common Fund for Commodities was made effective in 1989.

It was meant to be a revision of the international economic system in favour of Third World countries, replacing the Bretton Woods system, which had benefited the leading states that had created it–especially the United States.

Principles of NIEO

(1) Developing countries are allowed to control the activities of multinational corporations operating within their territory. (2) They would allowed to nationalize or expropriate foreign property on conditions that they deem fit. (3) They can set up associations of primary commodities producers similar to the OPEC. (4) International trade should be based on the need to ensure stable, equitable and remunerative prices for raw material, generalized non-reciprocal and non-discriminatory tariff preferences. The transfer of technology to developing countries would also be facilitated, as per NIEO norms. Economic and technical assistance would be given to such countries without any qualms or hidden costs.

Resource Allocation Mechanisms

An authoritative allocation mechanism involves direct control of resources. But more market-oriented private allocation mechanisms are to be created to balance the functioning of the economic order, say Haggard and Simmons aver. The nations of the southern hemisphere countries wanted authoritative solutions while deciding on resource allocation. North thought the opposite, though.

Central Planning and Free Market Mechanism

NIEO proposes central planning, as opposed to free markets. Tensions and disagreements between developed and developing countries continue. Developing block expects a greater degree of special treatment than industrialized one. This demand was expressed through the NIEO and Charter of Economic Rights and Duties of States (promoted by UNCTAD in 1970s). The Charter was never accepted by developing countries and is now defunct. But political, economic and social concerns that inspired it are active. The Charter called for restitution for economic and social costs of colonialism, racial discrimination and foreign domination. It would have imposed a duty on all states to adjust the prices of exports to their imports. The realization of NIEO was an impetus for developing country support for the Tokyo Round of trade negotiations. Critics of WTO comment that nothing came out of Tokyo and Uruguay Rounds of Talks for developing countries.

Price Regulation

The powerful countries of North America and Western Europe felt threatened by NIEO and tried to criticize and minimize it; according to professor Harry Johnson, the most efficient way to help the poor is to transfer resources from those most able to pay to those most in need. Instead of this, NIEO proposes that those poor countries that have monopoly power should be able to extort these transfers. In practice such power has caused most harm to other poor countries. Commanding prices above their natural level usually reduces consumption and thus causes unemployment among producers. Moreover, price regulation typically gives the extra income to those in control of who is allowed to produce, e.g., to governments or land-owners.

French Connection

NIEO is based on the (French) mercantilist idea that international trade would be a zero-sum game (i.e., causes no net benefits), and on the view that it benefits the rich at the expense of the poor. Some American economists challenge the idea of trade as a zero-sum game transaction.[2]

Central planning versus free markets

NIEO also proposes central planning, as opposed to free markets.

Conclusion

NIEO has been taken as a threat by North America and Western Europe. The best way to help the poor is to transfer resources from those most able to pay to those most in need. On the other hand, the NIEO proposes that those poor countries that have monopoly power should be able to extort these transfers. This power has harmed other poor countries, the West contemplates. Getting prices above their natural level usually reduces consumption and this can lead to causes high levels of unemployment among producers. Further, price regulation gives the extra income to those in control of who is allowed to produce. NIEO, in sum, is only in the nascent stage. We shall apprise our valued readers about its status in the subsequent editions of this very volume.

Chapter 22
BRICS

Introduction

BRICS is the joint forum of five countries viz, Brazil, Russia, India, China and South Africa. Member States discuss issues of bilateral and regional interests. The forum is viewed with respect in all diplomatic and global circles, primarily because of the presence of one superpower and two regional powers in it. Its efficacy has been proved over time. The member States are sincere and cooperative. The name was coined in 2001 by US investment bank Goldman Sachs to group together fast-growing economies and the group held its first summit in 2009. South Africa joined in 2011 at the third summit in China.

Theme

The Summit theme was: *BRICS Partnership for Global Stability, Security and Prosperity*.

Past Record

Dr. Manmohan Singh had met Dmitry Medvedev, Hu Jintao and Luiz Inácio Lula da Silva during BRIC summit in June 2009. The third summit was held in China in April, 2011. The fourth summit was organized in New Delhi from March 29 to April 3, 2012. The leaders of Brazil, Russia, India, China and South Africa attended the **Fourth** meeting of the bloc. It is being viewed as a stellar non-Western alliance. US and EU watched the proceedings carefully.

Members Agree to Set Up BRICS Bank

Presidents Dilma Rousseff of Brazil, Dmitry Medvedev of Russia, Hu Jintao of China and Jacob Zuma of South Africa attended the meet. Indian PM, Dr. Manmohan Singh, was the host member. Member Sates discussed the creation of a new development bank at the summit. They are also keen to strengthen collective diplomatic clout. The agenda was the creation of the BRICS Bank. It would fund development projects and infrastructure in developing nations. It could be an alternative to World Bank and the Asian Development Bank. The Delhi Declaration read (we quote): "The bank would mobilize "resources for infrastructure and sustainable development projects in BRICS and other emerging economies and developing countries, to supplement the existing efforts of multilateral and regional financial institutions for global growth and development.

China Grilled by Tibetans

BRICS started at Hotel Taj Palace in New Delhi. The demonstration by hundreds of Tibetan exiles protesting against the presence of Chinese President Hu Jintao was the sad issue. A 27-year-old activist set himself alight during an anti-Beijing demonstration before running screaming down a street in gruesome scenes captured by media. He died two days later. He became the first person outside China to self-immolate and added his name to a list of 29 others who have killed themselves since March 2012 to protest alleged repression by China in Tibet.

Commerce Vital for Members

The relationship "aspires to create a new global architecture." The Delhi summit is expected to focus on increasing intra-BRICS trade, which expanded by 28 percent last year to $230 billion. Two agreements to simplify processes and provide credit facilities for exporters were signed. Leaders also met in private to discuss bilateral issues.

Delhi Summit and Its Outcome

At the end of the summit, the Declaration discussed the bloodshed in Syria, the Iranian nuclear crisis and Europe's debt problems. US and EU monetary policies were indirectly censured. Brazilian President asked for making exports more competitive.

India and Brazil at the BRICS

A day after the BRICS summit, India and Brazil signed six pacts in areas ranging from science and biotechnology to cultural exchanges. They supported BRICS' stand on Syria and Iran. They called for resolving the crisis in West Asia through dialogue. Under **Science Without Borders**, they inked a pact that envisages placement of Brazilian students and young researchers in India. It will be funded by Brazil. Dr. Singh agreed to enhance consultations on reform of global governance system, especially in the context of the reforms of UN and in G-20 process. India, Brazil, Japan and Germany are part of the G-4 grouping that's pitching for a permanent seat in a reformed UN Security Council. The two leaders told their officials to launch an action plan to exploit the potential in areas like trade, education, science and technology, environment, defence, space and nuclear energy.

Conclusion

The summit was successful. The master agreement is aimed at reducing the demand for fully convertible currencies for transactions among BRICS nations. This would help in reducing transaction costs of intra-BRICS trade. The confirmation facility pact defines confirmation of credit lines on receipt of a request from exporter, exporter's bank or importer's bank. The pacts are expected to scale up intra-BRICS trade; currently, this value is $230 billion. BRICS has set a target of $500 billion by 2015. The pacts were finalized after a meeting of trade ministers of five countries. China did not flex its economic muscle during the course of talks. Hu Jintao agreed to play constructive roles in promoting global economic growth, improving global economic governance, strengthening multilateralism and democracy in international relations.

Chapter 23

UNFCC: UN Climate Talks (2011)

Introduction

The UN Climate talks concluded in Durban on December 11, 2011. The world agreed to implement global climate change regime from 2020. India became a force to reckon with in climate change talks and implementation of decisions taken by States present during the talks. India has become the moral voice of the developing world. US and EU were forced to listen to the demands of this most important block. Life was given to Kyoto Protocol; it would continue to be effective beyond 2012.

New Global Regime

From 2012, 195 parties to the UN Framework Convention on Climate Change (UNFCC) will start negotiating for a new global regime that would be made final by 2015. It would be implemented from 2020. A Green Climate Fund would be set up. Technology Centres would be established under the Cancun Agreements. Adaptation and transparency mechanisms would be put in place. Ms. Jayanthi Natarajan, India's Environment Minister, was present during the talks. She played a very crucial role to make the Talks a big success, especially for the developing nations. Ms. Natarajan made two demands. **Firstly**, she stated that the tenet of equity must remain intact in new climate regime. **Secondly**, she demanded that the new global deal be implemented from 2020. EU had asked for a roadmap to a new treaty and China and India had opposed its move. But China supported India and the latter forged the agreement in favour of the developing world. The final text of the Durban talks promised to create a protocol...with legal force. The term **legally-binding** was circumvented, much to the dismay of EU block.

Major Decisions

1. New deal to be finalized by 2015; to be launched by 2020. 2.

Second phase of Kyoto Protocol secured. 3. Green Climate fund launched. 4. Green tech development mechanism put in motion. 5. Equity finds place in future climate talks, yet again. 6. Transparency mechanism.

Repercussions of Agreement

1. India regains leadership of developing world, yet again. 2. EU gains at the cost of US; it also falls out with developing countries. 3. Small island states support EU front and so, they lose credibility. 4. Basic grouping more fragile than before; India China remain close but Brazil and South Africa move away from Talks results.

India's Advantages in Deal

(1) India wins in all major negotiations. (2) Ten years of economic growth of India and no cap on carbon generation. (3) Common but differentiated responsibility tenet retained.

India's Disadvantages in Deal

(1) IPR and technology not given a good seat in new deal. (2) Loopholes for developing world not fully blocked. (3) Agriculture brought under the gamut of climate change.

Key Concerns

India was worried about the acceptance of a "legally-binding" agreement, for it could hurt growth. There was a tussle between the India-China-Brazil block and US. The former block wanted a concerted effort to be made to keep temperature rising by more than 2 degrees Celsius over the pre-industrial level. Latter block (led by US) wanted symmetrical obligation from the first one. EU aligned with Alliance of Small island States. Jayanti Natarajan broke the impasse by adding the word 'equity' in the long-term cooperation agreement. So, India would have greater latitude to design its own response even if concrete cuts in carbon emissions are likely to be the new governing norms. That way, India can indulge in technological and business innovations without getting any kind of reprimand about carbon emissions from the developed world in general or EU block in particular.

India Faces New Challenges

The challenges before India are as follows: (1) India must fight to implement the principle of equity in the new deal. (2) It must negotiate for five years to chalk out the new global regime. (3) It must ensure that

Kyoto Protocol (Phase II) starts from 2012-17. (4) It must ensure that review of the existing commitments of the developing nations is done.

Conclusion

This is a major victory for India on the environmental front. It has proved that it can take care of the interests of all developing nations through its sheer guts and eco-friendly logic.

Chapter 24
Nuclear Summit (2012)

Introduction

The second NSS was organized in Seoul (South Korea) March 26-27 2012. In the second Summit, the heads of more than 53 country heads and organization CEOs too part. Besides, the heads of many concerned organizations were also present during the course of this Summit. From the Chinese side, Mr. Hu Jin Tao was present. Dr. Manmohan Singh was present, too; so was the US President, Mr. Barrack Obama. The Summit was organized at the Convention and Exhibition centre of Seoul. It was a grand success.

Agenda of the Summit (2012)

As per the statement of Mr. Obama, the agenda priorities at the 2012 summit were as follows:

(1) To deepen our cooperation and to strengthen the institutions and partnerships which help prevent nuclear materials from ever falling into the hands of terrorists. (2) To strengthen the International Atomic Energy Agency (IAEA) with the resources and authorities it needs to meet its responsibilities. (3) To take specific and concrete actions to secure the nuclear materials and to prevent illicit trafficking and smuggling.

List of Participants

(A) Republic of Korea, Algeria, Argentina, Armenia, Australia, Azerbaijan, Belgium, Brazil, Canada, Chile, China, Czech Republic, Denmark, Egypt, Finland, France, Gabon, Georgia, Germany, Hungary, India, Indonesia, Israel, Italy, Japan, Jordan, Kazakhstan, Lithuania, Malaysia, Mexico, Morocco, Netherlands, New Zealand, Nigeria, Norway, Pakistan, Philippines, Poland, Romania, Russia, Saudi Arabia, Singapore, South Africa, Spain, Sweden, Switzerland, Thailand, Turkey, UAE, UK, Ukraine, USA, Vietnam. (B) Heads UN, IAEA and EU. (C) INTERPOL.

History

The possibility of nuclear terrorism became a real threat after 9/11, which increased the importance of strengthening nuclear security to prevent nuclear materials from being misused by terrorist groups. The threat of **N-terrorism** could not be addressed by a single country or strategic alliance. The entire world was supposed to motivate to curb this deadly menace. On July 16, 2006, George W. Bush and Vladmir Putin jointly announced the organization of the Global Initiative to Combat Nuclear Terrorism (GICNT). It is a voluntary initiative aimed at fostering international cooperation to prevent terrorists from acquiring, transporting or using nuclear materials or radioactive substances. It is also designed to prevent hostile actions against nuclear facilities and to respond to incidents involving the use of radiological or nuclear materials. GICNT members work to combine experience and expertise from the nonproliferation, counter-proliferation, and counter-terrorism fields. They strengthen global institutions through integration of collective capabilities and resources. They maintain a network for partners to share information and expertise in a legally non-binding capacity. Thirteen nations gathered in Rabat (Morocco) on October 30-31 2006 for the first Plenary Meeting. They asked for a framework for partnership and a system for organizing events and charting progress. The Statement of Principles was the final product that guides GICNT efforts. Any country may choose to officially endorse in order to become a partner of the GICNT. In NSS (2010), hosted by USA, highlighted the contributions of GICNT to international efforts to combat nuclear terrorism. The most recent plenary meeting in Abu Dhabi resulted in several changes to the GICNT. The partnership adopted a revised Terms of Reference, activated an Implementation and Assessment Group (IAG). It selected Spain as Coordinator for IAG. It selected USA and Russia to continue serving as Co-Chairs. The first Nuclear Security Summit, the largest international meeting relating to the nuclear issue, was held in Washington in April 2010. The summit was attended by leaders from 47 states and 3 international organizations (UN, EU, and IAEA), including the P5 nations (nuclear weapons states) and states not party to the NPT, such as India, Pakistan, and Israel. The leaders discussed plans to strengthen nuclear security by preventing the misuse of nuclear materials by non-State actors.

Views of Heads

President Barrack Obama in his Prague Speech on April 5, 2009 called for making the GICNT a "durable international institution." Again, the importance of planning for conference was clarified when Obama explained his view (in 2012 Summit) that "we have the opportunity, as partners, to ensure that our progress is not a fleeting moment, but part of a serious and sustained effort."

The host country of the summit plays an important role in setting the agenda. The North Korean nuclear issue is expected to top the agenda of the 2012 summit; and the summit may attempt to deal with a broader spectrum of non-proliferation issues than in Washington. In advance of the meeting date, negotiations will take place primarily amongst multi-national civil servants. It is open to question that for Germany, the table lists the leader of their delegation to be their President, but not the normally more authoritative office of Chancellor; one can interpret this as the nation-state Germany contracting out its global security concerns and responsibilities to the European Union, an improvised aggregate state with features of a continuing experimental nature. In terms of other listed national leaders, the same matter concerning the de facto versus de jure authority is most relevant for Russia, a Permanent Member of the UN Security Council and the second Nuclear Weapon State. As Brazil and Vietnam are planning to increase their nuclear power plants significantly, questions can also be raised as to who is included in their delegations to the summit. Although Brazil is on a good overall economic trajectory, its culture has a history of coups, and securing enriched nuclear fuel and enrichment equipment practical knowledge can be a difficult task. It is open to question whether or not any Brazilian legislative leaders, not of Her Excellency President Rousseff's political party, will be at the Summit.

GICNT

The GICNT is an international partnership of 83 nations and 4 official observers working to improve capacity on a national and international level for prevention, detection and response to a nuclear terrorist event. Partners join it by endorsing the Statement of Principles, a set of broad nuclear security objectives. Nations organize and host workshops, conferences and exercises to share best practices for implementing the Statement of Principles. This organization holds plenary meetings to discuss improvements and changes to partnership. The Stimson Center stated that GICNT will be useful for countries to fulfill their UNSCR 1540 commitments. But many countries that have fissile material cannot afford the funds and manpower needed to implement necessary safeguards and GICNT does not provide a mechanism to address this shortcoming. This partnership of nations could impede nations' ability to "harmonize their long-term research and development programs as well as construct plans for dealing with the sources, magnitude, and appropriate responses to nuclear terrorist threats. It is an organization in a nascent stage, international political observers believe.

Statement of Principles

(1) Develop and improve accounting, control and physical protection systems for nuclear and other radioactive materials and substances. (2) Increase security of civilian nuclear facilities. (3) Improve the ability to detect nuclear and other radioactive materials to prevent illegal N-trafficking. (4) Improve capabilities of participants to search for, confiscate and establish safe control over illegally held nuclear or radioactive materials or devices using the same. (5) Prevent the provision of safe haven to terrorists and financial or economic resources to terrorists seeking to acquire or use nuclear and other radioactive materials. (6) Ensure adequate respective national legal and regulatory frameworks to provide for the implementation of appropriate criminal and civil liabilities for terrorists and those who facilitate acts of nuclear terrorism. (7) Improve capabilities of participants for response, mitigation and investigation in cases of terrorist attacks involving the use of nuclear materials. (8) Promote information sharing.

South Korea's Big Role

South Korea played a major role in organizing the NSS and deciding its agenda. It has gained even greater standing in international circles in the security field. It will play a leading role in establishing global governance in the security and political fields.

NSS Outcome

The Sous-Sherpas had reaffirmed the basic goals and principles on nuclear security agreed upon at the Washington Nuclear Security Summit (2010). In 2012, Seoul Nuclear Security Summit served as an opportunity for Korea to earn international recognition on its enhanced status following its hosting of the G20 Seoul Summit (2010). The stability of the Korean peninsula is vital for all powers of the world. The world has assured Korea that it would help it in case North Korea deliberately or inadvertently uses the nuclear option. NSS served as a forum for discussion of nuclear security issue as well as its interface with nuclear safety. The Fukushima nuclear accident, after the Tsunami attack on Japan (March 2011), was the issue under focus. In Seoul, the member countries have agreed to abide by the Statement of Principles. . The North Korean nuclear issue topped the agenda. The efforts to deal with non-proliferation issues than in Washington were viewed with warmth and mutual trust. All talks were held in a cordial atmosphere. The UN and its organs would fully support the initiatives taken at NSS (2012).

Plenary Meetings Venues

(1) June 30 2011 Daejeon (Korea) (2) June 29 2010 Abu Dhabi (3) June 16 2009 Hague (4) June 16-18 2008 Madrid (5) June 11-12 2007 Astana (6) February 12-13 2007 Ankara (7) October 30-31 2006 (Rabat).

Conclusion

The nations of the world have united against the menace of nuclear terrorism. Some terror elements have either procured or are trying to procure N-weapons. The countries of the world are fighting against them tooth and nail. NSS is the latest global initiative. With the cooperation of the members of NSS fold, the world would be able to nab the culprits before they are able to inflict any damage on the human race or the mother earth.

Chapter 25
UN: The Kashmir Imbroglio

Introduction

The relations between India and Pakistan have been affected by years of mistrust and suspicion ever since the partition of India (1947). The issue of contention between India and Pakistan is the Kashmir imbroglio. After an invasion by Pashtun tribesmen and Pakistani paramilitary forces, the Hindu Maharaja of the Dogra Kingdom of Jammu and Kashmir, Hari Singh, and its Muslim Prime Minister, Sheikh Abdullah, signed an Instrument of Accession with New Delhi. The First Kashmir War started after the Indian Army entered Srinagar, the capital of the state, to secure the area from the invading forces. The war ended in December 1948 when UN intervened. The Line of Control divided the Kashmir into territories administered by Pakistan (northern and western areas) and India (southern, central and northeastern areas). Pakistan contested the legality of the Instrument of Accession since the Dogra Kingdom has signed a standstill agreement with it. The Indo-Pakistani War of 1965 started following the failure of Pakistan's Operation Gibraltar, which was designed to infiltrate forces into Jammu and Kashmir to precipitate an insurgency against rule by India. The five-week war caused thousands of casualties on both sides. It ended in a United Nations (UN) mandated ceasefire and the subsequent issuance of the Tashkent Declaration. India and Pakistan went to war again in 1971, this time the conflict being over East Pakistan. The large-scale atrocities committed there by the Pakistan army led to millions of Bengali refugees pouring over into India. India, along with the Mukti Bahini, defeated Pakistan and the Pakistani forces surrendered on the eastern front. The war resulted in the creation of Bangladesh.

Conflict Can Have Nuclear Hues, Too

In 1998, India carried out the Pokhran-II nuclear tests which was followed by Pakistan's Chagai-I tests. Pakistan and India both have nuclear weapons and missiles to carry them. India has a nuclear submarine, too.

Ups and Downs Continue

After Lahore Declaration (February 1999), relations did improve. However, Pakistani paramilitary forces and Pakistani Army infiltrated in large numbers into the Kargil district of Indian Kashmir. This initiated the Kargil conflict after India moved in thousands of troops to successfully flush out the infiltrators. Although the conflict did not result in a full-scale war between India and Pakistan, relations between the two reached all-time low which worsened even further following the involvement of Pakistan-based terrorists in the hijacking of the Indian Airlines IC814 plane in December 1999. Attempts to normalize relations, such as the Agra summit held in July 2001, failed. An attack on the Indian Parliament in December 2001, which was blamed on Pakistan, which had condemned the attack caused a military standoff between the two countries which lasted for nearly a year raising fears of a nuclear conflict. However, a peace process, initiated in 2003, led to improved relations in the following years. Since the initiation of the peace process, several confidence-building-measures (CBMs) between India and Pakistan have taken shape. Samjhauta Express and Delhi–Lahore Bus service are two of these successful measures which have played a crucial role in expanding people-to-people contact between two countries. The initiation of Srinagar–Muzaffarabad Bus service (2005) and the opening of a trade route across the LoC (2008) reflect increasing eagerness to normalize relationship. The 2008 Mumbai attacks seriously undermined the relations between the two countries. India alleged Pakistan of harboring militants on their soil. Pakistan vehemently denied such claims. Relations are currently hampered since India has sent a list of 40 alleged fugitives in various terror strikes to Pakistan. Pakistan has declared that it has no intentions whatsoever of carrying out their extradition.

Conclusion

India wants 5180 sq. km. of Kashmir that have been given to China by Pakistan. ,In Muzaffarabad, the terror training camps continue. J&K is peaceful. The recent visit of the author and other journalists to Kashmir (March 8-11 2012) proves that Kashmiris want a peaceful solution to the problem. There are voices of dissent, though. However, these minor issues can be resolved, given that Kashmiris are basically peace-loving peoples. We hope that the Kashmir imbroglio would be resolved through tri-nation negotiations involving China, Pakistan and India. Kashmiris must be involved at every stage of the solution process.

Chapter 26
Sea Piracy

Introduction

Maritime piracy has been on the rise for much of the past decade, even as international efforts have helped reduce the number of successful hijackings, according to the International Maritime Bureau's (IMB) Piracy 2011 report. Large-scale attacks off the coast of Somalia in 2008 prompted the deployment of an ongoing international coalition of navies to the Gulf of Aden.

Glaring Data of Piracy

A report by OEF estimated the global cost of piracy for 2010 to be in the range of $7 to $12 billion. There were 439 worldwide piracy attacks in 2011, more than half of which were attributed to Somali pirates operating in the Gulf of Aden, the Red Sea, the Arabian Sea, the Indian Ocean, and off the coast of Oman. Other piracy hotspots for 2011 included the coast off Nigeria and Benin in West Africa, and Southeast Asia, near Indonesia. In the case of Somalia, analysts say one of the largest drivers of piracy is the lack of an efficient governing authority in the country.

Danger Zones

Pirate attacks are largely confined to four major areas: the Gulf of Aden, near Somalia and the southern entrance to the Red Sea; the Gulf of Guinea, near Nigeria and the Niger River delta; the Malacca Strait between Indonesia and Malaysia; and off the Indian subcontinent, particularly between India and Sri Lanka.

Somali pirates, by far the greatest global piracy threat, have increasingly pushed farther off the Somali coast. They have moved deeper into the Indian Ocean, off Seychelles and the Maldives, and further south along the East African coast, off Kenya, Madagascar, and Mozambique (2011). Somali piracy emerged as a potent force shortly after the regime of longtime Somali dictator Major General Mohamed Siad Barre collapsed in 1991. With the absence of any central governing authority, commercial fishing fleets began to exploit the country's coastline. Local fishermen responded by arming themselves, boarding illegal trawlers, and charging a fine of a few thousand dollars. Somali piracy tactics have centered on hijackings and kidnappings--lasting an average of six months--to extract large ransoms. Somali piracy has been largely free of violent tactics because it is in the pirates' interest to keep their hostages alive. In 2011, average ransom payments to Somali pirates were above $5 million. Piracy off West Africa has been driven much more by political and social grievances. In the Gulf of Guinea, many hijackings target oil tankers, with pirates seizing the oil and then selling it for a profit on the black market. There is evidence that Nigeria's rebel movement for the Emancipation of the Niger Delta (MEND)--which has pressured the Abuja government to more equitably allocate oil revenues--has been involved in attacks on oil tankers off the coast. In early March 2012, MEND claimed responsibility for shooting four police officers on a boat patrolling the Nembe river in Bayelsa state while indicating ties with pirate groups (al-Jazeera) in the region. Many Indian ships were also caught by Somali pirates in not so distant past. Many were able to come home after paying hefty ransom amounts. Some others were not so lucky, though.

Asian Connection

In Southeast Asia, piracy has focused on the ransacking of cargo fishing products. While attacks in the South China Sea decreased in 2011, the number of incidents off Indonesia rose for a second consecutive year, according to the IMB. These attacks have largely taken place in the Malacca Strait, through which 30 percent of the world's trade (VOA) and half of the world's oil shipments pass. In September 2011, Indonesia and Malaysia deployed two warships to the strait as part of a joint patrol targeting pirate attacks. The countries have also developed an "Eye in the Sky" operation with Singapore and Thailand, by which they jointly carry out air patrols above the strait. In late September 2011, Indonesian police arrested four suspected pirates thought to be part of an organized crime network (Jakarta Globe) operating across the strait.

Governance and Piracy

Many experts opine that the root of Somali's piracy problem has been the lack of an effective central government in Mogadishu, tied with limited economic opportunities throughout the country. Somalia is composed of a large number of clan groups, and the law is largely implemented at the local level. For many of these groups, particularly those in the Puntland province, piracy provides an economic lifeline, and so local authorities, if not directly involved, are willing to look the other way and refrain from prosecuting pirates. Somali pirates are able to sail hijacked ships back to the Somali shore and hold them there for months because there is no central government to enforce the rule of law in many coastal communities.

Global initiative to Combat Piracy on High Seas

The international community has taken a number of steps to tackle piracy since Somali pirates emerged as a threat to international maritime security four years ago. In 2008, the UN Security Council passed a series of measures targeting Somali piracy, culminating in the unanimous approval of U.S.-led Resolution 1851. The move authorized states with navies deployed in the Gulf of Aden to, with the permission of Somalia's Transitional Federal Government, take action against pirates and armed robbers within Somalia. Resolution 1851 facilitated the creation of the Contact Group on Piracy off the Coast of Somalia (CGPCS) in January 2009. The group was told to "address military and operational coordination, build capacity, address judicial issues and send public information related to piracy." Since January 2009, nine east African countries have signed the Djibouti Code of Conduct. This agreement was engineered by UN's International Maritime Organization.

UK hosted an international conference on the future of Somalia (Guardian) in London in February 2012 which focused on new international measures for combating and prosecuting piracy off the Somali coast. The steps included a joint Memorandum of Understanding between the British and Tanzanian governments allowing the British Royal Navy to transfer suspected Somali pirates to Tanzania for prosecution; an agreement that will see convicted pirates captured off the coast of Seychelles transferred to Somaliland for imprisonment; and the formation of an international task force on pirate ransoms. The international community also has at its disposal the UN Convention on the Law of the Sea. The treaty, which came into effect in 1994, is binding for 154 nations and the European Union. The United States has yet to ratify the agreement. The Convention governs "all aspects of ocean space," including the "settlement of disputes relating to ocean matters." It also makes "piracy a universal crime, and subjects pirates to arrest and prosecution by any nation," writes Georgetown University's Mark V. Vlasic for the Huffington Post. The Convention "provides the legal foundation to help combat piracy and prosecute piracy cases," he writes. The United States' refusal to adopt the treaty, despite support in the U.S. Senate and by the Obama administration, has complicated Washington's ability to tackle piracy with its international partners, Vlasic argues.

UN Resolutions

Connoisseurs emphasize that most of the current tactics do not address the state instability that allows piracy to flourish. After 2008 UN resolutions, 3 main naval missions have been deployed to Gulf of Aden, including NATO, EU, and U.S. operations. There are also independent navy ships-- including those of Australia, China, India, and Russia-- patrolling the corridor from all over the world. Many Somali pirates have adjusted their tactics and managed to avoid naval patrols by operating farther offshore, outside the Gulf of Aden. There are also too few ships patrolling the Gulf, writes the Atlantic Council's Murphy in a December 2011 piece for the Rusi Journal. "The current military response--with only a handful of navy ships available to provide protection on any given day--has just been a sticking plaster on a gaping wound," Spyroa Polemis, the chairman of the International Chamber of Shipping. Due to these challenges, many ships have started hiring armed guards as a preemptive deterrent for would-be attackers. However, while this tactic can be quite effective, Anyimadu cautions, there is not yet a process for regulating these guards, creating potential legal complications. As an example, she cites an incident off the coast of India whereby two Italian marines aboard a cargo ship (FT) shot and killed Indian fishermen suspected of being pirates. Shipping industry and national governments should coordinate their responses to the menace of sea piracy.

Conclusion

Somalia is creating trouble in Kenya and on high seas. The roots of bomb blasts in Nairobi can be traced to Somalia. Rebels have killed many people most of who are civilians. If this hunger problem is not solved, the world community may take a harsh action against pirates.

Chapter 27

ECOSOC: Global Recession

Introduction

In February 2008, Indian bourses crashed after the crash of home loan markets in the USA. It was triggered by the home loan crisis of the USA. The home loan parties (users of home loan) refused to pay loan and instead told the creditors to take homes because the home cost had gone down drastically. The stock markets of USA crashed. Later, Indian bourses came on their knees. Today, in 2012, we have not been able to overcome recessionary trends in India, Europe and the US.

Poor Economic Scenes

Greece, Italy and Spain are bankrupt. Germany and France are earning in Europe. They are supporting EU and handing out dole to countries like Greece through EU. In US, Wall Street firms, which were hitherto drivers of world economy, are bankrupt. Precious funds of the common man are in the drain. US economy has not recovered. EU's economy also does not show any signs of recovery. Indian economy is much, though.

What to Do?

Countries must remove their sight from luxuries and focus on normal production, the production that should focus on the needs of the masses. Luxury car production must be stopped. Alternatives of oil must be found out. The countries with oil reserves must be appeased at the earliest possible date. Reduce expenses on luxuries and produce more agricultural and industrial products that are of use to the common man. There is no alternative to hard work. The corporate sector thought that it can invest money and the profit would automatically come around. That is not so. Even industrial nations would have tpo work hard to earn their bucks, financial experts say.

Bourses, a Farce!

The firms that did not perform well had high bourses ratings in 2008. There is a difference between the real performance of a firm and its annual financial performance that is much hyped. Firms do not earn profits but their share prices shoot up. Firms do earn profits but their share prices are low. What is this? Man was by nature a theatrical anima. The failure of Wall Street firms has amply demonstrated this glaring fact to us all.

Conclusion

India has learnt its lessons. That is why its economic system is better than those of EU, US and Latin America. We have withered many a storm, too would pass. The corrections in stock markets ought to be real. What you earn must be yours; it must also accrue to you. Work and Survive attitude is better than Feign and Fail Posture, aver experts. Companies cannot see their profits soaring, their stock values skyrocketing and finally their investors biting the dust in a span of two or three years. Stock values adopt herculean values (positive and negative). Somehow, this trend does not seem to align with the actions and output trends of industrial and trade organizations. Business firms give concocted and window-dressed financial results so that the stock values may go up. That is why Wall Street failed in the middle of 2011. Today, people hate stock investments and trust gold as the single largest investment option. If global recession is to end, the private sector must come to terms with the realities of market earnings (must moderate), stock price rise (must be rational) and costs incurred (must be reasonable). If private firms do not get vital tips from the gloomy economic scene of today, they may be wiped off pretty soon, just like Ford, Gm, Chrysler, Citibank and other major player have been after the super crash of home loan markets in the Us (in February 2008).

Chapter 28

Democracy Knocks at the Door of Libyans

Introduction

On July 11, 2012, the UN Security Council welcomed the holding of Libya's first national elections during July 1-8 2012. This is an achievement for Libya's people in 50 years."The members of the Security Council congratulate the Libyan people on this occasion and commend their peaceful participation in the process, while strongly condemning the isolated incidents of violence that occurred," the 15-member UNSC said in July 2012.

Libya has Started Its Marathon Run on a Democratic Path

Elections are a milestone for Libya's democratic transition. Qadaffi had killed all democratic ambitions of the Libyan people. But now they can heave a sigh of relief. Council members praised the Libyan authorities, especially the High National Electoral Commission of Libya. The elections were smooth and fair, the observers noted.

Support was given by the UN Support Mission in Libya (**UNSMIL**) during the electoral process. Note that UNSMIL would give support to Libya during the next phase of its democratic transition, too. The actions would include the: (a) a process of preparing a new constitution; (b) promoting rule of law and protecting human rights; (c) restoring public security; (d) countering illicit arms proliferation; and (e) coordinating international assistance.

Secretary-General Ban Ki-moon and the head of UNSMIL (Ian Martin) congratulated the Libyan masses. Mr. Martin highlighted challenges an incoming government will face. He averred that elections "must not blind any of us to the enormous challenges that still lie ahead," particularly that of building security institutions. He had voiced concern over incidents of renewed fighting throughout Libya and called on authorities to address the causes of the conflicts and protect civilians. Armed clashes in recent months between various groups have tested the reach and authority of the government's security apparatus and ability to impose the rule of law.

Lesson for Other African and Asian Countries

The people's power and efforts of UNSMIL led to the concrete results for the Libyans. At last, they are breathing free air now. The UNO has made it possible for them to think and decide on their own. Qaddafi would never have allowed this to happen. It is time for the nations of Asia and Africa to follow this example and become democratic countries in the true sense of the world.

Conclusion

Democracy alone is the solution of most of the problems of humanity. Rational thinking, a check on free market mechanism and control over human greed are the three tenets that must be followed by all leaders and their followers alike. Libya would emerge as a major player in the affairs of the globe simply because its peoples would realize how much important democracy is for a nation.

Chapter 29

UN: Peacekeeping, Peacemaking and Peace-building

Introduction

UN armed forces were first used in 1948 to observe ceasefire in Kashmir and Palestine. It has been mentioned in the UN Charter that the use of such forces is allowed as a buffer between warring parties. This is called Peacekeeping. It was formalized in 1956 during the Suez Crisis between Egypt, Israel, France and the United Kingdom. Peacekeeping missions have taken many forms. They involve military troops from several countries. They work under the UN Security Council. Indian forces have taken part in such missions many times.

A Diary of Peacekeeping

In 1988, the UN Peacekeeping Forces were awarded the Nobel Prize for Peace. During the Cold War, peacekeeping was used in wars in the Middle East and Africa. Between 1948 and 1988, the UN undertook 13 peacekeeping missions involving lightly armed troops from neutral countries other than the permanent members of the Security Council. Canada, Sweden, Norway, Finland, India, Ireland and Italy have contributed their troops. Troops called "Blue Helmets" were allowed to use force only in self-defense. The missions enjoyed the consent of the parties at war. The blessing of the UN Security Council is a prerequisite.

Post Cold War Operations

With the end of the Cold War, the challenges of peacekeeping became complex. In order to respond to situations in which internal order had broken down and the civilian population was suffering, "second-generation" peacekeeping was developed to achieve multiple political and social objectives. The second-generation peacekeeping regime involves civilian experts and relief specialists as well as soldiers. In second-generation peacekeeping soldiers are authorized to employ force for reasons other than self-defense. In the 1990s, second-generation peacekeeping missions were undertaken in Cambodia (1991–93), former Yugoslavia (1992–95) and Somalia (1992–95). They did include troops from the permanent members of the UN Security Council and the developed and developing world (Australia, Pakistan, Ghana, Nigeria, Fiji and India).

In Bosnia and Herzegovina, the Security Council created safe areas to protect the predominantly *Bosniac* (Bosnian Muslim) population from Serbian attacks. UN troops were authorized to defend the areas with force. Between 1988 and 2000, more than 30 peacekeeping efforts were authorized. In 1993, more than 80,000 peacekeeping troops representing77 countries were deployed on missions around the globe. After 2000, annual UN expenditures on peacekeeping operations exceeded US$2 billion.

Since 1990, UN forces have supervised elections in many parts of the world, including Nicaragua, Eritrea and Cambodia. They encouraged peace negotiations in El Salvador, Angola and Western Sahara. They also distributed food and supplies in Somalia. UN troops acted well in Yugoslavia during its disintegration. In 1992, the UN created the Department of Peace Keeping Operations (DPKO). This organ of the UNO gives administrative and technical support for political and humanitarian missions and coordinates all mine-clearing activities conducted under the aegis of the UN.

Disarmament Is Still Utopian Concept

UN's founders wanted to maintain international peace and security. They thought that this would lead to the control and eventual reduction of weapons. UN Charter empowers the General Assembly to consider principles for arms control and disarmament. It can recommend to member states and Security Council. The Charter gives the Security Council the responsibility to formulate plans for arms control and disarmament. UN was in the centre of negotiations of many multilateral arms control treaties. The atomic bomb usage during World War II wreaked havoc in Hiroshima and Nagasaki. The General Assembly in created the Atomic Energy Commission (1946) to control atomic energy and reduce atomic weapons. USA promoted the Baruch Plan, which proposed the elimination of existing stockpiles of atomic bombs only after a system of international control was established and prohibited veto power in the Security Council on the commission's decisions. The Soviet Union, proposing the Gromyko Plan, wanted to ensure the destruction of stockpiles before agreeing to an international supervisory scheme. USSR also wanted to retain Security Council veto power over the commission. The conflicting positions of the two superpowers prevented any accord on the international control of atomic weapons and energy.

In 1947 the UNSC organized the Commission for Conventional Armaments to deal with armaments other than weapons of mass destruction. Progress on this issue was hampered by disagreement between USSR and the West. In 1952, the General Assembly voted to replace both of these commissions with a new Disarmament Commission. Comprising the members of the UN Security Council and Canada, this commission was directed to prepare proposals that would regulate, limit and balance the reduction of all armed forces and armaments; eliminate all weapons of mass destruction; and ensure international control and use of atomic energy for peaceful purposes only. Then, Strategic Arms Reduction Talks (START I) started in early nineties of the century gone by. USSR and USA agreed to cut down the number of nuclear weapons. START II followed START I during the late nineties and the early years of the new century. These talks also yielded some results but not so powerful that the world could become a safe place, sans nuclear weapons. Presently, the nuclear weapons are in the hands of USA, UK, Britain, China and France. India and Pakistan either have such weapons or can make them at short notices. Terror elements may have some nuclear detonator devices of fissile material. They may have made crude nuclear weapons in West Asia or North Africa. Arms reduction talks go on between Russia and USA from time to time. We shall keep our valued readers informed about those developments in the next edition of this very volume.

Limitations

UN's peacekeeping, peacemaking, and peace-building activities have suffered due to serious logistical and financial snags. This is the recession phase. The costs and controversies have multiplied. The UN reimburses countries for the use of equipment. However, these payments have been limited because of the failure of many member countries to pay their UN dues. Currently, the USA is the largest contributor to Un Funds. It is reeling under recessionary pressures. How can it contribute to UN if its own coffers are empty? The same is the case with India, Australia and other economies.

Latest Interventions

UNO has been able to establish democracy in Libya. It is working in Congo through MONUSCO. It has set up its mission in Syria, too. It is negotiating with Israel regarding the Palestinian issue. It has dealt with Somali sea pirates with a tough hand. It is tracking Indo-Pak negotiations on Kashmir. The 9/11 attacks and 26/11 attacks are very much on its agenda. The concerned parties are being contacted and debates and discussions are on.

Conclusion

In sum, the UNO has been able to suppress violence in many parts of the world. UN tries to maintain and bring about peace in all corners of the world. It is a weak negotiator because its founders have not disseminated powers to other member countries. But still, UN is doing commendable jobs on the peacekeeping fronts around the world. All nations must support it in military and logistic and financial terms because it is in our best interests to do so.